Oracle8*i*™ & UNIX®
Performance Tuning

ISBN 0-13-018706-2

90000

9 780130 187062

THE PRENTICE HALL PTR ORACLE® SERIES
The Independent Voice on Oracle

Oracle8*i*™ & UNIX® Performance Tuning

Ahmed Alomari

PH
PTR

Prentice Hall PTR
Upper Saddle River, NJ 07458
www.phptr.com

Library of Congress Cataloging-in-Publication Data

Alomari, Ahmed.
  Oracle8i and UNIX performance tuning / Ahmed Alomari.
    p. cm.
  ISBN 0-13-018706-2
  1. Oracle (Computer file) 2. Relational databases. 3. UNIX (Computer file) I. Title.

QA76.9.D3 A519 2000
005.75'85--dc21

                                                    00-056668

Editorial/Production Supervision: *Vincent Janoski*
Acquisitions Editor: *Tim Moore*
Marketing Manager: *Bryan Gambrel*
Manufacturing Manager: *Maura Zaldivar*
Cover Design Director: *Jerry Votta*
Cover Designer: *Nina Scuderi*
Interior Formatting: *Vanessa Moore*

© 2001 Prentice Hall PTR
Prentice-Hall, Inc.
Upper Saddle River, New Jersey 07458

Prentice-Hall International (UK) Limited, *London*
Prentice-Hall of Australia Pty. Limited, *Sydney*
Prentice-Hall Canada Inc., *Toronto*
Prentice-Hall Hispanoamericana, S.A., *Mexico*
Prentice-Hall of India Private Limited, *New Delhi*
Prentice-Hall of Japan, Inc., *Tokyo*
Pearson Education Asia Pte. Ltd.
Editora Prentice-Hall do Brasil, Ltda., *Rio de Janeiro*

CONTENTS

LIST OF FIGURES

LIST OF TABLES

PREFACE

The purpose of this book is to share my experiences in the areas of UNIX and Oracle performance and tuning. The chapters of this book provide a tremendous level of detail on the internal workings of the Oracle and UNIX kernels. The purpose of including so much detail is to give the reader a complete understanding of Oracle and UNIX. It is this understanding that will enable the reader to apply these concepts to specific applications and/or user environments, thus enabling the reader to maximize the performance of his or her environment.

It is a key characteristic of this book that only the latest versions of Oracle and UNIX are discussed, such as Oracle8*i* and Solaris 8. This will enable the reader to focus on the functionality and enhancements of the new versions, avoiding discussion of old releases.

Another characteristic of this book is that I have organized it into two major areas: data warehousing and Online Transaction Processing (OLTP). This edition of the book places more of an emphasis on application tuning since the application has the most control over the overall performance and scalability. It is important that the application be well designed and highly optimized.

Recommended prerequisites for this book are a basic understanding of SQL, UNIX shell language, and experience with UNIX system and Oracle database administration.

I have been a user of Oracle and UNIX across many different platforms including Sun, Sequent, HP, VAX/VMS, MS-DOS, Windows, and IBM RT. I hope you enjoy this book and find it useful in mastering the areas of performance and tuning. Good luck, and away we go!

COMPLEMENTARY MATERIALS

An ftp directory has been created to accompany this book at *ftp://ftp.pren-hall.com/pub/ptr/database.w-050/alomari*. The directory contains white papers, utilities, and scripts available for download. The material in the ftp directory offers additional information associated with Oracle8 such as architecure white papers, product features, and performance tuning tips. There are also SQL scripts that can be used to monitor database performance.

ACKNOWLEDGMENTS

This book is dedicated to the people of Iraq who continue to suffer due to the economic sanctions imposed on the country. A decade of economic sanctions has severely impacted the families and the common person in Iraq. Politics aside, the human suffering in Iraq due to the lack of food and medicine is alarming, and the death rates of infants continues to increase on a monthly basis. I hope that the sanctions can be lifted soon so that the human suffering can be eliminated.

Special thanks to my parents, Mukarram Alomari and Dr. Suha Alomari, and to my wife Lana, who give true meaning to the words commitment, dedication, and excellence. Their values and encouragement keep me constantly striving to excel.

Thanks to the rest of my family, Mustafa, Mohammed, May, and Munna, for their support and encouragement.

I would also like to thank the Oracle engineers and support staff with whom I have had the pleasure of working. Thanks also to the Sun, Hewlett-Packard, and Sequent engineers and support staff. Thanks to Vincent Carbone for his contributions on the Sequent architecture and performance tuning recommendations.

I would also like to thank the reviewers, Michael Machowicz, Graham Wood, Somu Rajarathanam, Dave Harris, Alex Tsukerman, and Mohammed Ziauddin. Their diligent and careful review helped me improve the format and organization of the book.

Thanks also to Tim Moore of Prentice Hall and the Prentice Hall staff for the editing and publishing efforts of this book.

Best Regards,

Ahmed Alomari

Ahmed.Alomari@oracle.com

INTRODUCTION

Tuning is by no means a science—meaning that it is not exact. Tuning is, however, similar to science in that tuning should follow the scientific technique. Science calls for defining the problem, followed by the formation of a hypothesis, and finally the performance of a series of tests on the hypothesis. Tuning is, in fact, very similar. Tuning should begin with the system and database administrator not necessarily defining the problem, but defining the goal. Then the system and database administrator must continue to develop test cases until the goal is reasonably achieved. For example, if the goal of a particular application is to achieve 1,000,000 transactions per second as the system throughput, the database administrator should execute as many test cases as necessary until the transactions per second (TPS) rate is achieved. The database administrator and developer should continue to tune the database and the application parameters until the desired TPS rate is achieved.

TUNING BY ITERATION

Tuning is definitely an iterative process that requires precision, analysis, and focus. One key element is that you must tune in a controlled environment. In other words, you should not change 20 different parameters at once and then reexecute the benchmark tests. Although you may have achieved the level of performance you desire, you will not have a concrete analysis as to which parameters directly affected the system performance. During the tuning process, try to minimize the amount of change per test (or benchmark) so that you can quantify each change in terms of its effect on performance. For example, if you are experiencing a low buffer cache hit ratio in the UNIX kernel, do not alter all the parameters associated with the buffer cache and paging at once. Try to increase the size of the buffer cache at a nominal rate at each iteration and measure the performance at each iteration. For example, consider the following system.

```
Iteration:          Parameter:              Performance Metric:
===============================================================
    1          db_block_buffers=10000    Buffer Cache Hit Ratio=85%
    2          db_block_buffers=12000    Buffer Cache Hit Ratio=96%
```

In this example, increasing the size of the Oracle buffer cache by 20 percent resulted in a 13 percent performance gain in terms of the buffer cache hit ratio. However, tuning is not this simple. The 13 percent buffer cache hit ratio gain may have caused a performance degradation in other areas.

The goal of performance and tuning is twofold. First, the obvious one, is to achieve the desired performance metrics for the system; the second is to qualify and quantify in detail the environment that helped achieve the desired performance levels. The result of the summarized findings should also help in capacity planning for future projects.

TUNING BY UNDERSTANDING

Another problem with performance and tuning that I have both witnessed and heard from customer sites is that the database and/or system administrator alters system and/or database parameters without a clear understanding of the purpose of the parameters. Each parameter in the UNIX kernel and the Oracle Database Management System (DBMS) has a specific purpose and performance can be seriously affected if care is not taken to understand its purpose before its value is altered.

My advice to you is to gain as much understanding of the details of your environment by learning the concepts and the purpose of the tunable parameters before you embark on your performance tuning efforts. For example, if you are running Oracle8 on an HP-UX Version 11 V2200 server, you should first learn the V2200 architecture so that you can take advantage of your system's architecture, then learn the concepts of the HP-UX Version 11 Operating System (OS), and finally learn all of the Oracle HP specific features.

TUNING AND TRAINING

Similar to performance and tuning, training is also a continuous iterative process. A great philosopher once said that life is simply one large classroom where lessons are taught and learned continuously. If you are going to be the person primarily responsible for system performance, I encourage you to work with your management to seek approval for formal training courses. Do not try to learn everything by yourself. This may result in a painful and time-consuming experience. The trainers who teach the advanced courses of operating system concepts and performance tuning have a tremendous amount of knowledge, expertise, and valuable experience that can help make your efforts more successful. I especially recommend that you take the formal Oracle training courses such as *DBA I, DBA II,* and *Performance and Tuning.* Also, I strongly recommend that you take a course in operating system concepts and hardware architecture from your particular hardware vendor. For example, Sun offers an excellent course on the internals of the Solaris operating system that provides the student with detailed knowledge of the internal workings of the Solaris UNIX operating system. If you are trying to maximize the performance of your particular environment, you will definitely need to learn the details of your specific environment. And who better to learn the details from than the people who engineered the original software and hardware.

GETTING THE MOST FROM YOUR ENVIRONMENT

As you begin tuning on different platforms and environments, you will find that you can increase performance by taking advantage of platform-specific features. Oracle is an excellent example of a single product providing the same functionality on more than 92 different platforms. Oracle provides extensions for each platform in order to take advantage of that platform's capabilities. You must make a serious effort to understand your platform so that you can tune the system accordingly and thus take advantage of your platform's features. For example, some UNIX platforms do not provide asynchronous I/O on file systems (a more detailed discussion on asynchronous I/O will follow in Chapter 3). Sun, however, does provide asynchronous I/O on both raw (character) devices and file systems (block devices). Using this feature can increase your system's performance if you use file systems for your database files.

In Oracle7, you may discover that `init.ora` parameter files are not straight-away portable to other platforms. For example, you will probably receive some errors when you try to use an `init.ora` startup file taken from a Sun Solaris platform to a Sequent Dynix platform. This further illustrates Oracle's platform-specific extensions that take advantage of the respective platform. In Oracle8, platform-specific `init.ora` parameters were made generic. This ensures that the parameter has the same effect regardless of the platform.

TUNING ON THE PROJECT LOG

One of the major problems associated with performance and tuning is that it is usually left as a post-project task rather than a pre-project task. Consequently, the database and system administration staff are left to deal with this issue after the application has been moved into production. This is a difficult task because once the system is serving a production workload, it is nearly impossible to alter system parameters and restart the system. Or, if there is a service window whereby the system can be brought down for maintenance or backups, the window is usually too small to allow for benchmarking or performance testing.

Therefore, it is critical that the effort of tuning the system be made part of the project plan before the project is launched. In other words, the application or database system should not be launched until the level of performance is acceptable and all reasonable workloads have been tested fully. For example, if you plan to launch a decision-support data warehousing system that will support an average of 100 concurrent users, testing the system with a few users running a few queries is far from sufficient. You must test the system by scaling from one user all the way up to as many as 150 users in order to measure contention, scalability, and response time as the user community continues to grow.

THE TEAM

Another major problem associated with tuning is the lack of human resources to perform the tasks associated with tuning. This is due largely to the fact that tuning is viewed as a task of the system and database administrator. Tuning is neither a task for one person nor for one particular group. Tuning must be viewed as a task in which all groups participate and should include the application group, the system test group, the system administration group, the network administration group, the database design group, and the database administration group. All of these groups must act as a team so that the desired level of performance can be achieved in all areas, starting with the desktop all the way through the servers and including all the layers in between.

RESOURCES

In my experience dealing with various performance issues, I have come to the conclusion that there are two major issues: insufficient time to conduct different test cases, and insufficient resources (people and hardware). As for the first problem—insufficient time to proactively performance test the system before the application is moved into production—I can recommend only that the project members request an appropriate period of time for performance testing as part of the development project plan. At the majority of sites I have visited, very little (if any) time was dedicated to performance testing. This book will help eliminate the growing pains that individuals involved in performance testing and tuning are forced to undergo due to the lack of good reference material.

As for the problem of insufficient resources, it is critical to the success of the project that appropriate resources be both dedicated and available. Do not try to launch a 200 GB database in production after testing only on a single-CPU system with a 1 GB database. Another example is testing the application with 300 simulated users when you actually expect several thousand users to access the system once in production. It is vital that a test environment exists and that it mirror the production environment. This will help facilitate testing and benchmarking without affecting production. It will also strengthen the value of the tests and the benchmarks because the production environment and test environment will be similar. By similar, I mean that if the production environment consists of a 200 GB database and 500 users, the test environment should mirror the production environment in size, workload, and user counts.

VERSION CONTROL

Do you remember the times when you have said, "I changed something, but I do not remember what, and now performance is worse"? For this reason, and many more, I seriously encourage you to use a version control system for maintaining changes to the database and OS configuration files. Using a version control system makes performance tuning easier because you can check in and check out configuration files of your choice easily without the pain of maintaining different configuration files manually. Whether you choose PVCS, RCS, or any other version control system, the important thing is that you do choose and use one. A version control system also facilitates ease of communication between teammates because all changes are documented and checked into the version control system. You may also want to consider developing a basic GUI front end for the `init.ora` parameters using something like Oracle Forms. This would enable you to make changes to the parameter file through a GUI tool and store each revision in the database. The version control system also will help management understand more clearly the efforts involved with performance and tuning and can also act as a documentation repository for system configuration.

THE REPOSITORY

In conjunction with a version control system, you should also use a repository manager such as the Oracle Repository tool. This will help you maintain more specific information regarding your Oracle database, such as database creation scripts, SQL (Structured Query Language) scripts, and user-related information such as tables, indexes, users, and permissions. The repository can be used to maintain sizing information on tablespaces, data files, tables, indexes, and other database objects.

STAYING CURRENT

It is critical that you try to keep your computing environment current. Do not fall behind and find that you are running old and unsupported releases of software. You need to stay current with both the operating system versions and the Oracle software. The Operating System (OS) vendors are continuously enhancing their operating system and fixing bugs. Oracle also is constantly expanding its products' features and functionality. Both the OS vendors and Oracle continually improve the performance of their products through the inclusion of new features and functionality. Therefore, it is key that you maintain a current environment, thereby enabling you to utilize the new features and performance enhancements. The current release of the database is Oracle8*i* release 2 (8.1.6). Oracle8*i* provides a tremendous number of new features for data warehousing and OLTP environments. Part of a systems or database administrator's role is to study the latest versions and maintain a current operating environment. OS versions are also extremely critical because OS patches are periodically released from the OS vendor that fix critical bugs, such as memory leaks and system panics, and often correct performance problems.

The task of remaining current is twofold. First, you must study the latest version in detail to determine the functionality and enhancements provided; and second, you must maintain a separate test environment. The test environment should be similar (if not identical) to your production environment. The test environment will enable you to test the new versions of the different products thoroughly. This will facilitate a smoother transition when you upgrade production systems since you will be familiar with any bugs, issues, or problems that the new version may introduce. The test environment will also help you work closely with the product vendor by reporting any bugs or issues that you may encounter during testing. The problems you report may be known already, and fixes might be immediately available; or, you may have to work closely with the vendor and provide them with a reproducible test case if the problem you discover is new. Testing new releases and keeping your environment current is a rather large task. For this reason, it is necessary to distribute the workload. For instance, you may have one person or a few people responsible for testing, and another group of people responsible for studying the new releases in detail before testing begins. When you consider an upgrade to a new release of a product, it is important that you work closely with the vendor and inform the vendor of your plans to upgrade. The vendor may have a migration path document, explaining the recommended approach to the migration, as well as a list of the known bugs and issues. In some cases, the vendor may discover critical problems in the new release and may issue a general warning to customer sites informing them thereof.

If you have a large number of systems, upgrading can be a tedious process. For this reason, you should try to automate the upgrade process as much as possible. Try to have, at a minimum, one NFS server that has all the product releases on at least one system organized by product and version. Using multiple NFS servers reduces the dependency on one system and increases the performance of the installations since not all installations will access only one NFS server. Then, you can simply NFS-mount the necessary partition on the system you want to upgrade. This avoids having to use CDs or tapes to install or upgrade software. Also, using the NFS technique, you can develop scripts to upgrade multiple systems simultaneously. As always, remember to perform a complete system backup before you upgrade to a new version of software. You may need to roll back to the backup in the event that the new version introduces some problems.

Chapter 1

INSIDE THE UNIX KERNEL

Despite the simplicity of the UNIX operating system at its inception, UNIX has evolved into a very complex, versatile, and scalable operating system. This complexity is due to the fact that the kernel manages a wide variety of services including Network File Systems (NFS), Input/Output (I/O), sockets, and process and memory management. The UNIX operating system is highly tunable and supports many different types of configuration. This chapter is not meant to be an introduction to the UNIX operating system. On the contrary, this chapter requires that you have a good working knowledge of the UNIX operating system. If you find this material overwhelming or difficult to understand, please consider reading a book on the fundamentals of the UNIX operating system (see the References section).

1.1 UNIX INTERNALS

The UNIX kernel is the central core of the operating system. It provides an interface to the hardware devices as well as to process, memory, and I/O management. The kernel manages requests from users via system calls that switch the process from user space to kernel space (see Figure 1.1).

Each time a user process makes a system call such as `read()`, `fork()`, `exec()`, `open()`, and so on, the user process experiences a *context switch*. A context switch is a mechanism by which a process switches from one state to another. The process may be either suspended until the system call is completed (*blocking*), or the process may continue and later be notified of the system call completion via a signal (*nonblocking*). Figure 1.2 shows an example of a context switch.

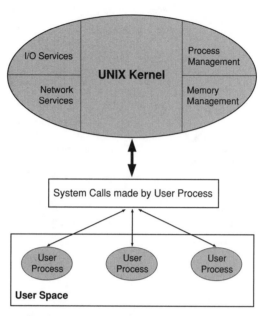

FIGURE 1.1   System calls and the UNIX kernel.

Figure 1.2 demonstrates a user process issuing a system call, in this case the `read()`[1] system call. The `read()` system call takes a file descriptor, buffer, and the number of bytes to be read as arguments. The `read()` system call forces the user process to block until the completion or timeout of the `read()` system call. Most UNIX operating system vendors provide a library for performing nonblocking (*asynchronous*) I/O calls since the traditional UNIX I/O calls of `read()` and `write()` are blocking (*synchronous*). See Chapter 3 for a more detailed discussion on the UNIX I/O model.

The UNIX kernel provides services to different system resources including I/O, memory management, process management, and network services. A particular application or user process accesses the system resources and services via system calls. The performance of the application is highly dependent on the type of system calls used and the number of system calls per application. Kernel resources are expensive and should be regarded as a valuable and limited set of resources. In order to maximize performance, the application should minimize the amount of system calls used, thereby reducing kernel space overhead and maintaining the user process in user space for most of the time. However, certain applications, such as a database management system heavily dependent on I/O, cannot avoid system calls. The goal in this situation is to tune the UNIX kernel and the system to respond as quickly and efficiently as possible so that the kernel resources can be freed quickly to service other requests. In other words, the goal of the application should be to minimize the amount of time spent in kernel space while maximizing throughput in the user space.

---

1.   Refer to the manual pages on the `read()` system call.

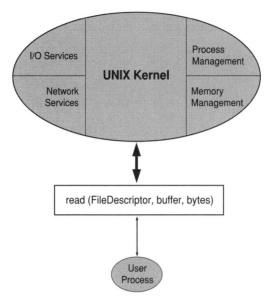

FIGURE 1.2   User process issues `read()` system call.

One of the major system calls central to the UNIX operating system is the `fork()` system call.[2] The `fork()` system call creates another process known as the *child* process, while the process that issued the `fork()` system call becomes the *parent* process. The `fork()` system call duplicates the entire process structure and the process address space of the parent process. The child process inherits the job class characteristics and environment of the parent process. The child process also inherits open file descriptors from the parent process. You can reference the parent process ID of a process using the `ps -ef` command.[3] The `fork()` system call enables one process to create another process either synchronously by waiting on the child process, or asynchronously by continuing the execution of the parent process. The `fork()` system call takes no arguments and returns an integer. The return value can represent one of three distinct values.

1. **0**, meaning the `fork()` call successfully created a child process, and 0 refers to the child process within the parent process;

2. **−1**, meaning the system was unable to create another process. In this case, you can use the `perror()`[4] system call to output the exact error message that caused the `fork()` call to fail; or

---

2. Refer to the manual pages on `fork()` (i.e., man fork) for a detailed description of the `fork()` system call.
3. Refer to the manual pages on `ps` for platform-specific options.
4. Refer to the manual pages on `perror()` for a complete description.

3. A default positive integer greater than 0 that is returned to the parent process which represents the process ID of the child process. The parent process can then wait on this child process, thereby blocking until termination of the child process, or the parent process can continue execution without waiting on the child process. This would be an asynchronous event, and the parent process can be signaled when the child process terminates. The parent process would need to establish a signal handler code segment to trap and interpret the signal from the child process.

The fork() system call is not only used within application programs to create subprocesses and subtasks, but also within the kernel itself to create subprocesses. For example, consider the output in Table 1.1 from the ps -ef command.

TABLE 1.1   Output from the ps -ef command

UID	PID	PPID	TIME CMD
root	0	0	0:01 sched
root	1	0	0:01 /etc/init -
root	2	0	0:00 pageout
root	3	0	3:27 fsflush
root	131	1	0:01 /usr/sbin/inetd -s
root	289	1	0:00 /usr/lib/saf/sac -t 300
root	112	1	0:02 /usr/sbin/rpcbind
root	186	1	0:00 /usr/lib/lpsched
root	104	1	0:12 /usr/sbin/in.routed -q
root	114	1	0:01 /usr/sbin/keyserv
root	122	1	0:00 /usr/sbin/kerbd
root	120	1	0:00 /usr/sbin/nis_cachemgr
root	134	1	0:00 /usr/lib/nfs/statd
root	136	1	0:00 /usr/lib/nfs/lockd
root	155	1	0:00 /usr/lib/autofs/automountd
root	195	1	0:00 /usr/lib/sendmail -bd -q1h
root	159	1	0:00 /usr/sbin/syslogd
root	176	1	0:07 /usr/sbin/nscd
root	169	1	0:13 /usr/sbin/cron

In Table 1.1, the sched process has the Process ID (**PID**) 0 and a Parent Process ID (**PPID**) of 0, meaning the sched process is the base process. The init process has a process ID of 1 and a parent process ID of 0, meaning that the init process was inherited by the sched process. The sched process is the scheduler process that is responsible for scheduling processes on the run queue. The inetd daemon has a process ID of 131 and a parent process of 1, meaning the inetd daemon was inherited by the init process. The init process is the system initializer process responsible for spawning and initializing processes with certain defaults.

Therefore, it is apparent that the fork() system call plays a large role in the UNIX operating system and is used frequently in both user applications and system applications. Consider the following program segment that summarizes the fork() system call and its use.

File: sample1.c

```
#define FORK_ERROR      -1

#include <stdio.h>
#include <unistd.h>

main ()
{

    int lpid;

    lpid=fork();  /* fork() issued, return code is checked below */
    switch(lpid)  /* for success or failure. */
    {

        case 0:  /* Child Process section - fork() succeeded, call
                     execl(). */
            execl ("sample2",arg*0,arg*1,....,arg*n, NULL);

        case -1:  /* Unable to create process */
            perror ("Unable to create process");
            exit (FORK_ERROR);

        default:  /* Return to Parent Process */
            /* Either continue or wait on child process. */
          /* Value returned here is process id of child process. */

    }

}
```

The process flow of this program would appear as in Figure 1.3 if compiled and executed.

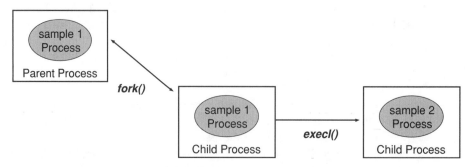

FIGURE 1.3   Process flow.

1.2   UNIX ARCHITECTURE

The UNIX operating system consists of many different layers that manage different resources and services. The basic architecture of the UNIX operating system (OS) consists of two main layers: the system or kernel layer, and the user layer.

Figure 1.4 illustrates the different layers of the UNIX operating system.

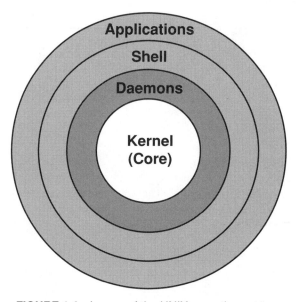

FIGURE 1.4   Layers of the UNIX operating system.

1.2.1 KERNEL LAYER

The kernel layer is the core of the operating system and provides services such as process and memory management, I/O services, device drivers, job scheduling, and low-level hardware interface routines such as test and set instructions. The kernel layer consists of many different internal routines that process the user requests. Access to the kernel is indirect via system calls. You cannot call the internal kernel routines directly. The system calls provide a mechanism by which a user process via the system call can request a kernel resource or service. The kernel itself is relatively small in terms of its disk and memory storage sizes. On Sequent systems, the kernel is located in the root directory and consists of a single file named unix (/unix). The size of the UNIX kernel on Sequent systems varies depending on the system configuration and the number of device drivers configured. A typical size may range from 1 MB–5 MB. On Solaris 7 (2.7) systems, the file path for the UNIX kernel is /platform/<platform_type>/kernel/unix. The <platform_type> indicates the type of system architecture such as sun4m or sun4u. It is important to note that when the operating system is installed on the machine, you must allocate enough space for the root file system. If you do not allocate sufficient space, you may not be able to rebuild the kernel because rebuilding the kernel requires a temporary staging area to hold both the new kernel and the previous kernel file. In addition, you may also not be able to install operating system patches if sufficient free space does not exist in the root file system. I recommend that you always leave at least 500 MB free in the root file system. Although this may seem high, rebuilding the root file system to increase its space is not an easy task. It is better to have extra space than be short a few megabytes.

The kernel also provides services such as signal handling, synchronization, interprocess communication, file system services, network services, and hardware monitoring. Each time a process is started, the kernel has to initialize the process, assign the process a priority, allocate memory and resources for the process, and schedule the process to run. When the process terminates, the kernel frees any memory and/or resources held by the process. The UNIX process model will be discussed in greater detail later in section 1.2.5.

1.2.2 FILE SYSTEMS

The UNIX file system is a hierarchical file system that begins with the root (/) file system. Each file system is mounted at a mount-point. For example, the /(root) file system is mounted on the / mount-point. The /usr file system is mounted on the /usr mount-point. Figure 1.5 shows the hierarchical directory structure of the UNIX file system.

In Figure 1.5, the /usr, /var, and /opt directories are subdirectories of the /(root) file system. The /usr, /var, and /opt subdirectories may each be separate file systems from the root file system; however, the hierarchical file structure still applies. In fact, it is recommended that the /(root), /var, /opt, and /usr subdirectories all be separate file systems. This helps prevent the root file system from being filled up with patches, system log files, E-mail, and user software packages. This also increases the performance of the root file system since the overhead of maintaining a larger file system is reduced by separating the operating system (OS) binaries and executables from user software packages and system log files.

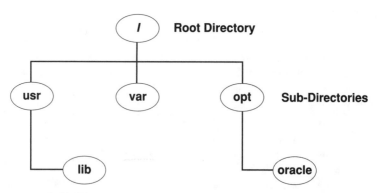

FIGURE 1.5   Directory structure of the UNIX file system.

The UNIX file system has many different file system types such as `ufs` (UNIX file system), `NFS` (Network file system), `vxfs` (Veritas file system), and `cdfs` (CD-ROM file system). The `ufs` file system type is the most standard UNIX file system consisting of super-blocks, inodes, offsets, and storage blocks. Reads and writes to a `ufs` file system are done in blocks depending on the size of the file system block size. Block sizes can range from 1 KB to 8 KB depending on the file system type selected. `NFS` is a remote file system that is exported to other client systems. These client systems may mount the remote file system from the server that is exporting the file system. There are system daemons on both sides (`NFS` server daemons and `NFS` client daemons) that communicate with each other via RPC (Remote Procedure Call). `NFS` packets are IP (Internet Protocol) packets that utilize the UDP (User Datagram Protocol) datagram.[5] The `vxfs` file system type is a file system based on the Veritas Volume Management software.[6] The `cdfs` file system type is a CD-ROM–based file system, also referred to as `hsfs` (High Sierra file system) and ISO 9660 CD-ROM file system.

1.2.2.1   `ufs`

The `ufs` file system is the most common UNIX file system type and consists of a block-based file system that contains offsets, super-blocks, cylinder groups' maps, inodes, and storage blocks. Figure 1.6 shows the `ufs` file system type structure.

Each ufs file system consists of multiple cylinder groups with each cylinder group consisting of the structure diagrammed in Figure 1.6. The boot block is contained only in the first cylinder group of the file system (Cylinder Group 0). The boot block is 8 KB in size and contains the boot strap used during the system boot process. If the file system is not used for booting (i.e., other than the root file system), the boot block is left blank.

---

5.   Solaris 2.5 changed the NFS code (NFS Version 3) to utilize TCP/IP instead of UDP.

6.   Veritas provides disk volume management software for UNIX platforms.

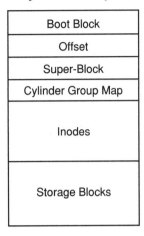

Cylinder Group n:

Boot Block
Offset
Super-Block
Cylinder Group Map
Inodes
Storage Blocks

FIGURE 1.6   The `ufs` file system type structure.

The super-block consists of information about the file system, such as

❑ Status of the file system (used by `fsck`)
❑ File system label (name)
❑ File system size in logical blocks
❑ Date and time stamp of the last update
❑ Cylinder group size
❑ Number of data blocks per cylinder group
❑ Summary data block

The cylinder group map is a specific feature of the `ufs` file system type and consists of a block of data per cylinder group that maintains block usage within the cylinder. The cylinder group map also maintains the free list of unused blocks, as well as monitors disk fragmentation.

The inode layer is one of the most important layers within the file system. The inode layer contains most of the information about a file with the exception of the file's name. The name of the file is maintained in a directory. An inode is approximately 128 bytes long. By default, an inode is created for every 2 KB of storage in the file system. The number of inodes can be specified during the file system creation phase by using the `newfs` or `mkfs` command.[7] See Chapter 3 for more details on tuning file systems. An inode in the `ufs` file system contains the following information.

---

7.   Refer to the manual pages on `newfs` and `mkfs` for specific parameters and options.

❏ Mode and type of the file

❏ Number of hard links to the file

❏ User ID of the owner of the file

❏ Group ID of the group to which the file belongs

❏ Number of bytes in the file

❏ Two arrays comprising a total of 15 disk block addresses

❏ Date and time stamp of last access

❏ Date and time stamp of last modification

❏ Date and time stamp of file creation

The core of an inode is two arrays that together consist of 15 disk block addresses. The first array is comprised of 12 direct addresses. These direct addresses map directly to the first 12 storage blocks of the file. If the file size exceeds 12 blocks, the first address of the second array refers to an indirect block. This indirect block consists of direct addresses as opposed to file contents. The second address refers to a double indirect block containing addresses of indirect blocks. The third address references a triple indirect block containing addresses of indirect blocks. Figure 1.7 portrays the ufs addressing scheme.[8]

Table 1.2 shows the maximum number of bytes addressable by each level of indirection.[9]

TABLE 1.2   Maximum file addressable size

Logical Block Size	Direct Blocks	Single Indirect Blocks	Double Indirect Blocks	Triple Indirect Blocks
2 KB	24 KB	1 MB	512 MB	256 GB
4 KB	48 KB	4 MB	4 GB	4 TB
8 KB	96 KB	16 MB	32 GB	64 TB

Note: TB (Terabyte)

The maximum file size in a ufs file system is 2 GB, which is addressable through triple indirection. Triple indirection is a signed 32-bit field, hence the 2 GB file limit as most UNIX operating systems are 32-bit.[10] Most UNIX vendors are currently working to convert to a 64-bit–based operating system. The 64-bit operating system will eliminate the 2 GB file limit, thus allowing terabyte size files. Although the logical file system block size ranges from 2 KB to 8 KB, ufs provides a smaller subset of a block known as a fragment or chunk. The fragment or chunk is usually 1 KB in size but can be set to a multiple of the operating system block size of 512 bytes. Fragments are used to accommodate smaller files in order to avoid a wastage of space. The maximum length of a ufs filename is 255 bytes.

---

8. Kulihin, Julia, Fox, Mary L., Nester, Joan. *System Administration*, Vol. 2. UNIX SVR4.2 MP, pp. 3–18.

9. Kulihin, Julia, Fox, Mary L., Nester, Joan. *System Administration*, Vol. 2. UNIX SVR4.2 MP, pp. 3–18.

10. Digital has the DEC-Alpha UNIX Servers, which are based on Digital's 64-bit operating system.

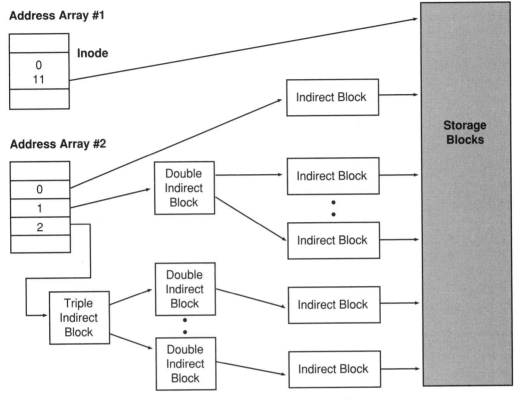

FIGURE 1.7 The ufs addressing scheme.

Each time a ufs file system is mounted, the state of the file system is checked. If the file system state is stable or clean, the file system is mounted and made available for use. If the file system state is unstable, an fsck is performed on the file system. The fsck utility scans the file system and corrects any discrepancies found between the inode information and data storage blocks. The fsck utility may cause a loss of data if certain inconsistent files are truncated. For large file systems, fsck may take a long time because fsck is a synchronous process and must scan the entire file system. For this reason, you may choose to use a journaled file system such as vxfs.

1.2.2.2 vxfs

The vxfs file system is based on the Veritas Volume Management software. The vxfs file system offers several enhancements over the ufs-based file system. It provides extent level allocation and a journal feature. The extent level allocation reduces the alloca-tion workload by allocating an extent (many blocks) at once, as opposed to the ufs-based file system which allocates in increments of blocks. The journal feature is similar to the concept of the Oracle redo log. As changes are made to the file system, those changes are recorded in the journal. Therefore, if the system were to crash or panic, an `fsck` would not be necessary since the journals need only to be applied to restore the file system's state of consistency. This significantly reduces the length of recovery time following a system crash or panic. Figure 1.8 details the structure of the `vxfs` file system.[11]

1.2.2.3 NFS

NFS (Network file system) is a remote file system that is accessed by client systems over the network. NFS file system types are extremely common and popular in the UNIX environment. NFS allows multiple client systems access to a common file system from an NFS server. It also provides heterogeneous systems the ability to share files and data. This centralizes system administration since only the NFS server needs to be backed up. This of course also leads to a single point of failure. NFS file systems typically are used for development, home directories, and software distribution. Figure 1.9 shows how an NFS file system works.

In Figure 1.9, the NFS server—that is, the system exporting the file system for remote mounting (access)—is running the NFS server daemons which service NFS client requests. On the client side, the client—a workstation or another server—mounts the file system as an NFS file system and accesses the NFS file system through the NFS client daemons. The NFS client daemons communicate with the NFS server daemons via RPC (Remote Procedure Call). Remote procedure calls enable applications to call procedures (functions) on a

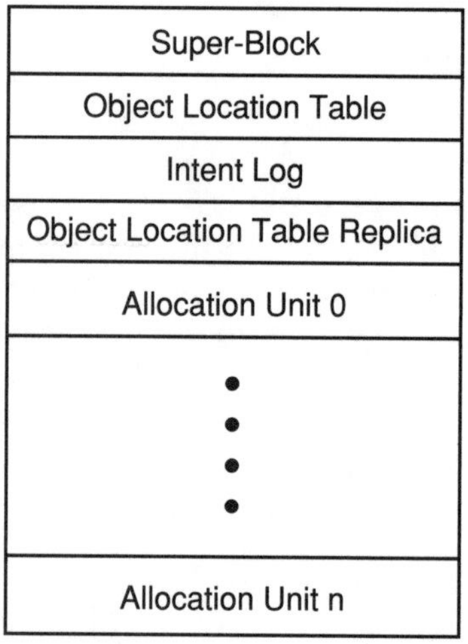

Super-Block
Object Location Table
Intent Log
Object Location Table Replica
Allocation Unit 0
• • • •
Allocation Unit n

FIGURE 1.8   Structure of the `vxfs` file system.

---

11. Kulihin, Julia, Fox, Mary L., Nester, Joan. *System Administration*, Vol. 2. UNIX SVR4.2 MP, pp. 3–33.

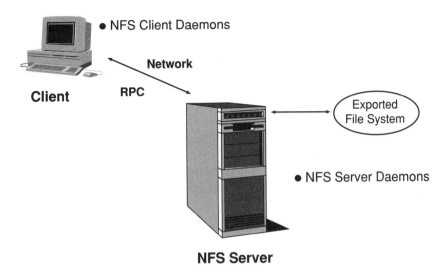

FIGURE 1.9 The NFS file system concept.

remote system. RPC uses the XDR (External Data Representation) protocol for data exchange. For more information on XDR or RPC, refer to the respective manual pages, or refer to a programmer's guide on RPC. A heavily hit NFS server can significantly increase the network traffic. This can affect network and NFS performance. There are many performance issues to consider when using NFS file systems. Performance issues pertaining to NFS are discussed in Chapter 3.

1.2.2.4 cdfs

The cdfs file system is a CD-ROM–based file system that is used to mount CDs for the purposes of installing software and/or data. These file systems are read-only and provide specific options during mounting[12] that control the format of the files on the CD.

1.2.2.5 The vnode

Internally, UNIX manages file systems using *vnodes*. Vnodes are known as virtual nodes and act as a higher-level object to the inode. The UNIX operating system uses the inode object to manage files and file systems. Vnodes are virtual nodes which then map to the specific object type depending on the use of the vnode. For example, for the ufs file system, a vnode consists of an inode. For an NFS file system, the vnode is an rnode (remote node). For more information on the vnode structure, you can browse the vnode header file

---

12. Refer to the manual pages on the mount command.

`/usr/include/sys/vnode.h`. The vnode structure allows for a generic file system implementation regardless of the specific type of file system.

1.2.2.6 Large Files

In the race to provide support for large files (files larger than 2 GB in the 32-bit world), operating system vendors have recently provided APIs allowing applications to manage large files. Solaris 2.6, HP-UX 10.2, and Dynix ptx 4.4 provide APIs that support 64-bit file offsets. Many vendors such as Sun, HP, Sequent, Oracle, and Veritas participated in the Large File Summit. The Large File Summit (LFS) is an industry initiative to develop a generic specification for the support of files larger than 2 GB. The LFS specification extends the current interfaces to behave differently when dealing with large files. For instance, the `open()` system call will set errno to `EOVERFLOW` if the file is greater than or equal to 2 GB.

The LFS draft defines a set of additional 64-bit API functions that provide support for regular size and large size files. In essence, the LFS draft defines a new set of functions named `xxx64()` corresponding to the existing set of functions named `xxx()`. For example, `open64()`, `creat64()`, `lstat64()`, and `lseek64()` are a few of the 64-bit functional interfaces added by the LFS specification. There is also a 64-bit file offset data type, namely `off64_t`.

In Solaris 2.6, setting `_FILE_OFFSET_BITS` to 64 in your application source before including system headers enables the 64-bit interfaces. Setting `_FILE_OFFSET_BITS` to 64 results in `off_t` being type-defined as a `long long` 64-bit data type. In addition, the existing file I/O function calls –`xxx()`– will be mapped to their 64-bit counterpart –`xxx64()`. In order to utilize the large file functionality, refer to your platform-specific documentation. Each platform may have a different set of APIs and commands for dealing with large files.

Solaris 2.6 also provides a new mount option which enables or disables large file support. If the file system is mounted with the `largefiles` option, then files larger than 2 GB can be created in the file system. The `nolargefiles` mount option disables support for large files. The system administrator can use these mount options on a per file system basis in order to manage large file support.

Large files are useful because they improve system administration and performance. System and database administrators now have the ability to reduce the number of files by utilizing large files. This helps reduce the complexity of backups and restores in dealing with a large number of files. However, large files also reduce the amount of file I/O parallelism. For example, two 2 GB files may be backed up or restored concurrently as opposed to a single 4 GB file. Large files may also improve performance by allowing wider stripes. The 2 GB file size restriction limited the sizes of disk partitions and thus the width of the stripe. By using the large file feature, more disks can be added to the stripe. For instance, instead of creating a 2 GB stripe consisting of three disks, you can create a 4 GB stripe consisting of six disks. The large file option has its advantages and disadvantages, but for the most part it is a useful feature enabling UNIX applications to manage large files.

1.2.2.7 UNIX Buffer Cache

UNIX employs a file system buffer cache to cache file system information such as directory name lookups, inodes, and file control block data. The actual file data blocks are part of the virtual memory pages, not the buffer cache. The concept of the UNIX file system cache is simple: data from reads and writes is maintained in the cache in the event that subsequent reads may request data that is already in the cache. This significantly increases performance since access to the cache is in the time order of nanoseconds (memory access speeds), and access to the disk is in the time order of milliseconds (disk access speeds). This is an order of magnitude 100,000 times greater since milliseconds have a base of 10^{-3}, and nanoseconds have a base of 10^{-9}. When a user process issues a read, the kernel first scans through the UNIX file system cache to determine if the data is already in the cache (*cache hit*). A cache hit means that the read request found the data in the cache, thereby avoiding physical disk I/O. If the data is in the cache, the kernel copies the data from the file system cache into the user's workspace. Although this is a memory-to-memory copy, system performance can suffer during periods of high file system activity. This can also lead to increased levels of paging. See Chapter 3 for a discussion of the performance tuning tips for the UNIX file system cache. If the data was not found in the cache (*cache miss*), the kernel issues a physical read to the disk drive(s) containing the data and brings the data into the UNIX file system cache. A cache miss means that the data was not found in the cache, and physical I/O was necessary to bring the data into the cache. The kernel then copies the data from the UNIX file system cache into the user's workspace. Figure 1.10 shows a cache hit and Figure 1.11 shows a cache miss. Each time a user process issues a write to a file system–based file, the data is written to the file system cache and later flushed to disk. Depending on the flags used to open[13] the file, physical writes to the file may be deferred. If the writes are deferred, the data is written only to the cache and is later flushed out to disk by the file system flush daemon. If the file was opened with the flag that requests writes to not be deferred, writes to the file are physically written to the disk. However, all file system reads are always read from the UNIX file system cache, unless specific calls are used to bypass the UNIX file system cache. The size of the UNIX file system cache is controlled by kernel-tunable parameters. On Solaris, the `bufhwm` kernel parameter controls the maximum size of the file system buffer cache. Another related parameter, `npbuf`, controls the number of physical I/O buffers allocated each time more buffers are needed (provided the total amount does not exceed `bufhwm`). These parameters can be set in the `/etc/system` file.

The UNIX file system cache uses a least recently used algorithm to age data out of the cache. The file system cache is maintained by a system daemon that is both time-driven and space-driven. The daemon wakes up periodically and scans for *dirty* pages to be written out. A dirty page is a page that has changed and has been marked as dirty, meaning that the page should be written out to disk upon the next write-out scan. The daemon also ensures that there is sufficient space for reads and writes by flushing dirty disk pages to disk or aging out least recently used data. The file system daemon is tunable, and performance gains can be achieved by tuning the file system daemon appropriately.

---

13. Refer to the manual pages on the `open()` file system call.

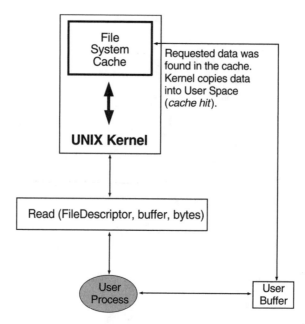

FIGURE 1.10   A cache hit.

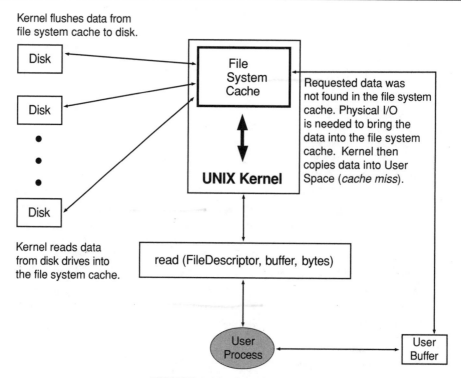

FIGURE 1.11   A cache miss.

1.2.3 VIRTUAL MEMORY

The UNIX operating system is based on the virtual memory model. The virtual memory model allows a process or a system to address more memory than physically exists. The UNIX virtual memory model consists of a set of memory pages, usually 4 KB each. Older versions of UNIX had page sizes of 8 KB. You can determine the page size on your platform by using the `sysconf()`[14] system call. The UNIX operating system uses a swap device in addition to physical memory to manage the allocation and deallocation of memory. For example, a machine with 64 MB of physical memory and a 192 MB swap device supports a virtual memory size of 256 MB. Earlier versions of UNIX did not provide a finer level of memory management than swapping. Swapping is the process by which the system no longer has enough free physical memory available, and processes are completely swapped out (written) to the swap device. Once the process has been completely written out to the swap device (i.e., swapped out), the physical memory occupied by the process can be freed. The swap device can be a single file or series of files, and each swap file can be no larger than 2 GB.[15] Therefore, the UNIX kernel virtual memory is based on both the physical memory and swap device. Figure 1.12 illustrates the virtual memory and swap device.

Because the UNIX operating system is based on the virtual memory model, a translation layer is needed between virtual memory addresses and physical memory addresses. This translation layer is part of the kernel and is usually written in machine language (Assembly) to achieve optimal performance when translating and mapping addresses. Figure 1.13 illustrates the virtual to physical translation layer within the kernel.

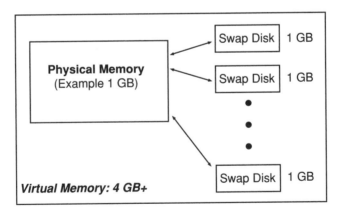

FIGURE 1.12   Virtual memory model.

---

14. Refer to the manual pages on the `sysconf()` system call.
15. This is due to the limitation that a single file on 32-bit UNIX platforms cannot exceed 2 GB. Most OS vendors currently provide large file support.

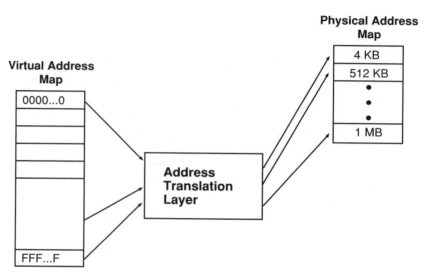

FIGURE 1.13   Virtual to physical memory address translation layer.

In Figure 1.13, each time a user process accesses memory, the kernel uses the address translation layer to map the virtual memory address into a physical memory address. Virtual addressing makes it possible to address larger amounts of memory than physically exist. As long as the virtual memory address scheme supports large memory configurations, adding additional physical memory is straightforward. Most 32-bit UNIX kernels support a maximum of 4 GB of direct addressable memory per process, and extensions are provided to address memory beyond 4 GB.

Current versions of UNIX provide a more granular approach to swapping known as *paging*. Paging swaps out various different pages in memory to the swap device rather than the entire process as in swapping. This not only increases performance by minimizing the time needed to load a process into memory, it can also provide more physical memory to other processes. In certain instances, a process might allocate a large section of memory upon process invocation. However, most of this memory may remain unused during the life of the process. For example, declaring a large System Global Area (SGA) when only a small section of the SGA is actively used could cause the unused portions of the SGA to be paged back to the free list. This allows other processes access to these physical memory pages. Hence, paging not only minimizes the chances of a complete swapout, it also provides higher availability to memory by utilizing idle memory pages. The UNIX kernel maintains a free list of memory pages and uses a page daemon to periodically scan the memory pages for active and idle pages. The page daemon uses a clocklike algorithm to maintain pages in memory. Figure 1.14, shows the paging algorithm.[16]

---

16. SunService. *SunOS 5.X Internals Guide SP-365*, Revision B.1, September 1993, pp. 5–6.

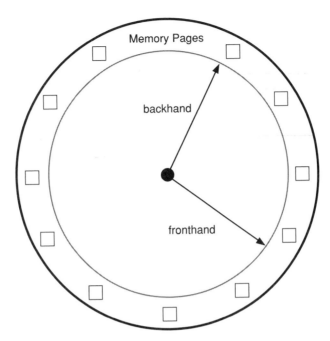

FIGURE 1.14 The paging algorithm.

In Figure 1.14, the `page` daemon using the minute hand (fronthand) scans the page list and examines the reference bit. If the reference bit is active, the page's reference bit is set to idle. If the reference bit is marked idle (meaning that no references have been made to this page), the page becomes a candidate for the page free list. During the second phase, the hour hand (backhand) scans the page list. If the reference bit is still idle and was set to idle during the previous scan, the page becomes a candidate for the free list. If the page reference bit is set (meaning that the page is active and has been referenced), the page is left alone. This algorithm's goal is twofold: to ensure that the system has plenty of free memory, and to minimize paging and swapping. There are system thresholds that control the frequency of the `page` daemon. As the available free memory closely approaches these thresholds, the `page` daemon will increase the frequency of its scans in order to increase the amount of free memory. The thresholds include limits such as the amount of memory that is always left free, the desired or ideal amount of free memory, and the amount of free memory before swapping occurs. All of these limits control the activity of the `page` daemon. Higher limits cause an active `page` daemon. Lower limits reduce the activity of the `page` daemon. Tuning the `page` daemon is discussed in Chapter 2.

Paging and swapping can severely impact the performance of your system, and efforts must be made to ensure that swapping never occurs and that paging activity is minimized. It should be noted that swapping is an act of desperation by the UNIX kernel to free memory immediately. This act of desperation causes processes to be completely swapped out in order to free memory. Thrashing occurs when even swapping was not successful in freeing memory, and memory is needed to service critical processes. This usually results in a system panic, as this is the last action that the kernel can take to free memory. Swapping needs to be avoided at all costs as this is evidence of insufficient memory. You may need to tune your system and/or application to use less memory or you may need to add additional physical memory to accommodate the workload.

1.2.4 SHARED MEMORY

The UNIX System V Release 4 operating system standard provides many different mechanisms for interprocess communication. Interprocess communication is required when multiple distinct processes need to communicate with each other either by sharing data or resources or both. Interprocess communication is also used when processes are dependent on one another. For example, one process may be responsible for updating files while another process is responsible for receiving the updates. Once received and verified, the process that receives the updates may forward the updates on to the other process to process the updates. These two processes need a method to share data. Shared memory is one of the methods of UNIX System V Release 4 interprocess communication. Shared memory, as the term suggests, enables multiple processes to "share" the same memory, in other words, multiple processes mapping into the same virtual address map. Shared memory avoids expensive memory-to-memory copies when processes need to share data in memory. Shared memory also increases application portability because most platforms support shared memory. Figure 1.15 illustrates the concept of shared memory.

Many applications use shared memory as a technique for interprocess communication. Oracle uses shared memory to hold the SGA. This enables Oracle processes and Oracle user connections to attach to the same SGA without having to copy the SGA between each process. Having to copy the SGA between processes not only would be time consuming, but memory requirements would also grow at an explosive rate.

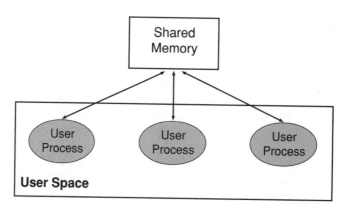

FIGURE 1.15   Shared memory concept.

1.2.5 PROCESS MODEL

The UNIX operating system uses a priority-based round-robin process scheduling architecture. Processes are dispatched to the run queue based on priority and are placed on the sleep queue based either on the process' completion of its time slice or by waiting on an event or resource. Processes can sometimes result in a deadlock when waiting on a resource. Hence, user applications need to provide deadlock detection to ensure that user processes do not deadlock on resources.

```
machine1% myprogram
```

When a user issues the command myprogram at the UNIX prompt, the kernel places the request for myprogram on the dispatch queue with a certain level of priority. The default priority for the particular job class is assigned assuming that no specific priority has been requested either through the nice[17] command or priocntl()[18] system call. The internal kernel routines scan the dispatch queue and the sleep queue to ensure that processes are not starved from the CPU and that processes do not exceed their time slice. Do not confuse internal kernel routines with system calls. Internal kernel routines are routines that can be used and called only by the kernel. System calls are the user interface to the kernel system services. For example, fork() and read() are examples of user system calls, while getpage() and putpage() are examples of internal memory management routines. Figure 1.16 illustrates the process scheduling cycle of the UNIX OS.

Figure 1.16 shows both the dispatch (i.e., run) queue and the sleep queue as containing processes. The dispatch queue contains processes marked as ready to run. Once a process is marked as runable, the process will begin execution on a CPU as soon as a CPU becomes available. In Figure 1.16, three processes are shown on the dispatch queue that then begin execution on the three available CPUs. Once the time slice (time-share job class) of the process is exceeded, the process is migrated to the sleep queue in favor of other processes which have been sleeping and are now marked as ready to run. The process scheduling algorithm in the UNIX kernel tries to balance CPU time collectively with other processes in order to avoid CPU starvation and CPU saturation. Once on the sleep queue, the process with the highest priority will be scheduled to run. The same holds true of the dispatch queue. The kernel may also *preempt* processes by reducing their priority. Preemption is a technique used by the UNIX kernel to stop a currently running process or set of processes and schedule other processes to run. A process can be preempted under many different circumstances, such as when the process has exceeded its time slice, a higher priority process needs to be scheduled, a system event or interrupt occurred that needs to be serviced, or the process appears to be waiting on a resource that is busy. The kernel maintains information about processes including the current process state. Using the ps command, you can obtain the process state of a particular process or list of processes. For example, Table 1.3 shows the output listing from the ps command.

---

17. The nice command enables a user to change the priority of a particular user process. Only the superuser or root account can increase the priority of a process using nice.

18. The priocntl() system call provides a system call interface to user process priority management.

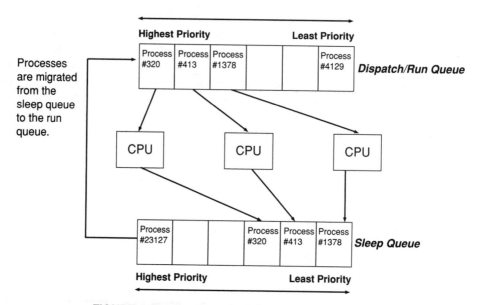

FIGURE 1.16   Process scheduling cycle of the UNIX OS.

TABLE 1.3   Output listing from the `ps` command

ST	UID	PID	PPID	TIME	CMD
S	root	0	0	0:01	sched
S	root	1	0	0:01	/etc/init -
O	root	2	0	0:00	pageout
R	test	281	280	0:01	xterm
Z	test	282			<defunct>

The process state can be classified as one of the following:

S — Process is currently sleeping.

O — Process is currently running on a CPU.

R — Process is ready to run.

I — Process is idle; currently being created.

T — Process is being traced.

X — Process is awaiting memory.

Z — Process is a zombie.

In a process state of S, the process is sleeping and is waiting on an event. The event could be waiting on an I/O request completion, waiting for a locked resource, or waiting on some data that is not yet available. A swapped process will also have a state of S (sleeping). Putting a process to sleep and later awakening the process is an expensive operation and can lead to performance problems—especially when a high number of process sleeps occur. A process state of O means the process is active and is running on a CPU. The process state R indicates that the process is ready to run, and as soon as a processor becomes available, the process will run (assuming it is not preempted in favor of a higher priority process). A process state of I indicates that the process is idle and is being created or initialized. A process state of T indicates that the process is being traced. This is common during debugging mode when parent processes trace child processes to detect problems. X refers to the state when the process is awaiting additional memory. Lastly, Z refers to the zombie process state. The zombie process state has two main meanings: the first is that the process (child process) has terminated and has a parent process. The second is that the process is marked to be killed by the UNIX kernel. Each process has a complete process structure associated with it when it is created. This process structure has a link to the address space of the process. During the zombie state, the process structure and address space are removed and freed back to the system. The only information remaining in the kernel for a zombie process is an entry in the process table. The kernel is responsible for cleaning up the process table and removing zombie entries. Figure 1.17 shows the process map within the kernel.

The process structure contains many different fields, including process information and process statistics. Each time a process is created, a separate process structure for the process is created. To learn more about the process structure, I encourage you to read the <proc.h> header file located in the /usr/include/sys directory. This header file is platform-specific, and it provides a complete listing of the process structure.

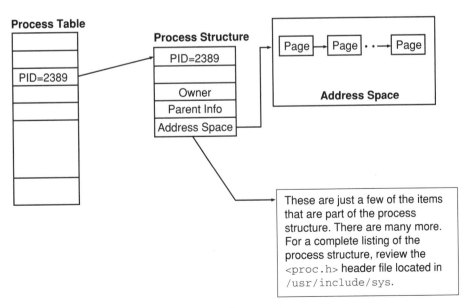

FIGURE 1.17 Process structure.

1.2.6 THE JOB SCHEDULER

The UNIX operating system job scheduler provides three different types of job classes as listed in Table 1.4. Each class listed in Table 1.4 has a discrete set of global priorities that control the scheduling order of the tasks (processes) within the particular job class. The job classes listed in Table 1.4 are listed in order of increasing priority. It is critical to understand the purpose as well as the properties of each job class. The understanding of the different job classes will enable you to further understand the kernel's job scheduling policy. I must emphasize that extreme care must be taken before altering the job class and/or priority of any particular process. Doing so without a full understanding of the possible effects could cause system instability, possibly forcing the system to panic. Please consult with your hardware and OS vendor before altering job-class parameters. Figure 1.18 summarizes the UNIX job scheduling classes.[19]

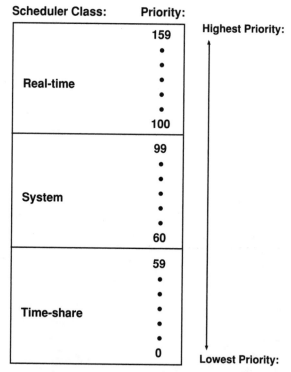

FIGURE 1.18   UNIX job scheduling classes.

19. SunService. *SunOS 5.X Internals Guide SP-365*, Revision B.1. September 1993, pp. 6–7.

TABLE 1.4 Job classes provided by the UNIX operating system job scheduler

JOB CLASS	PRIORITY RANGE
Time-share	0 through 59 (59 being the highest); default job class
System	60 through 99; reserved for system daemon processes
Real-time	100 through 159; highest priority job class

1.2.6.1 Time-Share Job Class

The time-share job class is the default job class and has priority 0 through 59, with 59 being the highest priority. In this job class, each process is assigned a time slice (or quantum). The time slice specifies the number of CPU clock ticks that a particular task (or process) can occupy the CPU. Once the process finishes its time slice, the process priority usually is decreased and the process is placed on the sleep queue. Other processes waiting for CPU time may have their priority increased, thereby increasing their likelihood to run. Unless specified through the dispadmin[20] or priocntl command, any time a new process is created, it will be assigned to the time-share job class with a default priority. You can use the ps -c command to list the job class and priority of a process.

For example,

```
myhost%> ps -c
    PID   CLS   PRI   COMD
   2403   TS    59    csh
  15231   TS    48    ps
```

In this example, the output from the ps -c command shows the Process ID (PID) of the current shell as well as the ps command itself. Both processes are in the Time-Share (TS) job class, and have a priority of 59 or less.

1.2.6.2 System Job Class

The system job class is reserved for system daemon processes such as the pageout daemon or the file system daemon. The priority range for the system job class is between 60 and 99. The system job class has a higher priority than the time-share job class. This is to ensure that the system can provide services to the time-share job class processes when system services such as memory, and/or file I/O are requested. Although it is possible to alter the job class of a time-share process to real-time, it is not recommended because the process would run at a higher priority than the system daemons. Use extreme care before altering the job class or priority of processes.

---

20. The dispadmin command is the Solaris utility used for process scheduler administration while the system is running. You can use this command to change job classes. Refer to the manual pages on dispadmin for a complete listing. On Sequent, use the priocntl command. On HP, use the rtsched to schedule a real-time job.

1.2.6.3   Real-Time Job Class

The real-time job class is the highest priority job class and has no time slice. Real-time process priorities range between 100 and 159. The fixed-priority job class (real-time) ensures that critical processes always acquire the CPU as soon as the process is scheduled to run—even if processes in other classes are currently running or scheduled to run. Again, use caution when switching priorities or job classes of processes. Consult with your vendor before switching processes into different job classes. There may be some operating system–specific issues when the job class or priority of a process is altered. Because there is no time slice with real-time processes, the number of context switches is reduced significantly, which can increase performance. More discussion on process management as it pertains to performance follows in Chapter 2.

1.2.7   THREADS MODEL

Several UNIX operating system vendors support the threads model either through a vendor-supplied library, or by supporting and supplying the POSIX[21] threads library. Sun Solaris 2.X provides a Solaris threads library as well as the POSIX threads library. HP-UX 10.X provides user threads and HP-UX 11.0 provides both user and kernel threads. The threads model consists of an LWP (Light-Weight Process) structure. A thread is a unit of control or execution within a process. A thread can be thought of as a subtask or subprocess. Unlike the process model, which creates a separate process structure for each process, the threads model has substantially less overhead than a process. A thread is part of the process address space; therefore, it is not necessary to duplicate the process address space of the process when a new thread is created. The `fork()` system call creates a new process and duplicates the process address space of the parent process. However, when a thread is created, it is part of its process address space. This significantly reduces memory consumption as well as creation time for the thread. There is an order of magnitude of difference between creating a process versus creating a thread. It takes approximately 1000 times longer to create a full process than it does to create a thread.

Each thread can be bound to a CPU, thereby enabling parallel processing. There are various routines such as `thr_create()`, `thr_suspend()`, `thr_join()`, and `thr_continue()` that create a thread, suspend a thread, block until thread termination, and continue execution of a thread, respectively.[22] Threads are extremely efficient but also are extremely complex. There are many issues such as signals, stacks, and synchronization that have to be considered carefully when using the threads model as opposed to the process model. The threads model calls for high-throughput low-overhead asynchronous processing. By default, threads are asynchronous and careful thought has to be given to the design of a threads application with respect to synchronization. While the concepts of threads and

---

21. POSIX is the Portable Operating System for the UNIX Standards Committee.

22. For more information on these Solaris thread system calls, refer to the manual pages on either `thr_create()`, `thr_continue()`, `thr_join()`, or `thr_suspend()`. The POSIX thread calls start with `pthread`, such as `pthread_create()`.

threads programming are certainly beyond the scope of this book, I intend to discuss the basic concepts of threads as well as the performance gains associated with threads. I encourage you to obtain a more detailed text on threads and threads programming.

Prior to the availability of threads, parallelism and asynchronous processing were accomplished by using the fork() system call. Using the fork() system call, a process created another process allowing both the parent and child process to execute simultaneously (assuming enough CPUs were available to handle multiple processes). The fork technique generates tremendous system overhead because separate process structures must be created and additional memory must be allocated. Solaris 2.X is a multithreaded operating system and most of the system daemons use threads to service requests.

1.2.8 SIGNALS AND INTERRUPTS

Fundamental to any operating system are the concepts of signals and interrupts. Signals are software events and interrupts are hardware events. Signals can be asynchronous or synchronous. Asynchronous signals can occur at any point. Asynchronous signals are things like the QUIT signal (CTRL-\), software interrupt signal (CTRL-C), or hang-up signal. Synchronous signals are caused by an invalid operation such as a floating-point exception, a divide-by-zero error, a segmentation violation, or a bus error. Signals are commonly used within applications as a method of communication between processes. Applications also use signals to trap certain events such as a user issuing the kill command on a specific process. The application could trap the kill signal and then shut down cleanly, as opposed to not trapping the signal and immediately aborting due to the kill request. You can use the signal(), sigset(), or sigaction() system calls to establish a signal handler in your application. You may choose to take a certain action upon receiving a certain signal or choose to ignore the signal and allow your application to continue. Certain signals, such as fatal hardware events, cannot be ignored and usually result in a core dump with the application being terminated. You can refer to the manual pages on signals or refer to the /usr/include/sys/signal.h file for system-defined signals. You can also define your own application user-specific signals.

Interrupts are kernel events that are used to notify the kernel when an event has occurred. A user application may issue a series of I/O calls and the kernel will pass these I/O calls to the I/O queue. The I/O devices involved will then process the I/O requests and then send an interrupt to the kernel, notifying the kernel that the I/O requests have completed. The kernel may then send a signal to the user process notifying the process that its I/O requests have completed. The user process can then check the error code of the I/O system calls to determine if the I/O requests have completed successfully. The kernel also uses interrupts to preempt processes or take a processor off-line.

1.2.9 NETWORK SERVICES AND COMMUNICATION

The kernel provides various network services including remote login, file transfers, *connectionless* connections, and NFS. The kernel provides a system daemon—the inetd daemon, to provide network services such as `rlogin`, `rsh`, `ftp`, and many other TCP/IP–based services. The default networking stack protocol for the UNIX kernel is TCP/IP. TCP/IP works in two parts: TCP (Transmission Control Protocol) is responsible for the virtual circuit layer that provides bidirectional data transmission; IP (Internet Protocol) is responsible for packet transmission between the user processes and the networking layer. Figure 1.19 shows the relationship between TCP and IP.

When the system is booted in multi-user mode, the `inetd` daemon is started. The `inetd` daemon is the Internet services daemon responsible for `telnet`, `rlogin`, `rsh`, and other types of Internet services. Upon a `login` or `telnet`, the `inetd` daemon forks and execs the appropriate daemon such as `in.telnetd` for a `telnet` session. The `/etc/inet/inetd.conf` file is the configuration file used to configure the `inetd` daemon. You can use this file to restrict certain Internet services such as remote shell (`rsh`) or finger. Upon an Internet service request such as `ftp`, the `inetd` daemon forks and execs the appropriate service daemon such as `in.ftpd` in the case of an `ftp` request. Using the `ps` command, you can verify this as there should be a process for the `ftp` session (`in.ftpd`), and the parent process ID should be the process ID of the `inetd` daemon. Most system administrators disable certain Internet services such as the remote shell and finger in order to increase the security of the system.

The raw IP layer consists of connectionless sockets. Sockets are a low-level method of communication using endpoints. With sockets, you can specify the type of protocol to use within the communication endpoint.

The UNIX kernel also supports other methods of communication such as pipes, named pipes, sockets, and messages. Messages are another method of interprocess communication. Messages typically are used to send special data to processes. A pipe is a unidirectional mechanism used to send streams of data to other processes. Named pipes are also another method of interprocess communication that provide a permanent path, as opposed to the traditional pipe. Sockets are bidirectional and are generally used for network communication between clients and servers. The client opens the communication endpoint via a socket, and the server listens on the socket to receive the communication.

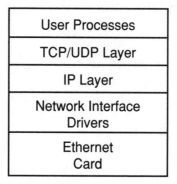

FIGURE 1.19 The networking layers.

1.2.10 I/O SERVICES

The UNIX kernel provides many different types of I/O including the standard synchronous I/O that consists of the read() and write() system calls, asynchronous I/O, streams I/O, and network I/O. Network I/O consists of the various different network services such as ftp, telnet, and other TCP/IP or other protocol-driven I/O services. Stream I/O is a mechanism for character-based I/O between the kernel and user processes. Examples of a stream are network connections, tape media, and other character devices. Asynchronous I/O is an enhancement to the standard synchronous I/O that allows nonblocking reads and writes. The kernel performs the asynchronous reads and writes and returns control to the calling program immediately following the asynchronous I/O system call. In the synchronous model, calling the system call read() or write() would not return control to the calling program until the completion of the read() or write() call. With asynchronous I/O, calls to aioread() or aiowrite() return immediately following the call.[23] If a signal handler has been established, the user process is later signaled when an outstanding asynchronous I/O call completes. Solaris 2.X provides a user library for writing applications using asynchronous I/O. The full path of the library is /usr/lib/libaio.so (shared library). Sequent also provides the library /usr/lib/libseq.a that contains the asynchronous I/O system calls.

The Sun Solaris library provides the aioread() and aiowrite() system calls for initiating asynchronous reads and writes, respectively. Sequent's library, libseq.a, provides DIO_Read() and DIO_Write() which, in addition to asynchronous I/O, provide direct I/O to file systems. Direct I/O bypasses the file system cache and accesses the disks directly.

1.2.11 SYNCHRONIZATION

The UNIX kernel provides several different methods of synchronization. Synchronization is the process of locking a resource to ensure consistency so that two or more processes do not invalidate each other's modifications. Although multiple processes can execute concurrently, locks are needed when a process wants to protect a resource such as a file, data block, and/or section of memory. For instance, consider the standard banking transaction: An individual is withdrawing money from his or her account, while another relative is depositing funds into the same account simultaneously. Without synchronization (locking), the end balance may not be reflected correctly.

The Solaris kernel provides the following methods of synchronization:[24]

1. mutex locks
2. condition variables

---

23. The aioread() and aiowrite() calls are provided by the Solaris asynchronous I/O library (libaio.so). For more information on the calls, you can refer to the manual pages on aioread() and aiowrite().

24. SunService. *SunOS 5.X Internals Guide SP-365*, Revision B.1. September 1993, pp. 2–31. Refer to the manual pages on mutexes, condition variables, semaphores, or reader/writer locks for detailed information on the related system calls.

3. semaphores

4. multiple-reader single-writer locks

Mutex locks are mutual exclusion locks and can be used at the process level or at the individual thread level. Mutex locks are simple and efficient low-level locks. Condition variables are used in conjunction with mutex locks to verify or wait on a particular condition. Semaphores are a standard method of synchronization and are part of the System V Release 4 interprocess communication kit. A semaphore is a nonnegative integer count of available resources. The integer count is either incremented or decremented as resources are freed or obtained, respectively. A semaphore count of zero indicates that no more resources are available. Multiple-reader single-writer locks are more complex than the other three types of synchronization as they provide multiple-reader locks as well as a writer lock. Multiple-reader single-writer locks are primarily used for data that is queried more often than updated. No reader locks can be obtained while a writer lock is held. Writer lock requests are favored over readers.

1.2.12   SYSTEM DAEMON LAYER

The concept of daemons is fundamental to the UNIX OS. A daemon is simply, as the term suggests, a task acting on behalf of another task or entity. In other words, a daemon is nothing more than a background job or process responsible for a certain task or set of tasks. The UNIX kernel consists of numerous system daemons that are responsible for memory management, file system management, printer jobs, network connections, and several other services. For example, consider the output shown in Table 1.5 from the ps command.

The listing in Table 1.5 from the `ps` command shows some of the system daemons that are running.[25] The `pageout` daemon (in Table 1.5 with `process ID=2`) is responsible for writing modified (i.e., dirty) pages to the file system. The `page` daemon, under certain conditions, will scan the memory page list and determine if the page is currently in use or has been recently referenced. Depending on the paging algorithm used,[26] the `page` daemon either will skip the memory page or return the page to the free list. The main goal of the `page` daemon is to ensure that the system does not run out of memory. After the page has been flushed out to disk by the `pageout` daemon, the page is placed on the page free list. The `pageout` daemon continues to run as long as there are pages to be written out to disk.

Another system daemon is the `fsflush` daemon. This daemon is responsible for flushing dirty disk pages from memory to disk. The UNIX kernel employs a UNIX file system cache for managing file systems. All writes to a file system–based file are first written to the file system cache, assuming the writes do not explicitly bypass the UNIX file system cache. The goal of the `fsflush` daemon is to ensure that dirty file system pages are written to disk.

---

25. The preceding output from ps was generated from a Sun Server running Solaris 2.5.

26. Paging algorithms are discussed in detail in Chapter 2.

TABLE 1.5 Output from the `ps` command

UID	PID	PPID	TIME	CMD
root	0	0	0:01	sched
root	1	0	0:01	/etc/init -
root	2	0	0:00	pageout
root	3	0	3:27	fsflush
root	131	1	0:01	/usr/sbin/inetd -s
root	289	1	0:00	/usr/lib/saf/sac -t 300
root	112	1	0:02	/usr/sbin/rpcbind
root	186	1	0:00	/usr/lib/lpsched
root	104	1	0:12	/usr/sbin/in.routed -q
root	114	1	0:01	/usr/sbin/keyserv
root	122	1	0:00	/usr/sbin/kerbd
root	120	1	0:00	/usr/sbin/nis_cachemgr
root	134	1	0:00	/usr/lib/nfs/statd
root	136	1	0:00	/usr/lib/nfs/lockd
root	155	1	0:00	/usr/lib/autofs/automountd
root	195	1	0:00	/usr/lib/sendmail -bd -q1h
root	159	1	0:00	/usr/sbin/syslogd
root	169	1	0:13	/usr/sbin/cron
root	194	186	0:00	lpNet

System daemons are critical to the operating system and service requests both from the kernel and from the user. The goal of these daemons is to satisfy these requests while maintaining the integrity of the system. System daemons generally close the standard files `stdin`, `stdout`, and `stderr`.[27] The file descriptor values for `stdin`, `stdout`, and `stderr` are 0, 1, and 2, respectively. Output from system daemons is usually directed to the system console or specific system administration files.

---

27. `Stdin`, `stdout`, and `stderr` are the default file descriptors associated with each process. `Stdin` refers to standard input. `Stdout` refers to standard output, and `stderr` refers to standard error.

1.2.13   SHELL LAYER

The UNIX operating system also provides different types of shells that act as a command interpreter and an interface to the OS. UNIX provides three standard types of shells: The Bourne shell (`sh`), the Korn shell (`ksh`), and the C-shell (`csh`). The Bourne shell and C-shell seem to be the most common. You may use the shell of your choice and customize it accordingly using the dot (.) files such as `.login`, `.cshrc`, and `.logout` for the C-shell. The `.cshrc` is the C-shell resource file invoked each time a C-shell is created. You can set objects such as environment variables, aliases, and file locations. You can also use your shell to invoke specific startup scripts or programs. Your default shell can be set by the UNIX system administrator in the `/etc/passwd` file or equivalent namespace in NIS or NIS+. Some UNIX vendors also provide a restricted shell (`/usr/lib/rsh`). This should not be confused with the standard remote shell (`rsh`), which is a remote login facility. The restricted shell is a special shell that restricts the user from changing environment variables and from changing directory locations. Under a restricted shell, the user may execute only commands found in the $PATH environment variable. This shell is often useful for secured accounts that need to run certain applications only. The system administrator can use a restricted shell to increase system security, permitting the user to run only certain commands and applications.

1.2.14   APPLICATION LAYER

The application layer within the UNIX architecture consists of user-level programs or scripts that are written in some sort of programming or script language. These programs or scripts tend to be executable or binary files used within an application. If a programming language such as C or C++ is used, the source code for the application is compiled using the C or C++ compiler. The compiler then generates object code specific to the platform and architecture. For example, compiling C code on a Sequent machine using DYNIX/ptx 4.4 generates object code based on the Intel architecture and the DYNIX/ptx operating system. Linking the object code produces a DYNIX/ptx format executable.

The application layer is an important layer within the UNIX architecture as it is responsible for running database software such as the Oracle8*i* Enterprise Edition, business-specific applications, graphics tools, and development and debugging tools. It is important that you understand this layer and all the layers beneath. This solid understanding will help you understand the Oracle architecture, thereby maximizing your ability to successfully tune your Oracle and UNIX environment.

Chapter 2

MEMORY AND PROCESSOR TUNING

The previous chapter explained the fundamentals of the UNIX operating system. This chapter covers the performance issues associated with memory and multiple processors. This chapter covers the Symmetrical Multiprocessor (SMP), and the Nonuniform Memory Access (NUMA) architectures.

Memory and processors are expensive system resources and should be regarded as such when tuning a system. Although systems can often become memory- or processor-bound, the answer is not always to add more hardware. The application may not be scalable or may not be using memory efficiently; therefore, additional hardware upgrades may not offer any gain.

There are two methods of tuning memory and processors: the *poor man's technique* and the *right-sizing technique*. The poor man's technique assumes that no additional hardware can be purchased or allocated, and the system administrator must use all means necessary to tune with what is available. In other words, adding memory or adding processors is not an option. For this technique, a conservationist approach must be taken to utilize memory as efficiently as possible while minimizing an application's CPU time. In this way, processes will be short transactions that occupy the CPU for a minimal period of time. Because the processes are short transactions, the system can handle multiple processes since each process occupies the CPU for only a small amount of time. The right-sizing technique, on the other hand, requires a greater effort in capacity planning. Right-sizing requires the collection of a tremendous range of statistics detailing scalability, performance metrics, application and database workload, and system utilization rates. Collectively, these statistics will help size a system accordingly with respect to the amount of physical memory, number of processors, number of disk drives and controllers, and number of media backup devices (tape drives).

2.1   UNIX MEMORY MODEL

The UNIX memory model is based on the virtual memory model which combines physical memory as primary storage and physical disk as secondary storage. This combination of primary and secondary storage represents the total virtual memory available to the system. Figure 2.1 demonstrates the concept of the virtual memory model.

In Figure 2.1, the total amount of memory available to the system is the total amount of virtual memory. Therefore, virtual memory = physical memory + swap device(s). In this example, the total amount of virtual memory available is 4 GB. The virtual memory consists of memory pages, usually 4 KB in size. The memory pages are managed by the `page` daemon, and a free list of free memory pages is maintained. The goal of the `page` daemon is to maintain a certain level of free memory as specified by the tunable thresholds and to maximize memory performance by maintaining active memory pages in physical memory for as long as possible.

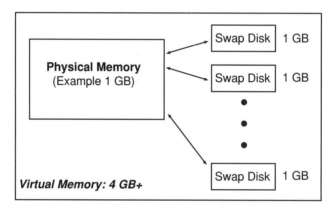

FIGURE 2.1   The virtual memory model.

2.1.1   PAGING

As discussed in Chapter 1, paging is the mechanism by which memory is divided into memory pages, typically 4 KB in size. The memory pages are then managed by the `page` daemon. The best way to think of the `page` daemon is as a cache manager for the virtual memory pool. Before a discussion on the `page` daemon commences, a review of some common terminology is in order. Table 2.1 defines these terms.

The `page` daemon is responsible for scanning the memory page reference bit to determine whether a page is active or idle. The `page` daemon uses a clocklike algorithm. Figure 2.2 details the clocklike algorithm of the `page` daemon.

In Figure 2.2, the total system memory is divided into smaller memory units known as pages. The `page` daemon scans through the memory pages periodically to determine the activity of the pages. The clocklike algorithm uses a two-phase scan. Upon the first scan, the memory page's reference bit is checked. If found to be idle, the page becomes a candidate for the free list. If found to be active, meaning the page is currently being accessed, the page reference bit is set to idle. Upon the second scan, if the page's reference bit is still found to be idle and its reference bit was set to idle during the first phase scan, the page becomes a candidate for the free list, possibly resulting in a *page-out*. If, however, the page reference bit is set to active, meaning the page has been referenced, the page is left untouched.

There are several paging parameters that control both the action and the frequency of the `page` daemon. The paging parameters are `lotsfree`, `desfree`, `minfree`, `slowscan`, `fastscan`, and `handspreadpages`.[1] In Solaris, you can set these parameters in the `/etc/system` kernel configuration file. You must reboot the system for your changes to take effect.

TABLE 2.1 Common Paging Terminology

TERM	DEFINITION
Page-in	Means that a page was requested and was subsequently brought into main memory.
Page-out	Occurs when a page is written out to disk (handled by the `pageout` daemon).
Page fault	Occurs when a page that has been requested had been returned to the free list, and the reference to the page forced the page to be reclaimed and brought back into main memory. There are two types of page faults: *minor page faults* and *major page faults*.
	Minor page fault—occurs when a page request was made for a page that has been returned to the free list. The minor fault indicates that although the page has been returned to the free list, it has not yet been reused. Hence, the page is brought back into the address space of the requesting process.
	Major page fault—occurs when a page request was made for a page that has been returned to the free list, but the page has been already reused by another process. This means that a new page would have to be allocated and the page data would have to be restored from the swap device, translating into physical I/O from the swap device.
Page attach	Occurs when a request for a page determines that the page is already in memory, and the process simply attaches to the page and increments the reference count by one. A large number of attaches is common during shared library usage and/or the use of shared memory by different programs.

---

1. The kernel paging parameters are operating system-specific, and you should refer to the system administration manual for your specific platform.

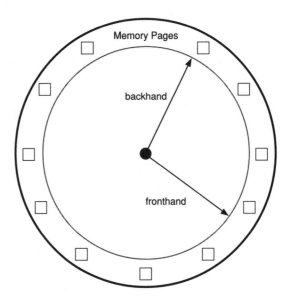

FIGURE 2.2   The clocklike algorithm of the `page` daemon.

The `lotsfree` parameter specifies (in number of pages) the upper-bound threshold of the amount of free system memory. If the available free memory is maintained above this upper bound, the `page` daemon will be idle until the available free memory falls below this parameter. To set this parameter on Solaris, edit the `/etc/system` file and enter the following line.

```
set lotsfree=<# of pages desired>
```

Example: `set lotsfree=256`

In order for the change to take effect, you must reboot the system. You can verify that the change took effect by issuing the following command.

```
mysystem# adb -k /dev/ksyms /dev/mem   * must be executed as root

    physmem 3e09                     * Output from adb
    lotsfree/D                       * enter lotsfree/D
    lotsfree:
    lotsfree:    256                 * value displayed in decimal
```

The `adb` utility is the Solaris general debugger and can be used to attach to the kernel to obtain kernel parameter values. The `/dev/ksyms` device is the kernel symbol table driver. The `/dev/mem` is the device that maps to the system's physical memory. After you issue the adb command, adb outputs the total physical memory being used.[2] Output from adb defaults to hexadecimal, but you can request decimal values by placing the /D switch after the respective kernel parameter. For example, lotsfree/D reports the value of the lotsfree parameter in decimal. For more information on the use of adb, refer to the manual pages on adb.

In Solaris 2.6, the default for lotsfree is 1.5 percent of physical memory. When the available free system memory is equal to lotsfree, then the page daemon uses the slowscan rate. The kernel checks to see if the available free system memory is less than lotsfree four times per second during the 100-Hz clock routine. If so, the pageout daemon is signaled.

The desfree parameter specifies (in number of pages) the middle bound value for the page daemon. If the available free system memory falls below desfree when pages are grabbed from the page free list, the pageout daemon is awakened. If the available free system memory remains below desfree for an average of 30 seconds, processes will selectively be swapped out to the swap device. The default for desfree is half the value of lotsfree.

The minfree parameter specifies (in number of pages) the absolute minimum amount of free system available memory. On Solaris, if the free system available memory is lower than minfree for an average of five seconds, the swapping out of processes will begin until the amount of free memory is restored to at least minfree. If the free available system memory falls below minfree, the *swapper* will continue to work aggressively until the minimum amount of free memory exists. The default for minfree is half the value of desfree.

The slowscan parameter defines the number of pages scanned per second by the paging algorithm when the available free memory is equal to lotsfree. The default for slowscan is 100. The frequency of the page daemon increases linearly from slowscan to fastscan as the available system memory drops from lotsfree to zero.

Fastscan, similar to slowscan, specifies the number of pages scanned per second when the available free memory is near zero. In other words, as the available memory drops from lotsfree to zero, the frequency of the page daemon in terms of pages scanned per second will increase from slowscan to fastscan. Since Solaris 2.4, the default for fastscan is physmem/4 with a maximum limit of 16384.

Handspreadpages specifies the distance (in pages) between the page daemon's fronthand scan and backhand scan. Higher values for handspreadpages increase the likelihood of pages remaining in main memory. Smaller values will result in the fronthand scan and backhand scan being closer to each other. This will increase paging activity and possibly increase the occurrence of page faults. On Solaris, you can set the handspreadpages kernel parameter in the /etc/system file. The default value for handspreadpages is typically set to the value of fastscan.

On Solaris, the page daemon is awakened by the page_create() routine when insufficient memory exists to satisfy the page_create() request. The page daemon can also be awakened by the page_create() routine if, after satisfying the memory request, the available free system memory falls below the value of desfree. The page daemon is

---

2. You can decrease the amount of physical memory by setting the kernel parameter physmem. Although this is not recommended, you can use this feature for benchmarking or testing.

also signaled by the `schedpaging()` routine, which calculates the number of pages to be scanned in the current scan cycle. The `schedpaging()` routine is scheduled via the `callout_thread()` routine. The two-handed paging clock algorithm is implemented by the `pageout_scanner()` routine. The `pageout_scanner()` routine initializes the clock hands and then sleeps until the amount of available free system memory falls below the value of `lotsfree`. The `pageout_scanner()` maintains two key variable counters: pushes and count.

The pushes variable contains the number of pages needed to be flushed out to disk. The count variable indicates the number of times that the `pageout_scanner()` routine completed an entire clock cycle without freeing any memory pages. If the value of count exceeds two, `pageout_scanner()` sleeps. The count variable is used to prevent the `pageout_scanner()` from occupying CPU time when no work is being performed by the `pageout_scanner()`. The `pageout_scanner()` will continue to scan until either enough free memory exists or the number of pages to be scanned is completed. The internal routine used by the `pageout_scanner()` routine to determine whether or not a page should be placed on the free list is the `checkpage()` routine. The `page_free()` routine places a page on the free list.

On Dynix/ptx 4.4, the header file `/usr/include/sys/mc_vmprvpm.h` defines the default values for the `minfree` and `desfree` paging parameters. You can also use the `/etc/vmtune` utility to set the value of `desfree` or `minfree`. The `/etc/vmtune` utility is described in greater detail in section 2.4.

Figure 2.3 summarizes paging parameters and `page` daemon scan rates.[3]

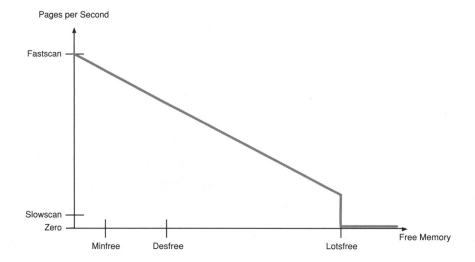

FIGURE 2.3　Paging parameters and the `page` daemon scan rates.

3.　Cockcroft, Adrian. *Sun Performance and Tuning*. Prentice Hall. 1995. p. 204.

2.1.2 SWAPPING

Swapping is the process by which all of the memory pages of a given process are written out to the swap device (swapped out). Swapping is generally an act of desperation by the operating system to free memory if the `page` daemon has failed to do so during its normal scanning process. The swapper process is activated by the `sched` system daemon when the free available memory falls below `desfree` and `minfree` for a specific time quantum. Figure 2.4 illustrates the concept of swapping.

In Figure 2.4, process 3485 is swapped out, meaning that all memory pages used by process 3485 are written out to the swap device. The kernel then returns all the memory used by the process to the free list. The kernel will continue swapping out processes until the available free system memory is at least equal to `minfree`. The swapper process is also invoked whenever a thread that is not currently loaded in memory is added to the dispatch queue.[4] Each scheduling class has its own swapping routines. When a swap-out takes place, the swapper calls the job class specific swap-out routine. The swap-out routine nominates a thread to be swapped out from each respective job class. The swap-out routine then swaps out the process structure and associated kernel stack of the thread with the lowest priority.

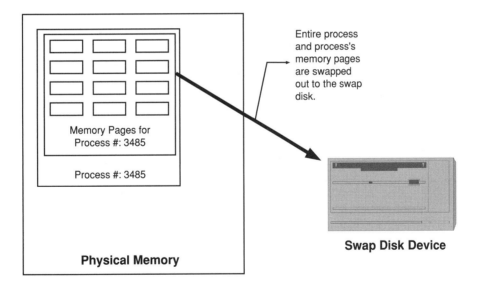

Entire process and process's memory pages are swapped out to the swap disk.

Memory Pages for Process #: 3485

Process #: 3485

Physical Memory

Swap Disk Device

FIGURE 2.4 The concept of swapping.

---

4. SunService. *SunOS 5.X Internals Guide SP-365*, Revision B.1. September 1993, pp. 5–15.

In Solaris, the two routines responsible for swap-outs are `ts_swapout()`, and `rt_swapout()` for the time-share job class (`ts`) and real-time job class (`rt`), respectively. The `ts_swapout()` routine does not consider threads that have any of the following conditions:

❑ The thread is in the process of being created.

❑ The thread is not currently loaded into memory.

❑ The thread's `t_schedflag TS_DONT_SWAP` is set.

❑ The thread's `t_proc_flag TP_LWPEXIT` is set

❑ The thread was recently swapped in.

Real-time threads are never swapped out. Real-time processes and their associated kernel stack are locked in memory. Because real-time threads are not swapped out, the `rt_swapin()` routine simply indicates whether or not there are currently runable threads in the real-time scheduling class that are loadable into memory.

2.2   PROCESS MEMORY MODEL

The UNIX operating system process memory model is based on the virtual memory model. In addition to the address space of a given process consisting of memory pages, the kernel also provides an *anonymous* memory layer. The anonymous memory layer is used to manage anonymous memory pages by using anonymous structures that map to the anonymous pages by means of hash tables.

Figure 2.5 shows the different segments that are associated with a process such as the user stack segment, hole segment, data segment, and text segment. The kernel, of course, is separate from the user process and contains two main stacks: the kernel stack and the interrupt stack. The user stack segment is used to store local variables and is also used during function calls. The user stack is dynamically allocated and dynamically adjusted. The typical default for a user stack for a process is 8 MB.[5] The hole segment is where the local memory storage is managed. Calls like `malloc()` and `mmap()` are serviced through the hole segment. The data segment contains items such as global variables and static variables. A static variable maintains its last value. A nonstatic variable is not exported to the linker. The text segment contains the actual code of the process. Each segment is responsible for managing its respective memory pages. Within the stack segment, there are four different types of stacks:

1. User stack

2. Kernel stack

3. Alternate signal stack

4. Interrupt stack

---

5.   You can use the `sbrk()` routine to alter the size of the stack. For more information on the call, refer to the manual pages on `sbrk()`.

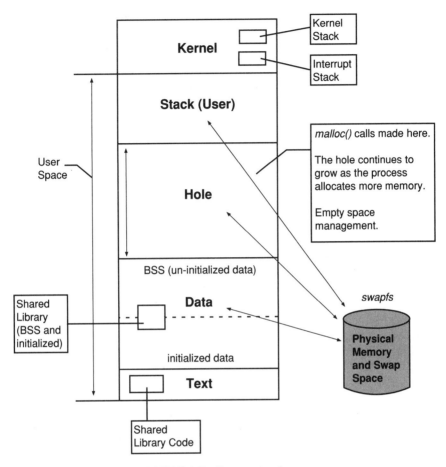

FIGURE 2.5   Segments of a process.

The data and stack segments' pages consist of *anonymous* memory. Anonymous memory is used for the uninitialized section (bss) of the data segment, the stack segment, and a copy-on-write (COW). A copy-on-write occurs when a change to a private page is made, causing a private copy of the page to be created and leaving the original page intact. The change then is made to the private copy of the page. This is done for reasons of consistency when pages are mapped as private. If the page is mapped as shared, the change is made to the original page. Anonymous memory can exist either in the main memory or on the swap device. However, anonymous memory is not identifiable through the file system. Anonymous memory is located using the anonymous memory structures that in turn use hash tables. Each memory page consists of a vnode and an offset. Memory pages are located using hash tables and the offsets. Anonymous pages must first reserve permanent backing store via the swap device, even if the backing store is not used. This is to guarantee that upon a `fork()` and/or `exec()`, sufficient memory exists up front to successfully complete the `fork()` and/or `exec()`, avoiding situations in which the `exec()` call fails at some point later in the execution due to insufficient memory and/or swap space. The `tmpfs` file system provides a file system layer for anonymous pages. Upon process termination, all anonymous memory pages are zeroed out using the `/dev/zero` device before the pages are returned to the free list. This is done for security reasons to prevent data from being read from the anonymous pages.

When the `fork()` system call is issued, the address space of the parent process [the process issuing the `fork()`] is duplicated for the newly created child process. The data pages are marked as copy-on-write. Figure 2.6 illustrates the duplication of the parent process address space for the child process that results from the `fork()` call.

Typically following a `fork()`, an `exec()` is performed to make the child process execute another program. The `exec()` system call takes an executable as its first argument as well as any arguments passed to the executable. When the `exec()` call is issued following the `fork()`, the child process' stack, data, and text segment layers are overlaid with the new executable as passed in to the `exec()` call. Only data pages and stack pages are saved to memory. Shared libraries (text and data segments) are also a part of the process structure address space. Shared libraries are paged in dynamically from the file system. Program text and file data are also paged in from the file system. File data can also be paged out as well. Because text pages are not modified (meaning the executable does not modify itself while running), the loaded executable's text segment will not generate any dirty file system pages. Text segments are not backed by swap as opposed to data and stack segments. Hence, executable text segments avoid the flushing of dirty file system pages to disk because no dirty pages exist for a text segment. A page that is resident in the file system

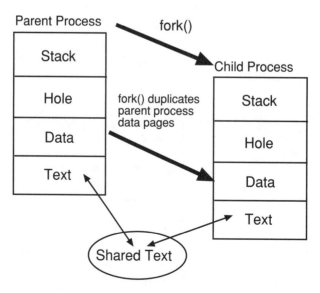

FIGURE 2.6   The `fork()` system call.

cache may also have several references from multiple processes. As part of a performance optimization, the page scanner now ignores a page if eight or more references to that page exist, irrespective of page activity. This optimization improves the performance of shared libraries and processes which execute the same code by maintaining these sets of pages in memory.

Solaris 7 optimized the virtual address space mapping of a process by not requiring that the top 256 MB of virtual address space be reserved, since it is not necessary on the sun4u kernel architecture. Hence, for 32-bit sun4u kernels, it is possible to have a virtual address space of 4,090 MB as opposed to the earlier limit of $3.75 \times 1,024$ MB. This allows an extra 256 MB of process address space. For example, in Solaris 7, shared libraries will be mapped 256 MB higher than they were in Solaris 2.6.

Shared libraries provide a significant performance gain as well as a substantial reduction in memory requirements. When a program that uses shared libraries is executed, the OS will mmap() the shared library into the user's process address space. The mmap() system call maps a file system–based file directly into user space without the overhead of first copying the file into the UNIX file system cache, followed by another copy into the user's address space. The mmap() call eliminates copy overhead by directly mapping the file into the user's address space. This not only saves CPU cycles but also reduces memory requirements by eliminating buffer copies. Shared libraries also allow multiple processes to share the same code (functions and modules). If an executable were statically linked (meaning that the executable contains, as part of the executable, all the referencing objects and libraries), multiple processes running the same executable may have to allocate the memory address space necessary to hold the objects and libraries that were invoked by the main executable. If, on the other hand, the executable were linked dynamically (or shared), each process that invoked the library would simply mmap() to the address where the library is loaded. This means that the shared library needs only to be loaded into memory once. For a large shared library, this can result in significant memory savings. If you are developing a large application that will serve many users, the libraries that you develop should be developed as shared libraries.

2.3 MONITORING PAGING AND SWAPPING

By now, you should be familiar with the basic concepts of paging and swapping. In order to maximize the performance of your system, you should monitor the paging and swapping activity by using sar or vmstat. The sar utility is a generic reporting utility available on UNIX platforms. The vmstat utility is available with Solaris. You can monitor paging activity by using the sar -p command. For example, on a Sequent system,

```
myhost> sar -p 1 5

DYNIX/ptx myhost 4.0 V4.1.3 i386
```

```
vflt/s   pflt/s   pgfil/s   rclm/s
51.24     0.00      0.00      0.00
 4.96     0.00      0.00      0.00
 7.56     0.00      0.00      0.00
 2.50     0.00      0.00      0.00
 5.83     0.00      0.00      0.00
```

In this example, the `sar -p` (paging) option is used to collect paging activity statistics. The first parameter following the `-p` option is the polling interval, in seconds. In this case, `sar` reports paging statistics every second. The second parameter following the `-p` option is the number of iterations of particular statistics that `sar` reports. Therefore, in this case, `sar` reports paging statistics every second for five iterations. The `vflt/s` column reports the number of virtual faults per second. A virtual fault is the result of an address translation page fault, meaning that a virtual address no longer maps to a valid physical page. The `pflt/s` column reports the number of page faults per second. The `pgfil/s` is the number of virtual faults per second that were handled by pages being paged in from the file system. The `rclm/s` column reports the number of page reclaims per second. A page reclaim occurs when a page that was *stolen* has to be brought back into main memory after being placed on the page free list. You can also use the `/etc/monitor` utility on Sequent to monitor paging and swapping. For example,

```
myhost> /etc/monitor

usr %      389      pgdrec   80      semops   552
sys %      320      pgin     0
tot %      709      ppgin    0
procs     1339      pgout    0
on p      5         ppgout   0
runq      0         sw in    0
wait      6         pswin    0
sleep     1328      sw out   0
swapped   0         pswout   0
fs io     2         fs brd   8
phys io   4         fs bwt   0
sysc      13414     fs rdh   100
csw       1068      fs wth   100
intr      754       raw rd   294
traps     63369     raw wt   72
fork      1         raw rKB  1591
vfork     1         raw wKB  289
exec      3         lckcnt   12
dk xf     542       %locks   0
dk KB     2882      deficit  0
ttyin     0         free     512418
ttyout    0         dirty    18
pf        796       tot vm   52280584
pg rec    127       msgops   1
```

On Sequent, the /etc/monitor utility also reports paging statistics such as page-ins, page-outs, the amount of free memory, and the number of dirty pages. For more information on the /etc/monitor utility, refer to the manual pages on /etc/monitor (i.e., man monitor). The /etc/monitor utility reports free memory in units of 1 KB. You can also use the sar -r command on Sequent systems to determine the number of free memory pages available for user processes (freemem), and number of free disk blocks available from the swap device for swapping (freeswap).

In Solaris, you can use the sar -p command to monitor paging.

```
myhost> sar -p 1 5

SunOS myhost 5.7 Generic_sun4u

            atch/s   pgin/s   ppgin/s   pflt/s   vflt/s   slock/s
             0.00     0.93      0.93     114.81   469.44    0.00
             0.00     0.00      0.00      10.37    47.41    0.00
             0.00     0.00      0.00     141.12   362.62    0.00
             0.00    23.58     90.57      94.34   705.66    0.00
             0.00    23.36     88.79      24.30   185.98    0.00

Average      0.00     9.06     34.10      73.71   338.54    0.00
```

In this example, the atch/s column indicates the number of times per second that processes attached to shared pages already in memory. The pgin/s column indicates the number of page-in requests per second. The ppgin/s column is the number of page-ins per second. The pflt/s column reports the number of page faults per second. The vflt/s column reports the number of virtual faults per second. Virtual faults occur when a translation from a virtual page to its corresponding physical memory page determines that the physical page is no longer in memory. The slock/s column reports the number of page faults incurred per second as a result of software locks that require physical I/O. In the above output, an average of 9.06 page-ins per second occurred over a 5 second interval. An average of 338.54 virtual faults per second occurred over a 5 second period.

In Solaris, you can also use the vmstat utility to monitor paging and/or swapping. For example,

```
myhost> vmstat 1 10

 procs     memory            -------- page -----------   disk          faults          cpu
 r b w     swap     free re    mf   pi  po fr de sr s6 s3 s3 s3    in    sy    cs us sy id
 0 0 0    12624     2824  0  2466  281  11 34  0 24  0  0  0  3  1516  1033  2797 19 12 69
 0 0 0 20122768  3303664  0   124    0   0  0  0  0  0  0  1  0   977 23287  5867 20 11 68
 1 0 0 20123272  3303960  0     0    0   0  0  0  0  0  0  0  0   823 13497  5449 18  1 81
 0 0 0 20123520  3304152  0     4    0   0  0  0  0  0  0  0  0   811 13609  5631 19  2 80
 1 0 0 20119064  3300816  0  1345 1208   0  0  0  0  0  0  0  0  2506 23903 10833 22 12 66
 0 0 0 20118512  3298568  0   460    0   0  0  0  0  0  0  0  0  1405 32066  6485 21 20 59
 0 0 0 20118560  3298664  0     4    0   0  0  0  0  0  0  0  0  1117 19008  6071 20  7 73
 0 0 0 20118560  3298664  0     0    0   0  0  0  0  0  0  0  0  1169 14697  6520 19  3 78
 0 0 0 20118496  3298600  0     3    0   0  0  0  0  0  0  0  0  1168 15788  6642 19  4 78
 0 0 0 20119256  3299280  0     0    0   0  0  0  0  0  0  0  0  1361 16941  7216 19  9 72
```

2.3.1 INTERPRETING vmstat OUTPUT

The vmstat utility, similar to sar, reports the number of page reclaims (re), minor page faults (mf), page-ins (pi), page-outs (po), kilobytes freed (fr), the anticipated amount of short-term memory shortfall (de), and the number of pages scanned (sr). It is important to note that vmstat reports memory statistics based on the deltas between two snapshots of kernel counters. Since the first line is the current snapshot minus zero, you should discount the first line of output from vmstat as this largely represents data from the last reboot. In addition, if you use small polling intervals such as 1 second, you may observe tangible discrepancies between each line of vmstat output. This could be due to system peaks or spikes in memory usage. A polling interval of 5 or 10 seconds is reasonable to monitor memory utilization for a relatively short amount of time. For periodic system monitoring over longer periods of times, such as several hours, you may want to use several minutes as the polling interval.

The main statistic to monitor from vmstat output is the scan rate (sr column). This statistic will help you gauge the paging activity on the system. If the value of the scan rate column is mostly zero for each line of vmstat output, then the page daemon is mostly idle. The page-out, page-in, and page fault columns also help identify the paging frequency. If the scan rates (sr) and page-out (po) rates constantly exceed 20, then excessive paging is occurring. In addition, you should monitor the I/O statistics for the swap devices to determine if I/Os are occurring. If a significant number of I/Os are occurring on the swap devices, this indicates that paging is occurring and that there is a shortage of memory.

To monitor swapping, use the following sar command.

```
myhost> sar -w 1 5

SunOS myhost 5.7 generic sun4u

        swpin/s bswin/s swpot/s bswot/s pswch/s
         0.00     0.0    0.00     0.0     3905
         0.00     0.0    0.00     0.0     5068
         0.00     0.0    0.00     0.0     5179
         0.00     0.0    0.00     0.0     4348
         0.00     0.0    0.00     0.0     5190

Average  0.00     0.0    0.00     0.0     4729
```

The sar command shows the number of swap-ins per second (swpin/s) and swap-outs per second (swpot/s). You can also use the Solaris vmstat command with the -S option (vmstat -S 1) to monitor swapping activity. On Sequent, you can use the /etc/monitor utility to monitor swapping as well as paging. In the /etc/monitor example given previously, swap-ins and swap-outs are reported along with paging statistics. On HP, you can use sar or the HP Glance Plus tools to monitor paging and/or swapping.

To adequately tune paging and swapping on your system, you should use the sar and/or vmstat utilities to monitor paging and swapping. There are also graphical user interface (GUI) tools from Sun, HP, LandMark, and BMC Software[6] that provide graphical displays of paging and swapping. These tools provide additional performance monitoring features that are extremely useful. I strongly encourage you to purchase a complete and concise set of GUI performance monitoring tools. If you administer a mixed environment such as a combination of Sun, Sequent, and HP, you may want to consider purchasing a cross-platform tool. This will provide you with a consistent level of administration and monitoring tools for your heterogeneous environment. While `sar` and `vmstat` can provide useful information, they are less user friendly than GUI monitoring tools. And, as the old saying goes, "a picture is worth a thousand words." In this case, a GUI graph of your system's performance makes a magnitude of difference over character-mode tools that require you to compute percentages and/or conversions manually. The majority of the GUI monitoring tools also provide client and server agents that enable you to monitor all of your systems from a single console.

2.4 TUNING PAGING

2.4.1 PHYSMEM

The `physmem` kernel parameter sets the total amount of physical memory in the system. This value is set automatically when the kernel boots. You should not need to set this parameter. Many kernel variables are dependent on `physmem`, and if `physmem` is set inappropriately, it may cause abnormal system behavior. However, if you are benchmarking an application or a system, you may want to set this value to reduce the amount of memory available. You can then increase the value of `physmem` for each iteration at some nominal rate and document the performance gains of increasing system memory. For example, suppose your system has 1 GB of memory. You may want to set `physmem` to the equivalent of 128 MB and run the application. Then, you can continue to increase the value of `physmem` in increments of 128 MB until you finally reach 1 GB. At each iteration, you will be able to measure the effects of adding memory to the system. You may find that little if any gain is offered by increasing the memory. This tends to indicate that either the application utilizes a very small amount of memory, or that the application may be heavily dependent on other resources such as disk I/O and/or the CPU. Before you launch your application, you should thoroughly review the complete application memory requirements with the application staff and system administration staff. You can do this by examining the different data structures within the application and any dynamic memory allocations. Be especially careful when looking for dynamic memory allocation routines. Programmers often use elegant techniques to allocate memory, and it may not be directly obvious to the reader. In Solaris, you can set `physmem` by placing a line in the `/etc/system` file as follows:

```
set phsymem=262144
```

---

6. BMC Software offers the Patrol (GUI) Software Suite.

Remember that `physmem` (as are most other Solaris kernel paging parameters) is represented in pages, not in bytes. The preceding example sets the physmem to 262,144 pages, each 4 KB in size.[7] This translates into 1 GB of available memory. For your change to take effect, you must reboot the system. Following the reboot, you can verify that your change took effect by using the `adb` command.

2.4.2 LOTSFREE

The `lotsfree` kernel parameter sets the upper bound of free memory that the system tries to maintain. If the available free memory is always above `lotsfree`, the `page` daemon will remain idle until the amount of free memory falls below `lotsfree`. If your system has plenty of memory, such as 1 GB or higher, you may want to consider setting `lotsfree` to a low value to avoid unnecessary paging. However, on systems where memory is scarce you may want to set `lotsfree` to a higher value than the default. This will cause the `page` daemon to be much more active and will help ensure that processes are not starved of memory. This also means that cache hit rates will be much lower since the `page` daemon will more than likely continue to return pages to the free list until the system has sufficient free memory.

2.4.3 DESFREE

The `desfree` kernel parameter sets the middle bound of free memory that the system tries to maintain. The value of `desfree` also causes the system to choose between paging and swapping. If the available free memory falls below `desfree` and remains below `desfree` for more than a certain period of time, swapping is employed in place of paging. Again, if your system has plenty of free memory, you should set the value of `desfree` to a low value to prevent an overactive `page` daemon. If your system has a limited amount of memory, using the default or increasing `desfree` helps avert memory deprivation.

On Sequent systems, `desfree` is the amount of free memory (expressed in kilobytes) that the swapper would like maintained on average. The default of `desfree` is 2 percent of the real memory available following the system boot. You can use the `/etc/vmtune` utility on Sequent to set or to view the paging kernel parameters. For example, to set `desfree` to 10 MB on your Sequent system, issue the following command as root:

```
myhost {root}-> /etc/vmtune -desfree 10240
```

The `/etc/vmtune` utility then shows all the values of the paging parameters, including your recent change, and asks you to confirm the change. For more information on the `/etc/vmtune` utility, refer to the manual pages (i.e., man `vmtune`).

---

7. The sun4u architecture (Ultra series) uses an 8 KB page size. This increases the performance of large memory allocations.

```
myhost{root}-> /etc/vmtune -desfree 10240

      128 minRS
  1902808 maxRS
       20 RSexecslop
        4 RSexecmult
        5 RSexecdiv
      100 dirtylow
      200 dirtyhigh
      128 klout_look
      100 PFFvtime
        8 PFFdecr
        2 PFFlow
       20 PFFincr
       15 PFFhigh
     1088 minfree
    10240 desfree    * (new desfree value)
      400 maxdirty
      Ok? y
```

2.4.4 MINFREE

The minfree kernel parameter sets the absolute lower limit of free available memory. If free memory drops below minfree, swapping of processes begins until the amount of free memory is at least equal to or greater than minfree. After that point, the page daemon resumes its normal algorithm. Be extremely careful when you set minfree, as this represents the lowest limit. For large-scale systems with an abundance of memory, set minfree to a low value such as 1 MB or 2 MB. The default is usually lower than this value. Nevertheless, setting the value of minfree to a reasonable value reduces the likelihood of the system swapping and possibly thrashing. If your system has 4 GB of memory or more, 1 MB–2 MB is relatively small compared to the total amount of available memory. Allowing the amount of free memory to approach minfree when minfree is very small, such as 512 KB, is quite dangerous and can lead to excessive swapping. Minfree needs to be set reasonably so that swapping is avoided, and so the system always has a legitimate amount of free memory available. On Solaris, you can set the value of minfree in the /etc/system file.

On Sequent, minfree is expressed in kilobytes and represents the lowest amount of free memory maintained on the average before desperation mode swapping is initiated. Desperation mode swapping sorts the list of processes by resident size and by the amount of time the process spent sleeping and then swaps out the selected processes accordingly. The resident size is the amount of memory pages of a process that are resident in real memory. It is important to note that a process may not necessarily be entirely resident in real memory. You can tune additional parameters using vmtune, such as the minimum resident set size (minRS), as well as the maximum resident size (maxRS). If you are not able to lock the SGA, you may want to consider setting the maxRS parameter to the maximum size of the Oracle SGA in order to ensure that the entire SGA is resident in real memory. Never set maxRS to an amount larger than the amount of physical memory. A larger maxRS reduces paging activity and page faults by maintaining more of the processes' memory pages in real memory. Use caution when setting maxRS as it is a global setting and can cause excessive paging if many processes are allocating large amounts of memory. Sequent provides the flag SHM_HARDLOCK to the shmget() system call which allows shared memory segments to be hardlocked. This prevents the shared memory segment from being swapped out or paged out. Using this feature alleviates the need to set maxRS to achieve the goal of maintaining the SGA memory pages in real memory.

The PFFvtime is the number of CPU clock ticks between page fault frequency checks. The default is usually 100 clock ticks (or one second). The PFFlow parameter is the minimum page faulting rate per second before the resident set decreases. The PFFdecr parameter is the number of kilobytes to decrease the resident set size. PFFhigh is the maximum page faulting rate per second before the resident set increases. PFFincr is the number of kilobytes to increase the resident size. The dirtyhigh and dirtylow parameters specify the maximum and minimum size (in kilobytes), respectively, of the dirty memory list. The maxdirty parameter specifies the maximum size of the dirty memory list (in kilobytes) before aggressive swapping begins. You can set the value of minfree using the /etc/vmtune utility. For example, the following command (which must be executed as root) sets minfree to 1 MB.

```
myhost {root}-> /etc/vmtune -minfree 1024
```

2.4.5 MAXPGIO

The maxpgio parameter regulates the number of page-out I/O operations per second that are scheduled by the system. On Solaris, the default is 40 pages per second on older systems and 60 pages per second for Sun4d systems. The default is based on the 3600 rpm disk drive. However, most new disk drives are either 7200 or 10000 rpm. Therefore, you can increase the value of maxpgio in accordance with your disk drive speeds. Avoid setting maxpgio too high so that the disk is not saturated with page I/O requests. On Solaris, the formula for maxpgio is disk rate (in revolutions per second) x 2/3. If your swap disk drives are 7200 rpm, set maxpgio = 120 rps x 2/3 = 80.

2.4.6 PRIORITY PAGING

Priority Paging is a new feature in Solaris 7 which improves memory utilization for file system-prevalent systems. Priority Paging helps address the performance issue of normal file system activity adversely affecting application memory utilization. Since Solaris caches file system pages as part of the virtual memory pool, it is very likely that a substantial amount of memory will be consumed for file system pages if the applications perform frequent file system I/O across a large working set. For example, consider a database server on which the database files are based on file system files and there exists a large number of concurrent users on the system. For a large database with many data files, it is likely that the data working set will be large since users will be operating on different data sets (random I/O). In this case, caching the file system pages may interfere with the memory components of the database server and may result in application memory pages being paged out. Using priority paging, the system administrator can place an upper limit on the file system cache so that pages are not effectively "stolen" from the application memory working set. A large amount of file system I/O will result in inundating the memory with file system pages, which will invoke the page scanner when the amount of available memory drops to the threshold defined by `lotsfree`. The scanner will then attempt to page out nonrecently referenced pages. Since a large amount of random I/O is occurring, the file system pages will most likely be "hot" (recently referenced). Hence, the page scanner may decide to age out the heap and stack address space of the application. If the system was serving an Oracle database, this could result in portions of the SGA or PGA being paged out.

Priority paging defines a new tunable parameter, `cachefree`, which defaults to 2 × `lotsfree`. If priority paging is enabled, the system attempts to maintain the number of pages defined by `cachefree` on the freelist. In addition, the file system pages will only be freed when the amount of free memory falls between `cachefree` and `lotsfree`. The priority paging algorithm introduces the new page scanner threshold `cachefree`. When the amount of free memory falls below `cachefree`, the page scanner will attempt to free only file system pages, excluding shared libraries and executables. This improves overall memory utilization by trying to avoid paging out application related memory pages. If priority paging is disabled and the amount of free memory drops to `lotsfree`, executables and anonymous memory may be paged out even with an insignificant amount of file system I/O.

Priority paging is available in Solaris 7 and Solaris 2.6 as part of the kernel patch 105181-09 (or higher). You can enable priority paging by setting the parameter `priority_paging` in the `/etc/system` file as follows.

```
set priority_paging=1
```

2.4.7 THE PAGING PARAMETERS RANGE CHECK

When tuning the kernel paging parameters, you must maintain the following range check:

```
cachefree > lotsfree > desfree > minfree
```

It is extremely important that your settings meet the above constraint check. Otherwise, the system might experience atypical paging behavior. Improperly setting the paging parameters might also cause the system to panic. Use care before altering the values of the kernel paging parameters. You should also maintain a reasonable multiplying factor between the kernel paging parameters. In other words, `lotsfree` should be a positive multiplier of `desfree`, and `desfree` also should be a positive multiplier of `minfree`.

This ensures that the values of each are not so close to each other that swapping is triggered by a hairline memory allocation. The value of the multiplier depends on the amount of physical memory available on the system. For systems with large amounts of memory (2 GB or more), you may want to use a higher multiplier. For a system with a small to medium amount of memory, use a smaller multiplier. For example, on a system with 2 GB of physical memory, if minfree is set to the equivalent of 1 MB, you may want to set desfree to 2 MB or a higher multiple of 1 MB, and lotsfree to 4 MB or a higher multiple. Avoid using large multipliers, otherwise you may have too large a gap between idle paging and swapping.

I would suggest that before altering the paging parameters, you review your settings with your hardware vendor's OS engineers. They will help you verify the settings and review in detail any associated implications. When tuning paging parameters, make sure you study the system default values, as well as examine any additional parameters that are dependent on the paging parameters. Default values often change between OS versions as the OS becomes more and more efficient. Parameters often become obsolete and are replaced with new parameters. Therefore, you should always study the new OS version in detail before you apply settings from an older OS release.

2.4.8 CYCLICAL PAGE CACHE

Solaris 8 replaces the priority paging algorithm with a more sophisticated file system caching architecture known as the Cyclical Page Cache. The new cyclical Page Cache method in Solaris 8 uses a dedicated file system free list to maintain file system data pages. Memory pages for other objects such as binaries, shared libraries, applications, and the kernel are managed by a separate free list. This avoids situations where heavy file system activity may cause competition for memory and result in paging. Using a separate free list avoids situations where memory pages used by running applications are aged out of the cache in order to satisfy file I/O requests. The new cyclical cache method in Solaris 8 improves performance for systems based primarily on file system files such as web servers or database servers.

The cyclical page cache architecture improves the ability to differentiate between a system experiencing heavy file I/O and a system experiencing a true shortage of memory. The vmstat utility can be used to monitor the memory utilization on the Solaris system. In Solaris 8, the vmstat utility has been extended to report memory utilization statistics for the cyclical page cache. The -p option of vmstat can be used to monitor paging activity for file system I/O and applications. Higher page reclaim rates in Solaris 8 simply reflect heavy file system activity. The free memory counter now also includes a the file system cache which will generally result in more memory being reported as available. The scan rate (sr column of the vmstat output) in Solaris 8 will generally be close to zero since a separate free list is used for the file system cache. Hence, non-zero values for the scan rate in Solaris 8 indicate a legitimate shortage of memory.

Solaris 8 greatly improves the optimization of virtual memory, and Solaris 8 should not require the manual tuning of virtual memory. In addition, the priority paging option should not be used in Solaris 8 since the cyclical page cache architecture is much more efficient.

2.5   SWAPPING

The swapper is run by the `sched` daemon. A process or thread is not considered swappable if the process or thread

❑ is part of the system scheduling class;

❑ is part of a process being forked;

❑ is in the zombie state; or

❑ has its address space in the kernel's address space.

Swapping is triggered when the average amount of free memory (`avefree`) is less than `desfree` or `minfree`. There are two types of swapping: leisure and desperate swapping. Leisure swapping begins when the amount of free memory falls below `desfree`. The swapper selects the processes to be swapped out. Usually the most idle processes (sleeping) are selected for swap-out. Desperate swapping begins when the amount of free memory falls below `minfree` (the absolute minimum). Processes are selected for swap-out based on the resident size, idle time, and priority. Desperate swapping is much more aggressive than leisure swapping because the swapper must restore the amount of free memory to at least `minfree`. Although processes may reserve swap space upon startup, a page of swap is not generally allocated until the page has to be flushed out. Also, some of the UNIX kernels allow swap space to be part of the physical memory pool because the kernel considers the physical memory and swap space as one large virtual memory pool (physical plus swap device). For example, Solaris allows reserved swap space to be part of physical memory. This improves the speed of swap reservation since the reservation may be done in physical memory rather than on physical disk. Swapping can severely impact performance.

Excessive swapping can also cause the system to appear unstable and can result in a panic. Recall that swapping is an act of desperation by the operating system to free memory immediately. Hence, the system selects processes to be swapped out, subsequently flushing these selected processes out to the swap device. The memory used by these processes can then be returned to the free list. Although swapping is commonly an outcome of a system lacking sufficient memory, swapping is often caused by *runaway* programs. Programs sometimes cause memory leaks due to improper process cleanup or by forgetting to free memory structures during the life of a process. Memory leaks are generally difficult to detect, especially in daemon programs that run continuously and `fork()` children to parallelize requests. There are numerous tools available on the market that help detect memory leaks and memory access violations. Rational Software offers the Purify tool, which detects memory leaks and access violations. Bounds Checker is another tool that also provides similar functionality. I cannot overemphasize the importance of such tools. These tools save programmers days and weeks of searching through code to find memory leaks. The time and effort saved by these tools well outweigh the cost of these tools. There are also regression testing tools such as SQA Team Test that thoroughly test the application. Testing tools may not pinpoint the exact location in the code that is causing the memory leak. However, through continued regression tests, you stand a higher chance of reproducing the memory leaks and locating the cause. Testing tools, coupled with the memory leak detection tools such as Purify, provide a robust and proper development environment.

On Sequent, you can tune the swap allocation policy. The kernel parameter SWAP_ALLOC_POLICY controls the swap allocation policy. If set to 0 (the default), swap space is allocated at process startup. If insufficient swap space exists to invoke the process, the process is terminated. If SWAP_ALLOC_POLICY is set to 1, swap space is allocated for processes upon startup except for paged incarnation virtual segments, mmap() or anonymous map objects, address space page tables, and the U-block of a process. If SWAP_ALLOC_POLICY is set to 2, no swap space is allocated at process startup except for shared pagable kernel objects. Setting SWAP_ALLOC_POLICY to 2 could lead to termination of a process throughout the execution of the process due to insufficient swap space. A value of 0 ensures that enough swap space exists to start the process. You should set the value of SWAP_ALLOC_POLICY to 0. This guarantees that if sufficient swap space exists, the process will start successfully. Although a value of 0 may increase process startup time, it is a much safer setting, and the time needed to reserve swap space during process startup is extremely minimal.

In order to avoid high paging and swapping, you should study in complete detail the applications that will be running on the system. Items of concern are the lifetime of the process, memory requirements of the application, allocation and deallocation routines, and process termination mechanisms. The more detailed information you have about the applications that will be running on your system, the easier it will be to tune your system in accordance with its requirements. I am constantly surprised by the reply that a system administrator receives after asking a developer, "How much memory does your application need?" The surprising reply is that a developer is often not sure how much memory is being used in the application. However, as the system administrator, you must work closely with the development staff to find the answers to the items of concern listed in this paragraph. The tuning advice with regard to swapping is: *avoid it at all costs.*

2.5.1 CONFIGURING SWAP

The UNIX operating system generally reserves (not allocates) swap space when processes are invoked. This ensures that the process can be swapped in and swapped out. The rule of thumb for configuring swap space is two to three times the amount of physical memory. I recommend that you create a swap device three to four times the amount of physical memory. For example, if you have a system that has 512 MB of memory, you should create a swap device of 1.5 GB–2 GB in size. This helps reduce the likelihood of your system's running out of swap space. Although the physical swap device should not be used frequently, since the goal is to keep processes in real (physical) memory, it is a good idea to have a more than sufficient amount of swap space in the event that it is needed. Also, some installer programs and applications require a generous amount of swap space upon startup. I also recommend that you distribute your swap files across different disk drives and controllers. You should create many smaller swap devices rather than one large swap device. For instance, in the previous example, do not create a swap device on only one disk drive of 2 GB in size. Create at least four different swap files on different disk drives to distribute the swap I/O.

This will also improve the performance of the `page` and the `pageout` daemons when pages need to be brought in from the swap device or written out to the swap device (a more detailed discussion on I/O tuning follows in Chapter 3). To list the currently configured swap devices, use the `swap -l` command.

```
myhost>  swap -l

path                    dev      swaplo    blocks
/dev/dsk/qd0s1          101,1     0        204800
/dev/vol/v_swap01       121,60    0        204800
/dev/vol/v_swap02       121,225   0        204800
/dev/vol/v_swap03       121,69    0        204800
/dev/vol/v_swap04       121,78    0        204800
/dev/vol/v_swap05       121,58    0        204800
/dev/vol/v_swap06       121,67    0        204800
/dev/vol/v_swap07       121,76    0        204800
```

In this example, eight swap devices of 100 MB each are configured. Try to keep swap disks separate from other disk drives. In other words, try to dedicate at least several disk drives to swap. To add swap devices, use the `swap -a` command, and update the necessary files so that the swap devices are brought online when the system boots. For example, to add an entire partition to the swap device, issue the following command as root.

```
myhost{root}->  swap -a /dev/dsk/c1t1d0s4
```

For systems with large amounts of physical memory, such as 32 GB or 64 GB, a relatively small amount of swap space, such as 3 GB or 4 GB, should suffice. Configuring the amount of swap space is dependent on the amount of physical memory. In essence, create a reasonable amount of swap space and be sure to distribute the swap files.

2.6 MEMORY SHORTAGES

The virtual memory model allows processes to allocate more memory than physically exists. While this may be possible, it is certainly not optimal. It is important that the development and administration staffs completely understand both the memory requirements of the application(s) being deployed, and the memory availability of the systems running the application(s). Using `sar`, `vmstat`, and/or other performance monitoring tools, you can determine whether or not the system is experiencing high amounts of paging and/or swapping. High amounts of paging and swapping indicate either that the system lacks sufficient memory to accommodate the memory allocation requests of the application(s), or that the kernel paging parameters need to be tuned. If the former case, you may need to consider adding additional physical memory, or reducing the amount of memory used in the application. If the latter case, you can tune the kernel paging parameters by following the guide-lines listed above. When you monitor paging and swapping, do not be alarmed by high rates in the areas of page faults, virtual faults, page-ins, and/or attaches if they occur only for a brief moment. This is usually a result of application startup latency in which memory struc-tures are allocated and initialized. Only be concerned with high rates that continue for a rea-sonable amount of time. You should try to monitor the paging and swapping activity throughout the entire lifetime of the application, inclusive of startup and shutdown. For an application that runs in nonstop mode, try to choose several periods of low, medium, and high usage to monitor the paging and swapping activity. For a system running the Oracle7 or Oracle8 DBMS, monitor paging and swapping while user applications are in progress. You should also monitor paging and swapping during peak periods to determine if adding more users increases the paging and/or swapping activity.

2.7   MEMORY SURPLUS

On systems where memory is abundant, it is important that this memory be utilized effi-ciently, and thus to its full potential. Applications should not be developed on the premise of "do not worry about memory allocation and deallocation, the system has plenty of mem-ory." This premise often leads to memory leaks and the inefficient use of a precious and expensive resource like memory. The application should never take for granted that plenty of memory will always exist, and therefore the application will always be able to run. There may be other applications running concurrently that also use large amounts of memory that may preclude your application from running. You should avoid using static memory decla-rations for application structures. Always allocate the memory dynamically, and free the memory once the structure is no longer needed. You can use the `malloc()` system call, or `shmop()` system call to allocate memory within your process.[8] Statically allocating an array in a program assumes that the structure is created and allocated. If for some reason the array could not be allocated upon execution, you may receive all sorts of strange errors ranging from segmentation violations and bus errors to arithmetic errors when you try to manipulate a nonexistent array. Using the `malloc()` or `shmop()` system calls to allocate the memory as soon as it is needed ensures that if the object could not be allocated due to insufficient memory, the application can trap the allocation error and terminate the applica-tion gracefully. Remember to use the `free()` system call to free memory when it is no longer needed. Consider memory as a resource similar to energy. You turn on lights when needed, and you increase the degree of lighting until it is suitable. Similarly, use memory when it is needed, and free it when it is no longer needed just as you turn off lights when leaving a room. There is no benefit to allocating memory that is never used. In fact, it may impede other users from obtaining the memory that their application needs.

---

8.   The `malloc()` call is the generic memory allocation system call. The `shmop()` system call allows the caller to perform shared memory operations such as creating a shared memory segment, attaching to the segment, or removing the segment. For more information, refer to the manual pages on `malloc()` or `shmop()`.

2.8 MONITORING APPLICATION MEMORY

Solaris provides the `pmap` tool which lists the different memory areas of a process. The `pmap` tool is extremely useful and it can be used to monitor the amount of memory used by an application. The `pmap` tools lists the different memory segments of a process and reports the size of each segment.

In the example of `pmap` output on the following page, the process (pid=12157) is attached to a shared memory segment (shmid=0x65) of size 30 MB (31,112 KB). In addition, the heap of the process accounts for approximately 1 MB (1,072 KB). The `pmap` command also shows the space consumed by the different shared libraries as well as the actual executable code of the oracle binary. Using the `pmap` command, you can identify the different memory segments of a process as well as determine the size of the different segments. The `pmap` `tool` can help you monitor the memory utilization of application processes. You can also use the `pmap` tool to monitor the memory utilization of the Oracle server processes in order to determine the amount of memory being used for process private areas. There is a bug in `pmap` which results in the incorrect reporting of memory related to text segments and shared libraries. The bug is fixed in Solaris 7, as well as in Solaris 2.6, with the application of the Solaris 2.6 kernel patch 105181-15 or higher.

The `top` command can also be used to monitor the memory utilization of the overall system as well as individual processes. The `top` command provides the ability to sort the output by different metrics: size (process memory size), cpu (percentage of CPU), res (resident memory size), and time (amount of CPU time). The following example illustrates how to use the `top` command to display the processes which consume the most amount of memory. The output is ordered by the process memory size:

```
myhost> top

last pid: 11453; load averages: 1.61, 2.17, 2.16
234 processes: 231 sleeping, 3 on cpu
CPU states: 80.1% idle, 15.4% user, 3.4% kernel, 1.2% iowait, 0.0% swap
Memory: 10G real, 172M free, 164M swap in use, 25G swap free

PID      USERNAME   THR  PRI  NICE   SIZE   RES    STATE  TIME  CPU     COMMAND
9036     oracle8    1    58   0      1612M  1580M  sleep  4:19  0.00%   oracle
10260    oracle8    1    58   0      1528M  1507M  sleep  1:49  0.00%   oracle
9505     oracle8    2    58   0      1525M  1504M  sleep  0:35  0.00%   oracle
4502     oracle8    1    58   0      1525M  1505M  sleep  1:58  0.00%   oracle
22583    oracle8    2    58   0      1513M  1492M  sleep  1:34  0.00%   oracle
27378    oracle8    1    58   0      1512M  1491M  sleep  1:57  0.00%   oracle
27384    oracle8    1    58   0      1511M  1490M  sleep  8:50  0.00%   oracle
27370    oracle8    1    58   0      1510M  1490M  sleep  8:13  0.00%   oracle
27372    oracle8    1    58   0      1510M  1489M  sleep  1:06  0.00%   oracle
27376    oracle8    1    58   0      1510M  1489M  sleep  5:32  0.00%   oracle
27382    oracle8    1    58   0      1510M  1490M  sleep  4:40  0.00%   oracle
20965    oracle8    2    58   0      1509M  1487M  sleep  1:03  0.00%   oracle
15192    oracle8    2    58   0      1506M  1486M  sleep  4:11  0.00%   oracle
27430    oracle8    1    58   0      1506M  1485M  sleep  0:16  0.00%   oracle
27422    oracle8    1    58   0      1506M  1485M  sleep  0:36  0.00%   oracle
```

Example of pmap output

```
myhost> /usr/proc/bin/pmap -x 12157

12157:   oracleprod81  (DESCRIPTION=(LOCAL=YES)(ADDRESS=(PROTOCOL=beq)))
```

Address	Kbytes	Resident	Shared	Private	Permissions	Mapped File
00010000	25232	10336	4832	5504	read/exec	oracle
018C2000	232	232	168	64	read/write/exec	oracle
018FC000	1072	1056	-	1056	read/write/exec	[heap]
6F950000	16	16	16	-	read/exec	libc_psr.so.1
6F960000	16	16	16	-	read/exec	libbmp.so.2
6F972000	8	8	-	8	read/write/exec	libbmp.so.2
6F980000	592	560	560	-	read/exec	libc.so.1
6FA22000	32	32	-	32	read/write/exec	libc.so.1
6FA2A000	8	8	-	8	read/write/exec	[anon]
6FA40000	8	8	8	-	read/exec	libkstat.so.1
6FA50000	8	8	-	8	read/write/exec	libkstat.so.1
6FA60000	24	24	24	-	read/exec	libposix4.so.1
6FA74000	8	8	-	8	read/write/exec	libposix4.so.1
6FA80000	448	400	400	-	read/exec	libnsl.so.1
6FAFE000	40	40	-	40	read/write/exec	libnsl.so.1
6FB08000	24	16	-	16	read/write/exec	[anon]
6FB20000	8	8	-	8	read/write/exec	[anon]
6FB30000	24	16	16	-	read/exec	libaio.so.1
6FB44000	16	16	-	16	read/write/exec	libaio.so.1
6FB50000	8	8	8	-	read/exec	libsched.so.1
6FB60000	8	8	-	8	read/write/exec	libsched.so.1
6FB70000	8	8	8	-	read/write/exec/shared	[anon]
6FB80000	3480	840	760	80	read/exec	libjox8.so
6FEF4000	88	56	-	56	read/write/exec	libjox8.so
6FF0A000	8	-	-	-	read/write/exec	[anon]
6FF20000	32	32	32	-	read/exec	libsocket.so.1
6FF36000	8	8	-	8	read/write/exec	libsocket.so.1
6FF38000	8	-	-	-	read/exec	[anon]
6FF40000	32	16	-	8	read/exec	libdsbtsh8.so
6FF56000	8	8	-	8	read/write/exec	libdsbtsh8.so
6FF58000	8	8	-	8	read/write/exec	[anon]
6FF60000	8	8	8	-	read/exec	libwtc8.so
6FF70000	8	8	-	8	read/write/exec	libwtc8.so
6FF80000	8	8	8	-	read/exec	libskgxp8.so
6FF90000	8	8	-	8	read/write/exec	libskgxp8.so
6FFA0000	8	8	8	-	read/exec	libdl.so.1
6FFB0000	8	8	-	8	read/write/exec	[anon]
6FFC0000	120	120	120	-	read/exec	ld.so.1
6FFEC000	8	8	-	8	read/write/exec	ld.so.1
80000000	31112	31112	-	31112	read/write/exec/shared	[shmid=0x65]
EFFF6000	40	40	-	40	read/write/exec	[stack]
--------	-----	-----	-----	-----		
total Kb	62840	45120	7000	38120		

In the output on page 57, the process that consumes the most amount of memory is `pid=9036`, which consumes 1,612 MB of memory with a resident working set size of 1,580 MB. The majority of the `oracle` processes consume an average of 1,510 MB of memory. This is because each process represents the dedicated server processes for user connections, and each dedicated server process is attached to the SGA. Hence, the memory size reported includes the size of the SGA (shared memory) as well as any private memory. If we assume for example that the size of the SGA is 1,485 MB, then `pid=9036` uses approximately 127 MB of private process memory.

The `pmap` and `top` utilities can be used to monitor the memory utilization in order to determine the distribution and consumption of memory. Using `top` with the order option can quickly identify processes which consume large amounts of memory. This may help identify applications that leak memory.

2.9   KERNEL MEMORY ALLOCATOR

The kernel memory allocator (`kma`) is responsible for servicing all memory allocation and deallocation requests. The `kma` is also responsible for maintaining the memory free list. On Solaris, you can monitor the activity of the `kma` using the `kma` command. Using `sar -k`, you can monitor the workload of the `kma` by observing the amount of allocations for small and large requests for memory as well as the number of memory requests that failed. You can also obtain statistics on the amount of memory allocated for oversize requests, and the number of failures for oversize requests. You should monitor `kma` activity in conjunction with paging and swapping activity in order to determine the occurrence of memory shortages.

2.10   LARGE MEMORY MODEL

Hardware vendors continue to make major advancements to enterprise servers, including the ability to support larger amounts of memory and larger disk farm configurations. In order to utilize more server memory effectively, operating system vendors have provided extensions for large memory support in a 32-bit world. This allows applications such as Oracle to create an SGA larger than 4 GB and maintain more data in memory, thereby reducing physical I/O. In the 32-bit virtual memory model, a user process's address space is limited to a maximum of 4 GB minus the kernel overhead. For those system architectures employing a 32-bit chip, OS vendors need to provide extensions for an extended cache in order to work around the 32-bit virtual address limit.

Depending on the platform-specific implementation, the concept of an extended cache model on a 32-bit architecture centers around the ability to map in memory pages to the user process during use and unmap the memory pages when they are no longer needed by the process. This essentially takes the burden of having to deal with extended caches off the application and places it on the OS. The application simply makes a system call to map the memory page in and unmaps the page when no longer needed. The overhead of mapping and unmapping buffers is relatively trivial when compared with the overall gain of extended caches. In most cases, mapping a buffer is an inexpensive operation involving mostly L2 cache page table translations from virtual to physical addresses. Solaris 8 provides extended memory (XMEM) support by allowing a 32-bit process to access more than 4 GB of physical memory. Solaris 8 uses a file system (xmemfs) to implement extended memory access. Until chip manufacturers and OS vendors migrate to a 64-bit environment, the extended cache feature is critical to large-system performance. This allows large-scale size databases to utilize a large extended cache and reduce physical I/O by maintaining more data in the cache.

Solaris 7 provides 64-bit capabilities as well as a 64-bit development environment. The 64-bit option of Solaris 7 requires a 64-bit chip architecture such as the UltraSPARC. For Intel platforms, the Solaris 7 64-bit option will require Intel's new generation IA-64 (64-bit) microprocessors.

Sequent provides extended cache functionality via the `virtwin()` and `shmatvw()` system calls to handle mapping extended cache buffers into the user process address space. Oracle8 on the Sequent NUMA-Q systems has been optimized to take advantage of the extended cache feature. Oracle8's extended cache feature allows the SGA buffer pool layer to reside outside the process' virtual address space. Buffers are mapped, only when needed, into a set of *window panes*.

HP-UX 11.0 also provides 64-bit OS functionality including features such as large memory segments, and large files. HP-UX 11.0 allows a shared memory size of 8 TB, a maximum file system and file size of 128 GB, and a 4 TB process data space. The V2200 HP Enterprise server supports 64-bit HP-UX 11.0 and provides a significant performance increase over the T-Class servers. HP is also working jointly with Intel and also helped design the Intel IA-64 architecture.

There are 64-bit versions of Oracle8 and Oracle8*i* available on platforms providing 64-bit support such as Solaris 7 (SPARC) and HP-UX 11.0. The 64-bit releases of Oracle8 and Oracle8*i* allow you to increase performance and scalabilty by taking advantage of your 64-bit platform, such as allowing larger memory configurations, more users, and more processes. This allows for larger database configurations as well as larger memory pools.

2.11 LARGE PAGE SIZES

Another useful feature that helps increase the performance of large SGAs is the large page size feature. This allows a page size of 1 MB or 4 MB for example, rather than the default page size of 4 KB or 8 KB, depending on the platform. Using the large page size feature reduces the work on the kernel memory allocator and `page` daemon, and results in improved efficiency of virtual memory. The large page size feature is most useful for large SGAs.

In Solaris 2.6, a large page size of 4 MB is used when a large shared memory segment is created. When attaching to the shared memory segment via the `shmat()` call, you should set the `SHM_SHARE_MMU` flag. In addition, the virtual address you specify should be 4 MB aligned and ISM (Intimate Shared Memory) should be enabled.

HP-UX 11.0 provides a variable page size option which allows you to specify the size of the page depending on the type of workload. Large page sizes may be used for process text, process data, process heap, shared memory, and shared libraries. Using the `chatr` command, you can specify the text or data page size. The kernel also chooses the page size transparently for executables with a *default* page size. The kernel uses the size of the object at the time of creation to determine the optimal page size. In order to use the large page size, the virtual address must be aligned with the page size being specified. HP-UX 11.0 provides large page size tunables including `vps_pagesize`, `vps_ceiling`, and `vps_chatr_ceiling`. The `vps_pagesize` parameter specifies the default page size to use for all objects created. The `vps_ceiling` parameter specifies the maximum size allowed for transparently selected pages. The `vps_chatr_ceiling` specifies the maximum page size that can be set for an executable via the `chatr` command.

2.12 SHARED MEMORY PARAMETERS

As stated previously, shared memory is a System V Release 4 method of interprocess communication. It allows multiple processes to attach to the same memory segment and allows the sharing of data. This avoids having to perform memory-to-memory copies from one process to another in order to share data. This reduces the `kma` workload as well as CPU cycles of copying data. Shared memory is no different than regular memory in the sense that it still consists of memory pages and is also managed by the `page` daemon in the same manner that regular memory is managed. When you start the Oracle8 instance, the Oracle kernel creates at least one shared memory segment to hold the SGA. Then, when users connect to the database, the user's respective server process attaches to the shared memory segment to access the SGA. Shared memory pages can be locked in memory upon creation by using the `lock` flag in the `shmget()` or `shmctl()` system call. The `mlock()` system call locks the memory pages specified in the `mlock()` call in main memory. This prevents the pages from being swapped or paged-out.

Using the `mlock()` call can have dangerous repercussions unless used properly. Preventing memory from being paged out may cause the system to become unstable if the amount of free memory available to the system drops below the specified paging limits. Sequent Dynix 4.2 provides a mechanism by which a shared memory segment can be locked into memory thereby increasing performance. This also increases the performance of Oracle by pinning the SGA into main memory, and preventing it from being paged out. In order to enable shared memory use on your system, you must set several kernel parameters. The kernel parameters associated with shared memory are `shmmax`, `shmmin`, `shmni`, and `shmseg`. The `shmmax` kernel parameter controls the maximum size, in bytes, of a single shared memory segment. The `shmmin` kernel parameter specifies the minimum size of a shared memory segment in bytes. The `shmni` kernel parameter specifies the number of shared memory identifiers. The `shmseg` kernel parameter specifies the number of shared memory segments per process. Set the value of `shmmax` to the maximum size of your SGA so that the SGA can fit into one contiguous shared memory segment. This ensures that the SGA is held in one shared memory segment. Otherwise, if your SGA is larger than `shmmax`, multiple shared memory segments will need to be allocated. Do not set `shmmax` to an amount larger than the amount of physical memory existent on the system. On HP, use the SAM tool to set the shared memory kernel parameters and reboot the system. On Sequent, use the menu tool to configure the kernel and set the shared memory kernel parameters. The menu tool also prompts if you want to rebuild the kernel and reboot the system for the changes to take effect. On Solaris, you can set these parameters by editing the `/etc/system` file and placing the entries that follow in the file. You must reboot your Solaris system for the changes to take effect.

Example /etc/system file

```
set shmsys:shminfo_shmmax=104857600
set shmsys:shminfo_shmmin=1
set shmsys:shminfo_shmni=100
set shmsys:shminfo_shmseg=10
```

On Sequent, you can set the following parameters to enable shared memory locking: SHM_LOCK_OK, SHM_LOCK_UID, SHM_LOCK_MIN, and SHM_LOCK_MAX.

2.13   TUNING SHARED MEMORY

Oracle uses shared memory to hold the SGA. User processes (connections) attach to the shared memory segment via their corresponding shadow process. The shadow process then can access the SGA to perform the client requests.

Solaris provides the *intimate shared memory* (ISM) option. The ISM option allows processes attaching to the same shared memory address to share the same page table entry, which avoids having to duplicate page table entries for each process, thereby reducing memory consumption. Applications which use shared memory on Solaris can also make use of ISM by specifying the SHM_SHARE_MMU flag as part of the `shmat()` call for processes which attach to the shared memory segment. The SHM_SHARE_MMU flag allows the page table entries for the shared memory mappings to be shared, thereby reducing overall memory consumption, especially when a large number of processes are attached to the shared memory segment. In addition, the use of the SHM_SHARE_MMU flag causes the shared memory segment to be "wired," or locked down, in physical memory. This prevents the shared memory segment from being paged out.

The following OS kernel parameters can be used to enable or disable the use of ISM.

```
set shmsys:ism_off=1             *** Disables ISM
set shmsys:ism_off=0             *** Default behavior
set shmsys:share_page_table=1    *** Always forces ISM
set shmsys:share_page_table=0    *** Default behavior
```

To force the use of ISM in the Solaris kernel, edit the `/etc/system` file and place the following entry:

```
set shmsys:share_page_table=1    *** Always forces ISM
```

If the `ism_off` parameter is set to one, ISM attaches are disabled despite the application's request for ISM. If the `share_page_table` parameter is set to one, all shared memory attaches will use ISM despite the application. The parameter `share_page_table` takes precedence over the parameter `ism_off`. Hence, if both parameters are set to the value of one, then ISM is forced. Since applications typically control the use of ISM, it is not necessary to utilize these `/etc/system` kernel parameters. For the Oracle Server, setting the `init.ora` parameter `use_ism=TRUE` or `_use_ism=TRUE` (Oracle8*i*) causes ISM to be used (if possible).

To enable the use of ISM within the Oracle Server, set the `init.ora` parameter `use_ism=TRUE`. Enabling the ISM feature can increase performance dramatically on Solaris systems with a large number of concurrent users. In Oracle8*i*, the `use_ism` `init.ora` parameter is an underscore parameter (i.e., `_use_ism`), and the default value is that ISM is enabled.

You can verify whether ISM is actually being used by using either the `/usr/proc/bin/pmap` utility or the `truss` utility. The `/usr/proc/bin/pmap` utility displays the process address space map for a given process. The `pmap` utility will list the shared memory segments which are attached by the process. For example, obtain the process ID of the database writer process for the instance using the `ps` command. Then use the `pmap` utility to report the process address space map for the database writer as follows.

```
myhost> /usr/proc/bin/pmap -x 27103
```

```
27103:   ora_dbw0_test81
Address   Kbytes  Resident  Shared  Private  Permissions            Mapped File
00010000   25232    11696    8888    2808    read/exec              oracle
018C2000     232      216     168      48    read/write/exec        oracle
018FC000     776       40       -      40    read/write/exec        [ heap ]
2D000000  200000    30912     440   30472    read/write/exec/shared [shmid=0x130]
39350000       8        8       8       -    read/shared            [shmid=0x130]
39352000   30704     8104    3504    4600    read/write/exec/shared [shmid=0x130]
3B14E000       8        8       8       -    read/shared            [shmid=0x130]
3B150000    2936     1888       -    1888    read/write/exec/shared [shmid=0x130]
3B42E000       8        8       8       -    read/shared            [shmid=0x130]
3B430000     512       24       -      24    read/write/exec/shared [shmid=0x130]
3B4B0000      24       24      24       -    read/shared            [shmid=0x130]
3B4B6000       8        8       8       -    read/write/exec/shared [shmid=0x130]
```

In the above output, the shared memory segment identified by the `shmid=0x130` appears multiple times in the `pmap` output. This indicates that ISM is not being used and that the shared memory segment is not mapped as a contiguous segment in the process address space of the database writer.

The other method which can be used to verify that ISM is being used is via the `truss` utility. The `truss`[9] utility traces system calls from a process and can be used to determine which system calls are being issued by the process. In the case of ISM, the process attaching to the shared memory segment will issue the `shmat()` call with the `SHM_SHARE_MMU` flag, which is equivalent to 040000 as defined in the header file `/usr/include/sys/shm.h`. For example, using SQL*Plus on the database server to create a new local connection, you can determine if ISM is being used.

```
myhost> truss -aefo run.out sqlplus test/test
```

The above example will truss the execution of SQL*Plus as well as the child process created by SQL*Plus, which will represent the dedicated server process. Once you are connected and the SQL*Plus prompt appears, you can exit immediately and then examine the file `run.out`. The `run.out` file generated by the `truss` command will contain the system calls issued by the SQL*Plus process. The `-f` switch informs `truss` to traverse child processes, which will include the system calls issued by the dedicated server process. You can then scan the `run.out` file for the `shmat()` system call and examine the arguments as well as the return values. For example, consider the following sample output from the `run.out` file.

```
27070:   shmat(204, 0x2D000000, 040000)              Err#12 ENOMEM
27070:   shmat(204, 0x2D000000, 0)                    = 0x2D000000
```

In the above output, the first `shmat()` call with the `SHM_SHARE_MMU` flag (040000) failed with the error ENOMEM, which means that not enough physical memory exists to wire down the shared memory segment. Oracle then attached to the shared memory segment without the ISM option which then succeeded. The return value for the second `shmat()` call represents the starting data address of the attached shared memory segment. Using either the `pmap` utility or the `truss` utility, you can determine whether the ISM feature is being used. In Oracle8*i* release 8.1.7, Oracle will automatically log a warning message in the `alert.log` file if for some reason ISM cannot be enabled.

There were several known bugs with ISM on Solaris 2.6 which resulted in system panics and memory corruption. The Solaris 2.6 kernel patch (105181) revision 17 or higher seems to have resolved these issues. Solaris 7 improved ISM handling and does not require specific patches for ISM.

---

9.   For more information on the `truss` utility, refer to the man pages. Solaris 7 expanded the `truss` utility to include user level tracing via the `-u` switch. This allows you to `truss` user library calls in addition to system calls.

Another init.ora parameter, pre_page_sga, enables you to increase the performance of the SGA for those platforms that do not support shared memory segment locking. In Solaris, if the init.ora parameter use_ism=TRUE or _use_ism=TRUE, the SGA shared memory segments are locked in memory. Sequent also locks shared memory segments. Locking shared memory prevents the shared memory segments (i.e., SGA) from being paged out. If your platform does not support the locking of shared memory, you can use the init.ora parameter pre_page_sga to try to keep the SGA memory pages warm. If pre_page_sga=TRUE, the SGA memory pages are touched upon connection and instance startup. This increases instance startup time and user connection time, but can help reduce the number of page faults thereafter by causing all SGA pages to be brought into memory. This maximizes the performance of the SGA by bringing all the SGA pages into memory upon startup or user login as opposed to incrementally. If your system does not support shared memory locking, set pre_page_sga=TRUE to increase the utilization of the SGA.

The maximum amount of shared memory allowed in the system is determined by the kernel parameters shmmax, shmmin, shmseg, and SHMMNI, shown in Table 2.2.

TABLE 2.2 Shared memory kernel parameters

PARAMETER	DEFINITION
shmmax	Specifies the maximum size of a single shared memory segment.
shmmin	Specifies the minimum size of a shared memory segment.
SHMMNI	The maximum number of shared memory identifiers.
shmseg	The maximum number of shared memory segments that can be attached by a process.

On Sequent, there are also memory limits per process that will need to be increased if you are configuring a large SGA. The kernel parameters SVMMLIM and HVMMLIM control the soft and hard limits, respectively, of virtual memory available per process. You should set these parameters to the maximum amount of memory addressable by your system. The maximum amount of shared memory available to a single process is equal to the value of shmmax × shmseg. Declaring a large SGA may require you to relocate the base address of the SGA. The base address of the SGA is defined in the file ksms.s ($ORACLE_HOME/rdbms/lib). If you change the base address of the SGA, you will need to relink the Oracle Server executable.[10]

---

10. Check with Oracle support and your OS vendor's support to ensure that the correct base address is selected when remapping the SGA.

2.14   SEMAPHORE PARAMETERS

Semaphores are also one of the System V Release 4 mechanisms of interprocess communication. Semaphores are used to protect resources. As resources are allocated, the semaphore counter is decremented. As resources are freed, the counter is incremented. A count of zero indicates that no resources are available. By default, the Oracle8 Server uses semaphores. There are also kernel parameters associated with semaphores that you may need to set. The semaphore kernel parameters—SEMMAP, SEMMNI, SEMMNS, SEMMNU, SEMMSL, SEMOPM, SEMUME, SEMUSZ, SEMVMX, and SEMAEM—are defined in Table 2.3.

On HP, use the SAM tool to set the semaphore kernel parameters and reboot the system. On Sequent, use the menu tool to set the semaphore kernel parameters. The menu tool will also prompt if you want to rebuild the kernel and reboot the system for the changes to take effect. You can monitor semaphore activity by using the sar -m command. On Solaris, you can set these parameters by editing the /etc/system file and placing the entries that follow in the file. You must reboot your Solaris system for the changes to take effect.

```
Example /etc/system file
set semsys:seminfo_semmap=10
set semsys:seminfo_semmni=10
set semsys:seminfo_semmns=60
set semsys:seminfo_semmnu=30
set semsys:seminfo_semmsl=25
set semsys:seminfo_semopm=10
set semsys:seminfo_semume=10
set semsys:seminfo_semusz=96
set semsys:seminfo_semvmx=32767
set semsys:seminfo_semaem=16384
```

TABLE 2.3   Semaphore kernel parameters

PARAMETER	FUNCTION
SEMMAP	Defines the number of entries in the semaphore map.
SEMMNI	Defines the number of semaphore identifiers.
SEMMNS	Defines the number of semaphores in the system.
SEMMNU	Specifies the number of undo structures in the system.
SEMMSL	Defines the maximum number of semaphores per user ID.
SEMOPM	Defines the maximum number of operations per semop call.
SEMUME	Specifies the number of undo entries per process.
SEMUSZ	Defines the size of the undo structure, in bytes.
SEMVMX	The maximum value of the semaphore.
SEMAEM	The amount used to adjust the maximum value of the semaphore upon exit.

2.15 PROCESSOR ARCHITECTURE

The processor and memory architecture of a symmetrical multiprocessing system relies on the *shared everything* architecture. In the shared everything architecture, a single system runs a single operating system consisting of processors, memory, and disk that are shared among the users and processes. Figure 2.7 highlights the shared everything architecture.

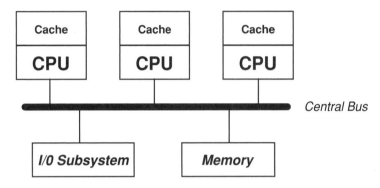

FIGURE 2.7 The shared everything architecture.

In Figure 2.7, the total system memory is shared between the processors and processes. The shared everything architecture requires an *affinity* algorithm. The affinity algorithm, sometimes referred to as the loose affinity algorithm, is responsible for transferring processes and/or threads from one CPU to another. For example, suppose a process is running on CPU 1 and then goes to sleep. When the process is later awakened, another process may be occupying CPU 1. Therefore, the process will have to be assigned to another CPU. On a uniprocessor system, affinity and cache coherency are not an issue since there can be only one active process or thread at any one moment. On a multiprocessor system, however, this is an issue that the OS has to deal with. For example, suppose a process running on CPU 1 requires data from memory or disk that is already in another CPU's cache. Rather than requesting the data from memory, it can request the data from the other CPU's cache. This is significantly faster because cache chips typically use SRAM (Static Random Access Memory). SRAM speeds range from 10 to 50 nanoseconds. Main memory typically uses DRAM (Dynamic Random Access Memory). DRAM speeds generally range from 60 to several hundred nanoseconds.

2.15.1 CACHE CONCEPTS

The concept of the cache is to substantially accelerate successive access to the same data. In other words, the very first access to data requires physical I/O (assuming the data is stored on some sort of physical media device) to bring the data into main memory. If the process accessing the data is currently running on a processor, the most recently accessed data may be in the CPU's cache. Therefore, subsequent access to the data will not require physical I/O because the data is in either the CPU's cache or the main memory. This significantly reduces physical I/O and increases overall performance.

Cache memory has several characteristics. First, cache memory is expensive relative to regular DRAM memory. For this reason, you will not find huge amounts of on-chip cache memory on the CPU versus off-chip cache. A typical size for an on-chip cache is 20 KB. Typical off-chip cache sizes range from 512 KB to 4 MB, depending on the hardware vendor of the processor. Second, cache memory requires more physical space and expends more power than DRAM chips. Finally, there is a point of diminishing return. The point of diminishing return occurs when adding additional cache memory provides little, if any, gain. In some cases, adding additional cache memory may actually reduce system performance.

The *cache hit ratio* is the number of times the data was found in the cache versus having to read the data from outside the cache (main memory or physical I/O to the disk). A higher cache hit ratio is always desirable and increases system performance. A cache miss results when the data requested was not found in the cache and had to be read either from main memory or disk. On the Sun SuperSPARC processor, the on-chip cache incurs a ten cycle cost for a cache miss. If your SuperSPARC processor contains SuperCache, data can be transferred from the SuperCache to the on-chip cache in five CPU cycles. Hence, it is apparent that cache misses can increase the CPU workload by a tangible factor.

There are two main types of caches: a *direct-mapped* cache and a *set-associative* cache. A direct-mapped cache maps each memory location to a single cache line. Off-chip caches (secondary caches) often use a direct-mapped cache algorithm. A cache line consists of a cache tag and data. The cache tag identifies the process ownership of the cache data. The cache is flushed upon the occurrence of a context switch. In a set-associative cache, a line can exist in the cache in many different locations. The cache lookup must search all possible locations in parallel to find the data. Because the data can be in numerous places in the cache, contention for the cache resource is reduced. However, because the data can be located in several different locations, the logic to manage a set-associative cache is much more complex than that of a direct-mapped cache. Set-associative caches are generally used for on-chip caches. The degree of the set-associative cache is determined by the number of possible locations for the cache line. For example, if there are three possible locations for a cache line, then this cache would be referred to as a three-way set-associative cache. The Sequent Symmetry systems use a two-way set-associative secondary cache for each CPU.

In addition to the mapping styles of the cache, there are also two main cache write algorithms: *write-through* cache and *write-back* cache. In a write-through cache, a write to main memory is always initiated simultaneously with a write to the cache. In a write-back cache, the write is written only to the cache. The write-through cache ensures consistency between main memory and the cache. However, write-through caches can reduce performance by issuing many writes to main memory. The advantage of a write-back cache is that subsequent cache writes need not wait on previous cache writes to update main memory.

2.15.2 CACHE COHERENCY

In a multiprocessor system, it is necessary to synchronize data among processors. For example, if a process on CPU 2 modifies some data resident in CPU 2's cache, and another process on CPU 3 needs to read the same data, CPU 3 would need to read the latest change from CPU 2's cache in order to maintain consistency. In order to accomplish cache coherency, the OS kernel employs a cache snooping algorithm. Typically, each CPU module has a *snooping* cache. The snooping cache listens for cache data across the bus. If a CPU writes to a shared cache block, the CPU can choose one of two actions: force every other CPU to nullify their entries pertaining to this cache data, known as the *write-invalidate* protocol; or, another alternative is to force the other CPUs sharing the cache block to update the CPU's copy of the cache block with the new data. This technique is known as the *write-update* protocol.

2.15.3 CENTRAL BUS

In the shared everything architecture, there is a central bus linking the system's processors, memory, and I/O subsystems. The Sequent Symmetry Server uses the Symmetry System Bus (SSB) or the Symmetry Highly Scalable Bus (HSB). The SSB is a synchronous, pipelined, and packet-switched bus. The bus clock rate is 10 Mhz for the SSB, and 30 Mhz for the HSB. The peak data transfer rates are 80 MB per second for the SSB, and 240 MB per second for the HSB. SSB devices use a 32- or 64-bit data path with a 32-bit address path, thereby yielding a sustained data transfer rate of up to 64 MB per second. HSB devices use a 32- or 64-bit data path and a 32-bit address path as well. The sustained data transfer rate for HSB devices can be up to 107 MB per second. Because operations are pipelined, the bus can service other transactions following a read or write request, even before the system memory issues its response. Sequent announced the new NUMA-Q (Nonuniform Memory Access) Server series, which introduces a new system architecture that permits substantially larger system configurations (up to 256 processors) and larger transfer rates.

The Sun SPARC Server 1000 and SPARC Center 2000 use the XDBus as the primary system bus. The XDBus is also a packet-switched bus and has a peak data transfer rate of 320 MB per second with a 40 Mhz system bus speed. The SPARC Center 2000E increased the system bus speed to 50 Mhz. A typical sustained transfer rate is 250 MB per second on the SPARC Center 2000. The SPARC Center 2000 uses a dual XDBus as opposed to the single XDBus in the SPARC Server 1000. The speed of the Sun SPARC processors typically range from 40 Mhz–60 Mhz. The Sun Enterprise Servers such as the E6500 use the *gigaplane* bus as the main system interconnect. The gigaplane bus allows transfers of up to 2.6 GB per second. This is a major improvement over the XDBus. Sun continues to improve the performance of the UltraSPARC processor. The 600 Mhz UltraSPARC-III processor is yet another improvement of the clock speed over the UltraSPARC II processors, which were 250 Mhz, 300 Mhz, or 450 Mhz.

Solaris 8 provides the ability to monitor bus traffic and utilization via the `busstat` utility. The `busstat` utility can be used to gather bus level statistics for devices such as SBus or PCI. The `busstat` utility gathers statistics such as memory bank reads and writes, number of interrupts, and clock cycles. The `busstat` utility allows system administrators to monitor bus traffic and identify possible performance issues.

2.15.4 NUMA-Q ARCHITECTURE

NUMA-Q is Sequent's implementation of the Nonuniform Memory Access (NUMA) architecture. Figure 2.8 illustrates the NUMA-Q architecture which consists of a series of quads linked together using a high-speed interconnect. The high-speed interconnect, IQ-Link, connects the quads and allows data transfers between the quads at a rate of 1 GB per second. IQ-Link also maintains the cache coherency for the system. The IQ-Link is not a backplane, rather a daisy chain connection between quads. When an application requests some data, the IQ-Link scans its own cache (L3) to determine if the data is present. If the data is not found in the IQ-Link's cache, IQ-Link sends a request to the other quads. The NUMA-Q architecture helps overcome the single large backplane bus bottleneck that typically occurs in large SMP systems. NUMA-Q allows hardware vendors to build large-scale SMP systems by adding more quads to the system. However, as more quads are added, more work is placed on the SCI-based interconnect (IQ-Link). Therefore, it is important that continual improvements be made to the interconnect in order to prevent the interconnect from becoming a bottleneck, thereby allowing high-performance and scalable NUMA-Q systems. The idea of NUMA-Q is to offer a model with low latency and high throughput. NUMA-Q offers low latency and high bandwidth by positioning groups of distributed memory in proximity to each processor, referred to as quad local memory. Quad local memory is a significant improvement over the traditional SMP model in which memory access must travel over the shared central bus. Also, data residing in remote memory that is frequently accessed is cached in the local quad in order to improve performance and maintain a high bandwidth.

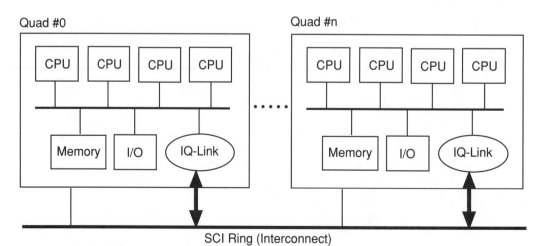

FIGURE 2.8   NUMA-Q architecture.

Oracle and Sequent continue to work together to optimize Oracle for NUMA-Q systems, including such things as the placement of SGA memory and Oracle processes and extended cache capabilities. Since the design goal of NUMA-Q is to localize operations per quad, it is important that applications avoid remote operations, if possible. This requires a sophisticated binding between the application and its data access methods. On Sequent NUMA-Q systems, Oracle8*i* distributes the SGA shared memory segment across the quads in order to balance memory usage and access. Using the `ipcs` command, you can see the different shared memory segments across the different quads after starting the Oracle instance. Sequent provides the `shmgetq()`[11] system call which extends the functionality of the standard `shmget()` system call by allowing you to distribute shared memory segments across the quads.

2.15.5 NEXT GENERATION PROCESSORS

Hardware vendors are working vigorously to deliver 64-bit processors to the marketplace in order to couple the chip with the 64-bit operating systems. Sun currently offers the 64-bit UltraSPARC processor in its Enterprise servers and recently announced the UltraSPARC-III 600 Mhz processor which includes the VIS instruction set and 2.4 GB per second memory bandwidth. Sun also plans to release the UltraSPARC IV and UltraSPARC V processors which will consist of speeds of 1.0 GHz and 1.5 GHz, respectively. Intel is developing the IA-64 processor architecture and plans to release Itanium as the first IA-64 generation processor. Sun and HP are working with Intel to deliver IA-64 based systems. The Intel Pentium III Xeon processor supports speeds of 600 Mhz and 733 Mhz. The Xeon processor enhances the Pentium II processor by taking the Pentium III processor to 0.18μ process technology and expands the system bus speeds to 133 Mhz. In addition to much higher clock frequencies, the Xeon and Itanium processors support larger L2 cache sizes of 2 MB which is a significant improvement over the previous Intel processor predecessors which typically had L2 cache sizes of 512 KB or 1 MB. The larger L2 cache size increases application performance by reducing data cache misses.

2.16 SOLARIS AND 64-BIT COMPUTING

One of the major features of Solaris 7 is the ability to develop and deploy 64-bit applications. Solaris 7 provides both a 32-bit and a 64-bit environment. Solaris 7 allows 32-bit and 64-bit applications to coexist. Solaris 7 64-bit requires 64-bit capable hardware such as the Sun systems based on the UltraSPARC chip. Solaris 7 provides a new set of 64-bit libraries which are used to build 64-bit applications. For example, the default c run-time library exists in the directory `/usr/lib/libc.so.1`, and the 64-bit equivalent exists in the directory `/usr/lib/sparcv9/libc.so.1`. The link `/usr/lib/64` points to the 64-

---

11. For more information on the `shmgetq()` system call, refer to the manual pages on `shmgetq()`.

bit set of libraries located in the directory `/usr/lib/sparcv9`. The Solaris 7 kernel is based on a 64-bit implementation, which means that applications dependent on third-party drivers or STREAMS modules will require 64-bit versions of these drivers. Applications built as 64-bit applications cannot use the 32-bit libraries. Figure 2.9 illustrates the overall architecture of the 64-bit and 32-bit environments in Solaris 7.

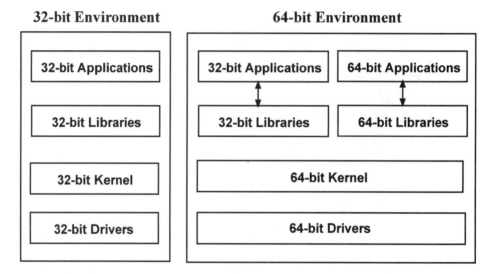

FIGURE 2.9   Overall architecture of the 64-bit and 32-bit environments in Solaris.

There are many benefits of a 64-bit application, such as the ability to handle a much larger address space, native large file processing and 64-bit math operations, and the ability to configure larger systems. The Solaris 64-bit model defines 32-bit applications as ILP32 and 64-bit applications as LP64. In the 64-bit world, longs and pointers become 64-bit while floating point types remain unchanged. The Table 2.4 summarizes the data type semantics for 32-bit and 64-bit environments.

TABLE 2.4   Data type semantics for 32-bit and 64-bit environments

IPL32	LP64
8-bit char	8-bit char
16-bit short	16-bit short
32-bit int	32-bit int
32-bit long	64-bit long
32-bit pointer	64-bit pointer
64-bit long	64-bit long
long	long

In order to compile applications with the 64-bit libraries on Solaris 7, you need to specify the `-xarch` compiler option. For example:

```
myhost>  cc -xarch=v9 -o test64 test64.c
```

The `-xarch=v9` compiler option uses the 64-bit set of libraries to build the application. The ability to develop and deploy 64-bit applications lifts the barriers on the maximum size of a process's memory address space and file sizes which, were previously 4 GB and 2 GB in the 32-bit world, respectively. The ability to significantly increase the process address space via 64-bit allows database engines, Web servers, and a wide range of other applications to take advantage of the large amounts of memory typically present in servers. For example, with the 64-bit release of Oracle8*i*, it is possible to configure a very large SGA beyond 4 GB.

2.17 THREADS MODEL

The threads model enhances the process model by defining further granular levels within a process known as a thread, and an LWP. A thread is a unit of control, or execution sequence. A thread can also be thought of as an abstraction of the processor. There are several threads standards organizations. UNIX International Threads (UI Threads) was an organization formed by Sun and AT&T. The Sun Solaris threads library (`libthread.so`) is based on UI threads. There is also the OSF DCE (Open Software Foundation Distributed Computing Environment) threads standard. POSIX also developed threads standards, and most vendors are moving toward adopting the POSIX threads. POSIX has released formal threads standards for platforms such as UNIX and Windows NT.

Threads are used to increase the level of concurrency and parallelism and at the same time reduce the process overhead. Prior to threads, parallelism and concurrency were achieved through creating multiple processes [i.e., `fork()`]. Creating multiple processes introduces substantial overhead relative to the threads model as separate stack, data, and text segments must be maintained for each process. Threads share the same address space as the process creating the thread. This significantly reduces memory and CPU overhead. A process consists of a Process Control Block (PCB) as well as its address space. A thread consists of a Thread Control Block (TCB), a stack, operating system control state, and a Kernel Thread Control Block (KTCB). Creating a thread is substantially quicker than creating a process, since the process already exists during thread creation. The time it takes to create a thread is on the order of 1000 times less than the time it takes to create a process. Threads also help reduce context switch overhead and kernel system call overhead because the majority of threads tend to remain in user space. Switching between threads does not involve the switching of address spaces as with the switching between processes. Interthread communication is much easier than interprocess communication because threads share the same address space.

The kernel provides support for threads via the threads library. As part of the kernel support for threads, the kernel provides virtual processors known as LWPs, or Lightweight Processes. By default, there is no fixed assignment of threads to the LWPs. Figure 2.10 diagrams the threads model.

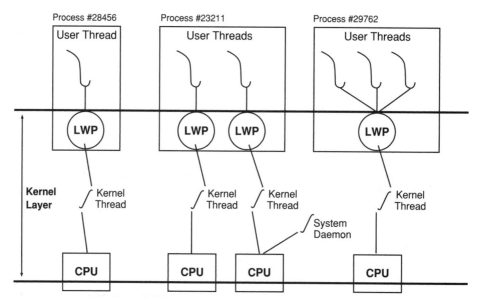

FIGURE 2.10   The threads model.

Figure 2.10 illustrates that user threads (application threads) are part of the user space and use no kernel resources. Application threads are therefore extremely lightweight. User threads are managed by the application threads library. The LWP can be thought of as a virtual CPU. Application threads are scheduled onto the LWPs via the threads library. If an application thread is bound to an LWP, the LWP is not available for use by other application threads. The kernel thread is the central scheduling object, and a kernel thread is associated with each LWP. Figure 2.10 shows a kernel thread with no corresponding LWP. This kernel thread is referred to as a *system thread* (or `system` daemon), meaning that no corresponding LWP exists. Examples of such daemons are the `pageout` daemon and the `clock` daemon. Every process consists of at least one kernel thread.

On Solaris, you can set the level of concurrency in your multithreaded application by using the `thr_setconcurrency()` system call. For example, `thr_setconcurrency(10)` sets the level of concurrency to ten by allocating ten LWPs. To maximize parallelism in this example, ten threads would be created, with each one being bound to a separate LWP.

Threads programming can offer significant performance gains over the traditional UNIX process model. Threads have less overhead and share the same address space as the process creating the thread. Creating a thread is approximately 1000 times faster than creating a process.

2.17.1 THREADS SAFETY

In order to develop a threads application, it is essential that the application be thread-safe. Since most of the libraries and applications were developed using the single-threaded model, care must be taken when calling library calls and system calls from a threaded application. There are four main issues with threaded programming versus the single-threaded model:

1. Global variables
2. Static storage
3. Synchronization
4. Signals

Global variables pose the biggest problem for threaded applications because multiple threads can modify the global variable. Therefore, the integrity of the variable is not guaranteed. Take for example the `errno` global variable. This global variable is used to set the error code following a system call. Suppose that several threads are concurrently issuing system calls. The value of `errno` could be set by any one of the threads issuing system calls. Therefore, synchronization is needed to lock the global variable before it is modified. This protects the variable from being modified from other threads. The same problem of global variables applies to static storage in a threaded application.

Synchronization also poses a problem. For example, many system calls return pointers to standard structures and objects. The application then usually manipulates these structures and objects throughout the course of the application. In a single-threaded process model, this is not an issue since the address space is local per process. However, when multiple subprocesses (threads) share the same address space and run concurrently, the likelihood of these common structures being overwritten by each other is extremely high. For this reason, many of the OS libraries have been rewritten to be thread-safe. On Solaris, you can determine if a system call is thread-safe by viewing the manual pages of the system call. Under the section titled MT-LEVEL, the system call will be labeled as either safe or unsafe. It is important that you determine whether the system call you are using in your threaded application is thread-safe. If not, you will either have to use another equivalent system call that is thread-safe or provide some sort of locking mechanism to prevent one thread from interfering with another.

Signals also must be dealt with carefully in a threaded application. In the process model, signals are process-wide. In other words, if you trap the `<CONTROL><C>` termination signal anywhere in the process and choose the default signal action for the termination, the entire process will terminate. For a single-threaded process this is not an issue, since signal handlers are established at the process level. However, with threads, each thread has its own signal mask. Remember, receiving signals at the single-threaded process level is quite simple, since the process has only one thread. However, in a multithreaded application, any one of the threads can receive the signal. If the thread receiving the signal does not deal with the signal properly by establishing a per thread signal handler, the entire process may be terminated causing termination of all threads. Therefore, it is important that each thread establish a separate signal mask. This allows each thread to deal with signals appropriate to the particular thread. For example, there is no sense in a thread waiting for I/O signals if no I/O is done by the thread.

2.17.2 THREADS PROGRAMMING

This section on threads is extremely brief and is not intended to be a programmer's guide to threads. For more detail on programming using threads, you should seek out additional text on threads programming.

You should try to use POSIX threads in order to increase the portability of your application. Solaris threads run only on Solaris. Many platforms now support POSIX threads. The threads section is intended to provide you with the basic architecture and concept of threads. I sincerely encourage you to consider threaded programming in any new application design. Some applications are better suited as a single-threaded process. However, the majority of business applications requiring high scalability and high throughput could definitely benefit from a threaded implementation. I do not want to imply that threaded programming is by any means simple and straightforward. On the contrary, threaded programming is probably the most complex method of user-level programming—requiring precision, accuracy, expertise, and extreme care. There are several texts available on threads programming that provide examples and detail the relevant thread system calls. For a developer who likes a challenge, threaded programming will definitely keep you challenged and excited. Many software vendors have projects underway to make use of threads within their software products in order to increase performance and throughput. The Oracle Server on NT uses a multithreaded model via NT threads.

One other key element to threads programming is testing and debugging. Debugging and fully testing a threaded program is quite difficult. Debuggers are now providing the ability to trace threads. However, because threads can execute in a different order each time the application is executed, it may not be easy or obvious to reproduce or detect a bug. Regression testing tools help by constantly running regression tests on the application. If you are developing a multithreaded application, you should obtain a complete set of debugging and regression testing tools that support threads. Maintaining proper threading coding practices and thorough testing will help foster a high-performance bug-free application. Threaded programming is elegant and challenging, and I encourage you to consider using threads for applications that require a high level of performance.

2.18 PROCESSOR TUNING

Hardware vendors are constantly improving processor technology. Sun has introduced a new series of servers called the Ultra Enterprise Series. These systems use the UltraSPARC 400 Mhz processor for the 3500, 4500, 5500, 6500, and 10000 (Starfire) Series Servers. This is an enormous improvement over the Sun SPARC 1000 Server and SPARC Center

2000 Series Servers. Not only has Sun increased the processor speed by a factor of almost ten, the backplane bus has also been expanded to sustain larger transfers at higher speeds. HP has also recently announced the V-Class and N-Class Enterprise server series. Sequent has also introduced the NUMA-Q systems and continues to enhance performance and scalability. HP and Sequent both plan to move to the new high-end Intel processors for their next generation of servers. Processor architectures and speeds will continue to improve, and it is critical that the software systems utilize these high-powered systems as efficiently as possible. For example, if an application does not scale, or does not make use of parallel processing, there will be little gained by adding additional CPUs. Processors are an expensive and vital resource and need to be utilized to their full capacity. The Oracle8*i* DBMS is one good example of a large-scale application (in this case a database management system) that not only scales but also benefits enormously from the addition of processors.

Right-sizing a system with the proper number of CPUs and memory requires legitimate performance metrics. The application that the system will be serving must be thoroughly benchmarked. CPU utilization statistics must be gathered, and scalability must be measured in terms of adding users and increasing the system workload. Do not rely on industry standard benchmarks or processor benchmarks such as SPECInt. While these benchmarks are useful as a generic baseline measurement, they cannot measure the scalability or performance of a custom application effectively. You must benchmark your application(s) extensively in your environment to determine scalability and performance.

To determine the CPU utilization of an application, use the `sar -u` command. For example,

```
myhost> sar -u 1 5

SunOS myhost 5.7 Generic_sun4u

        %usr     %sys     %wio     %idle
         19       15        1       66
         17        1        0       82
         17        0        0       83
         18        8        0       75
         18       17        0       65

Average   18        8        0       74
```

The `sar` command (`-u` option) reports CPU utilization. The `%usr` column reports the percentage that the processor was running in user time; `%sys` is the percentage of the processor running in system time; `%wio` is the percentage the processor spent waiting on I/O requests; and `%idle` reports the percentage that the processor was idle. On Sequent, you can also use the `/etc/monitor` utility to monitor CPU utilization. The `/etc/monitor` utility provides a line graph format of CPU utilization per processor. On Sun Solaris, you can also use the `mpstat` command. For instance,

```
myhost> mpstat 5 2
```

CPU	minf	mjf	xcal	intr	ithr	csw	icsw	migr	smtx	srw	syscl	usr	sys	wt	idl
0	182	0	687	828	801	508	29	104	270	0	2689	17	12	2	69
1	247	0	815	43	0	575	36	116	290	0	568	20	12	2	65
4	178	0	777	41	0	592	34	118	272	0	2427	16	11	3	70
5	309	0	813	38	0	497	33	104	299	0	2279	24	13	2	61
6	185	0	731	36	0	538	29	113	252	0	2666	17	11	2	69
7	244	0	803	44	0	589	37	117	273	0	313	19	12	2	66
8	144	1	787	44	3	621	34	121	265	0	1149	13	11	3	74
9	244	0	835	45	6	539	34	111	274	0	53	19	12	2	67
10	179	0	787	40	3	525	31	104	260	0	2649	18	11	2	69
11	71	0	781	311	99	271	19	56	344	0	1282	30	10	2	58
12	170	0	785	41	0	620	34	120	265	0	1910	15	11	3	71
13	279	0	813	88	48	522	33	110	294	0	1117	21	13	2	64

CPU	minf	mjf	xcal	intr	ithr	csw	icsw	migr	smtx	srw	syscl	usr	sys	wt	idl
0	0	0	0	70	66	254	3	56	9	0	475	23	1	0	77
1	0	0	0	3	0	244	3	57	2086	0	3164	10	14	0	75
4	0	0	0	28	0	51	4	14	937	0	78	62	24	0	14
5	0	0	141	16	0	270	1	74	13	0	332	2	16	0	82
6	34	0	0	1	0	252	0	79	9	0	360	9	1	0	90
7	0	0	0	8	0	286	7	74	834	0	1534	7	7	0	86
8	0	0	0	4	1	244	2	71	48	0	334	14	1	0	84
9	0	0	19	2	1	268	1	82	14	0	273	3	2	0	95
10	0	0	0	2	1	370	1	81	19	0	482	1	1	0	98
11	0	0	87	300	100	202	0	57	47	0	201	0	1	0	99
12	0	0	0	2	0	293	2	97	16	0	380	14	0	0	86
13	0	0	0	11	5	105	6	39	10	0	135	75	0	0	25

The mpstat command is similar to the sar command in that the arguments to mpstat are the time in seconds at which mpstat should poll, and the second argument to mpstat is the number of iterations mpstat should report statistics. The mpstat utility reports the statistics per processor, as shown in Table 2.5.

TABLE 2.5 Statistics per processor, as reported by the mpstat utility

STATISTIC	DEFINITION
CPU	the processor ID
minf	the number of minor faults
mjf	the number of major faults
xcal	the number of interprocessor cross calls
intr	the number of interrupts

(continued)

TABLE 2.5 Statistics per processor, as reported by the `mpstat` utility (continued)

STATISTIC	DEFINITION
ithr	the number of interrupts as threads
csw	the number of context switches
icsw	the number of involuntary context switches
migr	the number of thread migrations to another processor
smtx	the number of spins for a mutex lock, meaning the lock was not obtained on the first attempt
srw	the number of spins on reader-writer lock, meaning the lock was not obtained on the first attempt
syscl	the number of system calls
usr	the percentages that the processor spent in user time
sys	the percentages that the processor spent in system time
wt	the percentages that the processor spent in wait time (waiting on an event)
idle	the percentages that the processor spent in idle time

In conjunction with monitoring CPU utilization (`sar -u` or `mpstat`), you should also monitor the run queue to determine if processes are waiting for an available processor. You can use the `sar -q` command to monitor the run queue. For example,

```
myhost> sar -q 1 5

DYNIX/ptx myhost 4.4

runq-sz %runocc swpq-sz %swpocc
   9.0      82
   7.0      83
   8.0     161
   9.0      83
   8.0      83

Average    8.2          99
```

The `runq-sz` column is the length of the run queue (processes waiting for CPU), and `%runocc` is the percentage of time occupied. The `swpq-sz` column is the number of processes that have been swapped out but are now ready to run, and the `%swpocc` column is the percentage of time occupied. In the preceding output from `sar`, it is obvious that additional CPUs are needed in the system in order to service the amount of processes. The run queue average length is 8.2 and the percentage occupied is 99. This indicates that, on the average, at least eight processes are waiting for CPU. If the run queue in your system consistently shows many processes waiting for CPU, you will need to add additional processors or reduce the amount of concurrent processes on the system.

In addition to monitoring processor utilization via the `sar` or `mpstat` utilities, you can also use the `top` utility to report overall system utilization. The `top` utility provides the ability to sort the output by different metrics such as by CPU percentage or CPU time. This allows you to identify processes which are consuming a large amount of processor cycles. It may also help identify runaway processes which are just spinning and occupying CPU time. The following example illustrates the use of the `top` command:

```
myhost> top          ** output is ordered by time

last pid: 11698; load averages: 0.95, 1.09, 1.39
232 processes: 231 sleeping, 1 on cpu
CPU states: 97.1% idle, 0.1% user, 2.1% kernel, 0.7% iowait, 0.0% swap
Memory: 8G real, 180M free, 164M swap in use, 24G swap free


PID    USERNAME THR PRI NICE  SIZE   RES STATE  TIME     CPU COMMAND
4851   oraprod    1   0    0 1688K 1336K sleep 226:00  0.66% top
27528  oraprod   11  58    0   90M   61M sleep  68:53  0.02% oracle
27212  oraprod    1  58    0 1498M 1477M sleep  62:35  0.00% oracle
1006   oraprod    1  48    0 9816K 3264K sleep  39:37  0.00% tnslsnr
27526  oraprod   11  58    0   90M   62M sleep  15:54  0.00% oracle
27460  oraprod    2  48    0 1498M 1476M sleep  11:26  0.01% oracle
676    root       7  58    0 2800K 1744K sleep   9:52  0.00% automountd
27384  oraprod    1  58    0 1511M 1490M sleep   8:50  0.00% oracle
27370  oraprod    1  58    0 1510M 1490M sleep   8:13  0.00% oracle
1      root       1  58    0  736K  168K sleep   8:06  0.00% init
26920  oraprod  258  58    0 1504M 1475M sleep   6:14  0.00% oracle
27376  oraprod    1  58    0 1510M 1489M sleep   5:32  0.00% oracle
26926  oraprod   11  58    0 1499M 1470M sleep   4:41  0.01% oracle
27382  oraprod    1  58    0 1510M 1490M sleep   4:40  0.00% oracle
16363  oraprod    1  58    0 1498M 1476M sleep   4:29  0.00% oracle
```

In the above output, process ID 4851, which refers to the `top` command itself, consumed the most amount of CPU time of all the running processes. This indicates that the `top` command has been running for over several hours since its process consumed over 226 minutes of CPU time. Using the `top` command, you can quickly identify those processes which are consuming a large amount of processor cycles.

On Sequent NUMA-Q systems, you can create user run queues to help balance process workload and improve processor utilization. You can use the `/etc/monitor` command to monitor processor and quad utilization. The `/etc/rqcreat` command can be used to create additional run queues. You can specify the processors to be included in the run queue. Use the `/etc/showquads` command to list the quads and processors on your system. The OS scheduler typically balances the workload optimally across quads. However, you may want to consider using the run queues option to improve application processor utilization. As a general rule of thumb when deciding to use run queues, you should create a run queue per quad and not per processor. Then assign your process or set of processes to the specific run queue by using the `/etc/rqadmin` (`-assign` option). You can use the `/etc/rqstat` command to monitor run queue statistics such as the number of processes active, number of pending processes, and priority of the run queue which can range from –32 to 31. The statistics reported by `rqstat` will help you determine if the run queues are balanced.

You can also use the GUI performance monitoring tools to monitor CPU utilization. These tools will usually display GUI charts and graphs of CPU utilization per processor. You should watch for high WIO percentages. This tends to indicate that I/O is a bottleneck, and processors are spending the majority of their time waiting for I/O completion. Refer to Chapter 3 for more information about tuning I/O. You should also look for high percentages in system time or idle time. High system percentages mean that the processor is spending a large amount of time in kernel space and therefore less in user space. High idle percentages may indicate that the application itself does not make use of multiple processors, and therefore the remaining CPUs on the system may be idle. You may have to consider redesigning the application to parallelize the work either by forking child processes or by creating threads. In general, the ideal goal is to have the application spend most of its time in user space. If the application performs a lot of system calls, then the system mode utilization may also be high. However, if the application is well written and utilizes multiple processors effectively, there should be a minimal amount of contention. User time percentages should range anywhere from 60 percent for applications that issue a large number of system calls to 95 percent for an application with a minimal number of system calls. Anything less than 60 percent is reason for concern and should be reviewed. When tuning an application with respect to its processor utilization, the goal is to maximize user time. This goal allows the processor to spend the majority of its time running the application in user space. System time and certainly I/O wait time need to be minimal so as to not result in an application bottleneck. You must also monitor the run queue to ensure processes are not waiting for CPU.

In order to maximize user time during application execution, several things must be considered. If the application is an I/O-intensive application, then I/O must be configured and tuned appropriately. I/O tuning is discussed in Chapter 3. It is important that you conclude that I/O is not a bottleneck before you begin to tune the CPU utilization of your application. To rule out I/O as a bottleneck, follow the guidelines laid out in Chapter 3. Once you have determined that I/O is configured and tuned appropriately and that the statistics from the I/O subsystem indicate relatively good performance, you must tune your application to maximize CPU utilization while in user space. In order to maximize user time, you should try to minimize the amount of system calls made in the application. System calls require kernel resources to service the system calls and can result in high system time percentages. In some applications, the system calls cannot be avoided. For example, an I/O-intensive application cannot avoid I/O. However, if the I/O system is tuned properly, the application should see little wait I/O due to the proper I/O distribution. However, there are things that an application can do to reduce system call overhead and user space overhead as well. For example, a typical I/O application that reads and writes randomly to files can make use of new system calls. Consider the following example.

```
lseek (File Descriptor, offset, whence)

write (File Descriptor, buffer, nbytes)
```

OR

```
lseek (File Descriptor, offset, whence)

read (File Descriptor, buffer, nbytes)
```

This example is typical of an application performing file I/O. The application will usually issue an `lseek()` call to position the file pointer to a specific offset within the file and then issue the write to that location in the file. The same strategy is taken when reading from the file. The `lseek()` call is used to position the file pointer to the specified offset, and then the `read()` call is issued from that offset location. This means that for random file I/O, a minimum of two system calls need to be made. A new set of system calls, now available on several UNIX platforms, eliminates the need for two system calls to perform offset-based reads and writes. You can use the `pread()` and `pwrite()` system calls which combine the `lseek()` call and `read()` or `write()` call into one system call, respectively. For instance,

```
pread(File Descriptor, buffer, nbytes, offset);
```

OR

```
pwrite(File Descriptor, buffer, nbytes, offset);
```

Using `pread()` and `pwrite()`, you can reduce the amount of I/O system calls by eliminating the `lseek()` call. This reduces context switch overhead and kernel system call overhead. There are many other similar techniques that can be pursued to reduce system call overhead within an application.

Other common methods of reducing overhead in the application are the C string processing routines such as `strcpy()` and `strcmp()`. A more efficient set of routines is provided that operate on areas of memory. These routines include such calls as `memcpy()` and `memcmp()`. Since a string is simply an array of bytes, the memory-based routines are much more efficient than the string routines.

Applications periodically require certain shared resources. These shared resources in turn require synchronization objects (i.e., locking) such as semaphores to protect the resources. For example, a process may be trying to read from a section of shared memory, while another process is currently writing to that same section. This means that the process that is reading may have to wait until the process that is writing is complete and releases the lock. A typical implementation includes the use of the `sleep()` system call to put processes to `sleep()` when an attempt to acquire a resource fails. Putting a process to sleep and later awakening the process is an expensive operation. If your system has many high-speed processors, you may obtain better performance by implementing a *spin lock* mechanism. A spin lock is a lock that, upon failure to acquire the lock, spins (takes CPU cycles) until the resource becomes available or spins for a specific amount of cycles. The logic is that after spinning some CPU cycles, the process may be able to obtain the lock. Spinning a few CPU cycles on a multiprocessor machine is faster than forcing a process to sleep and later awakening it.

Applications that require interprocess communication often use files or buffer copies to share data. A more appropriate implementation is to utilize one of the System V Release 4 methods of interprocess communication such as shared memory. The application can declare a shared memory segment upon startup, and then each process can attach to the shared memory segment to exchange data. This reduces memory-to-memory copies between processes, thereby increasing memory utilization efficiency.

2.18.1 PREEMPTION CONTROL

Solaris 2.6 provides a new service known as *preemption control* that allows an application to prevent preemption while holding a critical resource. The kernel cannot maintain state information of a user land lock object. Preemption control services addresses this problem by notifying the kernel when the process is holding a critical resource. The preemption control services are implemented as macros instead of library or system calls in order to minimize the performance overhead. The following are the preemption control macros:

- ❑ `schedctl_init (void)`
- ❑ `schedctl_start (schedctl_t *sched_p)`
- ❑ `schedctl_stop (schedctl_t *sched_p)`
- ❑ `schedctl_exit (void)`

An application that manages concurrent access to shared resources via locks can be enhanced to take advantage of this feature. By calling the preemption control macros in the application shared resource locking layer, the performance of critical sections in the application can be increased by minimizing the chances of preemption. This translates into the application holding locks for fewer periods of time which in turn increases concurrency throughput. Preemption control uses a set of memory pages shared between the kernel and the user address spaces. The `schedctl_init()` macro allocates the kernel data structures necessary for process preemption control and returns a descriptor to be used with the `schedctl_start()` and `schedctl_stop()` macros. The `schedctl_start()` macro informs the Solaris scheduler that the user process is entering a critical section and that the process should not be preempted. The `schedctl_stop()` macro informs the kernel that the process can be preempted because it is no longer in a critical section of code.

The `schedctl_exit()` macro should be called when the process no longer requires preemption control services. The `schedctl_exit()` macro removes the kernel data structures used by the process for preemption control services. Preemption control applies to processes running in the Timeshare (TS) or Interactive (IA) job classes. Preemption control macros have no effect on processes running in the Realtime (RT) job class.

On Sequent, you can enable user-level process dynamic preemption services by setting the value of `root_nopreempt` to zero in the PTX kernel source file `/usr/conf/uts/kernel/i386_space/param_space.c`, and subsequently rebuilding the PTX kernel.

For example, make the following change to the `/usr/conf/uts/kernel/i386_space/param_space.c` file:

```
--> bool_t root_nopreempt=1; /*must be root to do NOPREEMPT*/
```

change to:

```
--> bool_t root_nopreempt=0; /*must be root to do NOPREEMPT*/
```

After making the above change, applications can then use the `proc_ctl()` system call to alter process attributes, including preemption control. To enable preemption control in Oracle on your Sequent system, set the `init.ora` parameter `_no_preempt=TRUE`. This can help improve performance by not preempting an Oracle process while it is holding a critical resource such as a latch.

2.18.2 PROCESSOR-RELATED KERNEL PARAMETERS

There are several kernel-tunable parameters that pertain to a multiprocessor system. Some of the key parameters are `maxuprc`, `maxusers`, `maxup`, and `nproc`.[12] The `maxusers` kernel parameter originally was used in UNIX to configure the number of users that could log into the system. The `maxusers` kernel parameter has changed since then and is now used to determine the size of the internal kernel tables and process tables upon system boot. A higher number for `maxusers` allocates larger kernel and process tables under the assumption that there will be more users and processes. On Solaris, the default for `maxusers` is set to `physmem`—the amount of available physical memory on the system. For example, on a Sun Solaris system with 2 GB of memory, `maxusers` would be set to 2048. If you do not intend to have a lot of users, you may want to consider reducing the size of `maxusers`, thereby reducing the size of the kernel and process tables. On Solaris, you can set this parameter in the `/etc/system` file. The default for `maxusers` on Sequent is usually 64, and you can set this parameter through the `menu` utility. On HP, you can use the SAM utility to set the value of `maxusers`. On Solaris and HP, the `maxuprc` is the number of concurrent

---

12. These parameters are operating system-specific, and you should refer to your platform's system administration documentation.

processes per user. On Solaris, you can increase or decrease this value by setting `maxuprc` in the `/etc/system` file. If you have many processes running per user, you may need to increase the value of `maxuprc` on your system. On HP, you can set the value of `maxuprc` by using the SAM utility. On Sequent, the equivalent to `maxuprc` is `MAXUP` which is also the maximum number of processes per user. You can set this parameter by using the `menu` utility.

The `nproc` kernel parameter is the maximum total number of processes system wide. This parameter controls the size of the kernel process tables. Therefore, if your system will not have a lot of processes running concurrently, reduce the size of `nproc` to reduce the size of the kernel tables. If, however, your system will be running a large amount of processes, you must set `nproc` to the total amount of processes that will run concurrently on the system. The equivalent to `nproc` in Solaris is `max_nprocs`, which is the maximum number of processes. The default for `max_nprocs` is (10 + 16 × `maxusers`). For example, if you will have no more than 1,000 concurrent processes running on the system, set `nproc` to 1000. When setting `nproc` or `max_nprocs`, remember to account for the daemon processes and their children. Daemon programs often `fork()` child processes to service requests. If the maximum number of processes is not set appropriately, the daemons may not be able to create subprocesses.

On Solaris, set `max_nprocs=1000` in the `/etc/system` file if your system will have no more than 1,000 concurrent processes. You can set `nproc` through either the SAM utility, or the `menu` utilities for HP and Sequent, respectively.

2.18.3 THINK PARALLEL

Hardware vendors like Sun, HP, and Sequent provide extremely high-speed high-throughput systems. These systems are constantly being improved and enhanced. Therefore, it is critical that applications deployed on these systems make full use of the multitasking nature of these systems. If you are designing or deploying an application on a multiprocessor system, you need to *think in parallel*. In other words, do not design a synchronous application in which the bulk of the processing resides in one process. You need to parallelize the tasks by creating subtasks either through the use of threads (preferably) or through the use of `fork()` and `exec()` for systems that possibly do not support threads. For example, if you are writing a PRO*C application to load 10 million rows on a ten-processor system, design the program so that you can run at least ten of these processes in parallel with each process operating on a smaller batch size than the total. This will be much faster than waiting for one process that has to do all the work of loading 10 million rows. If you are designing a new application, avoid synchronous bottlenecks such as obtaining an exclusive lock on an object for an extended period of time. Exclusive locks prevent other processes from modifying the object concurrently, even if the other processes modify a different section of the object. Try to parallelize large requests as much as possible by subdividing the tasks into smaller tasks. The hardware that the vendors are releasing nowadays is quite impressive in terms of parallel computing power. However, this power is useless unless the application can push the system to its limit by maximizing the parallelism of the application. An analogy would be a house with a 100-gallon water heater. If only one person lives in this house and uses less than 5 gallons of hot water, the majority of the hot water is being wasted.

One other key footnote: when thinking in parallel, try to involve the vendors as much as possible when designing a large-scale application. The vendors will provide hardware and software engineers who can help explain the architecture of the system, and advise you on how you can utilize the system's features in your application. The vendors will also provide you with benchmark information that you can use to baseline scalability. Many times people complain that their system does not scale, but this may not be due to the hardware and OS itself. Rather, the configuration of the system and architecture of the application are the major contributing factors to scalability.

2.18.4   RIGHT-SIZING THE NUMBER OF PROCESSORS

The million dollar question of *how many processors should I buy for my system* is one that deserves an entire text dedicated to this topic. Indeed, capacity planning is not a simple task. Capacity planning requires prior experience with the platform that you are considering for deployment, as well as a firm understanding of the application(s) being deployed. If you are responsible for capacity planning, you should work closely with your hardware vendor. Your hardware vendor will provide the necessary technical staff that can help you right-size your environment. The hardware vendors also have a significant degree of experience in benchmarking and testing their products. They can advise you as to the number of processors, quantity of memory, and disk I/O subsystems needed to ensure a high-performance system and/or application.

In addition to the advice of the hardware vendors, you should conduct your own research as to the scalability of your application. You will need to spend a serious amount of time gathering detailed statistics using either `sar`, `vmstat`, `mpstat`, or other GUI performance monitoring tools about the performance of your system and application. These statistics will help you determine if you are CPU-bound, memory-bound, or I/O–bound. If you see high percentages of CPU idle time, then obviously, you are not processor-bound. In this case, adding CPUs will not offer any gain as the existing processors are not being utilized fully. If, however, you are seeing close to zero percentages for CPU idle and high user time percentages, this is an indication that you are either processor-bound, or wait-bound. The wait could be due either to the application waiting for I/O requests to complete, or waiting on busy resources. To determine if you are pure processor-bound, you need to ensure that I/O is not a bottleneck, and that system time is minimized. After tuning I/O and monitoring to see that I/O wait percentages are minimal, you should monitor CPU idle time and user time. If wait I/O time and system time are minimal, and CPU idle time is zero or close thereto, and user times are high, you are more than likely processor-bound. High run queue lengths contribute to the fact that not enough processors exist to service all the running processes. Therefore, the OS must time-slice each process to ensure that each process is getting adequate CPU time. If your application is processor-bound, try reducing the number of processes. This should improve user throughput. Continue reducing the number of processes until the user time percentage reaches its peak, the run queue length is near zero, and CPU idle time is minimal. After monitoring the CPU utilization and the run queue, you should have a clear idea as to the number of processors needed to achieve ideal performance. Once you have collected these statistics and tuned the number of running processes, you will have a good feel as to the number of processors and processes needed to achieve the best performance.

2.18.5 AFFINITY BINDING ON MULTIPROCESSOR SYSTEMS

Binding certain processes to a processor can considerably increase performance on a multiprocessor machine. Solaris provides the `pbind` command to bind particular processes to a specific processor. Sequent provides the `tmp_affinity()` system call to bind a process to a processor, as well as the ability to create user run queues. The core advantages of processor binding include providing higher priority and additional CPU time for critical applications, preventing context switching of processes, the symmetric distribution of application workload across multiple processors, and an increased cache hit ratio. Processor binding is not automatic in Solaris. On a multiprocessor system you must explicitly issue the `pbind` command (refer to the manual pages on `pbind`). Either the superuser (i.e., root) or the process' owner can bind a process to a particular processor. Child processes inherit processor binding. Therefore, any spawned processes from a process that is bound to a particular CPU will be bound to the same CPU as the spawning process.

It is recommended that before binding processes you consult with your hardware and OS vendor to discuss possible issues in more detail. In cases where processes are experiencing an imbalance in processor utilization, it is recommended to bind the various Oracle background processes, with the exception of DBWR and LGWR, to different processors. You should leave at least one processor free to service DBWR and other processes. DBWR should not be bound to one particular CPU because this means that only that CPU can service I/O requests. Binding DBWR to a CPU may result in an I/O bottleneck because all DBWR I/O requests would be serviced by only one CPU. LGWR, for the same reason as DBWR, also should not be bound. Oracle8 introduces the concept of I/O slaves which allows for multiple DBWR, LGWR, ARCH, and BACKUP slaves. The I/O slaves can be used to parallelize I/O requests for those platforms that may not provide asynchronous I/O. Avoid binding I/O slaves to specific processors for the same reason as not binding DBWR and LGWR. Keep in mind that binding a process or set of processes to a specific processor does not guarantee exclusive use of the CPU by the binding set of processes. The CPU can still service requests from other nonbounded processes. Study your system and application in detail before you consider processor binding. An application may become CPU-bound under processor binding even if additional processors are available and idle. The performance gain seen by processor binding ranges from 0 to 15 percent. System scalability could also increase by 20 to 30 percent on systems with many processors and an intense workload.

In a multiprocessor system, the UNIX OS scheduler handles the scheduling of processes and ensures that each processor run queue is balanced, thereby avoiding CPU starvation and/or CPU gluttony of certain processes. Use `sar -q`, `sar -u`, and/or `mpstat` to monitor CPU utilization and the run queue. The resulting statistics indicate if processor binding will offer any gains.

2.18.6 PROCESSOR SETS

Solaris 2.6 offers the ability to create processor sets and bind processes to a set of processors rather than just a single processor. There are two types of processor sets: user-created processor sets and system processor sets. User processor sets can be created and managed by using the `psrset` command or `pset_create()`[13] system call. Processors that are assigned to user-created processor sets will only service LWPs that have been bound to that processor set. System-created processor sets may service other LWPs. System processor sets may not always exist on a particular system. System processor sets can be useful in situations where certain processors can communicate more efficiently with each other than with other processors in the system. System-created processor sets can neither be modified nor removed, but you may bind processes to them.

2.18.7 BENCHMARKING PROCESSORS

Once you have tuned your application, you should test your system for scalability in terms of processor scalability. This can be done on Solaris by using the `psradm` command. The `psradm` command must be executed as the root user (`psradm` can be made a `set-uid` program). For example,

```
* takes CPU ID=2 offline
myhost{root}->  /usr/sbin/psradm -f  2

* brings CPU ID=2 online
myhost{root}->  /usr/sbin/psradm -n  2
```

On Sequent, you can take a processor off-line or bring the processor on-line by issuing the following commands.

```
* takes CPU ID=3 offline
myhost{root}->  /etc/offline 3

* brings CPU ID=3 online
myhost{root}->  /etc/online 3
```

My recommendation is that you use the respective platform commands to on-line and off-line the system processors. For example, if you have an eight-processor Sun Ultra Enterprise Server 6000, you should turn all but CPU ID=0 off.[14] Then, with at least one processor on-line, run the application and gather the performance metrics. Then, at each

---

13. For more information on the processor set commands, please refer to the manual pages on the `psrset` command and the `pset_create()` system call.

14. You should never take processor 0 (CPU ID=0) off-line. The system must always have at least one CPU on-line. On some systems, CPU ID=0 is the base OS processor, and attempting to take it off-line may cause the system to hang or panic.

iteration, turn on one additional CPU and continue to run the application at each iteration until finally all processors are back on-line. At each interval you can measure the speedup factor of an additional CPU. For example, if running on two CPUs doubled your performance from that of running on one CPU, then you know that adding an additional CPU scaled linearly.

If, however, you begin to notice that after, say four CPUs, there is no performance gain, you can diagnose the problem further by examining the performance metrics from each successive run. This will allow you to measure not only the scalability of your application but the scalability of your system as well. I strongly recommend that you run your application by off-lining and on-lining CPUs to determine the speedup factor. Do not assume that because you only tested with all processors on-line that your application cannot run any faster. You may find that your application performs the same with four processors as it does with eight processors. You can automate the benchmark by creating a script that off-lines all the processors except CPU 0 and then runs the application, and at each iteration brings on-line one additional CPU. Then, you can review the performance metrics gathered by the benchmark script. If you suspect that additional processors are not yielding any gain, you can submit the output of the benchmark to the hardware or OS vendor for review. The performance metrics, specifically the speedup factor, will give you a reliable indication as to how the system will scale if you were to add additional processors. If you start to see that the speedup factor is decreasing or remains the same as more processors are brought on-line during the benchmark, your application may not benefit from additional processors. You may need to consider redesigning certain portions of the application in order to increase the application's scalability.

Memory and processor tuning are iterative processes that require precision and expertise. This chapter presented the processor and memory model of the UNIX operating system. Using the guidelines presented in this chapter, you should be able to monitor and tune your system and application(s) to maximize memory and processor utilization. In Chapter 3, I discuss I/O tuning in a format similar to this chapter. Other than the base system itself, processors and memory are the most expensive and most vital components. You need to utilize these valuable resources as effectively as possible, thereby maximizing your investment and system throughput.

CONFIGURING AND TUNING I/O

This chapter discusses the UNIX I/O model as well as techniques to tune I/O. Disk I/O is probably the most frequent bottleneck and performance issue reported by customer sites. I/O is one of the major contributors to performance for database applications. It is imperative that your I/O system be tuned so that I/O contention is minimal and that the system scales as more users are added to it.

3.1 UNIX I/O MODEL

In traditional UNIX, the I/O model consists of two main system calls: read() and write(). Both read() and write() take a file descriptor—either a buffer into which to read the data or a buffer that contains the data to be written—and the number of bytes that are to be read or written as arguments. These two system calls form the basis of the UNIX I/O model. The read() and write() calls are synchronous, which means that control is not returned to the calling process or program until completion of the read() or write() call. Both read() and write() return the number of bytes either written or read. If the read() or write() call fails, a -1 call is returned and errno is set to the error code that indicates why the read() or write() call failed. Figure 3.1 illustrates the UNIX I/O model.

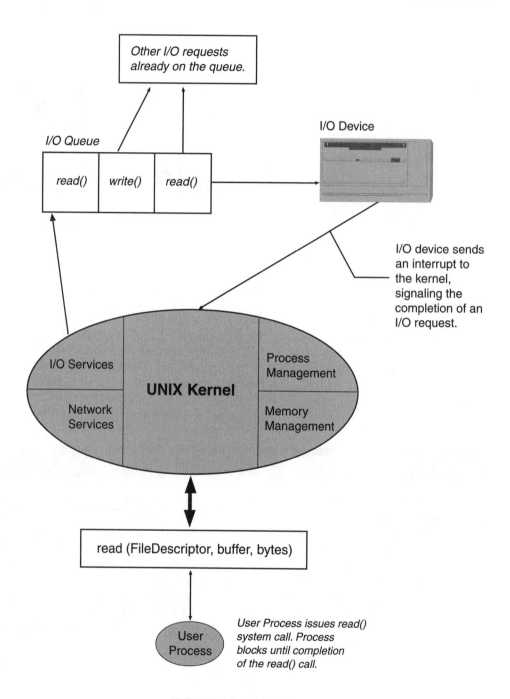

FIGURE 3.1   UNIX I/O model.

In Figure 3.1, a user process issues an I/O request via a system call. The kernel then forwards the I/O request on to the I/O queue. The I/O device then services the request from the queue and sends an interrupt to the kernel once the I/O request is complete. After processing the interrupt and completing the `read()` request, the kernel then returns control to the calling process and sets the I/O request error code appropriately. The user process can then check the error code to determine if the I/O call completed successfully. If the I/O queue is consistently long, it is an indication that a particular device is being saturated with I/O. This may lead to poor service times. The UNIX I/O model diagram shown in Figure 3.1 is a simplified diagram meant to illustrate the concept of the UNIX I/O model. In actuality, there are many more hardware and software layers involved when performing I/O. The importance is not necessarily to memorize all the different layers, but to be familiar with the basic concepts of I/O in UNIX.

For a system experiencing a tremendous amount of I/O, the synchronous `read()` and `write()` calls can cause an I/O bottleneck. Even if the data is distributed across multiple drives and spindles, there may be little benefit, since all `read()` and `write()` calls force the user process to block (meaning not return). For this reason, most UNIX vendors provide an asynchronous I/O interface layer. The asynchronous I/O interface layer enables processes to submit nonblocking I/O requests, allowing multiple reads and writes to be issued concurrently. In conjunction with asynchronous I/O, a volume manager can be used to distribute the data across multiple disk drives and controllers. The combination of a volume manager and asynchronous I/O maximizes I/O parallelism and I/O distribution.

3.2   LOGICAL VOLUME MANAGER

A Logical Volume Manager (LVM) provides a tremendous amount of functionality and performance features that substantially increase system throughput and I/O performance. The logical volume manager provides the capability to create and manage striped, mirrored, and RAID (Redundant Arrays of Inexpensive Disks) devices. The logical volume manager provides an interface between the physical devices and kernel I/O services. This interface provides for ease of system administration as well as load balancing in terms of I/O. Stripes and mirrored devices can help to greatly reduce the load on particular disks by employing a round-robin balancing algorithm.

The logical volume manager also allows reads and writes to proceed in parallel, thereby increasing I/O throughput. It also alleviates the need for manual striping, which is a tedious and complex process. The LVM offers tremendous benefits for system administration, performance, scalability, and reliability (mirroring and RAID devices). Figure 3.2 illustrates the use of a logical volume manager.

Figure 3.3 illustrates the relationship between the Oracle Server and the logical volume manager.

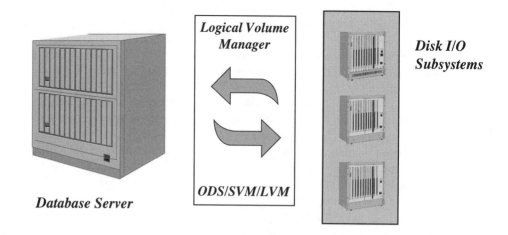

FIGURE 3.2 Logical volume manager.

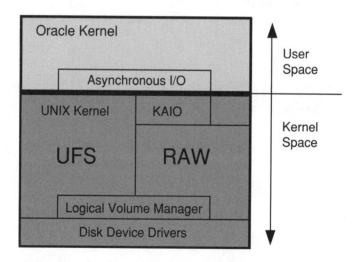

FIGURE 3.3 Logical volume manager and the Oracle Server.

3.2.1 STRIPING

Striping—also known as RAID 0 (meaning no redundancy)—is the process of spreading the data across multiple disk spindles. The goal of striping is to distribute disk reads and writes, avoiding *hot areas* and disk I/O saturation. Figure 3.4 illustrates the concept of striping.

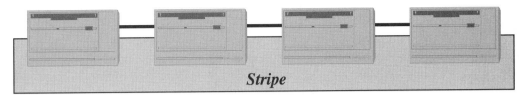

FIGURE 3.4 Striping.

Figure 3.4 shows the shaded area as the stripe across all the disk drives in the diagram. In a stripe, the data is spread across multiple spindles and controllers. A striped device consists of multiple partitions and an interleave. The stripe interleave value specifies the *hunt* size of the data. The hunt size is the number of bytes written to each partition. In other words, if you define a striped device that consists of three disk drives and the interleave value is defined to be 64 KB, then the first 64 KB of data is written to the first partition (or disk) in the stripe. The second 64 KB of data is written to the second partition (or disk), and finally the third 64 KB of data is written to the third partition (or disk) in the stripe. Then, the next 64 KB of data hunts back to the first partition and continues the round-robin algorithm, hunting to the next device as an interleave has been written. Figure 3.5 illustrates the stripe interleave.

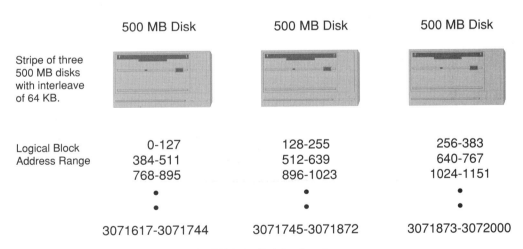

	500 MB Disk	500 MB Disk	500 MB Disk
Stripe of three 500 MB disks with interleave of 64 KB.			
Logical Block Address Range	0-127 384-511 768-895 • •	128-255 512-639 896-1023 • •	256-383 640-767 1024-1151 • •
	3071617-3071744	3071745-3071872	3071873-3072000

FIGURE 3.5 Striping interleave.

Figure 3.5 shows a striped device that consists of three disk partitions with an interleave of 64 KB. The logical block addresses show the hunting (round-robin) nature of the stripe. The first 64 KB is stored on the first disk, the second 64 KB is stored on the second disk, the third 64 KB is stored on the third disk, and then the data hunts back to the first disk and continues to round robin. The stripe interleave plays a major role in the performance of the stripe. Tuning the stripe interleave is discussed in section 3.4.

Striping improves performance by distributing the data across multiple disk drives and multiple controllers. Hence, if an I/O operation takes m time units to complete on one of the disks, then an I/O operation on the striped device should take m/n time units, where n represents the number of disjoint and distinct disk drives in the stripe.

Striping not only increases I/O throughput by n times, it also sustains a larger I/O workload as more users are added to the system. Striping, also known as RAID 0, offers the best performance over any other type of RAID. However, because striping is RAID 0, meaning no redundancy, most customer sites tend to choose a different level of RAID in order to maintain a higher fault tolerance during a media failure. In a striped device, only one disk drive failure is needed to invalidate the stripe. If a disk drive (or multiple disk drives) in a striped device fails, the data on the stripe is no longer available, and you will need to restore all stripes that contained partitions on the failed disk drive.

Although nothing surpasses the performance of a pure stripe (RAID 0), you must develop a robust backup and recovery strategy in order to avoid losing critical data. Media recovery performance and tuning are discussed in Chapter 7. If you run a mission-critical On-Line Transaction Processing (OLTP) application, you should consider either full mirroring (RAID 1), or some level of redundancy to protect against data loss. You will also need to make frequent backups in the event of a large-scale failure, or in the event that data is unintentionally deleted. If you are running a Decision Support System (DSS) that is primarily read-only, I recommend that you use full striping and schedule periodic backups. Since the data is primarily read-only, data redundancy is not as critical as it is in an OLTP mission-critical system. Whichever level of RAID you choose, try to distribute the data across as many spindles and controllers as possible. And, as always, schedule frequent backups and develop a legitimate and thorough backup strategy.

3.2.2 STRIPING ON SEQUENT

To take advantage of striping on Sequent, it is important that you understand the I/O subsystem in your Sequent Server. On Sequent Symmetry servers specifically, disks are organized in the manner shown in Figure 3.6.

In Figure 3.6, the QCIC (Quad-Channel I/O Controller) board is the main I/O controller and provides four SCSI-2 channels. Each channel is a fast-narrow (8-bit) SCSI providing a transfer rate of up to 10 MB per second. The QCIC-W (Wide Quad-Channel I/O Controller) board provides four-wide SCSI-2 channels. Each channel on a QCIC-W board is a wide channel (16 bits) that provides a fast-wide data transfer rate of up to 20 MB per second.

Both the QCIC and QCIC-W support the on-line replacement of disk and tape drives. This means that disks and tapes can be added and removed while the system is running without any disruption to the users. You should use the QCIC-W controller board in order to maximize your data transfer rate at up to 20 MB per second as opposed to the 10 MB per second offered by the QCIC. You can install up to eight QCIC or QCIC-W boards in the S2000 or SE60 system. The QCIC and QCIC-W use the Intel 80960CA microprocessor for on-board function control and coordination. An NCR SCSI controller is used for each SCSI channel on the QCIC and QCIC-W boards. Each SCSI channel on the QCIC-W or QCIC board connects to a SCSI peripheral bay (Pbay). The Pbay can be installed in an expansion cabinet or in the base system cabinet. Each Pbay can contain either six or twelve SCSI devices.

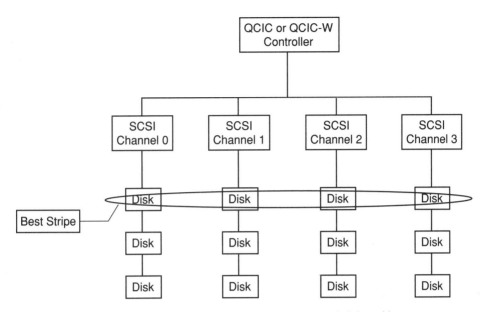

FIGURE 3.6 Sequent Symmetry system controller and disk architecture.

Although Figure 3.6 shows only three disks per SCSI channel, you can have up to twelve drives per SCSI channel. However, you should not have more than six. If you have more than six drives per SCSI channel, the SCSI channel controller may become saturated during concurrent access to the disks that are attached to that controller. Try to distribute the disks across many controllers, setting a limit of six disks per SCSI controller. This will distribute the I/O much more effectively than would having too many disks on one controller.

On Sequent NUMA-Q systems, disks are organized somewhat differently than the symmetry servers. Sequent NUMA-Q systems employ a full-speed (100 MB per second) fiber channel host connection to the disk I/O subsystem. Figure 3.7 illustrates a typical configuration.

In Figure 3.7, a single-connect/dual-fabric fiber channel configuration is shown. The configuration consists of a fiber channel PCI card on each quad, 100 MB per second-capable fiber optic link, 800 MB per second-capable fiber channel switch, and the Fiber Channel (FC) Storage Subsystem. In addition to the I/O subsystem itself, the FC Storage Subsystem consists of one or more fiber channel to SCSI bridges. Each switch connects to every FC Storage Subsystem in the Resource Domain. This allows each quad to have a direct path to every FC Storage Subsystem. If a direct path is not available, Dynix/ptx uses a *multipathing* technique, which routes an I/O request through the IQ Link and then through an available path. The direct path approach results in better performance than the multipathing technique. Nevertheless, each quad requires a direct path to every I/O device.

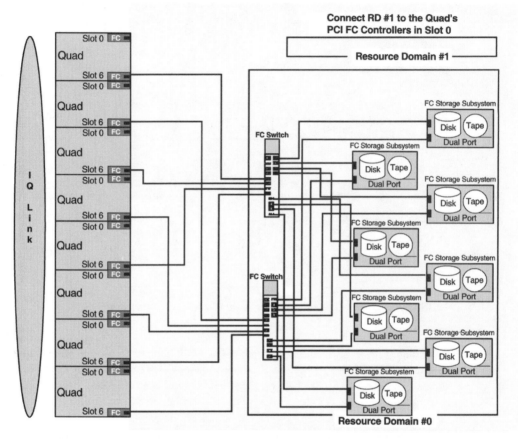

FIGURE 3.7   NUMA-Q fiber I/O subsystem architecture.

The logical volume manager on Sequent is known as the SVM (Sequent Volume Manager). The current version of SVM is Version 2. I recommend that you use the SVM volume manager to manage the disk subsystems in your Sequent system. Do not try to manage the disk partitions manually. Managing the disks manually is a tedious effort that will reduce your overall performance. Without the volume manager, striping has to be done manually, which will not avoid *hot files*. Hot files are data files that are being accessed concurrently by a large number of users. The manual stripe method would place Oracle data files on different disks. However, if a large number of users are querying the same data file, a hot file situation can occur, and disk I/O performance can suffer. With striping, you eliminate hot files because the data is interleaved and striped across multiple disks and controllers. This permits a single Oracle data file to be spread across multiple disks, as opposed to manual striping in which an Oracle data file maps to a single-disk partition. Configuring the SVM requires some basic knowledge of the SVM and its architecture. The SVM has three main object layers: subdisks, plexes, and volumes.

SVM objects are managed in terms of disk groups. A disk group is simply a collection of SVM disks. Disk groups allow you to group disks into logical collections for administrative convenience. For example, disks containing database applications could be placed together in a disk group. SVM requires the existence of at least one disk group, *rootdg* (root disk group). The rootdg disk group is created when SVM is configured for the first time. The rootdg disk group must contain only *bootable* local storage, including the root file system and the primary swap. The remaining SVM disks (i.e., not bootable local storage) must be placed into disk groups other than the rootdg disk group. Furthermore, a disk can only be in one disk group.

Disks in a disk group contain two regions: private and public. The private region contains the SVM configuration database, which is used to manage all the objects within a disk group. The public region contains the remainder of the disk, which contains the actual subdisk storage allocations. Public and private regions are allocated on each disk by disk type. There are three disk types:

❏ **Sliced**—The public and private regions of these SVM disks are on different disk partitions. The private region of the disk must be located on a type-8 partition. When you attempt to place a partition under SVM control, the software counts the total number of type-8 partitions on the entire disk and matches the type-8 partition with partitions that are neither type-9, type-8, nor type-3 (usually only type-1 partitions remain), in numerical slice order. If there are no type-8 partitions on the disk but the disk is partitioned, SVM labels the disk as type *nopriv* (described below).

❏ **Simple**—The public and private regions of these SVM disks are on the same partition. SVM automatically designates disks that are nonpartitioned as simple disks. The first part of the disk is private. The remainder of the disk is public.

❏ **Nopriv**—No private region exists on these SVM disks; therefore, the disks do not contain database configuration information.

Sliced and nopriv disk types are available mostly for compatibility with older versions of SVM. In general, simple disk types should be used. To create a disk group, you must first place the disks under SVM control. To create a simple disk, the disk's Volume Table of Contents (VTOC) partition map must first be removed using the `/etc/devdestroy` command. Then, using the `vxdisk` command, the disk can be placed under SVM control. For example:

```
myhost{root}-> /etc/devdestroy   /dev/rdsk/sd8
myhost{root}-> vxdisk -f init sd8 privlen=6000
```

The `privlen=6000` option, specifies that 6,000 disk blocks are to be allocated for the configuration database. The size of the private area can be estimated using the following formula.

```
private area size = (nobjects * .68) * 1.20
```

The value for the number of objects (`nobjects`) includes the estimated number of disks, subdisks, plexes, and volumes in the disk group. The additional 20 percent accounts for future growth. Once the disks are placed under SVM control, the disk group can be created as follows.

```
myhost{root}-> # vxdg -s init db01_dg sd8 sd9 sd10 \
                       sd11 sd12 sd13 sd14 \
                       sd15 sd16 sd17 sd18 sd19
```

The above statement creates the disk group `db01_dg` which includes disks `sd8` through `sd19`. Note that each simple disk has a private region reserved for the disk group's configuration database. The entire configuration database is contained within a private region. For redundancy purposes, multiple copies are maintained, however it is not necessary to maintain a copy on each disk. SVM, by default, maintains one copy of the configuration database for each SCSI bus of the disk group, with a minimum of four copies. For large systems with many SCSI buses, the default behavior may not be practical. In this case, the *nconfig* option of the `vxdg` command can be used to specify the number of configuration database copies. In general, four copies of the configuration database should be sufficient (*nconfig=4*).

A description file can be created with all the statements necessary to create subdisks, plexes, and volumes to be used as input into the `vxmake` command. The following is a description file that creates eight subdisks of 600 MB each, a striped plex using a stripe width of 64 KB, and the corresponding volume. The ownership of the volume is set to the Oracle user and the dba group. The `vxmake` command then uses the description file to create the subdisks, plex, and volume.

```
File: db01 dg.desc
sd sd8-0 disk=sd10 offset=0 len=12288
sd sd9-0 disk=sd10 offset=0 len=12288
sd sd10-0 disk=sd10 offset=0 len=12288
sd sd11-0 disk=sd11 offset=0 len=12288
sd sd12-0 disk=sd12 offset=0 len=12288
sd sd13-0 disk=sd13 offset=0 len=12288
sd sd14-0 disk=sd14 offset=0 len=12288
sd sd15-0 disk=sd15 offset=0 len=12288
plex item1-01 layout=STRIPE st_width=64 sd=sd8-0,\
        sd9-0,sd10-0,sd11-0,sd12-0,sd13-0, \
        sd14-0, sd15-0
vol item use_type=gen plex=item1-01 \
        user=oracle group=dba
```

The command `vxmake` is then executed to create the subdisks, plex, and volume.

```
myhost(root)-> vxmake -g db01_dg -d db01_dg.desc
```

3.2.3 STRIPING ON SUN

Sun provides a wide variety of storage solutions, such as the StorEdge A1000, A3500, and A5200 Arrays. The A1000 StorEdge Arrays provide the ability to configure a rack mount disk I/O subsystem containing, for example, 108 disk drives of 18.2 GB capacity. The A1000 Array consists of an Ultra SCSI interface and allows either software- or hardware-managed RAID to be configured. The A1000 StorEdge array can also be configured with battery backed cache ranging from 24 to 80 MB. Figure 3.8 illustrates the architecture of the A1000 Array.

In Figure 3.8, the interface board is supported by two Ultra SCSI Channels, each capable of 40 MB per second. The A1000 can be configured for hardware or software RAID, and can consist of either 18.2 GB or 36 GB capacity drives. An Enterprise expansion cabinet can be used to rack mount multiple A1000 Arrays. The A1000 Array also provides several high availability features such as the ability to hot swap power supplies, fans, or disk drives.

The A3500FC StorEdge Array is a high performance dual fiber channel array which supports numerous levels of RAID including RAID levels 0, 1, 1+0, 3, and 5. The A3500FC Array can be configured with up to 256 MB of controller-based cache. The A3500FC provides full redundancy, including dual hot-swappable controllers, power supplies, and hot-swappable disks. Figure 3.9 illustrates the architecture of the A3500FC StorEdge Array.

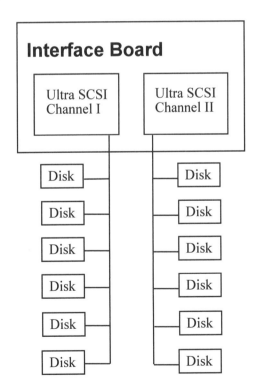

FIGURE 3.8 Sun StorEdge A1000 Array architecture.

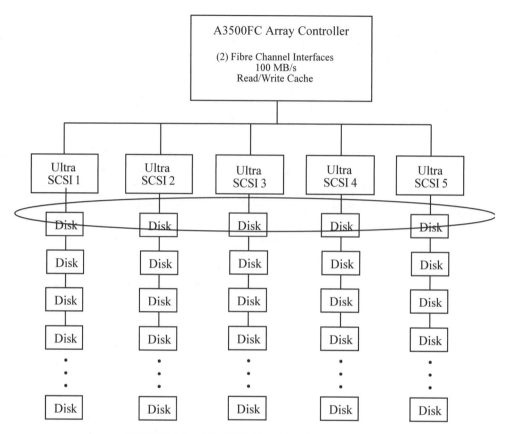

FIGURE 3.9   A3500FC StorEdge Array architecture.

The StorEdge A3500FC Array represents the new generation in fiber storage array technology. The storage array consists of five differential Ultra SCSI internal controllers that each provide maximum transfer rates of 40 MB per second. The connection between the storage array and the host computer is via a fiber channel FCAL (Fiber Channel Arbitrated Loop). The FCAL connection increases performance over the standard differential SCSI connection. The A3500FC Array supports two Fiber channels on the array controller. The A3500FC Array also allows two FCAL host adapters (SBus or PCI) to be used for the host system interface. This allows two systems to attach to a single storage array. The storage array can also be used in a Sun Cluster configuration and in an Oracle Parallel Server (SMP) environment. The Oracle Parallel Server for the SMP clusters requires that each node in the cluster share the same disks.

The A3500 StorEdge Array can be configured with either a Fiber Channel interface or a differential Ultra SCSI interface. In differential SCSI, the data signal (between –5.0 V and +5.0 V) is transmitted along with its inverse signal. A one or zero state is determined by comparing the signal with its inverse. In single-ended SCSI, the host adapter transmits data and ground signals. The one state is determined by the difference between the ground and data signals. Single-ended SCSI limits the physical length that the data can be transmitted, subsequently limiting the length of the single-ended SCSI bus to 6 meters. Single-ended SCSI cannot carry signals as far as differential SCSI. Differential SCSI can carry SCSI signals up to 25 meters. One important footnote is that the length limit of the SCSI bus (6 meters for single-ended and 25 meters for differential) includes the cable from the host adapter to the terminator and all the cabling connecting the peripherals. Attempting to exceed the physical length limits of the single-ended or differential SCSI bus may cause data unreliability and SCSI bus resets and/or timeouts.

The fiber channel interface consists of two fibers that allow signals to be carried in opposite directions. As opposed to SCSI, which uses the same set of wires for both directions, the fiber channel allows concurrent transfers of data in both directions. This increases I/O throughput and allows the A3500FC Array to sustain more than 3300 I/Os per second.

In order to create a striped device on the Sun storage arrays, you can use either the hardware volume manager to configure RAID stripe sets or you can use the Sun Solstice DiskSuite tool (SDS). The SDS tool enables you to create striped, mirrored, concatenated, and RAID-5 devices. SDS Version 4.1 provides the GUI Metatool which enables the user to manage SDS *metadevices* via a graphical user interface similar to that of Veritas. Disk Suite releases prior to 4.0 required manual commands in order to create and manage metadevices. Metadevices are SDS' logical devices. SDS' main configuration file is the `md.tab` file located in the `/usr/opt/SUNWmd/etc` directory. The `md.tab` file contains entries for each metadevice, as well as the complete definition of the device. SDS is an easy-to-use tool that enables the quick configuration of logical devices. Figure 3.10 shows the metadevice layer.

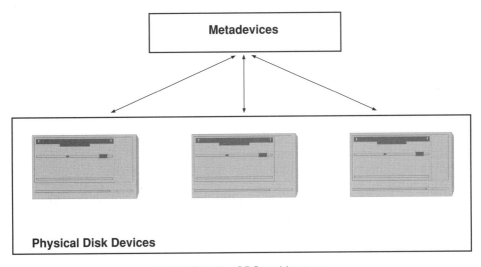

FIGURE 3.10 SDS architecture.

To create metadevices, you must first install the SDS software package. I recommend that you upgrade to the latest release of SDS (currently 4.1) if you are currently running SDS. SDS 4.1 provides additional performance enhancements as well as bug fixes to known problems. Once SDS is installed, you can create the database replicas by using the `metadb` command. For example,

```
myhost{root}-> metadb -a -f /dev/dsk/c1t1d0s7 \
                           /dev/dsk/c2t1d0s7 \
                           /dev/dsk/c3t1d0s7
```

In this example, the `metadb` command is used to create the metadevice database. The metadevice database is stored on the disk partitions listed in the preceding example. Each partition holds a replica of the metadevice database. In the case of the failure of a disk that contains a metadevice database replica, SDS will read the database information from the other replicas. Placing the database replicas on different disks and different controllers minimizes SDS downtime. Also, you should allocate 3 MB of disk space for each metadevice database replica. SDS 4.0 increased the size of the replica database from prior versions of SDS that used less than 1 MB. Therefore, when you upgrade to SDS 4.X, you may need to resize your database replica partitions. For this reason, allocate plenty of space upfront so that in the future if new versions of SDS require more space for database replicas, your partition size can handle the growth. I recommend that you allocate 3 MB for each SDS replica partition. Although this is more than is necessary now, it will foster a smoother migration to future versions that may require larger replica partition sizes. This avoids the nightmare scenario in which your disk partitions may have to be resized only because of the growth in the metadevice database replica size requirement. Once the metadevice database is created, you can start to create metadevices. You can do this either by editing the `md.tab` file or by using the GUI metatool that is provided with SDS 4.X. For example, to create a striped metadevice on a Sun Server using the disk trays, edit the `md.tab` file, and place the following entry:

Example md.tab file

```
d1 1 4 /dev/dsk/c2t0d0s3 \
       /dev/dsk/c3t0d0s3 \
       /dev/dsk/c4t0d0s3 \
       /dev/dsk/c5t0d0s3 -i 64k
```

Then save the changes, and exit the file. Now you can use the following SDS commands to create the metadevice:

```
myhost{root}-> metainit -n d1
myhost{root}-> metainit d1
```

The `metainit` command creates and initializes the metadevice by reading the corresponding entry from the `md.tab` file. The first `metainit` (-n option) example verifies the `d1` entry in the `md.tab` file but does not create a `d1` metadevice. The `metainit -n` option is frequently used to validate a metadevice entry without actually creating it. The second `metainit` command creates the metadevice `d1` as defined in the `md.tab` file. The `d1` metadevice is a striped device that consists of four separate disks on four separate controllers with a stripe interlace of 64 KB. This striped device offers the best performance because all disks in the stripe are on separate controllers.

The storage arrays typically follow a different device naming convention than that of directly attached disks. For example, in the traditional device naming convention of `/dev/dsk/cNtMdRsP`, N represents the controller number, M represents the SCSI target number, R represents the device number on the target, and P represents the slice or partition number. Therefore, `/dev/dsk/c2t3d0s1` refers to controller 2, SCSI target 3, device 0 on SCSI target 3, and slice or partition 1 on device 0, target 3. The storage arrays use a slightly different device naming convention since the base controller represents the fiber SBus or PCI slot in the host, and the storage array itself has five internal differential Ultra SCSI controllers. In the storage array, N represents the base controller number of the fiber SBus slot, M represents the internal controller number within the array, R represents the SCSI target of the device connected to the internal controller, and P represents the slice or partition number. For instance, `/dev/dsk/c2t3d3s2` refers to controller 2 as the fiber SBus controller; `t3` is the fourth internal storage array Ultra SCSI controller, `d3` is the fourth disk drive off of the `t3` internal controller, and `s2` represents slice 2. To create a stripe within a storage array, edit the `md.tab` file, and place the following entry into the `md.tab` file:

Example md.tab file

```
d1 1 5 /dev/dsk/c2t0d0s3 \
        /dev/dsk/c2t1d0s3 \
        /dev/dsk/c2t2d0s3 \
        /dev/dsk/c2t3d0s3 \
        /dev/dsk/c2t4d0s3 -i 64k
```

In this example, a stripe is created that consists of a disk drive (`d0`) from each internal storage array Ultra SCSI controller using an interleave value of 64 KB. The stripe is a five-device stripe spread across the six internal fast-wide SCSI controllers. There are two things you should avoid when striping. The first is never to create a stripe that consists of disks on the same controller. For instance,

Example md.tab file: <AVOID THIS KIND OF STRIPING>

```
d1 1 5 /dev/dsk/c2t0d0s3 \
        /dev/dsk/c2t0d1s3 \
        /dev/dsk/c2t0d2s3 \
        /dev/dsk/c2t0d3s3 \
        /dev/dsk/c2t0d4s3 -i 64k
```

In this example, a stripe device is created that consists of five disk drives on the same controller. This significantly reduces performance by saturating one controller. This example not only prevents parallel disk I/O, it also defeats the whole purpose of striping—to parallelize I/O across multiple controllers and disk drives. The second thing you should never do when striping is to stripe across storage arrays. For instance,

Example md.tab file: <AVOID THIS KIND OF STRIPING>

```
d1 1 5 /dev/dsk/c2t0d0s3 \
        /dev/dsk/c3t0d0s3 \
        /dev/dsk/c4t0d0s3 \
        /dev/dsk/c5t0d0s3 \
        /dev/dsk/c6t0d0s3 -i 64k
```

Assume that c2, c3, c4, c5, and c6 are each separate Fiber SBus controller cards for the five storage arrays. This creates a striped device across five storage arrays. Although this may seem optimal, it is not. The storage arrays are quite different from traditional SCSI controllers. In a traditional SCSI controller environment, this stripe is quite efficient. The storage array uses a fiber connection between the storage array and the host computer. The host computer communicates to the storage array using firmware drivers.[1] Each time an I/O request is issued to a storage array, the firmware drivers service the request by sending the I/O request down to the storage array across the fiber connection. Therefore, accessing a single striped device that consists of several storage arrays forces the I/O to the striped device to be broken down over several fiber buses. The latency overhead in this case severely impacts the performance of the stripe because the I/O has to be broken down over several SBuses. A much better approach is to define striped devices within each storage array and then separate I/O by using multiple striped devices from different storage arrays. However, no single striped device should span a storage array. For instance,

Example md.tab file: <Ideal Striping for Storage Array>

```
d1 1 5 /dev/dsk/c2t0d0s3 \
        /dev/dsk/c2t1d0s3 \
        /dev/dsk/c2t2d0s3 \
        /dev/dsk/c2t3d0s3 \
        /dev/dsk/c2t4d0s3 -i 64k

d2 1 5 /dev/dsk/c3t0d0s3 \
        /dev/dsk/c3t1d0s3 \
        /dev/dsk/c3t2d0s3 \
        /dev/dsk/c3t3d0s3 \
        /dev/dsk/c3t4d0s3 -i 64k
```

---

1. The storage array patches provide the latest firmware release for the particular array. You should ensure that the storage arrays contain the latest firmware release. The firmware patches typically include bug fixes and performance optimizations.

This example creates two separate striped devices, each of which stripes within a single storage array. You can then add these two data files to the Oracle database. This parallelizes Oracle writes to the d1 and d2 metadevices when written to simultaneously, thus maximizing I/O parallelism by distributing the I/O.

For systems which use regular disk trays, you should stripe across different SCSI controllers. For example, if your system has ten fast-wide SCSI or Ultra SCSI controllers, you can define striped devices to stripe across the ten controllers.

Example md.tab file: <Ideal Striping for Disk Trays>

```
d1 1 5 /dev/dsk/c2t0d0s3 \
        /dev/dsk/c3t1d0s3 \
        /dev/dsk/c4t2d0s3 \
        /dev/dsk/c5t3d0s3 \
        /dev/dsk/c6t4d0s3 -i 64k

d2 1 5 /dev/dsk/c7t0d0s3 \
        /dev/dsk/c8t1d0s3 \
        /dev/dsk/c9t2d0s3 \
        /dev/dsk/c10t3d0s3 \
        /dev/dsk/c11t4d0s3 -i 64k
```

This example creates two separate striped devices, with each stripe spanning five different disks and five different controllers. Again, if d1 and d2 were Oracle data files, this parallelizes Oracle writes to the d1 and d2 metadevices, thus minimizing contention. Another important consideration when striping is organizing the hardware SCSI controllers in such a way that no more than three fast-wide SCSI SBus controllers are installed per system board. The maximum SBus transfer rate is 50 MB per second. If each SCSI SBus controller is a fast-wide SCSI controller with a 20 MB per second maximum transfer rate capability, the third fast-wide controller on the same SBus will cause SBus saturation. For fast (single-ended) SCSI, you may use up to the maximum number of fast SCSI SBus slots on the system board since each fast SCSI will have a maximum transfer rate of 10 MB per second. With fast SCSI, it would take more than five fast SCSI controllers on the same SBus to induce saturation. If you have open slots on other system boards, try to balance the I/O by distributing the number of controllers across different system boards evenly. For example, if you have four system boards with four SCSI controllers or Fiber SBus controllers all on only one board, place a controller on each system board. This avoids SBus and system board bus saturation and distributes I/O much more effectively.

3.2.4 STRIPING ON HP

On HP, the logical volume manager is known as LVM. You can use the lvextend and lvcreate commands to create stripes and logical volume groups. For more information refer to the HP system administration manuals on LVM or to the manual pages on LVM (man lvm). Use the same tuning guidelines on HP as Sequent and Sun. Try to spread your data across multiple spindles and controllers.

3.2.5 MAXIMIZING THE PERFORMANCE OF THE STRIPE

To maximize performance when striping, you should define a striped device that concatenates disk drives with each disk drive being part of a different controller (i.e., channel). This avoids excessive I/O on one or a few controllers and allows for full parallelism by distributing I/O across multiple controllers. For example, if you create a striped device that consists of three disks on the same SCSI controller, reads and writes cannot proceed in parallel because disks in the striped device are on the same controller. Ensure that each SCSI controller has the same configuration in terms of hardware, software, and data transfer rates. Having different SCSI controllers each with different transfer rates would cause the stripe to operate at the slowest speed because the reads and writes are issued to the stripe. Therefore, try to balance the I/O as best as possible by creating stripes on different controllers and different disks per controller.

One other important footnote is that a single data file may not be able to exceed 2 GB in size on certain UNIX platforms due to the hard limit. Therefore, take this fact into account when you design and plan for stripes. However, Solaris 7, HP-UX 11, and Dynix/ptx 4.4 provide 64-bit interfaces to manage large files allowing you to create files larger than 2 GB. Make sure that when you partition the slices on the disk drives that each partition used in a striped device is of equal size; otherwise the striped device will be the size of the smallest partition multiplied by the number of partitions in the stripe. For example, if you were concatenating three devices of 10 MB, 500 MB, and 500 MB, the stripe device would be only 30 MB as opposed to 1010 MB. The common rule is to make the size of each partition in the stripe equal to the total desired size of the stripe divided by the number of partitions in the stripe. For example, if you are configuring a 2-GB stripe device, and you are striping over four disks, each of the four partitions should be sized at 512 MB.

3.3   PARTITIONING THE DISKS

On Solaris, you can have at most seven user-defined slices (0 . . . 8). On Solaris, slice2 (`/dev/dsk/c2t1d0s2`) represents the entire disk. Therefore, take this into consideration when you create stripes. For example, if you want to create 2-GB striped devices on a storage array, and each disk is 9 GB, if you stripe across all six controllers in the array, each partition on the disk will be approximately 341 MB. This means that with seven user slices, only 2387 MB will be used if each partition is 341 MB to be striped across six controllers not exceeding 2 GB. Therefore, a large portion of the disk space will be wasted. You can deal with this problem two ways: request smaller disk drives from your disk vendor, or create more logical volumes via the volume manager in order to fully utilize the space. Sequent allows a maximum of 255 partitions or slices on a single disk.

One important note is that if you intend to use raw devices, you must preserve cylinder 0 manually. Cylinder 0 holds the VTOC information, and if this is not preserved, the VTOC information will be overwritten when writes are performed to the raw device. You can use the format utility on Solaris or the `fmthard` utility to partition the disks. When you partition the disks, allocate one cylinder (the first cylinder—cylinder 0) to the first partition (slice 0). Then, you can partition the remaining slices, leaving you with up to six user-definable slices. Protecting the VTOC is necessary only if you are using raw devices. If you are using file systems, the OS protects the VTOC from being overwritten.

3.4 SETTING THE STRIPE WIDTH

The stripe interleave is an important factor in determining the I/O performance. In general, most sites have seen good performance with 32 KB or 64 KB interleaves. However, it is important to note that the interleave can drive the performance based on the following factors: the Oracle block size, the number of devices (partitions) in the stripe, and the DBMS and server workload. For example, a heavily hit OLTP system should use a different interleave size than a pure DSS (read-only) environment. Suppose, for example, the Oracle block size is 4 KB, and the stripe interleave is 32 KB. This information of itself is not sufficient to determine performance. More information is required about the physical layout of the disk drives. Suppose further that a striped device is made up of three disks. That means, in order to have full I/O parallelism (in this case three-way parallelism), a read or write request would have to be batched at a size of (stripe-size) × (number of members in the stripe). Or in this case, (32 KB) × (3) = 96 KB. This means that Oracle would have to read or write 24 data blocks in order to achieve full parallelism. If the workload were such that small number of rows were requested, the read requests would consist of small batch sizes. This would not make full use of the stripe itself.

For an OLTP system, the majority of I/O will most likely consist of random reads and writes as SQL statements are largely using indexes to access the data. Hence, the goal in an OLTP system is to minimize "hot files" by spreading the I/O across many of the available volumes. For an Oracle block size on UNIX, I recommend 4 KB or 8 KB for a mostly OLTP system. Then, to calculate the ideal stripe width, use a multiplier of the Oracle block size. Also, set `_db_block_write_batch=<Oracle block size>` × `<number of members in stripe>`. This helps set the optimal DBWR batch size. For an OLTP system, an Oracle block size of 4 KB or 8 KB with a stripe interleave of 32 KB resulted in optimal performance. Performance gains of up to 100 percent have been observed when using a volume manager with an OLTP system.

For a data warehousing workload, there will most likely be a tremendous amount of sequential large-scale reads. Items such as full-table scans and parallel queries are extremely common. Large joins and sorts are also common in a data warehousing workload. Therefore, the Oracle block size should be as large as possible, allowing more data to be read in per block. Oracle 7.3 allows for a maximum database block size of 16 KB (`db_block_size=16384`). In addition to the block size, set `db_file_multiblock_read_count=<block_size / 1024>` × `<number of members in the stripe>`. The Oracle server enforces several constraints pertaining to the maximum setting for `db_file_multiblock_read_count` such as the maximum I/O size. The maximum I/O size is platform specific and controls the maximum amount of bytes that can be read or written in a single I/O call. On Solaris, the maximum

I/O size is 1 MB. On Sequent the maximum I/O size is 128 KB. On HP, the maximum I/O size in Oracle is 2 MB. This means that `db_file_multiblock_read_count` cannot exceed 64 on a Sun Solaris system with a database block size of 16 KB. On a Sequent system with a 16 KB database block size, `db_file_multiblock_read_count` cannot exceed 8. Determining the optimal stripe width for a data warehouse is a little more complicated than in an OLTP system. In a data warehouse, you have two main choices: either parallelize an individual I/O request or parallelize a group of I/O requests. Parallelizing an individual I/O request involves selecting a small stripe width such as 32 KB or 64 KB, thereby causing a single I/O to span several spindles. Parallelizing a group of I/O requests involves selecting a large stripe size, such as 512 KB or 1 MB. This results in a single I/O being serviced by a single spindle but collectively servicing disjoint I/Os in parallel across different spindles. For example, suppose on a Sequent system that the stripe width is 128 KB, and `db_file_multiblock_read_count=8` and `db_block_size=16k`. During a parallel query, each I/O would be serviced by a single disk. However, because each parallel query slave will be issuing parallel I/Os, many spindles would be servicing I/O in parallel. If the stripe width is 64 KB, a single I/O during a parallel query would span two spindles. In general, a larger stripe size, such as 512 KB or 1 MB, is much more efficient for DSS systems. There is some overhead associated with striping when an I/O larger than the stripe interleave size is issued. In this case, the I/O needs to be broken into multiple I/Os of the interleave size. Therefore, you should measure and consider this overhead when choosing the stripe size. Performance gains of 500 percent have been observed when using volume management software to optimally stripe the database files in a data warehouse system.

On Solaris, if you are using SDS with file systems, you should set the stripe interleave to 56 KB or equal to the file system cluster write size for optimal performance. Solaris uses a memory stride when it writes to file systems so that blocks are written to contiguously before a rotational delay. For example, in a file system with an 8 KB block size, the default maximum number of contiguous blocks allocated for a file is seven. Therefore, I/O to the file is grouped into seven contiguous blocks, of 8 KB each. The memory stride used for such a write would be 56 KB. Therefore, your stripe width should be in sync with the memory stride. This allows contiguous one-pass I/O without having to break the stripe into smaller 56 KB fragments if your stripe is larger than 56 KB. You can set the maximum number of contiguous blocks allocated for a file before a rotational delay is inserted by using the `newfs` command (`-C` option) or `tunefs` command (`-a` option). For an 8 KB file system block size, the default of seven is fine. Setting the stripe width to 56 KB offers optimal performance within file systems.

3.5   MIRRORING

Mirroring, also known as RAID 1 (meaning full redundancy), consists of complete data duplication. In a striped device, a single loss of a disk within a stripe causes all files that are part of that stripe to become unavailable. Any data on the stripe is lost. In a mirrored device, an exact duplicate of the data is available on another device (the mirrored device). A mirrored device consists of at least two submirrors. The first submirror becomes the primary device, and the second submirror represents the secondary device, and so on. You can use the volume manager to create a mirrored device that has at least two submirrors. For example, using the Solstice DiskSuite tool, you can create a mirrored device.

Example md.tab file: <Mirrored Device>

```
d1 1 5 /dev/dsk/c2t0d0s3 \
        /dev/dsk/c3t1d0s3 \
        /dev/dsk/c4t2d0s3 \
        /dev/dsk/c5t3d0s3 \
        /dev/dsk/c6t4d0s3 -i 64k

d2 1 5 /dev/dsk/c7t0d0s3 \
        /dev/dsk/c8t1d0s3 \
        /dev/dsk/c9t2d0s3 \
        /dev/dsk/c10t3d0s3 \
        /dev/dsk/c11t4d0s3 -i 64k

d3 -m d1 d2
```

In this example, two striped devices, d1 and d2, are defined, and d3 is the mirrored device. The d1 device is the primary device of the d3 mirror, and d2 is the secondary device of the mirror. Once you create the mirror by issuing the metainit command, you will no longer be able to use the d1 and d2 devices because they are now part of the mirror. All reads and writes must be performed to the d3 device. The kernel SDS driver handles the duplication of the writes on d1 and d2 when writes are issued to d3. When you create mirrored devices, be sure that the devices that make up the mirror are configured equivalently in terms of size and I/O distribution. For example, do not mirror two metadevices in which one metadevice is striped across four controllers and the second metadevice is striped across two controllers. This reduces the performance of writes because a write to the second submirror may take longer than a write to the first submirror. When mirroring, ensure that the stripes that make up the mirror are configured equivalently. Also, be sure that the stripe widths of the mirrored devices are all equal in order to prevent unbalanced I/O. On Sequent, you can use the volplex utility to build mirrors by attaching a plex to an existing volume. The same logic applies, and you should build the striped plexes first, then build the volume, and attach the striped plexes that you want to act as the mirror to the existing volume. For more information on the Sequent SVM and mirroring, refer to the SVM system administration manuals or the manual pages on volplex. Since the theme of this text is performance and tuning, I assume most readers have a good background with the volume manager of the respective platform. If not, I recommend that you read the SVM (Sequent), SDS (Sun), and LVM (HP) administration and user guides to familiarize yourself with the respective local volume manager.

Mirroring degrades I/O performance due to the fact that each write I/O needs to be duplicated for each submirror. For this reason, you should create a mirror with each submirror striped. Also, each submirror should be on a different controller and on different disks than the other submirrors in order to minimize the performance degradation caused by mirroring. This also provides higher system availability in the event of a controller failure because the data is spread across multiple controllers. In a two-way mirrored device, the performance loss caused by mirroring is approximately 15 percent.

If you are configuring mirrored devices on the Sun StorEdge arrays, you should configure them so that the striped devices that make up the mirror are not part of the same tray. If your mirrored device consists of striped devices that are part of the same tray, you will not be able to replace the defective disk during a media failure on the mirror without having to shut the system down. If the submirrors in a mirrored device are part of the same tray, pulling the tray out while the system is running causes the entire mirror to be unavailable. You will certainly not be able to pull the tray if the mirror is in use. Therefore, by distributing the submirrors across different trays, you can pull the tray that contains the defective disk drive without disrupting the mirror because the functional submirror is on another tray. Ideally each submirror metadevice should be on a separate storage array to maximize mirroring performance. However, if this not possible due to a limited amount of storage arrays, spread the submirrors across different trays. Before you pull the tray, be sure to off-line the submirror that contains the defective disk. After you replace the failed disk drive with a new drive, you must issue a sync to the off-line submirror to force all the data from the on-line submirrors to the off-line submirror. The sync process can take a long time for a large mirror device, especially in an active system. However, if your submirrors are distributed properly, the sync time can be minimized by parallelizing I/O. In SDS, use the `metaonline` or `metasync` command to on-line the submirror and sync the mirror after the failed media problem has been corrected. `Metaonline` automatically issues a resync. `Metaonline` should be used in conjunction with `metaoffline`. On HP, use the `lvsync` command to sync the mirror.

Although mirroring decreases write performance, you can use mirroring to your advantage in a data warehousing (read-only) environment. Some volume managers support geometric reads, meaning that when data is needed from the mirrored device, the volume manager driver reads from whichever submirror is geometrically closer. For example, if the disk read/write heads on submirror 1 are positioned at cylinder 10, and the disk read/write heads on submirror 2 are positioned at cylinder 2200, and data needs to be read from cylinder 11, the geometric read option would use submirror 1 since it is geometrically closer. Geometric reads divide read operations among the submirrors by logical block addresses. For instance, in a two-way mirrored device, the disk space on the mirror is divided into two equally sized logical address ranges. Each submirror can then perform separate reads. Reads to the first section are handled by the first submirror, and reads to the second region are handled by the second submirror. In SDS, you can enable geometric reads through the `metatool` or `md.tab` file when defining the mirror. For example,

Example md.tab file: <Mirrored Device – Geometric Reads>

```
d1 1 5 /dev/dsk/c2t0d0s3 \
        /dev/dsk/c3t1d0s3 \
        /dev/dsk/c4t2d0s3 \
        /dev/dsk/c5t3d0s3 \
        /dev/dsk/c6t4d0s3 -i 64k

d2 1 5 /dev/dsk/c7t0d0s3 \
        /dev/dsk/c8t1d0s3 \
        /dev/dsk/c9t2d0s3 \
        /dev/dsk/c10t3d0s3 \
        /dev/dsk/c11t4d0s3 -i 64k

d3 -m d1 d2 -g
```

This example enables geometric reads for the mirrored metadevice d3. The performance gain offered by geometric reads is 5–10 percent. Geometric reads increase performance for sequential reads. For a DSS application, sequential reads occur frequently, and geometric reads can help increase performance. However, in a DSS environment, mirroring typically is not used because the data in a DSS environment is primarily read-only.

When you create a mirrored device, there are generally two write options: parallel writes and serial writes. On SDS, parallel writes are the default for mirrors. Parallel writes mean that writes to the submirrors are issued in parallel. The serial write option issues a write to each submirror in a serial fashion, waiting for each write to complete before the next write to the next submirror is issued. For best performance, use the parallel write option. This enables writes to the mirror to proceed in parallel, thus minimizing mirroring degradation.

3.6   RAID LEVELS

3.6.1 RAID-5

RAID-5 (Redundant Arrays of Inexpensive Disks) stripes data and parity across several disk drives. This eliminates the parity bottleneck introduced by previous types of RAID that stored the parity data on a single disk drive. RAID-5 treats multiple partitions as one large contiguous slice, which can contain data or parity information. No one single physical partition contains all the parity information—it is distributed across the multiple physical sections. If a disk drive were to fail, data is reconstructed dynamically by performing an XOR on the data and the parity bit. RAID-5 improves sequential read performance, but it may have an impact on overall write performance due to its inefficiency on small writes and the overhead of the parity-bit calculation. The main performance bottleneck of RAID-5 is due to the *read-write-modify* cycle in which a small write request involves two parity calculations and four disk I/Os: one I/O to write the new data, two I/Os to read the old data and old parity in order to compute the new parity, and one I/O to write the new parity. For small write requests, the parity is computed by comparing the new data with the old data and applying the differences to the parity block. For large write requests that involve many disks, parity is computed by performing an XOR on the new data on each disk. Therefore, RAID-5 can seriously reduce performance for frequent small write requests such as redo log writes. RAID-5 can be useful in a data warehousing environment where the majority of I/Os are reads and updates are minimal. RAID-5 offers good random I/O read performance and can also offer good sequential performance if the block sizes in the stripe are smaller than the average size of the I/O request.

In the case of a disk failure, reconstructing the data dynamically can seriously degrade performance, and a synchronization of the data once the defective drive is replaced is a lengthy and expensive operation. However, because the parity information is distributed, the dynamic reconstruction of the data will not be bottlenecked by a single drive. RAID-5 offers several advantages, including its ability to recover from a single disk failure, and it is more cost-effective than mirroring.

3.6.2 RAID-6

RAID-6 enhances the error recovering ability of RAID-5 in the case of multiple drive failures. RAID-5 recovers data from a failed disk by essentially reading the data and parity information from the remaining (available) disks in the stripe set. It is possible that additional disks in the RAID-5 stripe set may fail during the recovery phase, resulting in data loss. Hence, mission-critical applications may require stricter reliability in order to reduce system downtime. RAID-6 employs Reed-Solomon encoding on another drive to protect against any two disk failures. This improves the recoverability of the standard RAID-5 configuration. For small writes, RAID-6 offers less performance than RAID-5 due to the update of the additional parity information. The RAID-6 read-modify-write sequence for small writes requires six disk I/Os in order to update both sets of parity information.

3.6.3 RAID-7

RAID-7[2] is yet another improvement of the standard RAID configurations. RAID-7 provides asynchronous I/O access by utilizing a real-time event operating system local to the RAID-7 array known as the Array Management OS Software. The Array Management OS Software utilizes the CPU and memory buffer resources local to the array to process I/O requests in parallel. This enables I/Os to be queued to the RAID-7 array, thereby allowing the host application to continue processing without having to block on I/Os. The independent channel buffers, real-time OS, and separate control buses are critical to the asynchronous and independent nature of RAID-7. RAID-7 offers a high level of I/O throughput over the traditional RAID due to its ability to utilize an independent OS and hardware array resources to process I/O requests.

---

2. RAID-7 products are available from the Storage Computer Corporation (www.storage.com).

3.6.4 RAID-S

RAID-S[3], another level of RAID, reduces the overhead of the parity computation by performing the operation via the hardware on the disk drive rather than the controller microcode. RAID-S requires XOR capable disk drives. RAID-S does not stripe data across different disks as is done in a RAID-5 configuration. Instead, RAID-S allows standard I/O performance tuning techniques to be used to distribute the data. RAID-S increases I/O parallelism by performing the XOR operation on the disk drive itself, subsequently reducing the performance penalty associated with small writes.

3.7   HARDWARE VOLUME MANAGEMENT

The software logical volume manager (LVM) such as Veritas, SDS, or SVM adds overhead to I/O operations by consuming additional processor cycles for operations such as logical to physical disk address translations and I/O buffer alignments. In the case of mirroring, the LVM needs to propagate the write to the submirrors. In order to improve performance and reduce the server overhead introduced by the software LVM, many disk array vendors have provided hardware RAID functionality through the storage array itself. Typically, the storage array is configured with at least one processor and some local cache memory. This allows the storage array to handle the RAID functionality, off-loading the RAID work from the server. This is referred to as hardware-level RAID. In general, hardware-level RAID is faster and more efficient than the software equivalent. The hardware RAID functionality implemented in the storage array allows the server to focus on application processing rather than RAID operations. Software volume managers are typically used in place of hardware level RAID where the hardware level RAID functionality is limited and cannot meet the performance requirements of the application. Therefore, when evaluating storage arrays, make sure you investigate the configuration details, such as the amount of cache, number and type of processor, and level of RAID functionality provided.

In order to optimally configure your I/O subsystem, you should also benchmark your software LVM against the hardware level RAID provided in your storage array to determine which is more optimal. In some cases, a combination of both offers superior performance. For example, you may configure your system such that the storage array handles the hardware level RAID-1 for mirroring, and the software LVM is used for striping. As storage array technology continues to improve reliability, performance, and functionality, applications can reap the benefits of hardware level performance and powerful RAID functionality.

---

3.   RAID-S products are available from the EMC Corporation (www.emc.com).

3.8   NEW STORAGE ARRAY TECHNOLOGIES

Disk array vendors are constantly making major advancements in storage array technology in the areas of performance, reliability, administration, capacity, and interoperability. Customer database sizes continue to grow at explosive rates, raising the need for large-capacity, high-performance, reliable I/O subsystems. Disk drive vendors are also developing faster drives as well as using higher throughput interfaces such as 2 Gbit Fiber channel and Ultra160 SCSI. Coupling the disk drive technology breakthroughs with the storage array progression enables customers to build large-scale databases using the new array technologies yielding impressive I/O rates.

Seagate offers the new high-performance Cheetah X15 drive with 15,000 rpm and 48 MB per second data access rates. Ultra160 SCSI represents a massive improvement over the previous SCSI rates of 3 MB per second, by providing SCSI bus data rates of 160 MB per second. The increased bandwidth translates into optimal server performance for random access environments requiring swift response times. The technology behind Ultra160 SCSI consists of three core main features: double-edge clocking, cyclical redundancy checking (CRC), and domain validation. The double-edge clocking feature provides rates of 160 MB per second by doubling the data transfer rate without the use of additional internal clocking. The CRC feature increases data reliability by ensuring the integrity of the transferred data via error checking and reporting. The domain validation feature uses an intelligent algorithm to negotiate the data transfer rate in order to ensure each SCSI channel device uses the highest rates possible during communication. The Cheetah X15 drive is available in the 18.4 GB capacity. The Cheetah X15 drive offers a 2 millisecond average latency, an average read seek time of 3.9 milliseconds, and supports up to 16 MB of cache. The new Cheetah X15 drive rotates at 15,000 rpm and is capable of data access rates of 48 MB per second. The programmable multisegmented cache employed by the Cheetah family of drives enables substantial I/O throughput in multitasking environments. The disk cache buffer can also be divided into numerous segments for independent read and write caching.

Sun has made major breakthroughs in storage array technology. The new storage arrays from Sun offer significant performance gains as well as improved administration and reliability. Sun offers the StorEdge 7000, A5200, and A3500 arrays. The new StorEdge A5200 Array is capable of handling over 12,000 I/Os per second (IOPS), thereby enabling high-performance transaction and transfer rates. The StorEdge A5000 Array is capable of over 10,000 IOPS and supports a 100 MB per second full duplex fiber interface. The StorEdge A3500 can be configured with up to 256 MB of mirrored cache, which considerably increases I/O performance. In addition, the StorEdge 3500 Array provides added reliability and performance by utilizing dual active redundant controllers. The StorEdge Arrays provide the Sun Enterprise Volume Manager, which allows you to manage and configure different levels of RAID such as RAID-1, RAID-0+1, and RAID-5. The StorEdge A3500 and A5X00 series arrays are designed for applications requiring superior performance and high availability. The A5X00 StorEdge arrays represent Sun's second-generation fiber channel disk array. The A5X00 arrays support hot-pluggable power supplies, fans, interface boards, and disk drives. The A5X00 arrays use a 100 MB per second fiber connection to the host and consists of dual fiber channel loops. The A5X00 StorEdge arrays increase the transfer rate performance of the fiber connection over the original Sun storage arrays. The A5X00 arrays also support fully redundant RAID configurations. The Sun Enterprise Volume Manager can also be used to configure and manage different RAID level configurations. The Dynamic Multipathing (DMP) feature of the A5X00 Array increases availability via the auto loop failover and load balancing. The new storage arrays from Sun significantly improve performance, reliability, administration, and connectivity.

3.9   ASYNCHRONOUS I/O

The asynchronous I/O model provides system calls [for example, `aioread()` and `aio-write()`] that perform nonblocking reads and writes. These system calls return immediately following the call itself. If a signal handler has been established, the calling process is later signaled[4] notifying the calling process of the completion of the asynchronous I/O request. Using asynchronous I/O can improve the I/O performance of the Oracle Server drastically. Another way to think of asynchronous I/O is as parallel reads and parallel writes. If enabled, asynchronous I/O allows multiple reads and writes to proceed in parallel, thereby reducing I/O wait time. Using asynchronous I/O in conjunction with the volume manager (striping) maximizes I/O throughput by parallelizing reads and writes and avoids disk I/O saturation through the proper data distribution via the volume manager.

3.9.1   ASYNCHRONOUS I/O IN SOLARIS

To enable asynchronous I/O in the Oracle7 Server on Solaris, set the `init.ora` parameters `async_write=true` and `async_read=true`. In Oracle8 and Oracle8*i*, set the `init.ora` parameter `disk_asynch_io=TRUE`. On Solaris, asynchronous I/O is supported on both file systems and raw devices. Asynchronous I/O on Solaris is handled by the asynchronous I/O library (`libaio.so`). To initiate asynchronous I/O calls on Solaris, you can call the `aioread()` and `aiowrite()` functions that are provided with the Solaris asynchronous I/O library (`libaio.so`). The Solaris asynchronous I/O library uses threads to issue nonblocking reads and writes. Solaris 2.6 and Solaris 7 made major improvements to the asynchronous I/O layer. Solaris 2.6 provides support for the POSIX asynchronous I/O calls `aio_read()` and `aio_write()`. Using the POSIX asynchronous I/O calls increases application portability. The POSIX `aio_read()` and `aio_write()` calls are provided by the `libposix4.so` shared library. On Solaris, the Oracle Server uses the Solaris asynchronous I/O calls.

As of Solaris 2.5.1, asynchronous I/O on files larger than 2 GB is supported on the Sun Ultra systems (sun4u). Solaris 2.6 provides the ability to create files larger than 2 GB

---

4. Depending on the specific platform, typically the SIGIO or SIGAIO signal is used to signal a process when an asynchronous I/O request is completed.

by providing large file support via 64-bit file offsets. The standard Solaris asynchronous I/O calls of `aioread()` and `aiowrite()` support asynchronous I/O on files no larger than 2 GB. This is due to the fact that the `libaio.so` shared library uses the `lseek()` system call to position the file offset. The `lseek()` call supports only 32-bit file offsets, meaning that a file cannot be larger than 2 GB. The `llseek()` system call extends the `lseek()` system call by allowing 64-bit file offsets. The `aioread64()` and `aiowrite64()` system calls support asynchronous I/O for large files based on 64-bit file offsets. This not only allows larger size data files in Oracle, it allows asynchronous I/O on files larger than 2 GB. Oracle8 and Oracle8*i* on Solaris support asynchronous I/O on large files.

There were several issues surrounding the use of asynchronous I/O in Solaris 2.6 with file systems. It is recommended that asynchronous I/O be disabled via the `init.ora` parameter if you are running Solaris 2.6 and the database is based on file systems. Solaris 7 resolved these issues with asynchronous I/O on file systems. In addition, it is important to note that asynchronous I/O on file systems does not typically result in much gain because Solaris acquires an exclusive write lock on the vnode (i.e., file) when concurrent I/Os are issued to the same file. To work around this issue, you can either ensure that you create a lot of smaller files rather than fewer larger files, or use the Veritas Quick I/O option. Quick I/O simulates raw device behavior for file system-based files.

3.9.2 ASYNCHRONOUS I/O IN HP-UX

To enable asynchronous I/O on HP, set the `init.ora` parameter `use_async_io=TRUE` in Oracle7 and `disk_asynch_io=TRUE` in Oracle8 and Oracle8*i*. On HP, you must configure the async disk driver in the Drivers Area using the SAM tool. Following this you must regenerate the kernel and reboot the system. Use the SAM tool to regenerate the kernel. The new kernel will be located in `/stand/build/vmunix_test`, and the location of the corresponding configuration file used to create the kernel is `/stand/build/SYSTEM.SAM`.

To enable the new kernel changes to take effect, move the `/stand/build/vmunix_test` to the `/stand` directory using the `mv` command, and move the configuration file `/stand/build/SYSTEM.SAM` to `/stand/system`. Remember to back up the old kernel and the old configuration file before you move the newly generated kernel into the `/stand` directory. Once you have moved the newly generated kernel and corresponding system configuration file into the `/stand` directory, reboot the system to force the asynchronous I/O changes to take effect. Asynchronous I/O on HP will be used only when accessing raw (character) devices. This means that if your database consists of file system–based files, asynchronous I/O will not be used. Also, if using asynchronous I/O with raw devices, ensure that the `/dev/async` device is owned by the Oracle software owner and belongs to the dba group. If the `/dev/async` device driver does not exist, create the device driver by using the following command.

```
myhost{root}-> /sbin/mknod /dev/async c 101 0x0
```

The permissions on the `/dev/async` device should be read and write by the Oracle software owner. For example,

```
myhost%> ls -al /dev/async

crw-rw——   oracle   dba   /dev/async
```

If the file permissions are different than those listed in the preceding example, use the following commands to set the proper permissions.

```
myhost{root}> chown oracle /dev/async

myhost{root}> chgrp dba /dev/async

myhost{root}> chmod 660 /dev/async
```

In addition to creating the /dev/async device driver, you should also set the kernel parameter max_async_ports which specifies the maximum number of processes that can simultaneously open the /dev/async device driver. A low setting for max_async_ports may cause Oracle processes to fail when trying to open the asynchronous I/O device driver.

3.9.3 ASYNCHRONOUS I/O ON SEQUENT

To enable asynchronous I/O on Sequent, set async_write=TRUE in Oracle7 and disk_asynch_io=TRUE in Oracle8 and Oracle8*i*. Asynchronous I/O is supported only on raw character devices on Sequent. Asynchronous I/O is handled by the /usr/lib/libseq.a library through the DIO interface layer, which provides several routines that can perform direct I/O and asynchronous I/O. The DIO_Read() and DIO_Write() system calls are used to perform asynchronous I/O on raw devices. Sequent also provides large file asynchronous I/O support via the DIO_Read64() and DIO_Write64() system calls. If you plan to use asynchronous I/O, you should also set some kernel parameters that pertain to asynchronous I/O. The MAXAIO and NABUF kernel parameters specify the maximum number of concurrent asynchronous I/O requests, and the number of asynchronous I/O buffers, respectively. Set MAXAIO to the maximum number of asynchronous I/O requests. For a heavy I/O system, set MAXAIO to 512, and NABUF to 1024. Remember that asynchronous I/O requests hold the data memory image for the asynchronous I/O request resident until the request is completed or canceled. Hence, memory can diminish rather quickly when a large number of asynchronous I/O requests are issued. Make sure you have enough free memory when setting high values for NABUF and MAXAIO.

3.9.4 ASYNCHRONOUS I/O IN ORACLE

The Oracle Server provides asynchronous I/O on most UNIX platforms. Asynchronous I/O increases DBMS performance by performing nonblocking I/O. It also yields a high throughput DBWR by avoiding the standard (synchronous) I/O calls that block DBWR until each I/O is completed. The concept of asynchronous I/O is quite simple. In synchronous I/O, each write or read call would block until the completion of the call itself. This means that each time LGWR and DBWR issue writes to log files and data files, each respective process must wait (block) until the completion of each write call. This can cause a bottleneck for LGWR and DBWR, and can also cause other Oracle user processes to wait on space in the SGA because LGWR and DBWR have not yet completed their *dirty* writes. If you configure your Oracle Server to use asynchronous I/O, set the Oracle7 `init.ora` parameter `db_writers=1`. In Oracle8 (8.0.4), set the `init.ora` parameter `db_writer _processes=1`. Since asynchronous I/O is enabled, DBWR and LGWR will not block on writes. Therefore, there is no need to have multiple DBWR processes, unless a single DBWR is not keeping up with the buffer cache workload. You can determine this by querying the `v$system_event` view, and checking to see if a large amount of time is being spent in the "`free buffer waits`" event. Using asynchronous I/O and setting `db_writers=1` (Oracle7) or `db_writer_processes=1` (Oracle8 and Oracle8*i*) reduces the overhead of having multiple Oracle background processes. It also eliminates the amount of interprocess communication between the master DBWR and its slaves since there only will be one DBWR process when `db_writers=1`.

3.10   I/O SLAVES IN ORACLE8

Oracle8 provides the ability to utilize I/O slaves for those platforms that do not support asynchronous I/O. I/O slaves can also be used with asynchronous I/O. Several new `init.ora` parameters have been added to control the behavior of I/O slaves. The `init.ora` parameters `arch_io_slaves`, `backup_disk_io_slaves`, `backup_ tape_io_slaves`, `dbwr_io_slaves`, and `lgwr_io_slaves` specify the number of I/O slave processes to be used for archives, disk backups, tape backups, database file writes (DBWR), and log file writes (LGWR), respectively. If you enable `dbwr_io_slaves`, only one DBWR process is used, regardless of the setting of `db_writer_processes`. I/O slaves can be used to increase database I/O throughput by parallelizing I/O requests. This helps improve archiving and log write throughput by allowing the slaves to parallelize I/O requests as opposed to Oracle7 which used only a single archiver process (`ARCH`) and a single log writer process (LGWR). I/O slaves can also improve backup and restore performance for those platforms that do not support asynchronous I/O to tape devices. I/O slaves are dynamically allocated on an as needed basis. This reduces the overhead of spawning processes that are never used. The format of the process name for an I/O slave is as follows: `ora_iNnn_<SID>`, where "i" identifies the process as an I/O slave, "N" is the I/O adapter number, "nn" is the I/O slave number, and "SID" refers to the `ORACLE_SID`.

In Oracle8*i*, the I/O slave parameters such as `lgwr_io_slaves`, `arch_io_slaves`, and `backup_disk_io_slaves` were made underscore parameters (`_lgwr_io_slaves`, `_arch_io_slaves`, and `_backup_disk_io_slaves`). In general, multiple database writers are more efficient than DBWR I/O slaves. LGWR I/O slaves should typically not be needed as a single LGWR can generally keep up with the redo rate.

In order to determine whether or not you should configure your system to use I/O slaves, monitor the file I/O, DBWR, and LGWR statistics to determine if DBWR or LGWR are falling behind. I/O slaves use shared memory for the I/O buffers. Therefore ensure that your system can afford the memory and processor overhead of the additional processes. To choose an optimal number of I/O slaves, monitor processor, memory, and disk I/O utilization in conjunction with the Oracle I/O statistics. Query the views `v$sesstat` and `v$sysstat` and examine the statistics `physical writes`, `physical reads`, `logical reads`, and `write requests` to determine the I/O rates. You should also correlate the I/O statistics from the `v$sesstat` and `v$sysstat` views with the statistics from the `v$sess_io` and `v$filestat` views. The performance of the I/O slaves is also highly dependent on the data distribution. In order to maximize the performance of the I/O slaves, ensure that your Oracle data files and log files are optimally distributed and sized.

3.11 DIRECT I/O (DIO)

Direct I/O, as the term suggests, bypasses the UNIX file system cache and copies the file system-based file data directly into user space. Direct I/O on file systems is similar to raw devices. However, direct I/O on file systems is synchronous. If asynchronous I/O is not used, Oracle uses the `read()` system call to read from file system-based files. To force Oracle to use direct I/O on your Sequent system, set the Oracle7 init.ora parameter `_direct_read=TRUE`. Direct I/O reduces the file system overhead by eliminating file buffering. If your Sequent database uses file system files, you can use Direct I/O to improve file system performance over the traditional `read()` call.

Solaris 2.6 provides the ability to perform direct I/O via the `directio()` system call. Using the `directio()` system call, an application can perform direct I/O on a file thereby bypassing the UNIX file system cache. The mount command also provides the options `noforcedirectio` and `forcedirectio` which control whether or not direct I/O to the file system is forced. Direct I/O can improve large sequential I/O performance. If you are using UNIX file systems for your database files, you can take advantage of the direct I/O feature by mounting the file systems containing the Oracle database files with the `forcedirectio` mount option.

3.11.1 DIRECT I/O IN ORACLE

Oracle uses direct I/O for such operations as backup, restore, and parallel query execution. During parallel query execution, Oracle can read the data blocks directly into the PGA as opposed to the SGA. Oracle can also write data blocks directly to disk when performing large joins or sorts. This is known as direct I/O since Oracle reads and writes directly from and to the disk into the user buffers. The Oracle8 init.ora parameter `db_file_direct_io_count` specifies the number of blocks to be used for direct I/O operations. The size of the direct I/O buffer is a product of `db_file_direct_io_count` and `db_block_size`. The direct I/O buffer cannot exceed the maximum I/O size for your platform. You should set such `db_file_direct_io_count` to a multiple of the data file stripe size so as to maximize I/O throughput. For maximum performance, set `db_file_direct_io_count` such that the direct I/O buffer is equal to the maximum I/O size for your platform. This reduces the amount of I/Os needed since more data can be stored in the direct I/O buffer. This also reduces the number of system calls and reduces context switch overhead.

3.12 KERNELIZED ASYNCHRONOUS I/O (KAIO)

Solaris provides a further enhancement to asynchronous I/O (AIO), known as KAIO (Kernelized AIO). KAIO reduces the context switch overhead between kernel and user space by maintaining the AIO layer in the kernel itself. Traditional AIO is performed through a shared library API in which user calls (from Oracle) are made to the AIO API. These calls must then switch from user space to kernel space in order to perform kernel I/O services. KAIO eliminates this need by incorporating the AIO API services into the kernel itself. During AIO calls, the kernel can lock memory for AIO, thereby making the locked database buffers unswappable. Hence, be sure your system has sufficient free memory to hold the entire SGA and to service AIO requests. KAIO is enabled in Solaris by default. Solaris 2.6 and Solaris 7 improved the performance of KAIO, reducing kernel overhead and improving the speed of the KAIO services.

Solaris 2.6 dramatically improved the performance of raw device I/O by optimizing the low level I/O routines and rewriting the storage array device driver. KAIO is supported on raw devices only. The Quick I/O option of Veritas allows KAIO to be used on file system-based files. In benchmarks, KAIO has increased performance 30 percent over the standard asynchronous I/O. It also allows asynchronous I/O to tape drive devices. KAIO allocates internal buffers to service asynchronous I/O requests. Hence, make sure your system is not short of memory, otherwise KAIO requests may fail.

You can determine if KAIO is being used by trussing the database writer process. For example,

```
myhost> truss -aefp 9155    *** 9155 = pid of database writer

9155: kaio(AIOWRITE, 408, 0x9159E000, 8192, 16384, 0x019F9A0C) Err#48 ENOTSUP
9155: lwp_cond_signal(0xEEF45FA0)                               = 0
9155: lwp_cond_wait(0xEEF45FA0, 0xEEF45FB0, 0x00000000) = 0
9155: kaio(AIOWRITE, 406, 0x9029C000, 8192, 0x05364000, 0x019F78C4) Err#48 ENOTSUP
9155: lwp_cond_signal(0xEEF33FA0)                               = 0
9155: lwp_cond_wait(0xEEF33FA0, 0xEEF33FB0, 0x00000000) = 0
9155: kaio(AIOWRITE, 391, 0x90068000, 8192, 3555328, 0x019F577C) Err#48 ENOTSUP
9155: pwrite64(408, "0E02\0\0\0 @\00284AAFDF6".., 8192, 16384) = 8192
9155: lwp_cond_signal(0xEEF21FA0)                               = 0
9155: pwrite64(406, "0202\0\0\0C0 )B284AAFE U".., 8192, 0x05364000) = 8192
9155: lwp_cond_wait(0xEEF21FA0, 0xEEF21FB0, 0x00000000) = 0
9155: kaio(AIOWRITE, 386, 0x9362A000, 8192, 0x1754A000, 0x019F14EC) Err#48 ENOTSUP
9155: pwrite64(391, "0602\0\0048001B284AAFE ]".., 8192, 3555328) = 8192
9155: lwp_cond_signal(0xEEF0FFA0)                               = 0
9155: lwp_cond_wait(0xEEF0FFA0, 0xEEF0FFB0, 0x00000000) = 0
```

In the above `truss` output, the KAIO calls are failing and the operation-not-supported error is being raised (`Err# 48`). Upon further investigation, it was discovered that some of the files were based on file systems, and some of the database files were based on raw devices. The I/Os which failed above were I/Os to the file system-based files. If a KAIO request fails, Solaris spawns threads to perform the I/O if asynchronous I/O is being used. In this case, the KAIO write failed, hence Solaris spawned threads to perform the actual writes using the `pwrite64()` call. The following is a sample `truss` output which illustrates that KAIO is being used.

```
myhost> truss -aefp 5364

5364:    kaio(AIOWRITE, 408, 0x01917B40, 8192, 32768, 0x0191D1B4) = 0
5364:    kaio(AIOWRITE, 407, 0x01917B40, 8192, 32768, 0x0191CED4) = 0
5364:    kaio(AIOWAIT, 0xEFFFE330)                          = 26333620
5364:    kaio(AIOWAIT, 0xEFFFE330)                          = 26332884
```

In the above `truss` output, the KAIO write calls have succeeded because the return code is 0. The KAIO `wait` calls have also successfully completed, and the return values refer to a pointer to the result structure. You can use the `truss` utility to determine if asynchronous I/O or KAIO is being used.

3.13 LIST I/O (LIO)

List I/O (LIO), as the term suggests, builds a list of I/O requests and submits the list, asynchronously, to the kernel for processing. In the traditional asynchronous I/O model, a separate I/O call had to be made for each I/O request. For a heavy I/O database server, the traditional method generates significant process, system call, and context switch overhead. List I/O can alleviate this overhead by building a list of I/O requests and submitting the list to the kernel.

On HP-UX, LIO is supported only for database files created on raw devices. LIO is usually performed through a shared library in which user processes call the system call `lio_listio()`. Solaris 2.6, HP-UX, IBM AIX, UnixWare, and SGI all provide list I/O. Refer to the installation and configuration guide of your specific platform to enable LIO.

Oracle8*i* provides support for LIO on platforms which support list I/O, such as Sun Solaris 2.6 and above. List I/O is not enabled by default, and you need to explicitly enable LIO via the `init.ora` parameter `_enable_list_io`. If `_enable_list_io=TRUE`, then LIO is used for processes such as the database writer. If you are running Solaris 2.6 with Oracle8*i*, it is recommended that LIO be disabled (default) because of the performance implications. In Solaris 2.6 and Solaris 7, the use of list I/O results in an additional `fstat()` call per file descriptor for each submitted I/O. This extra `fstat()` call per member resulted in the performance of list I/O being worse than that of regular asynchronous I/O. In Solaris 8, the extra `fstat()` call has been eliminated, and the performance of LIO is faster than without LIO.

3.14 `readv()`

The `readv()` system call performs the same action as read but places the input data into the user buffers that are specified in the call to `readv`. Using `readv` (meaning vector read) reduces the CPU overhead of copying buffers from kernel space (UNIX file system cache) to user space (Oracle buffers). Although `readv()` reduces CPU overhead, the I/O workload is increased by the degree of the buffering (vector). For sequential access of UNIX file system-based files, `readv()` can increase I/O performance. On raw devices, `readv()` has shown a performance degradation on Solaris. Therefore, use caution when enabling `readv()` in the Oracle7 Server. The default value of `use_readv` is disabled. To enable `readv()`, set the Oracle7 `init.ora` parameter `use_readv=TRUE`. If your Oracle7 database uses raw devices, and asynchronous I/O is enabled, set `use_readv=FALSE`.

In Oracle8, the I/O subsystem in the database kernel was largely rewritten in order to improve the performance and provide the ability to dynamically choose the most appropriate form of I/O for a particular request. The I/O subsystem decides whether to use asynchronous I/O, synchronous I/O, or vectored I/O based on the type of request. For example, it does not make sense to use asynchronous I/O for a request which will read only one block due to the overhead of submitting the asynchronous I/O request and polling on the I/O request in order to verify the successful completion of the I/O.

3.15 ORACLE MULTIBLOCK READS

Oracle provides the ability to read multiple blocks in a single I/O for operations such as full-table scans. The `init.ora` parameter `db_file_multiblock_read_count` controls the number of Oracle data blocks read at each I/O read during a sequential (i.e., full-table) scan. For example, setting this parameter to 8 would cause Oracle to read eight blocks at each read request during the sequential scan. Therefore, this parameter can control the performance of sequential scans. A larger value of `db_file_multiblock_read_count` reduces the number of I/O calls needed to scan the object. For example, if set to 32, and the Oracle block size = 8 KB, then a sequential scan of a table of size 256 KB can be read in one pass. If you are using a volume manager, this parameter should be set so that `<db_block_size>` × `<db_file_multiblock_read_count>` is a multiple of the stripe size. For example, if your stripe width is 32 KB, and your block size is 8 KB, setting `db_file_multiblock_read_count=32` results in multiple spindles being accessed in parallel to satisfy the I/O read request.

The values for `db_file_multiblock_read_count` are operating system specific and cannot be larger than (`db_block_buffers`/4). The default value for `db_file_multiblock_read_count` is also operating system dependent. Typically on UNIX platforms, `db_file_multiblock_read_count` defaults to (`max_IO_size`/ `db_block_size`). The `max_IO_size` is the maximum size of a single I/O request. The max_IO_size is also operating system dependent. Oracle 7.3 enforces several constraints when setting db_file_multiblock_read_count. If the user-specified value exceeds the values of the internal constraint checks, db_file_multiblock_read_count defaults to (max_IO_size/db_block_size). Therefore, when upgrading to Oracle 7.3, you may notice that user-specified values for db_file_multiblock_read_count are being over-ridden. This is due to the enforcement of the constraint checks. For example, if max_IO_size is set to 128 KB and db_block_size=8192 (8 KB), then db_file_multiblock_read_count cannot exceed 16. A patch that increases max_IO_size to 1 MB is available for Oracle 7.3 on Sun Solaris. To obtain the patch, contact Oracle Customer Support, and refer to bug 433762. This patch allows a maximum setting for db_file_multiblock_read_count=128 when db_block_size=8K. However, even though the patch increases max_IO_size to 1 MB, db_file_multiblock _read_count is still restricted by (db_block_buffers/4). The patch can help increase the performance of large full table scans and parallel queries. In Oracle8 and Oracle8*i*, the maximum I/O size for an Oracle I/O on Solaris is 1 MB.

3.16 FILE SYSTEMS VERSUS RAW DEVICES

The debate over using raw devices instead of file systems is a popular one. The overall consensus seems to be performance versus ease of administration. Although file system technology constantly improves through vendor innovations, raw devices remain the leader in terms of performance and scalability. Figure 3.11 outlines the I/O cycle of raw devices and file systems.

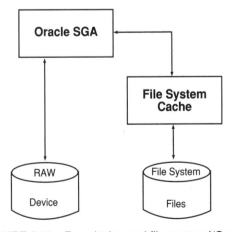

FIGURE 3.11   Raw device and file system I/O cycle.

3.16.1   UNIX FILE SYSTEMS

In Figure 3.11, any reads issued to a UNIX file system-based file cause the file metadata to be brought into the UNIX buffer cache, and the file data to be brought into virtual memory. The file data is then copied into the user space (in this case, the Oracle buffers). Therefore, each read translates into a read followed by a copy from kernel space to user space. Also, the UNIX kernel allocates file system buffers for data from the virtual memory pages. The UNIX buffer cache holds information such as inodes, indirect blocks, super-blocks, and cylinder group data. File data pages and directory block data are part of the virtual memory pages, not the buffer cache. Hence, a file system-based database server with a tremendous amount of I/O may experience a high amount of paging. The UNIX file system cache employs a least recently used algorithm to maintain the contents of the cache.

File systems have several advantages over raw devices, including sequential read performance, buffering, and ease of administration. The UNIX file system provides look-ahead read for sequential scans. This can help a DSS database when most queries result in full-table scans. Also, the data from the sequential scan, depending on the access frequency, may remain in the cache, and subsequent queries on the data will observe quicker execution times. File system-based files are also much easier to administer in terms of sizing, growth, and backups and restores. There are many backup and restore tools that do not yet support raw devices and that offer effortless automated backups and restores of file systems. The block size of the file system can be made to match that of the Oracle block size to minimize I/O during reads and writes. The `readv()` feature can also be enabled to take advantage of file system sequential reads.

Solaris and HP-UX support the Veritas file system (`vxfs`).[5] The Veritas file system (`vxfs`) provides additional features over the standard UNIX file system (`ufs`). The `vxfs` file system uses extent-level allocation rather than block-level allocation by grouping multiple blocks into a single extent. It also provides faster recovery following a system crash by providing journaling. The journaling feature avoids having to `fsck` the entire file system by applying the changes from the journals. On a large file system, this provides tremendous time savings following a system crash. It also provides a higher level of availability because the chance of losing the entire file system is minimal. If you are using file systems, it is recommended that you set the file system block size to the Oracle block size, but not smaller than 4 KB. The 4 KB lower limit is due to the fact that the virtual memory page size is 4 KB. A block size smaller than the page size forces a memory page to be broken down into the size of the file system block size during a write-out. For example, having a 2 KB Veritas block size would force a 4 KB memory page to be broken into two writes of 2 KB each. This would decrease I/O performance.

If you choose to use file systems on a large database, I recommend that you either create a Veritas-based file system, or use the equivalent file system journal feature provided in Sun's SDS 4.X product. This eliminates the need to perform an `fsck` on your file system since the journals only need to be applied to restore the consistency state of the file system.

---

5.   Using the Veritas Volume Manager, you can create a Veritas file system (`vxfs`).

Using the journal feature of Veritas or SDS can considerably reduce the time required to make a file system consistent. It also increases reliability because `fsck` may truncate files, thereby losing data.

3.16.1.1 Tuning the `fsflush` System Daemon

In Solaris, two kernel parameters control the rate of the `fsflush` system daemon: `autoup` and `tune_t_fsflushr`. Recall that the `fsflush` system daemon is responsible for flushing dirty file system pages to disk. If your database uses file systems, `fsflush` can use a considerable amount of CPU time. You can check the amount of CPU time being used by the `fsflush` daemon by using the `ps` command. For example,

```
myhost> /bin/ps -p 3    * fsflush always has PID=3


PID TTY       TIME   COMMAND
  3  ?       62:02   fsflush


myhost> uptime

        2:55pm  up 5 day(s), 21:17 users,
        load average: 0.01, 0.02, 0.02
```

In this example, `fsflush` has used over an hour of CPU time since the system was last rebooted. According to the `uptime` output, the system has been up for 508,620 seconds. Therefore, `fsflush` used 3,722 seconds of CPU time over a total elapsed system uptime of 508,620 seconds. This represents less than 1 percent of overall CPU utilization by the `fsflush` system daemon. If your system experiences high CPU usage times for the `fsflush` daemon, you may want to decrease the rate at which the daemon wakes up. The `autoup` kernel parameter controls the maximum age of any dirty memory resident file system page. The default for `autoup` is 30 seconds. You should set `autoup` to a larger value, such as five minutes (300 seconds). This reduces the `fsflush` workload and also increases the cache hit rate since dirty file system pages are more likely to remain in memory longer. The `tune_t_fsflushr` kernel parameter specifies how often the `fsflush` daemon wakes up. The default for `tune_t_fsflushr` is 5 seconds. Set `tune_t_fsflushr` to a higher value such as 60 seconds to reduce the overhead of `fsflush`. If your database server uses all raw devices, and file system activity is extremely minimal, increase `autoup` and `tune_t_fsflushr` to high values since file system activity is minimal. You can also disable page flushing by setting the kernel parameter `dopageflush` to zero.

3.16.1.2 Tuning the UNIX Buffer Cache

The UNIX buffer cache is used to cache the file metadata such as file headers, inodes, and indirect block addresses. The cache can significantly increase the performance of reads and writes as data may be held in virtual memory, thus avoiding physical disk I/O. Access time to the cache is in the order of nanoseconds (typical memory speeds) while physical disk I/O access time is in the order of milliseconds. If you are using file system-based files for your database, you need to tune the UNIX buffer cache to achieve a high read and write hit ratio. You can use `sar -b` to monitor the hit ratio of the buffer cache. Examine the `%rcache` and `%wcache` columns from the `sar -b` output to determine the cache hit ratios. If the percentages are low, you need to tune the buffer cache parameters if you are using file systems. Determine the hit ratio before modifying the size of the file system buffer cache. If `sar -b` reports poor hit ratios, increase the size of the file system buffer cache nominally until a hit ratio of 90 percent or higher is achieved. The kernel parameters that can be tuned to achieve a high-performance buffer cache are NBUF, NHBUF, NPBUF, and `bufhwm`. The two main parameters that affect the buffer cache are NBUF and `bufhwm`. The NBUF parameter controls the amount of block I/O buffers that are allocated dynamically at each interval when buffer headers are needed. NHBUF is the size of the hash table used to locate a buffer. NPBUF is the number of physical I/O buffers allocated. One I/O buffer is needed for each physical read or write. Increasing this parameter for a system with heavy reads and writes may yield tremendous improvements. bufhwm is the buffer cache high-water mark that specifies the maximum amount of memory that can be used for block I/O buffers. If you use raw devices for your database files, decrease the size of the buffer cache in order to make more memory available for Oracle and user processes.

In Solaris, `bufhwm` controls the high-water mark for the size of the buffer cache, expressed in kilobytes. The default for `bufhwm` on Solaris is 2 percent of physical memory. You can set the `bufhwm` parameter by placing a line the `/etc/system` file as follows.

```
set bufhwm=4096
```

This example sets the buffer cache high-water mark to 4 MB. If you are using raw devices and your system has a lot of memory, the 2 percent default can translate into a tangible amount. Therefore, if you use raw devices, reduce the size of `bufhwm` to 1 MB or less. The buffer cache grows dynamically up to the high-water mark. You can also set nbuf and p_nbuf in the `/etc/system` file. The p_nbpuf parameter specifies the amount of nbuf buffers to allocate in a single allocation.

On Sequent, the BUFPCT kernel parameter specifies the percentage of free memory that is available for the buffer cache. Again, if you use file systems, monitor the cache hit ratio through `sar -b`. If the hit ratios are low, increase BUFPCT at a nominal rate.

If you use file systems, tuning the buffer cache can increase performance. However, it is important that you balance the buffer cache with the Oracle SGA and user processes. If you increase the buffer cache, there will be less memory available for the SGA and user processes. It is key that you maintain a balance. When tuning the buffer cache, you should monitor paging and swapping in conjunction with monitoring the buffer cache (`sar -b`). Increasing the buffer cache too much may reduce performance due to increased levels of paging. Review the material that pertains to buffer cache kernel parameters of your respective platform in detail before you alter the buffer cache-related kernel parameters. Parameters and defaults often change with new releases.

3.16.1.3   Tuning the Inode Cache

The `ufs` file system uses inodes to manage files. The inodes reside on physical disk. When an operation is performed on a ufs-based file, the inode for the file is read into the inode memory cache. The idea is that if the inode is needed again, it will be found in the cache versus the inode having to be read from physical disk. You can increase your system's performance by tuning the inode cache. Use `sar -a` to monitor the inode cache. If `iget/s`, which is the number of inodes read per second, is high, it is an indication that the inode cache is too small. On Solaris, you can increase the size of the inode cache by setting the kernel parameter `ufs_ninode` in the `/etc/system` file. If the statistics from `sar -a` show a poor inode cache hit ratio, increase the value of `ufs_ninode`. On Sequent, the parameter `NINODE` sets the maximum number of inodes in the file system.

3.16.1.4   Tuning the Directory Name Lookup Cache

Each time a file is opened, the Directory Name Lookup Cache (DNLC) is scanned to determine if the file is in the DNLC cache. The DNLC associates a vnode with the name of a file. Typically, short file names are cached and file names that are too long to be cached are looked up by reading the directory. In Solaris 2, file names longer than 30 characters are not cached.

A cache miss translates into more CPU cycles, and possibly more physical I/O, in order to read the directory. In Solaris, you can set `ncsize` in the `/etc/system` file to set the size of the directory name lookup cache. Use the `sar -a` command to monitor the DNLC. The column `namei/s` reports the number of name lookups per second, and the `dirbk/s` reports the number of directory blocks read per second. To make use of the DNLC cache, you should try to minimize the length of file names to less than 30 characters. On HP and Sequent, use the SAM tool or MENU tool to set the `NCSIZE` kernel parameter.

3.16.1.5   Optimizing File Metadata Maintenance

Each time a `ufs`-based file is accessed, the file header is updated to reflect the timestamp of the last access. For frequently accessed files, the overhead of updating the last access time can be significant. Solaris 8 provides the ability to defer the update of the last access time attribute. The `ufs` file system mount options `dfratime` and `nodfratim` can be used to enable or disable the deferment of access time updates. Deferring the last access time update is useful for Web servers or NFS servers whereby the majority of the requests are read-only.

3.16.2   RAW DEVICES

Raw devices bypass the UNIX file system cache, thus eliminating the overhead of copying the data from kernel file system I/O buffers to user buffers. Using raw devices also reduces the workload of the `fsflush` daemon which flushes out file system dirty pages to disk. By using raw devices, less memory is used for the file system cache and file I/O buffers. This reduces system paging, and also makes more memory available for user and Oracle processes, thereby reducing the chances of swapping. Raw devices provide the advantage of utilizing AIO and KAIO.[6] Currently, AIO and KAIO are not supported against file systems.[7] By using asynchronous I/O and KAIO, raw devices can provide a significant performance increase. For an OLTP system where transactions usually result in random I/O, raw devices further increases performance.

There are a number of backup and restore tools that provide full support for raw devices. Consult with your OS vendor to obtain a list of backup and restore tool vendors. If you are not able to obtain a backup and restore tool, you can utilize the dd utility to backup raw devices. In nonarchive mode, shut down the database, and issue the following command.

```
myhost%> dd if=<raw device db file name> \
             of=<backup device name> bs=32k
```

I recommend that you use raw devices for your database in order to maximize performance. You should also use a volume manager to configure and to size your raw partitions appropriately. Make sure that you do not waste space when you create raw device partitions. Refer to the *Oracle8i Administrator's Guide* for exact sizing of database objects. If you are switching from file system files to raw devices, you may use the dd utility to do so—assuming you have enough space for the file system data and raw device data.

```
myhost%> dd if=/my_old_FS_file \
             of=/dev/rdsk/my_new_RAW_device bs=32k
```

Before you issue this command, be sure that the raw device is at least the same size as the UNIX file system file. The database must also be shut down. The permissions on the raw device file must be owned by the Oracle software owner, with read and write permissions granted to the owner. It is also recommended that you use symbolic links to reference the actual raw device names. This allows the symbolic links to be easily manipulated if the raw device names change during a reconfiguration, and/or OS upgrade. Please refer to the *Oracle Installation and Configuration Guide (ICG)* for your specific platform for more information on the operational issues involved in using raw devices.

3.16.2.1 Maximum Physical I/O Size

The maximum physical I/O size limits the size of a single I/O that can be issued to a device driver. The maximum physical I/O size is platform and driver dependent. For a DSS system in which large size I/Os are being issued, it is important that you set the OS kernel parameter accordingly. Generally, I/Os larger than the size of the maximum physical I/O size are broken down into several segments of the maximum physical I/O size. In Solaris, you can set the maxphys kernel parameter in the /etc/system OS kernel configuration

---

6. Kernelized Asynchronous I/O (KAIO) is available on Solaris 2.4 or higher.
7. Sun provides asynchronous I/O on both file systems and raw devices. Sequent and HP provide asynchronous I/O on only raw devices.

file. For example, you can set `maxphys` to 1 MB to ensure that Oracle multiblock I/Os to raw devices are not broken down into several I/Os. This helps increase I/O throughput and overall performance.

```
set maxphys=1048576       *** ( 1M raw I/O)
```

The Veritas Volume Management software also allows you to specify the maximum I/O size. For Veritas logical devices, the equivalent to `maxphys` is the `vol_maxio` parameter. The `vol_maxio` parameter is specified in units of 512-byte sectors. For example, to set `vol_maxio` to 1 MB, place the following entry in your `/etc/system` configuration file.

```
set vxio:vol_maxio=2048   *** (Veritas 1 MB I/O)
```

3.17   SEPARATE SEQUENTIAL AND RANDOM I/O

In order to achieve the best disk I/O performance, consider the following when laying out the data files and redo log files: redo log file access is completely sequential. Redo log files should be separated from the other database files. If possible, it is a good idea to dedicate a few disks to redo log files. If the same disks are used for both database and redo log files, the disk read and write heads may be constantly moving around the disk to satisfy random I/O requests. If you dedicate a few disks to the redo log files, the reads and writes can continue sequentially since redo log file access is purely sequential. This increases the performance of log writes by reducing the I/O service time.

The redo log files should also be mirrored to avoid loss of the database if a redo log file becomes unavailable due to a hardware failure. Preferably, the mirroring of the redo log file should be at either the hardware or OS level through the volume manager. Mirroring the redo files through multiple Oracle redo log members will cause Oracle extra overhead by issuing I/O to all members within the group. Mirroring at the hardware and/or OS level eliminates the Oracle mirroring overhead by handling the mirroring at the kernel or hardware level. However, keep in mind that with hardware or OS mirroring, any corruption to the Oracle log files will be propagated to the mirror. Therefore, it is a good idea to have at least one Oracle redo log member mirror per redo log group to help guard against redo log file corruption.

Access to data files is often random, and therefore the data files should be spread among the controllers and disk drives as best as possible. Refer to section 3.2.1 in this guide for helpful hints on striping. Proper data distribution and efficient use of the volume manager can ensure high I/O throughput. Avoid overloading any single disk drive with random I/Os. For a 4 GB or 9 GB disk drive, random I/Os should not exceed 60–70 I/Os per second. For a 18 GB or 36 GB disk drive, random I/Os should not exceed 90–100 I/Os per second. Disk drive manufacturers continue to enhance disk drive technology by improving disk drive spindle speeds, and I/O transfer rates as well as increasing the size of the disk drive cache.

3.18 TABLESPACE OPTIMIZATION

There are various items that need to be considered when optimizing the performance of a tablespace, such as the size of the extents, life expectancy of the extents, size of I/O requests, read and write rates, media recovery time requirements, level of concurrency, Oracle Parallel Server (OPS) traffic, I/O workload, and size of the tablespace. Segments that have different size extents should be placed in different tablespaces in order to improve space management and administration. Segments that are periodically dropped and recreated should be separated from other tablespaces so as to minimize tablespace fragmentation. This is the main reason for separating index and data segments since indexes are frequently rebuilt.

Tablespace performance can also be optimized by separating segments that experience different size I/O requests and setting the stripe interleave based on the size of the I/O request and level of concurrency. Read-only segments should be placed in read-only tablespaces. Also, read-only tablespaces can be placed on less expensive media devices such as CD-ROM or RAID-5. In order to improve free list management, place tables that experience a high degree of inserts in different tablespaces than tables that are update and delete intensive.

The level of concurrency should also be considered when designing and configuring tablespaces. For example, in Oracle7, the redo log files have a low level of write concurrency since only LGWR handles redo log file writes. Hence, a more granular level of striping can be used with redo log files. In Oracle8, LGWR I/O slaves can be configured which may require you to stripe your redo log files differently than in Oracle7 since multiple I/O slaves can be issuing concurrent log writes. In addition, LGWR often performs group commits which groups many redo writes together into a single-batch write. Therefore, you may want to set the stripe width for the redo log files according to the average redo write size which is based on your workload. You can calculate the average redo write size by looking at the ratio of `redo size`/`redo writes` from the `v$sysstat` view. Tablespaces experiencing a high degree of concurrency should be distributed across multiple disks and multiple controllers so as to minimize hot areas. In an OPS environment, it is important that tablespaces and segments be configured such that contention for the same data blocks is minimized. It is also key that you maintain reasonably sized tablespaces in conjunction with the recovery time requirements. Very large tablespaces may preclude you from being able to restore the entire tablespace in a reasonable time window.

3.18.1 LOCALLY MANAGED TABLESPACES

The default mechanism for tablespace management involves the use of the data dictionary, such as the dictionary tables `uet$` (used extents) and `fet$` (free extents). There is a single enqueue, the ST enqueue, which is used to coordinate space management operations. As extents are freed and allocated, the dictionary tables are updated accordingly using the ST enqueue. For operations such as parallel DML or parallel index create, contention for the ST enqueue can occur as multiple concurrent processes are attempting to update the space-management-related dictionary tables. In addition, applications which frequently create and drop objects may fragment the data dictionary, which will reduce the overall performance of the system. Oracle8i provides a new type of tablespace management known as locally managed, or bitmapped. The Oracle8i locally managed tablespace maintains a bitmap in each datafile of the tablespace, which is used to track the status of the free and used blocks in the datafile. The bits of the bitmap correlate to the block or group of blocks in the datafile. The bitmap is updated when extents are freed or allocated. Locally managed tablespaces do not use the data dictionary to manage space; hence contention for the ST enqueue is eliminated. In addition, the performance of space management operations improves since space management no longer requires recursive dictionary SQL; rather, the bitmap of the corresponding datafile is updated. Since recursive dictionary SQL is not needed for space operations on locally managed tablespaces, rollback data is not generated. The tablespace quota information, however, is still maintained via the data dictionary. Locally managed tablespaces automatically track adjacent free space. This avoids having to manually coalesce the tablespace free extents.

Locally managed tablespaces provide two types of extent management: uniform and system-managed. The uniform extent model uses the same size extent for all extent allocations. You can specify the extent size or use the default extent size of 1 MB. The uniform extent model is useful for tablespaces which require similar or exact storage properties such as temporary extents (temporary tablespaces). The uniform extent model also helps eliminate tablespace fragmentation since the extents will consist of the same size. The system managed extent model allows you to specify the initial extent size, and Oracle automatically determines the optimal size of the additional extents. The minimum extent size is 64 KB. The following example creates a locally managed tablespace using the uniform extent allocation model.

```
SQL> create tablespace TEST_LOCAL_UNIFORM
     datafile '/d1/dbs/sdprod/dbf/testuni_local1.dbf' size 200M
     extent management local uniform size 100K;
```

The following example creates a locally managed tablespace using the system-managed allocation model (i.e., autoallocate).

```
SQL> create tablespace TEST_LOCAL_AUTO
     datafile '/d4/dbs/sdprod/dbf/testauto_local1.dbf' size 500M
     extent management local autoallocate;
```

In general, locally managed tablespaces should be used in place of dictionary-managed tablespaces. Oracle is planning to migrate the system tablespace to locally managed in a future release. Locally managed tablespaces eliminate contention for the ST enqueue as well as eliminate tablespace fragmentation when using locally managed tablespaces with the uniform extent model. In addition, locally managed tablespaces improve the performance of space management operations and significantly reduce data dictionary modification.

3.18.1.1   Converting from Dictionary-Managed to Locally Managed

You can convert your existing tablespaces from dictionary-managed to locally managed using the Oracle8*i* space management API DBMS_SPACE_ADMIN. The DBMS_SPACE_ADMIN package provides the procedure TABLESPACE_MIGRATE_TO_LOCAL which can be used to convert dictionary managed tablespaces to locally managed tablespaces. The following example illustrates the use of the dbms_space_admin package to convert a dictionary managed tablespace to locally managed:

```
SQL> execute dbms_space_admin.tablespace_migrate_to_local ('TS_ORD_DATA');
```

The conversion largely involves the deletion of the entries from the uet$ and fet$ dictionary tables, and the creation of the bitmaps for each datafile in the tablespace. The execution time of the conversion largely depends on the number of segments and the number of extents present in the tablespace at the time of the conversion. For example, for a tablespace with 11,000 segments and 209,000 extents, it took approximately two hours to convert. In Oracle8*i* release 8.1.7, the performance of the conversion has been improved significantly, which will reduce the conversion time from two hours to 10 minutes for such a tablespace.

3.18.2   TEMPORARY TABLESPACES

Oracle uses temporary tablespaces for operations such as hash joins and sorts. In a data warehousing environment in which queries result in large table joins or large sorts, temporary tablespace extents may be needed if the operation cannot be completed entirely in memory. For systems which extensively use the temporary tablespace, such as in a data warehousing environment, it is important that you optimize the configuration of the temporary tablespace. It is also important that you ensure that the underlying data files making up the temporary tablespace have been optimally configured in terms of disk subsystem placement.

Oracle 7.3 allows you to create temporary tablespaces in addition to the permanent tablespaces. Temporary tablespaces reduce the storage management overhead since once extents are allocated, they are reused when other processes need temporary extents. This can help DSS workloads by reducing the amount of storage management performed in order to allocate and free temporary tablespace extents for sorting. To make use of this feature, use the alter tablespace command to mark your tablespaces as temporary. For example,

```
SQL> alter tablespace ts_temp temporary;
```

You can also mark a tablespace as temporary in the create tablespace command. To determine if a tablespace is permanent or temporary, query the dba_tablespaces view. For example,

```
SQL> select tablespace_name,
            contents,
            status
     from dba_tablespaces
     order by tablespace_name;
```

TABLESPACE_NAME	CONTENTS	STATUS
RBS	PERMANENT	ONLINE
SYSTEM	PERMANENT	ONLINE
TEMP	PERMANENT	ONLINE
TOOLS	PERMANENT	ONLINE
TS_TEMP	TEMPORARY	ONLINE
USERS	PERMANENT	ONLINE

You can also query the v$sort_segment view to obtain sort segment information for sorts to temporary tablespaces. The v$sort_segment view provides statistics such as the number of current users and total number of extents for a given sort segment as well as the number of extents allocated to sorts.

3.18.2.1 Temporary Files

Oracle8*i* provides a new feature, known as temporary data files, which can be used to further improve the utilization of temporary tablespaces. Temporary files are useful for temporary tablespaces because temporary files use the NOLOGGING mode, and they do not participate in media recovery. Adding a temporary file to an existing temporary tablespace is extremely fast and does not incur the same cost of data file initialization as does adding a regular data file. The following example illustrates the use of temporary files in conjunction with the temporary tablespace.

```
create TEMPORARY tablespace TS_P_TEMP
tempfile 'ts_p_temp1.dbf' size 500M
EXTENT MANAGEMENT LOCAL
UNIFORM SIZE 1M;
```

In the above example, a temporary file is created as part of the temporary tablespace TS_P_TEMP. The specified size of the temporary file is 500 MB. The elapsed time to create the temporary tablespace with the 500 MB temporary file is 0.08 seconds. This is significantly less time than the time it would take to create a regular 500 MB data file. The dictionary views DBA_TEMP_FILES or V$TEMPFILE can be used to report temporary file information. In general, you should use temporary files for all the files making up the temporary tablespace. Temporary files are faster in general, and they significantly reduce the time needed to recreate the tablespace should the need arise.

3.19 SETTING THE DATABASE BLOCK SIZE

The Oracle database block size can be optimally configured to achieve high I/O throughput. In UNIX, the logical block size of the file system depends on the file system type and the method of access. File system block sizes can be 1 KB, 2 KB, 4 KB, or 8 KB. If you use file systems, your database block size should be a multiple of the file system block size. Currently, the Oracle Server for UNIX-based platforms allows db_block_size to be set to either 2 KB, 4 KB, 8 KB, or 16 KB (maximum in Oracle8*i*). There are some platforms that allow 32 KB block sizes. If you are using raw devices, set db_block_size to a multiple of the OS physical block size (512 bytes). For an OLTP system, set db_block_size to either 2 KB or 4 KB. In an OLTP environment, the idea is to minimize block contention and free buffer waits. Therefore, a smaller block size such as 2 KB or 4 KB results in having more blocks in the buffer cache which helps reduce block-level contention. For a DSS workload, set db_block_size to 16 KB. In a DSS environment, typically large size reads and writes are occurring through complex queries, batch updates, or bulk data loads. Therefore, more rows (data) per block reduces the amount of I/O required because more data is read or written per block. For a mixed workload, set db_block_size to either 4 KB or 8 KB.

3.20 MONITORING I/O ACTIVITY

You should regularly monitor disk I/O statistics by using utilities such as sar -d, and/or iostat.[8] In Solaris 2.6, iostat provides an option (iostat -n) that displays the descriptive disk device name rather than the *sdnnn* format. This allows you to immediately identify the particular controller and disk for which the statistics are being reported. These utilities report useful performance statistics, such as percent busy, average service time in the wait queue, number of reads and writes per second, blocks per second, average wait, and average service time. The most important items of focus are average service time and average wait. The average service time is the average elapsed time (in milliseconds) that the disk drive takes to complete an I/O request. The average wait is the average amount of time requests were left outstanding. High averages for these two items indicates an I/O bottleneck. Average service times longer than 50 milliseconds are reason for concern if it continues over a long time. Do not be concerned with service times of 50 milliseconds or less for small intervals of time. This means simply that the system received a large I/O request at that point in time. Be concerned with high average service times that are continuously high. You may have to repartition the data and redo log files to eliminate the I/O contention. The following is an example of how to use the iostat command to monitor I/O utilization:

---

8. The iostat utility is available on Solaris and reports disk utilization statistics.

```
myhost> iostat -xn 1

        extended device statistics

 r/s   w/s   kr/s   kw/s wait actv wsvc_t asvc_t  %w  %b  device
111.0 1.0 3480.1  2.0  0.0  8.8   0.0   78.1    0 100  c0t1d0
106.0 1.0 3392.1  2.0  0.0  3.9   0.0   36.3    0  94  c2t0d0
 0.0  0.0    0.0  0.0  0.0  0.0   0.0    0.0    0   0  c1t1d0
 0.0  0.0    0.0  0.0  0.0  0.0   0.0    0.0    0   0  c1t6d0
 0.0  0.0    0.0  0.0  0.0  0.0   0.0    0.0    0   0  c1t10d0
 0.0  0.0    0.0  0.0  0.0  0.0   0.0    0.0    0   0  c1t11d0
109.0 0.0 3456.1  0.0  0.0  8.1   0.0   74.0    0 100  c0t1d1
106.0 0.0 3392.1  0.0  0.0  3.9   0.0   36.5    0  90  c2t0d1
```

The above `iostat` output shows that the devices `c0t1d0` and `c2t0d0` are experiencing longer than normal service times. The two devices, `c0t1d0` and `c2t0d0`, are busy 94 percent and 100 percent percent of the time, respectively. The device `c2t0d0` is averaging 106 reads per second, and the `c0t1d0` device is averaging 111 reads per second. The throughput for each device is approximately 3.3 MB per second. The average service time for the device `c0t1d0` is slightly more than double that of the `c2t0d0` device. The average wait is 0, meaning that the devices are not experiencing wait time due to long I/O queues. In this particular case, we need to investigate the device mapping for the `c0t1d0` device in order to drill down on the long service time. It may be necessary to reconfigure this device in order to improve the I/O utilization. The device `c0t1d0` maps to a hardware RAID device, which consisted of only two disks in the RAID set. Reconfiguring the device to include four disks in the stripe set significantly improved the I/O throughput. The following `iostat` output illustrates the difference in the I/O throughput following the reconfiguration.

```
myhost> iostat -xn 1 10

        extended device statistics

 r/s   w/s   kr/s   kw/s  wait actv wsvc_t asvc_t  %w  %b device
 97.9 1.0 6266.4   8.0  0.0  1.0   0.0   10.2    0  99 c0t1d0
122.0 1.0 7808.0   8.0  0.0  1.0   0.0    8.2    0  99 c0t1d0
117.0 2.0 7487.9  16.0  0.0  1.0   0.0    8.5    0  99 c0t1d0
117.0 2.0 7487.9  10.0  0.0  1.0   0.0    8.5    0  99 c0t1d0
117.0 1.0 7487.9   8.0  0.0  1.0   0.0    8.6    0  99 c0t1d0
125.0 0.0 7999.9   0.0  0.0  1.0   0.0    7.9    0  99 c0t1d0
124.0 1.0 7935.8   8.0  0.0  1.0   0.0    8.0    0  99 c0t1d0
108.0 0.0 6911.8   0.0  0.0  1.0   0.0    9.2    0  99 c0t1d0
123.0 1.0 7872.3   8.0  0.0  1.0   0.0    8.2    0  99 c0t1d0
125.0 1.0 7999.8   2.0  0.0  1.0   0.0    8.0    0  99 c0t1d0
```

In the above `iostat` output, the throughput increased from 3.3 MB per second in the earlier configuration to almost 8 MB per second, with an average of 125 reads per second. The average service time reduced to an average of 8.5 milliseconds versus 78.1 milliseconds with the earlier configuration. Using `iostat` or `sar`, you can identify the disks or I/O devices experiencing I/O contention. You will then need to analyze the configuration and possibly reconfigure the device or logical volume in order to improve I/O utilization. You can also use the GUI performance monitoring tools to monitor disk and I/O utilization. Whichever utility you use, it is important that you monitor the I/O subsystem periodically to ensure that I/O is not a bottleneck. Using the volume manager and raw devices with proper data distribution can help you avoid disk contention.

3.21   TUNING I/O

I/O is the single most critical component that pertains to performance in a database system. This section discusses the Oracle I/O-related issues that pertain to the overall performance of an OLTP system, such as the Volume Manager, raw devices, and file systems.

3.21.1   VOLUME MANAGEMENT

It is vital that your I/O subsystem be tuned as best as possible by either using the hardware volume management services or a logical volume manager (LVM). Hardware volume management is generally faster than software volume management. However, if your hardware volume manager is limited in functionality, then you may choose to utilize the software LVM or a combination of both. For example, in an OLTP mission-critical environment, mirroring is typically employed to provide high availability. In this case, using the hardware mirroring may be faster than the software equivalent. The LVM enables you to create stripes, mirrors, or RAID devices. For transaction-intensive systems, try to use striping or mirroring in place of parity-based RAID. Parity-based RAID introduces parity bit calculation overhead, and is often inefficient when performing small writes. Striping or mirroring offers the best performance in terms of I/O throughput. If you use mirroring, make sure your submirrors are separated across different controllers and different disks so that the overhead of mirroring is minimized. If the submirrors are not separated, mirroring can cause an I/O bottleneck by saturating particular disks.

3.21.2   STORAGE ARRAY CACHE

Storage arrays often contain on-board cache memory to improve the performance of reads and writes. Depending on the size of the cache and the sophistication of the storage array cache manager, reads and writes can generally benefit from the cache thereby increasing overall I/O throughput. If your storage array has cache memory, you should ensure that the cache is enabled in order to improve I/O performance. In certain cases, the storage array cache can be configured to maximize either read or write performance. For an OLTP environment, configuring the write back cache for maximum write performance improves the performance of transactions and commits. For a data warehousing environment, enabling the cache to maximize read performance helps improve query throughput and may also aid in asynchronous read ahead performance depending on the sophistication of the cache.

If you are using the Sun StorEdge arrays, you can increase performance by utilizing the cache that is provided on the storage array. The Sun A3500 StorEdge storage array can be configured with 256 MB of cache memory. The StorEdge arrays use an NVRAM cache, which can increase the performance of writes significantly because the data is written to the NVRAM cache (backed up by battery) and later is flushed to disk (i.e., write-back cache).

On the Sun A3000 Storage Array, you can use the `raidutil` command to enable the NVRAM cache. You can also use the `raidutil` command to tune several NVRAM cache-related parameters such as the read cache, mirroring, read-ahead prefetch, dynamic flush threshold, and dynamic threshold amount.

It is important that you become familiar with your storage arrays by fully understanding their capabilities and functionality. This allows you to tune your storage I/O subsystem in accordance with the system workload in order to maximize I/O throughput.

3.21.2.1   The StorEdge Fast Write Cache

Sun offers additional technology to increase I/O performance when using the A5X00 StorEdge storage arrays. The Fast Write cache for the A5X00 StorEdge storage arrays uses NVRAM (non-volatile memory) to cache data which can significantly increase the performance of user requests for data. Instead of writing the data to the disk physically, the data can be written to the Fast Write Cache and flushed out later. This improves the performance of the LGWR or DBWR by reducing the I/O wait time during writes. Writing the data to the Fast Write Cache, as opposed to the physical disk, is approximately 40 times faster for sequential writes.

3.21.3   RAW DEVICES

You should also use raw devices for your OLTP database. Raw devices provide the best performance for random reads and writes. Transactions generally result in random I/O as new records are inserted and existing records are queried, updated, or deleted. Using raw devices not only helps random I/O, it also reduces the memory and CPU overhead introduced by file systems. For a heavily hit OLTP server, paging levels can be very high when file systems are used due to the UNIX file system cache. Use the LVM to configure and set up raw devices. Make sure the raw devices are owned by the Oracle software owner and are part of the DBA group. You can do this by using the `chown` command followed by the `chgrp` command. The permissions on the raw devices should be 660 (read and write by only the Oracle software owner and the DBA group).

Although file system technology is continually being improved and the performance gap between raw devices and file systems is closing in, raw devices remain the leader in performance. File systems introduce extra overhead including file locking and maintenance of the file system cache and inode control block. Raw devices provide the database administrator with greater flexibility in sizing and database file layout. This allows the DBA to focus on distributing the I/O and sizing the files based on capacity and expected growth.

3.21.4 ASYNCHRONOUS I/O

Another benefit of using raw devices is the capability to use asynchronous I/O. If you are using raw devices, you should enable asynchronous I/O in the Oracle Server. On Solaris, set the `async_write=TRUE` and `async_read=TRUE` in Oracle7, and `disk_asynch_io=TRUE` in Oracle8 and Oracle8*i*. On HP, set `use_async_io=TRUE` in Oracle7, and `disk_asynch_io=TRUE` in Oracle8 and Oracle8*i*. On HP, you must configure the `/dev/async` asynchronous I/O device driver. Follow the instructions in Chapter 3 to configure the asynchronous I/O driver on HP. On Sequent, set `async_write=TRUE` in Oracle7 and `disk_asynch_io=TRUE` in Oracle8 and Oracle8*i* to enable asynchronous I/O if you use raw devices. Also, if you use asynchronous I/O, set the `init.ora` parameter `db_writers=1` in Oracle7 and `db_writer_processes=1` in Oracle8 release Oracle 8.0.4 or higher. In some cases, multiple database writers can improve throughput if a single database writer falls behind. The combination of asynchronous I/O and raw devices provides high I/O throughput and maximizes scalability as more users are added to the system.

3.21.5 ORACLE WRITES

When Oracle writes to data files or log files through its respective process, DBWR or LGWR, the writes are nondeferred. On most UNIX platforms, Oracle uses the O_SYNC flag when it opens files.[9] The O_SYNC flag causes the data and file control block information to be written physically to the disk (not the cache). The O_SYNC flag is used to guarantee consistency because Oracle must ensure that the data is physically written to the disk. For this reason, it is important that your data be striped and properly distributed in order to avoid I/O bottlenecks during writes. Even if you use file systems and have configured a large UNIX file system cache, writes will still be physically written to disk. The rate at which Oracle writes out is highly dependent on the configuration of the Oracle Server.

3.21.6 VERITAS FILE SYSTEM MOUNT OPTIONS

If you choose to use Veritas file systems (`vxfs`) as opposed to raw devices, make sure that the file system is mounted without the `mincache=closesync` (refer to the `vfstab` options file) option. The `mincache=closesync` option causes the file system cache to write any file updates to disk once the file is closed, thereby reducing the usefulness of the cache. The performance degradation caused by this option is approximately 10 percent.

---

9. For more information on the different types of flags, refer to the manual pages on the `open()` system call.

The `vxfs` file system type provides additional mount options such as `convosync` and `nolog`. You can mount the file system with either the `convosync=direct` or `dsync` option. The direct option causes reads and writes to bypass the UNIX file system cache and to read and write directly from the disk to the user space. During heavy I/O loads, using direct I/O over traditional file system I/O has seen a 50 percent performance improvement. The `dsync` option, when used in conjunction with the `open()` system call, causes writes to block until the data is physically written to disk, but not the inode information. The inode information is deferred and later written to disk. The `dsync` option can offer a 20–30 percent performance gain if a high degree of file system write concurrency is occurring. If your system and/or application does not benefit from the advantages of the UNIX file system cache, using direct I/O over the `dsync` option can increase I/O performance.

You can also use the `nolog` option which disables file system journaling. This increases performance; however, file system reliability is substantially reduced. With the `nolog` option, you must repair the file system using a full scan via the `fsck` utility. Without the journal logs, the file system may be unrecoverable following a crash.

The following are examples of how to utilize the `vxfs` mount options.

```
myhost {root}-> mount -F vxfs -o convosync=direct  \
                    /dev/vx/dsk/vol1 /mount-point
```

or

```
myhost {root}-> mount -F vxfs -o convosync=dysnc  \
                    /dev/vx/dsk/vol1 /mount-point
```

or

```
myhost {root}-> mount -F vxfs -o nolog  \
                    /dev/vx/dsk/vol1 /mount-point
```

3.21.7 VERITAS DATABASE EDITION FOR ORACLE

In addition to the Veritas file system, Veritas offers the Database Edition for Oracle and the Quick I/O Database Accelerator, which provide up to a 90 percent performance improvement over the standard UNIX file system (`ufs`). The Quick I/O Database Accelerator reduces read/write lock bottlenecks by allowing parallel updates to database files, supports asynchronous I/O, and eliminates double buffering. The Veritas Server Suite Database Edition for Oracle increases performance substantially over the traditional `ufs`. If you use file systems for your database and do not want to consider raw devices for whatever reason, you should consider using the Veritas Database Edition for Oracle and Quick I/O Database Accelerator to help increase your system's performance.

3.21.8   VERITAS FILE SYSTEM AND PAGE COLORING

Page coloring algorithms are used to improve file performance by laying out the files in a such a manner that certain hot blocks or pages are grouped together so as to minimize I/Os. If you are using Veritas file systems (vxfs), there is a known bug which severely degrades the performance of executables such as the Oracle executable (oracle). The bug is due to the page coloring algorithm which Veritas uses for files residing in a Veritas file system. The performance of your Oracle system can degrade by as much as 50 percent due to the Veritas page coloring bug. For example, if your $ORACLE_HOME resides in a vxfs file system, the performance of the database will continue to degrade over time. Many customers worked around this bug by periodically shutting down the instance, and copying the oracle binary ($ORACLE_HOME/bin/oracle) to a staging area, and then copying the binary back to $ORACLE_HOME/bin using the UNIX copy command (cp). Veritas File System release 3.3.2 resolves the page coloring performance issue; hence you should upgrade to Veritas 3.3.2 or higher. You can use the pkginfo command on Solaris to determine which release of the Veritas File System your system is running.

```
myhost> pkginfo -l VRTSvxfs

  PKGINST:  VRTSvxfs
     NAME:  VERITAS File System
 CATEGORY:  system,utilities
     ARCH:  sparc
  VERSION:  3.3.2 for Solaris 7 (32-bit/64-bit), 2.6 and 2.5.1
  BASEDIR:  /
   VENDOR:  VERITAS Software
     DESC:  Commercial File System
   PSTAMP:  12-02-1999
 INSTDATE:  Mar 09 2000 20:12
  HOTLINE:  (800) 342-0652
    EMAIL:  support@veritas.com
   STATUS:  completely installed
    FILES:      114 installed pathnames
                 19 shared pathnames
                  3 linked files
                 21 directories
                 28 executables
                  3 setuid/setgid executables
               9404 blocks used (approx)
```

3.21.9   EXCLUSIVE FILE WRITE LOCK

In an OLTP application in which a large number of random reads and random writes are occurring, you can increase performance by having more small-size data files rather than fewer large-size data files when you use file system-based files. This helps reduce the exclusive UNIX file system file write lock bottleneck. Solaris requires an exclusive write lock at the file level to ensure file consistency. The exclusive lock on the file can cause multiple simultaneous writes to the file to be serialized, thereby reducing I/O performance. The performance effect of the exclusive file lock is especially noticeable when asynchronous I/O is used on file system based files. If a batch of asynchronous I/Os are issued in parallel to the same file, the I/Os will be serialized as Solaris acquires an exclusive write lock on the vnode (i.e., file). Solaris 8 resolves the issue of the exclusive file system write lock, thereby significantly improving file system performance, especially for databases based on file system files. Since an exclusive lock is acquired, it is not recommended that asynchronous I/O be used on file system-based files, especially on databases where the majority of the I/Os are concentrated to a small set of files. The workaround is to create many small-size data files, thereby causing writes to be distributed across many different files. If a high degree of write concurrency to a single or a few UFS-based files is occurring, increasing the number of data files by creating many more smaller-size files can increase I/O throughput. For example, instead of creating a single 2 GB data file, create four 512 MB data files to help reduce contention for the file write exclusive lock. Another workaround to the exclusive write lock issue is the use of the Veritas Quick I/O option, which essentially treats the file system file as a raw device to the accessing application. This allows asynchronous I/O to be used efficiently as if the file was a raw device. In addition, the Veritas Quick I/O option allows kernelized asynchronous I/O to be used (KAIO), which further improves the performance of asynchronous I/O. Many Oracle customers use Quick I/O for the database files in order to simulate raw device-like performance, yet maintain the administration benefits of file system-based files.

3.21.10 CHECKPOINTS

A checkpoint occurs when DBWR writes all the dirty database buffers (including committed and uncommitted data) that are in the SGA to the data files. Checkpoints ensure that data blocks in the SGA that are modified frequently are written to disk periodically. DBWR uses a Least Recently Used (LRU) algorithm to age blocks out of the buffer cache. Therefore, an active block that changes frequently may not necessarily be written out to disk if checkpoints are not occurring.

Another advantage of a checkpoint is that, because all database changes up to the checkpoint have been applied to the data files, redo log entries prior to the checkpoint need not be applied in the event of instance recovery. Hence, checkpoints can help reduce the instance recovery time.

Checkpoints always occur during a log switch from one log group to another. When a checkpoint occurs, Oracle updates the headers of all the data files to indicate the occurrence of the checkpoint. The task of updating the headers of the data files is usually handled by the LGWR process. However, if your database has many data files, this can increase the workload of LGWR.

In order to separate the workload of the checkpoint from LGWR's primary work of maintaining the redo log buffer, you can enable the checkpoint process (CKPT) in Oracle7. If the checkpoint process is enabled, it handles updating the header files. To enable the checkpoint process, set the Oracle7 `init.ora` parameter `checkpoint_process=`

TRUE. Enabling the checkpoint process can increase performance by allowing a separate process to handle the data file header updates and allowing LGWR to manage the redo buffer. If, however, processors and memory are limited on your system, you may want to consider allowing LGWR to handle the data file header updates. If your system cannot afford the overhead of an additional process, set `checkpoint_process=FALSE`. In Oracle8, the checkpoint process (`CKPT`) is enabled by default and the `init.ora` parameter `checkpoint_process` has been made obsolete.

Oracle8*i* uses multiple queues of recovery dirty buffers to help reduce the time needed to complete recovery checkpoints. Prior to Oracle8*i*, multiple DBWR processes could experience contention for the checkpoint queue latch due to the single queue of recovery dirty buffers. Hence, the time needed to complete recovery checkpoints is directly proportional to the number of DBWR processes (`db_writer_processes`). The multiple queues of recovery dirty buffers improves recovery checkpoint performance by partitioning the recovery dirty queue across the DBWR processes.

You can also set the interval at which checkpoints are started. The `init.ora` parameter `log_checkpoint_interval` specifies the number of operating system blocks (usually 512 bytes per block) needed to trigger a checkpoint. If the number of redo log file blocks generated since the last checkpoint exceeds this number, a checkpoint is performed. Regardless of this setting, a checkpoint always occurs after a redo log switch. A redo log switch occurs when LGWR switches from one redo log group to the next, in circular fashion. You can reduce the frequency of checkpoints by setting `log_checkpoint _interval` to the size of each redo log file. In which case, checkpoints occur only during a log switch. However, keep in mind that this will result in increased recovery times if instance or media recovery is required since the frequency of checkpoints will be reduced. If your application requires swift recovery times, you may want to set `log_checkpoint_interval` to a smaller value. You should also set the `init.ora` parameter `log_checkpoints_to_alert=TRUE`. This will allow you to monitor the frequency of checkpoints by examining the `alert_SID.log` file located in the `background_dump_dest` directory.

It is also important that you size your redo log files appropriately so as to avoid constant checkpoints and long redo log I/O waits. The `redo size`, `redo entries`, and `redo wastage` statistics from `v$sysstat` aid you in properly sizing the redo log files as well as optimally configuring the checkpoint frequency by analyzing the redo workload. The average redo entry size is (`redo size` / `redo entries`). The `redo wastage` statistic reports the number of bytes of unused space in the redo log buffer at the time when the entire redo buffer is written out. Also by setting the `init.ora` parameter `log_checkpoints_to_alert=TRUE`, you can monitor the frequency of checkpoints. Examining the checkpoint frequencies and computing the average redo entry size should give you a good feel as to your system's redo workload, subsequently allowing you to accurately size your redo log files.

The `init.ora` parameter `db_block_max_dirty_target` specifies the amount of dirty buffer cache blocks that would need to be recovered if the instance were to fail. In other words, the parameter specifies the number of blocks that need to be read during instance recovery. DBWR will flush dirty buffers to disk in an attempt to maintain the number of dirty buffers below `db_block_max_dirty_target`. The `init.ora` parameter `db_block_max_dirty_target` does not impose a hard limit on the number of dirty buffers that can be resident in the buffer cache. By adjusting the value of `db_block_max_dirty_target`, dirty buffers can be written out more frequently, thereby reducing instance recovery time following a crash. The majority of the time consumed during recovery involves the work of recovering the data blocks by applying the redo records between the most recent checkpoint and the end of the log. Choosing an optimal value for `db_block_max_dirty_target` involves determining the amount of time needed to read one block from disk and the desired length of the recovery process. For example, if it takes 5 milliseconds to read one block from the disk I/O subsystem, and you would like the recovery period to last no longer than 45 seconds, set `db_block_max_dirty_target=9000`. A lower value for `db_block_max_dirty_target` results in more frequent writes of dirty buffers, but a reduction in the recovery time. This parameter can be dynamically altered by using the `ALTER SYSTEM` command.

The Oracle8*i* `init.ora` parameter `fast_start_io_target` specifies the number of buffer cache blocks that would need to be processed during instance recovery if the instance were to fail. DBWR will continuously flush dirty buffers to disk and advance the checkpoint position in an attempt to maintain the number of I/O operations necessary in the event of recovery below `fast_start_io_target`. The `init.ora` parameter `fast_start_io_target` does not impose a hard limit on the number of dirty buffers that can be resident in the buffer cache. By adjusting the value of `fast_start_io_target`, the checkpoint position can be advanced more aggressively, thereby reducing instance recovery time following a crash. The majority of the time consumed during recovery involves the work of recovering the data blocks by applying the redo records between the checkpoint position and the end of the log. Choosing an optimal value for `fast_start_io_target` involves determining the amount of time needed to read one block from disk and the desired length of the recovery process. For example, if it takes 5 milliseconds to read one block from the disk I/O subsystem, and you would like the recovery period to last no longer than 45 seconds, set `fast_start_io_target=9000`. A lower value for `fast_start_io_target` results in more frequent writes of dirty buffers, but a reduction in the recovery time. This parameter can be dynamically altered by using the `ALTER SYSTEM` command.

The `init.ora` parameters `log_checkpoint_interval` and `log_checkpoint_timeout` have been redefined in Oracle8*i*. Prior to Oracle8*i*, `log_checkpoint_interval` specified the amount of redo blocks that can be filled before an interval checkpoint was started. In Oracle8*i*, `log_checkpoint_interval` specifies the number of blocks by which the checkpoint position should not be behind the tail of the log. This helps ensure that no more than a fixed number of redo blocks will have to be read during recovery. The `log_checkpoint_timeout` now refers to the number of seconds ago that the target incremental checkpoint was at the same log position as the tail of the redo log. This ensures that no more than `log_checkpoint_timeout` seconds worth of redo data should need to be recovered. This is implemented by comparing the incremental checkpoint RBA and ensuring that it does not exceed the tail of the log by more than the number of blocks specified by `log_checkpoint_interval`.

3.21.11   MONITORING FILE I/O

You should monitor file I/O periodically to ensure that I/O to the Oracle data files is being distributed properly. You can use the File I/O rate monitor of the Enterprise Manager (Performance Manager) to obtain file I/O statistics. You can also query the `v$filestat` view. The reported columns and their definitions are listed in Table 3.1.

TABLE 3.1   Reported columns of file I/O statistics

COLUMN	DEFINITION
PHYRDS	Number of physical reads per second since the last sample.
PHYWRTS	Number of physical writes per second since the last sample.
PHYBLKRD	Number of physical blocks read since the last sample.
PHYBLKWRT	Number of physical blocks written since the last sample.
READTIM	Response times per read (in hundredths of a second). *
WRITETIM	Response times per write (in hundredths of a second). *

* Set the `init.ora` parameter `timed_statistics=TRUE`.

If you see a high number of read and write requests for a specific data file or limited set of data files, you may need to redistribute your data so that reads and writes are spread out as much as possible across the different data files. If you use a volume manager (hopefully), the file I/O statistics may not give you a clear indication of the back-end disk movement. All file I/O statistics are reported at the database file level. Hence, if you use a volume manager, you should also monitor the I/O using `sar -d` (or an equivalent tool) to determine if the I/O is being distributed across multiple disks within the single logical volume. The write times should be ignored since they reflect the times of the write batch. However, the read times can be used to monitor the amount of time being spent on file reads. In addition, the read times should be collaborated with the operating system I/O statistics. Using the Oracle read times along with the operating system I/O statistics, you can identify which Oracle data files are experiencing contention or poor I/O response times.

3.21.12   TUNING THE DATABASE WRITER

The database writer is responsible for writing dirty blocks from the Oracle buffer cache to the data files. It is also responsible for maintaining adequate space in the buffer cache so that the physical I/O is minimized and the buffer cache hit ratio is maximized. Database reads (both logical and physical) are performed by the user shadow process. To maximize the performance of DBWR, ensure that DBWR is not constantly being saturated with write-out requests, and while writing, try to minimize DBWR write time.

In order to minimize DBWR write time, it is critical that your data files be distributed. You should tune I/O following the methods outlined in this chapter to ensure that I/O is properly distributed. If your data is not distributed properly, DBWR may experience high wait times. Therefore, use the volume manager to distribute I/O so that writes can proceed in parallel. Another way to minimize DBWR wait time is to use asynchronous I/O and raw devices. Asynchronous I/O and raw devices provide the best combination for I/O performance. Using asynchronous I/O can reduce the DBWR wait time incurred by the standard synchronous `write()` system call. Asynchronous I/O allows DBWR to issue multiple writes in parallel without blocking.

If you are not using asynchronous I/O, you should set the Oracle7 `init.ora` parameter `db_writers=n` where n represents the distinct number of disk drives and controllers that your data spans. For example, if most of your data files consist of stripes across five disks, set `db_writers=5`. In addition, try to balance the number of DBWR processes with the number of disks, as well as the number of controllers. This allows high throughput DBWRs by parallelizing writes across controllers. For example, if your data spans ten disks, but only two controllers, setting `db_writers=10` may saturate I/O, causing disk waits, since there are only two controllers to service the I/O requests.

In Oracle8, you can set the `init.ora` parameter `dbwr_io_slaves` to enable DBWR I/O slaves. In Oracle 8.0.4, you can enable multiple DBWR processes by setting the `init.ora` parameter `db_writer_processes` to the number of DBWR processes desired. If asynchronous I/O is disabled or not supported on your platform, using multiple DBWR processes or I/O slaves can improve database I/O throughput. If you enable I/O slaves or multiple DBWR processes, monitor the `v$filestat` statistics as well as processor utilization to ensure that file I/O is being parallelized and processes are not waiting to run. Configuring too many DBWR processes or I/O slaves may cause a performance degradation if processes spend too much time waiting for processor time or data is not distributed properly.

Oracle8*i* made several improvements to the database writer in order to improve the overall performance. One such optimization included a change to the DBWR callback interval, thereby allowing DBWR to issue a batch of I/Os and begin accumulating buffers for the next batch without having to wait for the completion of the first batch of I/Os. This improves DBWR throughput and helps reduce free buffer wait events. In addition, DBWR's throughput will no longer be limited by a slow or busy disk(s). Previously, DBWR could not begin collecting buffers for the next batch until all the writes from the current batch completed. In the previous model, a slow or busy set of disks could cause a delay in the current DBWR write batch. This delay would then hamper DBWR's ability to assemble the next batch and issue new writes.

Oracle8*i* also added cold lists and reuse lists in order to improve DBWR and `CKPT` throughput. Cold lists contain clean buffers that have been scanned by DBWR on the LRU list and buffers that have been written from the LRU-W list (write list) for aging purposes. The cold list prevents DBWR from unnecessarily scanning the same clean and recently written buffers. Foreground processes first scan the cold list when looking for free buffers. A reuse cross instance call eliminates buffers belonging to a range of blocks or to an object which is to be dropped or truncated. Prior to Oracle8*i*, a cross instance call would be invoked on each DBWR process. In Oracle8*i*, the `CKPT` process services the cross instance call, flushes any clean qualifying buffers, and moves current qualifying dirty buffers onto the reuse queues. DBWR then writes the buffers from the reuse queues per its affinity.

3.21.12.1 Monitoring the Database Writer Activity

In order to be sure that DBWR is keeping up with the buffer cache workload, you should monitor the following server statistics that are available through the Enterprise Manager or v$sysstat view.

NAME	VALUE
DBWR buffers scanned	104248
DBWR checkpoints	90
DBWR cross instance writes	0
DBWR free buffers found	42069
DBWR lru scans	852
DBWR make free requests	348
DBWR summed scan depth	105038
DBWR timeouts	304495
background checkpoints completed	4
background checkpoints started	5
dirty buffers inspected	0
free buffer inspected	884
free buffer requested	117224
physical writes	14115
summed dirty queue length	644
write requests	2886

The following points summarize the preceding DBWR statistics:

❏ DBWR buffers scanned statistic reports the number of buffers in the Least Recently Used (LRU) section of the buffer cache scanned by DBWR when it searches for dirty buffers to write-out to disk. DBWR buffers scanned includes clean buffers as well as dirty buffers. You should divide DBWR buffers scanned by the value of DBWR lru scans to determine the average number of buffers being scanned.

❏ DBWR checkpoints reports the number of times DBWR was signaled to perform a checkpoint.

❏ DBWR free buffers found is the number of buffers that DBWR found to be clean when requested to make free buffers. Divide DBWR free buffers by the value of DBWR make free requests to determine the average number of free buffers at the end of the LRU.

❏ DBWR make free requests is the number of requests made of DBWR, including requests made by DBWR, to make more buffers free in the LRU section of the buffer cache.

❏ DBWR timeouts is the number of timeouts accumulated by DBWR during idle writes. Idle writes occur when DBWR scanned the buffers but found nothing to write-out. Do not be alarmed by a high number of DBWR timeouts. This simply means that DBWR found nothing to write out during its scan.

❏ Dirty buffers inspected reports the number of dirty or modified buffers found in the cache. If the value of dirty buffers inspected is large or continues to increase, DBWR is not keeping up with the workload.

❏ Physical writes, background checkpoints completed, and background checkpoints started will give you a good indication of the amount of physical I/O occurring. High numbers indicate that too much physical I/O is occurring, and that either DBWR is falling behind and/or the buffer cache is too small.

3.21.12.2   The Database Writer Parameters

The three primary Oracle7 and Oracle8 init.ora parameters that affect DBWR are db_block_write_batch, db_block_checkpoint_batch, and db_file_simultanenous_writes. The _db_block_write_batch parameter specifies the number of blocks to batch in each DBWR I/O.[10] A larger value for _db_block_write_batch means that more blocks are written out at each batch I/O. This reduces the overall activity of DBWR because when DBWR writes, it will write a larger batch. Smaller values for _db_block_write_batch may increase the activity of DBWR, since DBWR will have to write out many smaller size batches rather than fewer larger size batches.

To determine if _db_block_write_batch is optimally set, divide the summed dirty queue length by the number of write requests to determine the average length of the dirty list. The summed dirty queue length is the sum of the LRU queue length following the completion of every write request. In the previous example, the summed dirty queue length is 644, and write requests is 2886. Therefore the average size of the dirty queue length is 644/2886=.22. The free buffer inspected is the number of buffers skipped in the buffer cache by user processes attempting to find a free buffer. If the value of free buffer inspected is high, it means that the buffer cache consists of a large number of modified buffers. You should either increase the size of the buffer cache, or increase the _db_block_write_batch to force more dirty buffers to be written out. Free buffer requested is the number of times a free buffer was needed to create and/or load a block. Set _db_block_write_batch=128 and increase it if necessary. Continue to increase _db_block_write_batch until the summed dirty queue length and free buffer inspected are small. However, do not set _db_block_write_batch so high that the I/O subsystem is over saturated with too many I/Os thereby causing long I/O wait queue lengths.

---

10. Db_block_write_batch has been made an underscore parameter (_db_block_write_batch) because Oracle dynamically determines the optimal batch size based on db_file_simultaneous_writes.

The db_block_checkpoint_batch specifies the batch size of DBWR check-point writes. A high value for db_block_checkpoint_batch allows checkpoints to complete quickly. You should set db_block_checkpoint_batch such that check-points always complete before the next checkpoint. This will reduce the wait time between checkpoints.

The db_file_simultaneous_writes specifies the number of simultaneous batches issued by DBWR for each database file. If your operating system does not support multiple writes per device, then you should set db_file_simultaneous_writes=1. If you are using file systems, setting db_file_simultaneous_writes to a high value may have a negative effect due to the exclusive file-write lock that is used to guarantee file consistency. On raw devices with asynchronous I/O, set db_file_simultaneous _writes to at least twice the number of distinct members in the striped volume and to no more than five times the number of members. For example, if your striped data file consists of six distinct disk drives, set db_file_simultaneous_writes=12 (minimum set-ting) and no more than db_file_simultaneous_writes=30. Use larger values for db_file_simultaneous_writes for wide striped files (numerous members). Moni-tor the v$filestat view and disk I/O utilization (sar -d) to determine the optimal set-ting for db_file_simultaneous_writes. Storage arrays with large amounts of cache can typically sustain a large number of concurrent I/Os, therefore larger settings for db_file_simultaneous_writes can often increase database I/O throughput.

In Oracle8*i*, the init.ora parameters db_block_write_batch, db_block_ checkpoint_batch, and db_file_simultanenous_writes have been made obsolete. In Oracle8*i*, the buffer cache uses more of a dynamic model to adjust the optimal batch size as well as the other variables effecting the database writer(s). The Oracle8*i* init.ora parameter _db_writer_max_writes controls the maximum number of outstanding I/Os that a database writer can issue. However, you should not typically need to set this parameter.

3.21.12.3 Multiple Database Writers

Oracle8 release 8.0.4 introduced the ability to configure multiple database writers. Prior to multiple database writers, DBWR I/O slaves could be used to parallelize I/O requests if a single database writer process could not keep up with the buffer cache work-load. Multiple database writers are more efficient than I/O slaves because the buffer cache is effectively partitioned such that each database writer processor maintains a disjoint set of buffers. This allows the buffer cache processing to be parallelized across the available database writer processes. DBWR I/O slaves do not parallelize buffer processing because a single database writer is used to allocate work to the I/O slaves. In addition, I/O slaves do not allow requests such as ping requests or make free buffer requests to be parallelized since there is only a single database writer to field these requests. I/O slaves also result in a higher overhead than multiple database writers due to the IPC communication with the I/O slaves, which results in more context switches and memory copies for buffer writes.

Multiple database writers essentially divide the buffer cache into equal-sized groups of buffers termed as working sets. Each working set consists of the following queues: an LRU queue, a write-out queue (LRU-W), a ping queue (LRU-P), and checkpoint queues. The buffers are partitioned via the working sets amongst the database writers. The working sets are assigned to the different database writers in a round-robin fashion in order to ensure that each database writer process receives an equitable share of the different buffer pools such as the keep, recycle, or default buffer pool. The number of working sets is defined by the number of LRU latches (`db_block_lru_latches`). Each working set is protected by an LRU latch. For example, if four database writers were configured (`db_writer_processes=4`), and the buffer cache consisted of 50,000 buffers (`db_block_buffers=50000`), and there existed 16 LRU latches (`db_block_lru_latches=16`), then 16 working sets would be configured, each consisting of 3,125 buffers. Each database writer would manage four of the 16 working sets (i.e., 12,500 buffers).

NUMA platforms can take advantage of the multiple database writers by localizing the buffers within the same set to the node or quad. This reduces the need for remote node memory access when accessing or processing buffers. Oracle8*i* for the Sequent NUMA platforms provides a feature known as quad-local buffer access, which essentially localizes the buffers within a set to a specific node.

The maximum number of database writers which can be configured (`db_writer_processes`) is ten. In addition, the recovery time for temporary segment cleanup following a shutdown abort is proportional to the amount of database writers. Hence, if you perform a shutdown abort, you may want to consider starting up the database using a single database writer, and completing the recovery and segment cleanup. You can then shut down the instance and restart the database with multiple database writers. In general, try to use shutdown normal or shutdown immediate when shutting down the database (if possible).

3.21.12.4 The Optimal Number of Database Writers

In order to determine the optimal number of I/O slaves or database writers, you need to review the I/O statistics `physical writes`, `physical reads`, `logical reads`, and `write requests` from the `v$sesstat` and `v$sysstat` views to determine the I/O rates. In addition, you should compare the I/O statistics from the `v$sesstat` and `v$sysstat` views with the statistics from the `v$sess_io` and `v$filestat` views. Choosing the right number of I/O slaves and/or database writers involves reviewing the I/O rates and statistics. In a normal situation where your data files and redo log files are optimally striped and disk I/O contention is minimal, I/O slaves will more than likely not be needed when asynchronous I/O is enabled and is fast and efficient. However, if DBWR or LGWR are falling behind, and disk I/O contention has been resolved, you should enable multiple database writers to help parallelize the work of the buffer cache. It is important to note that if your disk contention is due to the fact that your database and redo log files are not optimally distributed and striped, starting additional database writers or I/O slaves can have a negative effect on performance since more processes will be issuing I/O. Multiple database writers and I/O slaves are primarily intended for workloads where a single database writer and a single log writer are not driving the I/O subsystem hard enough or a single database writer is not keeping up with the buffer cache workload. In these cases, additional database writers can help improve the buffer cache throughput as well as improve the utilization of the I/O subsystem.

3.21.13 TUNING REDO

For an OLTP system, it is critical that user processes and Oracle background processes are not waiting constantly on LGWR or space in the redo buffer. If the redo area is not properly tuned, it can cause high user process wait times, waiting on LGWR to make space available in the redo buffer or complete checkpoints.

The LGWR process writes to the redo log files in a circular fashion. Figure 3.12 shows the circular cycle of the LGWR.

The redo log files contain redo entries, which consist of data that is used to reconstruct changes made to the database, including rollback data. Redo entries also contain rollback segments as well as data. They are a low-level mapping of the database changes. The redo entries cannot be used by applications to show the user actions.[11]

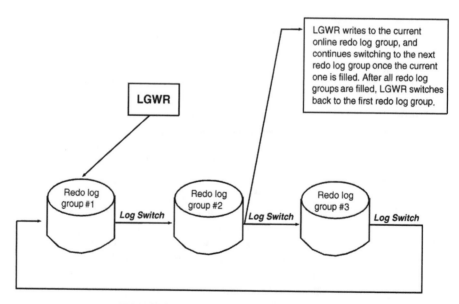

FIGURE 3.12 Circular cycle of the LGWR.

---

11. BMC Software offers the SQL*Trax tool that allows you to examine the Oracle redo log files to show detailed information on changes. For more information of the tool, contact BMC Software Company.

3.21.13.1 Configuring the Redo Log Files

Before you begin to tune the redo buffer in the SGA, it is critical that your redo log files be configured properly. Make sure that each redo log member file within a group is striped across multiple disks and multiple controllers. One thing to remember is that members of a redo log group are written to asynchronously (simultaneously), and redo log groups are written to synchronously. This means that redo log groups can be on the same set of disks as are other redo log groups since LGWR writes only to one active group at a time. Therefore, if you have multiple members within a group (Oracle redo log mirroring), make sure each member is on separate set of disks and controllers so that LGWR writes can proceed in parallel to each member. Figure 3.13 shows how redo log files should be configured.

In Figure 3.13, redo log members are separated across different disks and different controllers to ensure that LGWR writes proceed in parallel. If you are mirroring the Oracle redo members (meaning you have multiple members within a single redo log group), LGWR attempts to write to the members asynchronously (assuming asynchronous I/O is enabled). Therefore, if your members are all on the same disk, contention for the disk is likely to occur. The redo log groups, however, can be on the same set of disks as the other redo log groups because Oracle writes to only one redo log group at a time. As Figure 3.13 shows, redo log members of the same group are separated across different controllers and disks. However, each redo log group is on the same set of disks and controllers as the other groups. You should dedicate at least a few disks for redo log files. Try to avoid mixing redo disks with other data since this will reduce overall I/O performance.

Appropriately tuning your redo log files can ensure a high throughput LGWR. For an OLTP system, redo is one of the major contributors to the workload as rows are constantly being inserted, updated, and/or deleted. Remember to use `sar` or other I/O monitoring utilities to monitor redo disk utilization. The I/O statistics will allow you to identify the I/O bottlenecks (if any) for the disk drives containing the redo log files.

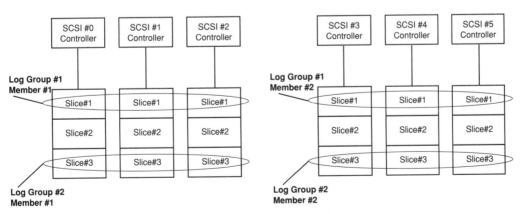

FIGURE 3.13 Ideal redo log file configuration.

3.21.13.2   Volume Management Mirroring Versus Oracle Mirroring

Another tuning technique you can use—if you are using a hardware or software volume manager that supports mirroring—is the mirroring functionality that is provided with
the hardware or software volume manager. Mirroring by the logical volume manager is
done in kernel space, and hardware mirroring is typically handled by the storage array,
which is much more efficient than user-space mirroring (Oracle issuing multiple writes).
However, keep in mind that in the case of corruption, hardware-level or OS-level mirroring
will duplicate the corruption across the mirror which may render your database useless if
only one redo log member exists per group. Oracle mirroring (meaning multiple redo members exist per redo log group) can add another level of safety by having multiple redo log
members. In the case of corruption, Oracle will likely detect the corruption and continue
writing to the valid redo log members. Therefore, it is a good idea to have at least two redo
log members per redo log group and allow the OS or hardware-level mirroring to handle
additional redundancy.

3.22   TUNING NFS

NFS file systems are extremely common, and performance can suffer during heavy NFS
use. My first recommendation for tuning NFS is to ensure that the back-end file system (the
file system being exported as an NFS file system) is striped across multiple disks and controllers. Follow the guidelines in section 3.2.1 to tune the file system itself. If the file system
is not distributed properly, performance of local access and remote access (NFS) of the file
system will suffer. Therefore, before you export the file system, use a volume manager to
stripe the file system.

In addition, tune the inode cache and DNLC. For heavy NFS activity, you should set
the DNLC and NCSIZE to larger values to accommodate the NFS traffic. NFS uses RPC to
communicate between the client and the server. NFS packets use the UDP datagram, and
client machines manage NFS inodes as an rnode (remote node). Solaris 2.5 introduced NFS
Version 3, which increased NFS performance and also switched from UDP to TCP/IP packets. Most other vendors' NFS utilities are still based on version 2.0. For an NFS server experiencing a lot of NFS traffic, increase the number of NFS server daemons (nfsd). This
allows more NFS client requests to be serviced in parallel. On Solaris, the nfsd daemon
uses kernel threads to service requests. The kernel threads do not experience context
switches between user space and kernel space because NFS remains in kernel space. This
allows the nfsd daemon to achieve high throughput. On Solaris and HP, you can use the
nfsstat utility to monitor NFS performance.

On the NFS server, use nfsstat -s, and on the NFS client, use nfsstat -c. On
the server, the calls column (output from nfsstat -s) reports the total number of RPC
calls received. The badcalls column reports the total number of RPC calls rejected. The
rejects could be due to security or to attempts to access an NFS file system for which the
client has no permission. The nullrecv column reports the number of empty RPC packets

received. The `badlen` column reports the number of packets received that were too short to be considered valid. The `xdrcall` column reports the number of RPC packets received that were poorly formatted, subsequently preventing the packet from being decoded.

On the NFS client, use `nfsstat -c` to monitor NFS performance. The `retrans` column (output from `nfsstat -c`) reports the number of retransmissions. The `timeout` column reports the number of calls that timed out after awaiting a reply from the NFS server. The `wait` column shows the number of times a call had to wait due to the unavailability of a client handle. The `badxid` reports the number of times that a reply received from the NFS server did not correspond to any outstanding call. If you are seeing a high number of retransmissions and `badxids`, your network may be dropping packets, thereby forcing the packet to be resubmitted. You should monitor your network traffic to determine if a lot of collisions or packet drops are occurring. If the value of timeout or wait is high, it is likely that there is a server bottleneck. Monitor the disk statistics on the NFS server to check for I/O bottlenecks.

3.22.1 NFS VERSION 3

Solaris 2.5 and HP-UX 11.0 include NFS Version 3. NFS Version 3 offers several performance enhancements over NFS Version 2 and increases read and write throughput. NFS Version 3 also improves local client cache utilization and reduces server lookup and write requests.

NFS Version 2 has a maximum buffer size limitation of 8 KB, subsequently limiting the amount of NFS data that can be transferred over the network at one time. NFS Version 3 relaxed this limitation improving NFS transmission efficiency by transmitting larger amounts of data. This also helps NFS to more effectively utilize high-bandwidth network communication such as FDDI and Fast Ethernet.

NFS Version 3 improves NFS performance by improving the client-side cache utilization, using the TCP/IP protocol instead of UDP, improving read and write throughput, and relaxing the network bandwidth restriction. Caching the NFS file data including pages, attributes and directory information on the client helps reduce the NFS overhead of transferring data across the network. The process can read and write to the local cache and avoid network lookups. This helps reduce the call frequency of popular NFS call procedures such as `read`, `readdir`, `readlink`, and `lookup`. Caching significantly increases NFS client performance and enhances server scalability. This translates into clients getting faster access to file data via a fast local cache. Also, the *read-ahead* feature helps NFS clients that are reading files sequentially. NFS detects that the file is being read sequentially and brings the data into the local client cache. Hence, when the process requests the next set of data, it is already present in the local cache. This increases the performance of sequential reads.

NFS Version 3 increases write throughput by eliminating the synchronous writes requirement while maintaining the advantages of the *close-to-open* semantics. The close-to-open semantics refers to when an application closes a file, all the outstanding data is written to the file on the server before the close can complete. This is done to ensure file data consistency. The NFS Version 3 client significantly reduces the number of write requests to the server by grouping multiple requests and then writing the batch through to the server's cache. A commit is then subsequently issued which causes the server to write all the data to stable storage simultaneously. This is known as *safe asynchronous writes*. Safe asynchronous writes considerably reduce the number of server write requests, thereby improving write throughput. The writes are considered safe because status information on the data is maintained which indicates whether or not the data has been stored successfully. The client can query the status information to determine if the server crashed before the commit request once the server is restored.

3.22.2   NETWORK APPLIANCE

Network Appliance offers a variety of products to improve the performance of file caching, including NFS. The Network Appliance file servers use a sophisticated cache to improve the response of NFS I/O requests by orders of magnitude. The Network Appliance file servers employ NVRAM to cache the data. For more information on Network Appliance file servers and products, visit the Network Appliance Web site at *www.netapp.com*.

3.23   NFS AND DATABASE

The NFS service is a kernel service and has a higher priority than user processes. Avoid mixing NFS servers with database servers. In other words, do not set up your database server to act also as an NFS server. NFS requests always take priority over user processes (in this case Oracle). Therefore, Oracle processes may see longer wait times due to NFS requests. In some cases, when NFS experiences timeouts and messages such as "NFS server not responding" appear on the client systems, it can cause the NFS server to halt all other processing until NFS services are restored. For this reason, you should not set up your database server as an NFS server. Separate your database servers from NFS servers.

   Do not use NFS file systems to create Oracle data files or redo log files. Oracle issues nondeferred writes to guarantee data consistency once data is written to Oracle files. NFS cannot guarantee this same level of consistency. Therefore, do not use NFS file system-based files within your Oracle database.

3.24   USING THE AUTOMOUNTER

The automounter is a daemon that handles the mounting and unmounting of NFS file systems. The automounter mounts the file system upon use, and unmounts the file system if it is idle for a period of time. This can increase performance by reducing the overhead of mounted file systems that are infrequently used and are idle most of the time. On Solaris, to set up the automounter, you need to configure the /etc/auto_master file to include the /etc/auto_direct file as a search path. Then, place your mount entries in the

`/etc/auto_direct` file. The automounter scans the `/etc/auto_direct` file and mounts and unmounts the specified file systems. You can also use the automounter equivalent namespace maps in the YP, NIS, or NIS+ naming service. On HP, you can configure the `/etc/auto.direct` file to set up the automounter. On HP, the automounter unmounts the file system if the file system is not accessed within the default five-minute interval. Using the automounter can reduce kernel resources and file system overhead by mounting the file system only upon use.

3.25 CONFIGURING AND SIZING THE DISK I/O SUBSYSTEMS

There are a tremendous number of disk I/O subsystem vendors, and it is often difficult to determine the appropriate vendor. Before you choose a vendor, it is important that you set some requirements for consideration.

First, the disk I/O subsystem vendor must support a volume manager. If the vendor does not support a volume manager, do not consider this vendor. Without a volume manager, striping and disk administration will be extremely difficult.

Second, for a database application, do not consider any vendor that insists on focusing on only capacity rather than performance and reliability. For example, a vendor attempts to sell you two 73 GB disk drives because you requested 140 GB of disk storage for a database application. For a database application, the best performance is obtained by distributing I/O across multiple spindles and controllers. The larger the size of the disk, the smaller number of disks you will have to distribute I/O. As far as optimal size, the Seagate Cheetah 18 GB 10,000 rpm or the Cheetah X15 18 GB 15,000 rpm disk are optimal disk drives for database applications. Try to avoid disk drives larger than 36 GB for a database application. Realizing that database sizes are growing at an exponential rate and disk drive and disk array vendors are focusing on capacity, small disk drives such as the 9 GB or even 18 GB may no longer be available. However, the logic is that the more spindles you have, the better your I/O performance since you will have more disks to spread your data across. For example, four 18 GB disks are better than having one 73 GB disk. Larger disks, such as the 73 GB drives, have their appropriate use, but a database server is not one of them. Larger disk drives work well for NFS servers, Web servers, file system staging areas, operating system binaries, software packages, and documentation.

Third, make sure that whatever disk vendor you choose, your system's hardware vendor (if different than the disk vendor) supports the configuration fully. If you intend to run Oracle, you should contact Oracle to verify that Oracle supports the disk vendor you are considering.

Fourth, avoid any nonopen proprietary disk I/O subsystem vendors at all costs. Not doing so may impede your future ability to migrate to newer server technologies. It may also hinder your ability to migrate the disk subsystems to different platforms. For example, avoid disk I/O subsystems that do not allow you to turn off certain options, such as mirroring or RAID. The disk I/O subsystem you purchase should allow you to configure the disk in many different ways. This enables you to configure the disks appropriately to an application's requirements.

Last, choose a disk vendor that has an extremely reliable product and an excellent track record for customer service. A reliable product will help foster a high system uptime percentage. The excellent customer service track record will help minimize downtime during media failures as the vendor will take all efforts to rush on-site to correct the problem. As a customer, the last thing you want is to sit idle and wait several hours for a service engineer to come and replace a disk, while your system remains down.

These are the five basic rules you should keep in mind when considering a disk I/O subsystem vendor. If you use Sun Servers, you should use the Sun StorEdge arrays. The Sun StorEdge storage arrays are highly reliable and provide a tremendous amount of functionality in terms of configuration options. The new StorEdge storage arrays use a fast 100 MB per second fiber optic connection between the server and the storage array. The storage arrays also allow you to easily migrate to the Sun Cluster environment should you decide to use Oracle Parallel Server in the future. If you use HP Servers, you can use either HP disk or EMC disk. EMC has a close partnership with many hardware vendors including HP. The EMC Symmetrix disk I/O subsystem uses a large cache (between 1 GB and 4 GB, depending on the configuration), which can increase database performance by reducing physical I/O. On Sequent, you can use the EMC Symmetrix Storage systems, or the Clarion Disk Arrays.

Choosing a disk I/O subsystem vendor can be difficult. Following the five guidelines listed previously can help make the decision quicker and clearer. For a database server, the core component is the disk I/O subsystem. An unreliable and poorly performing disk I/O subsystem can wreak havoc on your environment. If you are considering multiple disk I/O subsystem vendors, you may want to request that each vendor provide a loaner unit for benchmarking and testing. This will assist you in making the selection because you will have had hands-on experience in testing reliability, performance, openness, functionality, and scalability.

Chapter 4

APPLICATION TUNING

The application is a core component of any system. It is critical that the application obtain a high level of performance. A poorly designed application can hinder overall performance regardless of the computing power running the application. If the application does not scale or does not make use of parallel processing, adding more hardware provides little, if any, gain. It is important that the application be designed properly, and that it be implemented in such a way that it is permitted to scale and to maintain a high level of performance. In this chapter, I intend to offer recommendations on how to tune an application with the goal of maximizing scalability and performance.

4.1   APPLICATION ARCHITECTURE

When an application is designed, it is critical that its architecture be robust and solid. The architecture must allow the application to scale as more users are added. For example, designing a database application for which the majority of the processing is in one process hinders the application's scalability. You should distribute the application architecture as much as possible to allow for a more modular design. This also aids in debugging. If you are designing a multiplatform application, you may want to consider using a virtual layer and then allowing the virtual layer to call the platform-specific routines. A virtual layer helps isolate the application from the platform-specific issues by providing a consistent generic layer (virtual layer) on top of the platform-specific extensions. See Figure 4.1.

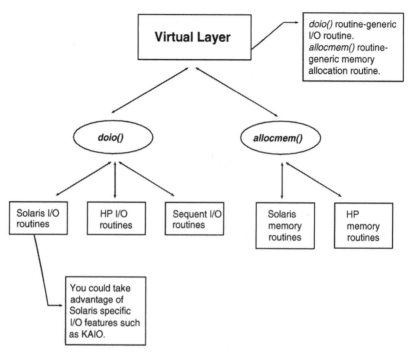

FIGURE 4.1   The virtual layer model.

The virtual layer not only allows you to take advantage of specific features of the platform, but it also provides for a very modular application in which specific platform layers can be modified without also changing the other layers. Although designing a virtual layer can be extremely complex, if you are designing a large-scale platform-independent application, it is well worth the effort.

The virtual layer should also be extended to error handling. Avoid hard-coding specific error numbers in the code. Use header files to store platform-specific error codes, or preferably store the error codes and descriptions in the database. This will allow you to change the error codes and descriptions easily by simply updating the database without recompiling code.

The performance of an application is highly dependent on its design and architecture. You need to spend a legitimate amount of time designing the application, and you must give careful thought to implementation issues, such as security, process management, memory management, error handling, and concurrency. You should also consider platform-specific issues, such as platform-specific performance features. The virtual layer enables your application to take advantage of platform-specific functionality while still maintaining the overall integrity of the application.

When you design the application, especially if it is a large-scale application, you need to think in parallel and asynchronously. Avoid coding practices in which routines wait a long time on processing or resources and thereby cause an application bottleneck. Divide larger tasks into many smaller tasks, and try to execute those tasks in parallel. For example, if you need to read data from two separate and independent tables, do not execute the queries serially. Execute the queries in parallel. For example, if writing a PRO*C program, you could `fork()` and `exec()` multiple processes, thus allowing the queries to execute concurrently. Or, a more preferred method is to create multiple threads within the PRO*C program itself. Oracle 7.3 provides PRO*C 2.2, which allows for the use of threads within a PRO*C program. If you use threads, you can create multiple threads and then have each thread execute a separate query.

4.2   DEVELOPMENT ENVIRONMENT

You should use a source version control system, such as PVCS or RCS, and a project management and methodology tool during application design and development. The source control system allows for version control maintenance of source code, as well as permitting multiple team members to work on the same application. The source code control system helps to prevent team members from overwriting one another's changes. The project management system helps the project leader track dates and deliverables. It also helps manage the workload by distributing modules of the application to the team members. The methodology tool helps foster a modular design by documenting the individual components and modules of the application. The methodology allows you to observe the dependencies between the modules.

In addition to the source control system and methodology tool, you also must have a complete set of GUI debugging and regression testing tools. These tools will allow you to debug your application as well as perform regression testing on the application. The regression testing helps you catch bugs before the application is moved into production. It can also help you measure scalability by simulating multiple users.

4.3   TUNING PRO*C APPLICATIONS

PRO*C is Oracle's precompiler for the C language. As of Oracle 7.2/ PRO*C 2.1, Oracle has provided support for C++, which allows you to code your application using C++ as well as C. The pre-compiler enables you to embed SQL statements as well as invoke PL/SQL statements that include stored procedures. The precompiler offers you SQL and PL/SQL functionality as well as the power of the host language itself. The flow of a PRO*C program is shown in Figure 4.2.

In Figure 4.2, the source code file (`mysource.pc`) is passed through the PRO*C precompiler, generating a modified source program file. The modified source program file contains library calls in place of the SQL statements. The modified source program then is passed through the compiler and/or linker, and an executable is produced. The linker uses the SQLLIB run-time library to resolve the calls.

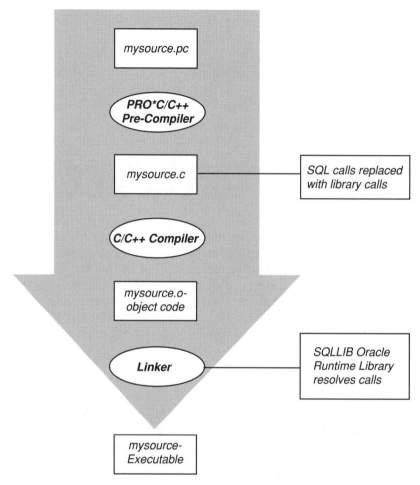

FIGURE 4.2   PRO*C process flow.

There are several techniques to increase performance that you can use to tune a PRO*C application, which include using the array interface, client-shared library, and reducing the SQL call overhead.

4.3.1   USING ARRAYS IN PRO*C

You should use the array processing feature of PRO*C when processing transactions. The array interface allows you to declare a local C array and populate it with values. Then the array can be used to perform an insert, update, or delete. You can also use arrays to fetch data from Oracle. The array interface increases performance by reducing the SQL calls from the number of records to be processed to a single call. For example, if you wanted to read 1,000 rows from the database, the traditional method is to open a cursor and loop through each fetch until all 1,000 rows are retrieved. This results in 1,000 SQL fetch calls. If you are running in a networked environment in which the application runs on a server other than the database server, this can increase the network traffic and reduce overall performance. Using an array of 1,000 elements results in only one SQL fetch call. The following is an example of array processing within PRO*C.

Example: batch_array.pc

```
#define BATCH_SIZE    1000
#define ORACLE_SUCCESS (sqlca.sqlcode == 0)
#define ORACLE_NUM_ROWS_PROCESSED (sqlca.sqlerrd[2])
#define ORACLE_CODE (sqlca.sqlcode)
#define PRODUCT_DESC_LEN   30

#define SUCCESS 0
#define FAILURE -1


int open_cursor (...........)
{

        EXEC SQL DECLARE lpcursor CURSOR FOR
            SELECT PRODUCT_NUM, PRODUCT_DESC
            FROM PRODUCT
            WHERE product_num = :lproduct_num;

        if (!ORACLE_SUCCESS)
        {
         fprintf (stderr,"Unable to Declare Cursor, Oracle Error#:
                 %d\n",ORACLE_CODE);
         return (FAILURE);
        }


        EXEC SQL OPEN lpcursor;

        if (!ORACLE_SUCCESS)
        {
         fprintf (stderr,"Unable to Open Cursor, Oracle Error#:
                 %d\n",ORACLE_CODE);
         return (FAILURE);
        }
        return (SUCCESS);


}
```

```
int fetch_cursor (.....................)
{


        /**** Declare the batch arrays and batch size variable  ****/

          int batch_size;

      #ifdef PROC8

          /** In PRO*C 8, we can take advantage of the array of
              structures feature.  **/

          struct sproduct
                  {
                      int product_num;
                      char product_desc[PRODUCT_DESC_LEN];
                  } asproduct[BATCH_SIZE];
      #else

         int product_num[BATCH_SIZE];
         char product_desc[BATCH_SIZE][PRODUCT_DESC_LEN];

      #endif /* PROC8 */

         /**** this routine assumes a database connection has
               been established *****/

         if (open_cursor() == SUCCESS)
         {

         batch_size=BATCH_SIZE;
         do
         {

      #ifdef PROC8

           /* Fetch into the array of structures */

             EXEC SQL FOR :batch_size
                     FETCH lpcursor INTO :asproduct;

      #else

             /* If not using PRO*C 8, fetch into the individual
                arrays */
```

```
                EXEC SQL FOR :batch_size
                        FETCH lpcursor INTO :product_num,
                                            :product_desc;

        #endif  /* PROC8 */


          /****** Code to Process the Array/Batch  ********/


          }
          while (ORACLE_SUCCESS)

          }


}

int update_batch (…………………….)
{


        int batch_size;
        int product_num[BATCH_SIZE];
        char product_desc[BATCH_SIZE][PRODUCT_DESC_LEN];



        /**** this routine assumes a database connection has been
              established *****/

        batch_size=BATCH_SIZE;     /** Set batch size **/

        EXEC SQL FOR :batch_size   /** Update Batch **/
                UPDATE PRODUCT
                SET PRICE = PRICE * 1.10
                WHERE PRODUCT_NUM = :product_num;


        if (!ORACLE_SUCCESS)
        {
          fprintf (stderr,"Unable to Update Batch, Oracle Error#:
                  %d\n",ORACLE_CODE);
          return (FAILURE);
        }


}
```

Using arrays to perform SQL operations can considerably reduce SQL call overhead as well as network overhead if running in a distributed environment. There are a few things to remember when using arrays in PRO*C. The first is that with PRO*C releases prior to PRO*C release 8, you cannot use an array of structures within PRO*C. You can, however, use arrays within a single structure to perform batch operations. PRO*C 8.0 does allow you to utilize an array of structures to perform batch SQL and other object-type operations. Using an array of structures allows for more elegant programming and also offers the application developer more flexibility in organizing the data structures. If you use array processing, remember to declare the same length for each array if you are using multiple items within a single batch operation. Therefore, declare a standard batch size, declare all arrays based on the batch size, and use the `FOR :batch_size` clause when you perform SQL operations to specify explicitly the number of rows to be processed. The second thing to remember is that for insert, update, delete, and select statements, `sqlca.sqlerrd[2]` reports the number of rows processed. For batch fetches, `sqlca.sqlerrd[2]` reports the cumulative sum of rows processed. In some cases, using the array interface increased performance 1000 percent. For more information on array processing in PRO*C, refer to the *Pro*C/C++ Precompiler Programmer's Guide* (Using Host Arrays section).

4.3.1.1   Selecting the Batch Size

Choosing the optimal batch size depends on many factors, such as the size of the data set being fetched, the performance characteristics of the network between the application server and the database server, and the latency of round trips. For example, in some cases large batch sizes can reduce overall performance if running in an environment where the network performance is poor. Larger batch sizes greatly increase the amount of network traffic between the application and the database server. For networks with heavy traffic or networks experiencing performance problems, using a large batch size can have a negative effect on performance. A large number of columns, especially those with long row lengths, can cause a slow batch operation. Therefore, choose an ideal batch size operation by making the batch size parameter dynamically configurable upon execution, either through some startup configuration file or an environment variable. My recommendation is that you start small, such as 500 for a batch size, and increment this figure nominally until you achieve the best performance. For SQL statements which need to operate on a large number of rows, batch processing can help improve the overall throughput of the application. It is best to perform numerous experiments with the batch size until an optimum value is reached.

When you use batch arrays to process SQL statements in your PRO*C application, do not statically allocate arrays or structures. Always allocate the arrays or structures dynamically by using a memory allocation routine such as `malloc()`. This enables you to free the batch array or structure once it is no longer needed. This also reduces application startup overhead by allocating only the amount of memory needed. The previously provided example statically allocates the arrays. However, this example is to show only the use of arrays in PRO*C. You should always allocate and deallocate the arrays or structures dynamically to ensure that sufficient memory exists. Also, use the `FOR :batch_size` clause when you perform SQL operations to specify explicitly the number of rows to be processed.

4.3.2 LINKING WITH THE SHARED LIBRARY

The PRO*C compiler version 2.1 and above (Oracle7 release 7.2 and above) added support for C++ as well as a client-shared library. In previous releases of PRO*C, all PRO*C executables were statically linked and subsequently resulted in executables of 2–3 MB in size on the average. In PRO*C releases 2.1 and above, a client-shared library, `libclntsh.so`, was provided so that PRO*C applications could be linked with this shared library. Linking with the shared library significantly reduces the size of PRO*C executables from 2–3 MB to 50–100 KB on the average. This results not only in massive disk storage savings but also saves compile time and execution time. Since the executables are linked with the shared library, only functions that are called are paged-in, which increases the performance of the executable since the memory requirements drop significantly. Also, because it is now a shared library, multiple users running PRO*C and OCI applications will benefit since the shared library enables multiple users to share the memory pages without having to separately reload the library in memory. In order to make use of the client-shared library, relink your PRO*C and OCI programs with the `libclntsh.so` library (`-lclntsh`) or `libclntsh.sl` on HP.

On UNIX platforms, use the `proc.mk` make file provided in `$ORACLE_HOME/precomp/demo/proc` directory for Oracle 7.3. For Oracle 8.0, use the `demo_proc.mk` file provided in `$ORACLE_HOME/precomp/demo/proc` to build the sample PRO*C programs or as a template make file for your application. PRO*C 8.0 and PRO*C 8i link with the client-shared library by default. For Oracle 7.2, the `proc.mk` file is located in `$ORACLE_HOME/proc/demo`. Set the environment variable `ORA_CLIENT_LIB` to shared before compiling. For example,

```
myhost> setenv ORA_CLIENT_LIB shared   (C-Shell)
myhost> make -f proc.mk EXE=mysample \   *** 7.2/7.3
        OBJS=mysample.o

myhost> make -f demo_proc.mk build   \   *** 8.0
        EXE=mysample OBJS=mysample.o
```

4.3.3 PRO*C COMPILE OPTIONS

There are several PRO*C compiler options that can increase cursor management performance. The `HOLD_CURSOR` compile option, when set to `YES`, causes Oracle to hold the cursor handle that is associated with the SQL statement in the cursor cache. This helps eliminate reparsing should the SQL statement be executed again later in the PRO*C application. This can increase performance by eliminating the need to reparse the SQL statement since the cursor can be reused. `HOLD_CURSOR` set to `NO` causes the cursor handle to be reused following the execution of the SQL statement and the closing of the cursor. Set `HOLD_CURSOR=YES` to increase the cursor cache hit ratio.

The `RELEASE_CURSOR` compile option, when set to `YES`, releases the private SQL area associated with the SQL statement cursor. This means that the parsed statement for the

SQL statement is removed. If the SQL statement is reexecuted later, the SQL statement must be parsed again, and a private SQL area must be allocated. When RELEASE _CURSOR=NO, the cursor handle and the private SQL area are not reused unless the number of open cursors exceeds MAXOPENCURSORS. Set RELEASE_CURSOR=NO and HOLD _CURSOR=YES to increase the cursor cache hit ratio. Set the MAXOPENCURSORS compile option to the maximum number of cursors used in your application. When setting MAX-OPENCURSORS, allow for recursive SQL cursors.

In PRO*C 8, you can increase the performance of the object cache by using the PRO*C compiler DURATION option to specify the duration of pinned objects in the object cache. The default value for DURATION is TRANSACTION which causes the object to be implicitly unpinned upon transaction completion. You can set DURATION=SESSION in order to allow the object to be unpinned following termination of the connection. Setting DURATION=SESSION can improve object cache performance if subsequent transactions need access to the same objects already pinned in the object cache.

PRO*C 8*i* provides the ability to reduce network round trips to the database server by prefetching rows of a cursor. The PREFETCH PRO*C compiler option allows you to specify the number of rows to be prefetched. The default value for prefetching is 1, and the maximum number of rows which can be prefetched is 65,535. Prefetching is primarily useful for cursors which do not perform array processing or fetch rows in batches. However, prefetching can also be used in conjunction with cursors which fetch in batches (i.e., array processing). For example, if your cursor fetches in batches of 100 rows, and the prefetch compiler option is set to 500, then after 500 rows have been fetched by the program, another database round trip will occur in order to fetch the next set of 500 rows.

4.3.4 PARALLEL PROCESSING USING PRO*C

It is important that you subdivide the tasks in your PRO*C application, allowing them to be parallelized. You can do this by using the fork() and exec() calls to invoke multiple PRO*C applications, or preferably by using the new threads feature provided with PRO*C 2.2/Oracle 7.3. Using the threads feature can help you parallelize your application by creating several threads. For example, you may have several inserter threads that insert data into different tables. You may also have multiple deleter or updater threads.

The new threads option allows a high degree of parallelism by establishing separate contexts via the EXEC SQL CONTEXT ALLOCATE statement, and each thread may use a different context to perform SQL operations. Refer to the section on threads programming in the *Pro*C/C++ Precompiler Programmer's Guide* for more information on the use of threads within PRO*C. Using threads can increase the performance of your PRO*C application significantly by processing SQL statements simultaneously via lightweight threads. Using threads is more efficient and elegant than the fork() and exec() technique that is often used to create multiple processes. Remember that when a fork() is issued from a PRO*C application following an established connection, the child process will not be able to make use of the connection. Although the connection to Oracle is treated as a file descriptor (socket), and fork() duplicates all open file descriptors, the Process ID (PID) of the process that establishes the connection is also used to manage the connection. Therefore, after the fork() and exec(), you may get errors such as ORA-1012 (not logged on) when SQL statements are issued from the child process. If you intend to use `fork()` and `exec()` within your PRO*C program, the preferred method is to issue the `fork()` and `exec()` before any connection is established, and then establish separate connections in each process (parent and child).

4.3.5 OBJECT CACHE

PRO*C 8 provides an area of client-side memory used to interface to the database objects known as the object cache. The two object interfaces, associative and navigational, are used to manipulate transient copies of the objects and persistent objects, respectively. Objects allocated via the `EXEC SQL ALLOCATE` statement are transient copies of persistent objects in the Oracle database. Once fetched into the object cache, updates can be made to the transient copies but require explicit SQL statements to make the changes persistent to the database. You can use the `EXEC SQL FREE` statement to free an object from the object cache. You can also use the `EXEC SQL CACHE FREE ALL` to free the entire object cache memory. The associative interface is typically used when accessing a large collection of objects or objects that are not referencable, or performing update or insert operations that apply to a set of objects. The navigational interface is generally used when accessing a small set of objects consisting of explicit costly join predicates or performing many small changes to distinct objects. In the navigational interface, the `EXEC SQL OBJECT FLUSH` statement flushes the persistent changes to the database.

Oracle8 provides two `init.ora` parameters that control the optimal size of the object cache. The `init.ora` parameters `object_cache_max_size_percent` and `object_cache_optimal_size` specify the maximum size of the object cache and the size that the object cache will be reduced to when it exceeds the maximum size, respectively. The `object_cache_max_size_percent` specifies the maximum size of the object cache as the allowed percentage of growth beyond the optimal size. When the size of the object cache exceeds the maximum size, it is reduced to the size of `object_cache_optimal_size`.

4.3.6 DML RETURNING

Oracle8*i* provides a feature known as `DML RETURNING` which allows a value to be returned as part of a DML statement (insert, update, or delete). The `DML RETURNING` feature essentially allows two SQL statements to be combined in one, thereby reducing server round trips. For example, an application typically inserts an empty LOB locator in the database, and then subsequently selects it back out in order to operate on the LOB locator. Using the `DML RETURNING` feature allows you to combine the `INSERT` and `SELECT` into a single statement as follows:

```
INSERT INTO mylobtab VALUES (:in_locator)
       RETURNING lob_col
       INTO :out_locator
```

The DML RETURNING feature can also be useful for returning the REF of an object that is being inserted or updated. The DML RETURNING feature can also be used to return the values of other columns without having to use a separate SELECT cursor. The DML RETURNING feature can help increase performance by reducing the number of SQL calls, server round trips, and cursors.

4.4   THE MAKE FILE

When you develop applications, always use make files to compile and link code. Do not use manual compile scripts to produce executables. This is especially true of Oracle PRO*C applications. Oracle often provides new make files with new releases that incorporate new functionality. Therefore, if you use manual compile scripts, code that you compiled under a previous release may not link properly under a new release of the Oracle products. If you are developing PRO*C applications, use the sample make files provided by Oracle (proc.mk or demo_proc.mk) to compile and link your application. Make files provide a tremendous amount of functionality by checking and resolving dependencies and reporting errors caused by dependency violation. Make sure you check your make files into your version control system so that you know which make file is needed to build certain applications.

4.5   SQL PROCESSING

There are many phases which an SQL statement undergoes before actual execution. It is essential that you understand these different phases of SQL processing. The understanding of these different phases will help you optimize the SQL statements in your application. The SQL processing phases are as follows.

❑ Parse
❑ Syntactic
❑ Semantic
❑ View processing
❑ Subquery processing
❑ Predicate pushing
❑ Constant folding
❑ Optimization
❑ Query Execution Plan (QEP) generation
❑ Query Execution Plan (QEP) execution

In the parse phase, the SQL statement is parsed and a shared cursor is built (if one does not already exist). The syntactic phase ensures that the SQL statement which was submitted is valid in terms of syntax; for example, if the SQL statement misspelled the FROM keyword. Semantic checking ensures that the SQL is semantically correct, such as ensuring that the columns which are being selected actually exist. Semantic checking also ensures that the user has the proper security privileges to access the objects being referenced. View processing unnests the view definition for SQL statements that reference views. The view processing phase also attempts to merge the view with the referencing query. Subquery processing attempts subquery transformations, such as converting a correlated subquery into a regular join. The predicate pushing phase pushes predicates, or filters, down into the view query block. The following query illustrates predicate pushing.

```
Query:
====================================================================
select  ai.invoice_id,ai.invoice_num,ai.amount_paid,ai.project_id,
        ah.hold_date,ah.postable_flag
FROM    ap_invoices ai,
        ap_holds_v ah
WHERE   ai.invoice_id = ah.invoice_id(+) and
        ai.invoice_num = :b1 and
        ah.line_location_id = :b2
```

The format of the execution plan output is as follows: operation followed by the Cost=<c>,<cardinality>,bytes=<b>. The value of c refers to the cost of the operation. The value for the estimated or computed cardinality appears after the cost value. The value for bytes (b) reports the number of bytes expected to be returned. For example, the line TABLE ACCESS BY INDEX ROWID AP_HOLDS_ALL Cost=3,1 bytes=47 means that the table AP_HOLDS_ALL is being accessed via index rowid, and that the cost of this operation is 3. The estimated cardinality of this operation is 1, and the number of estimated bytes being fetched for this operation is 47.

In the following example, the filter [ah.line_location_id = :b2] is pushed inside the query block of the AP_HOLDS_V view. This allows the index on LINE_LOCATION_ID (AP_HOLDS_N2) to be utilized despite that the view AP_HOLDS_V is not mergable. In this case, predicate pushing allowed the optimizer to utilize the index on LINE_LOCATION_ID, which reduces the answer set for the view AP_HOLDS_V. If the predicate was not pushed into the view query block, the answer set would be much larger and the predicate [ah.line_location_id = :b2] would be applied as a normal outer query block filter rather than as an indexed filter.

The constant folding phase folds constant expressions into a single constant to avoid reevaluation. For example, if a query contained an expression such as [col = (3*5.5) + 8], the expression ((3*5.5) + 8) would be folded into a single constant (24.5). This avoids having to recompute the expression for each row.

```
Execution Plan:
---------------
---------------

SELECT STATEMENT      Cost=21,1   bytes=63 ,
  NESTED LOOPS      Cost=21,1   bytes=63 ,
    TABLE ACCESS BY INDEX ROWID AP_INVOICES_ALL   Cost=2,1   bytes=26 ,
      INDEX RANGE SCAN AP_INVOICES_N6 Cost=1,1   bytes= ,
    VIEW AP_HOLDS_V Cost=,18   bytes=666 ,
      NESTED LOOPS OUTER  Cost=19,18   bytes=5886 ,
        NESTED LOOPS OUTER  Cost=19,1   bytes=322 ,
          NESTED LOOPS OUTER  Cost=18,1   bytes=313 ,
            NESTED LOOPS OUTER  Cost=17,1   bytes=304 ,
              MERGE JOIN OUTER  Cost=16,1   bytes=296 ,
                MERGE JOIN CARTESIAN  Cost=15,1   bytes=271 ,
                  NESTED LOOPS OUTER  Cost=13,1   bytes=236 ,
                    NESTED LOOPS OUTER  Cost=13,1   bytes=231 ,
                      NESTED LOOPS OUTER  Cost=12,1   bytes=221 ,
                        NESTED LOOPS OUTER  Cost=11,1   bytes=211 ,
                          NESTED LOOPS OUTER  Cost=11,1   bytes=206 ,
                            NESTED LOOPS   Cost=11,1   bytes=201 ,
                              NESTED LOOPS OUTER   Cost=10,1   bytes=192 ,
                                NESTED LOOPS OUTER   Cost=8,1   bytes=157 ,
                                  NESTED LOOPS OUTER   Cost=7,1   bytes=117 ,
                                    NESTED LOOPS OUTER   Cost=5,1   bytes=82 ,
                                      TABLE ACCESS BY INDEX ROWID AP_HOLDS_ALL   Cost=3,1   bytes=47 ,
                                        INDEX RANGE SCAN AP_HOLDS_N2   Cost=1,1   bytes= ,
                                      INDEX RANGE SCAN FND_LOOKUP_VALUES_U1 Cost=2,1   bytes=35 ,
                                    INDEX RANGE SCAN FND_LOOKUP_VALUES_U1 Cost=2,1   bytes=35 ,
                                  TABLE ACCESS BY INDEX ROWID AP_HOLD_CODES Cost=1,65   bytes=2600 ,
                                    INDEX UNIQUE SCAN AP_HOLD_CODES_U1 Cost=,65   bytes= ,
                                INDEX RANGE SCAN FND_LOOKUP_VALUES_U1 Cost=2,1   bytes=35 ,
```

```
TABLE ACCESS BY INDEX ROWID AP_INVOICES_ALL Cost=1,117 bytes=1053 ,
    INDEX UNIQUE SCAN AP_INVOICES_U1 Cost=,117 bytes= ,
  INDEX UNIQUE SCAN FND_USER_U1 Cost=,1086 bytes=5430 ,
  INDEX UNIQUE SCAN FND_USER_U1 Cost=,1086 bytes=5430 ,
  TABLE ACCESS BY INDEX ROWID RCV_TRANSACTIONS Cost=1,5604 bytes=56040 ,
    INDEX UNIQUE SCAN RCV_TRANSACTIONS_U1 Cost=,5604 bytes= ,
  TABLE ACCESS BY INDEX ROWID RCV_SHIPMENT_LINES Cost=1,2789 bytes=27890 ,
    INDEX UNIQUE SCAN RCV_SHIPMENT_LINES_U1 Cost=,2789 bytes= ,
  INDEX UNIQUE SCAN RCV_SHIPMENT_HEADERS_U1 Cost=,2612 bytes=13060 ,
SORT JOIN Cost=15,1 bytes=35 ,
  INDEX RANGE SCAN FND_LOOKUP_VALUES_U1 Cost=2,1 bytes=35 ,
SORT JOIN Cost=14,1 bytes=25 ,
  TABLE ACCESS BY INDEX ROWID PO_LINE_LOCATIONS_ALL Cost=1,1 bytes=25 ,
    INDEX UNIQUE SCAN PO_LINE_LOCATIONS_U1 Cost=,1 bytes= ,
  TABLE ACCESS BY INDEX ROWID PO_RELEASES_ALL Cost=1,5 bytes=40 ,
    INDEX UNIQUE SCAN PO_RELEASES_U1 Cost=,5 bytes= ,
  TABLE ACCESS BY INDEX ROWID PO_HEADERS_ALL Cost=1,67 bytes=603 ,
    INDEX UNIQUE SCAN PO_HEADERS_U1 Cost=,67 bytes= ,
  TABLE ACCESS BY INDEX ROWID PO_LINES_ALL Cost=1,82 bytes=738 ,
    INDEX UNIQUE SCAN PO_LINES_U1 Cost=,82 bytes= ,
VIEW HR_LOCATIONS Cost=,1833 bytes=9165 ,
UNION-ALL PARTITION Cost=, bytes= ,
NESTED LOOPS Cost=3,1 bytes=229 ,
  TABLE ACCESS BY INDEX ROWID HR_LOCATIONS_ALL_TL Cost=2,1 bytes=54 ,
    INDEX UNIQUE SCAN HR_LOCATIONS_ALL_TL_PK Cost=1,1 bytes= ,
  TABLE ACCESS BY INDEX ROWID HR_LOCATIONS_ALL Cost=1,1 bytes=175 ,
    INDEX UNIQUE SCAN HR_LOCATIONS_PK Cost=,1 bytes= ,
  TABLE ACCESS BY INDEX ROWID HZ_LOCATIONS Cost=2,1 bytes=109 ,
    INDEX UNIQUE SCAN HZ_LOCATIONS_PK Cost=1,2 bytes= ,
```

The optimization and QEP generation phases generate the optimal plan based on the optimizer environment. In the case of the RBO, the fixed rankings will be used to generate the execution plan. The CBO will use the cost model to generate the most efficient plan. Once a plan is generated, it becomes part of the shared cursor. For this reason, the optimizer environment is part of the criteria used for determining whether a cursor can be shared. After the execution plan is generated, the SQL statement is executed.

4.5.1 PARSING PHASES

The parsing phase of SQL processing includes many different subprocessing phases, such as the syntactical and semantical verification of the SQL statement, type checking, execution plan generation, and the building of a shared cursor. In general, parsing is mostly CPU intensive rather than I/O intensive. Shared cursors help reduce the impact of parsing by allowing a cursor to be shared across sessions. Hence, the first session to execute the cursor (assuming that the cursor does not exist in the shared cursor cache-shared pool) incurs the expense of parsing the SQL statement. Subsequent sessions simply refer to that shared cursor, and execute the SQL statement. This avoids having to reparse the SQL statement and incur the cost of plan generation.

Although it is most commonly understood that Oracle has two main modes of parsing known as the *hard parse*, and the *soft parse*, there are actually three modes of parsing: hard parse, *medium parse*, and soft parse.

4.5.1.1 Hard Parse

The hard parse mode occurs if parsing is done during the first execution of the SQL statement and if the objects being accessed by the SQL statement have not been previously referenced. For example, consider the following SQL statement (query).

```
select order_id, line_id, order_date, order_amount
from   orders o,
       order_lines l
where o.order_id = l.order_id and
      o.order_id = :b1
```

In the case of a hard parse, it is assumed that the above query is being executed for the first time and that the tables orders and order_lines have not been accessed by another SQL statement. This means that the objects do not exist in the data dictionary cache. Hence, the hard parse needs to read the object definitions from the data dictionary (i.e., system tablespace) and populate the dictionary cache with the relevant information, such as the table definitions, column metadata, object statistics if the Cost Based Optimizer is being used, synonym information if the references to these tables are via synonyms, and so on. Once the data dictionary has been populated with the necessary metadata, a shared cursor is built for the SQL statement. A hard parse is the most expensive mode of parsing as there is much more work involved than in the medium or soft parse case.

4.5.1.2 Medium Parse

A medium parse assumes that the SQL statement is being executed for the first time, as is the case with the hard parse mode; however, the necessary data dictionary information is already available in the data dictionary cache. Therefore, no physical disk I/O is needed to populate the data dictionary cache. In the medium parse phase, the SQL statement has not been previously executed and the SQL statement does not currently exist in the shared cursor cache. In addition, the medium parse phase eliminates the data dictionary cache population phase assuming that another SQL statement has already referenced those same objects. For example, consider the following two queries.

Query 1:

```
select order_id, line_id, order_date, order_amount
from   orders o,
       order_lines l
where o.order_id = l.order_id and
      o.order_id = :b1
```

Query 2:

```
select order_date, order_amount, ship_date, order_status
from   orders o,
       order_lines l
where o.order_id = l.order_id and
      o.order_status in ('OPEN','SHIPPING','HOLD')
```

Query 1 represents the hard parse phase, meaning that Query 1 is being executed for the first time, and no other queries have referenced the objects ORDERS and ORDER_LINES. If Query 2 is executed after Query 1 in serial, then Query 2 will incur a medium parse because Query 2 has not been previously executed; however, the objects ORDERS and ORDER_LINES have been previously referenced via Query 1. Therefore, the data dictionary cache will contain the metadata information for the ORDERS and ORDER_LINES objects. In general, when most people refer to a hard parse, they are actually referring to a medium parse since it is very likely that the metadata information will be present in the data dictionary cache even though the SQL statement is being parsed for the first time. A medium parse is also expensive because it includes the time to build a shared cursor and generate an execution plan. If the application is repeatedly performing hard or medium parses, the application will not scale and the application will induce the classic symptom of latch contention. It is important that you ensure that the application has a good degree of cursor sharing so that the number of parses is minimal compared to the number of executions.

4.5.1.3   Soft Parse

The soft parse phase is the least expensive mode of parsing compared to the hard parse and medium parse. In the soft parse mode, a client submits an SQL statement for execution or executes a cursor, and then Oracle performs a cache lookup in the shared cursor cache to determine if a shared cursor exists for that particular SQL statement. If a shared cursor already exists, then the shared cursor is used for execution. This is known as a soft parse, meaning that the parse phase did not actually perform a complete parse. Instead, a shared cursor for that particular SQL statement was found in the shared cursor cache, and that shared cursor can be used for execution without having to build a new cursor. Applications that have a good degree of cursor reuse, a relatively fixed number of SQL statements which are repeatedly executed, and that use bind variables will experience mostly soft parses. Although soft parses are inexpensive relative to hard or medium parses, soft parses can also be expensive when a large number of concurrent users are soft-parsing the same SQL statements. Many applications, such as Web-based applications, construct a cursor cache for the cursors of the application so that the cursors are effectively opened once, and repeatedly executed throughout the application. This avoids even the soft parse phase and improves application scalability and performance. PL/SQL provides an optimization whereby statically defined cursors executed within a PL/SQL block are soft parsed only once.

Applications which repeatedly soft parse the same set of SQL statements may limit the overall scalability since soft parses largely consume processor cycles. In addition, a soft parse also requires that a library cache pin be obtained on the cursor when binding a shared cursor to the executing session. A soft parse also includes some initialization steps for the cursor and the mutable frame.

4.5.2   VIEW MERGING

View merging is a component of the optimizer which unnests the body of a view and merges it with the body of the parent query. This results in the ability to consider more access paths than would be available if the view had not been mergable. For example, consider a query which joins table A with view V. Assume further that view V consists of a join between tables B and C. View merging would allow permutations such as A→B→C, B→A→C, C→A→B, etc. Without view merging, the only join permutation would be A→V[B→C] or A→V[C→B] assuming that A is the driving table. Hence, the lack of view merging limits the execution plan in terms of considering additional join permutations and possible driving tables. In this case, the driving table would either be the non-mergable view V or table A. However, it may be more efficient to drive from table B or table C in terms of overall selectivity and cost. View merging currently happens before plan generation.

The view processing layer probes inside the view query block and attempts to merge the view query block with the main query block. However, there are several restrictions which prevent certain types of views from being merged. In addition to view merging, complex view merging (_complex_view_merging=TRUE) relaxes the restrictions of view merging and enhances view merging. Complex view merging also imposes restrictions on which types of views can be merged. Complex view merging is a feature that was added in Oracle8 release 8.0.4. It has been further expanded in 8.1.6 to merge other types of complex views.

Currently, the optimizer merges the following types of views.

1. Simple views
   – select
   – project
   – join
2. Simple aggregate views
3. Outer-joins to single-table views

The optimizer currently (8.1.6) does not merge the following types of views.

1. Complex views containing aggregate functions (AVG, SUM, etc.)
2. Views containing set operators (UNION, UNION ALL, MINUS)
3. Outer-joins to complex views (nonsingle table views)
4. Outer-joins to views containing PL/SQL functions with constants
5. Outer-joins to a view containing a correlated subquery
6. Left-hand side outer-joined complex views

There are additional restrictions with view merging, such as views containing ROWNUM operators or views with hierarchical operators (CONNECT BY).

View merging is extremely critical because the lack of view merging can lead to a full-table scan on a large transaction table. Consider the following query, which outer-joins to a complex view in order to check if a project accounting entry exists for an accounts payable Web-expense.

```
SELECT START_EXPENSE_DATE,
       AERL.PROJECT_ID,AERL.TASK_ID,
       PATASK.TASK_NUMBER,EXPENDITURE_TYPE
FROM   PA_TASKS_EXPEND_V PATASK,
       AP_EXPENSE_REPORT_LINES AERL
WHERE AERL.REPORT_HEADER_ID = :b3  AND
      AERL.TASK_ID = PATASK.TASK_ID(+) AND
      AERL.PROJECT_ID = PATASK.PROJECT_ID(+)
ORDER BY DISTRIBUTION_LINE_NUMBER
```

The explain plan for this query is as follows.

```
SELECT STATEMENT   Cost=3176,1  bytes=131 ,
  SORT ORDER BY  Cost=3176,1  bytes=131 ,
    NESTED LOOPS OUTER  Cost=3170,1  bytes=131 ,
      TABLE ACCESS BY INDEX ROWID AP_EXPENSE_REPORT_LINES_ALL Cost=7,1
        bytes=91 ,
        INDEX RANGE SCAN AP_EXPENSE_REPORT_LINES_N1 Cost=3,1  bytes= ,
      VIEW  PA_TASKS_EXPEND_V Cost=,681315  bytes=27252600 ,
        TABLE ACCESS FULL PA_TASKS Cost=3163,681315  bytes=27252600 ,
```

As can be seen from the execution plan, the view PA_TASKS_EXPEND_V is not merged, and hence a full-table scan on PA_TASKS is performed. The cost of the full-table scan of PA_TASKS is 3,163, which indicates that the table is fairly large.

Currently, views which contain set operators, such as UNION, UNION ALL, MINUS, and INTERSECT, are not merged. A new feature in Oracle8*i* 8.1.6, known as the push join union view, allows join predicates from the referencing query to be pushed inside the view. The following query illustrates the lack of view merging due to the join to a view which contains a UNION operator.

```
select p.project_id,p.name ,p.segment1
from pa_projects_all p,
    (select pcdl.project_id
    from PA_COST_DISTRIBUTION_LINES_ALL pcdl
    UNION
    select pei.project_id
    from pa_expenditure_items_all pei) pv
where (p.project_id = pv.project_id) and
    (p.segment1 = :b1)
```

The explain plan for the above query is as follows.

```
SELECT STATEMENT   Cost=323,61  bytes=2745 ,
NESTED LOOPS    Cost=323,61  bytes=2745 ,
 TABLE ACCESS BY INDEX ROWID PA_PROJECTS_ALL Cost=2,1  bytes=32 ,
   INDEX UNIQUE SCAN PA_PROJECTS_U2 Cost=1,2  bytes= ,
 VIEW   Cost=,41917  bytes=544921 ,
   SORT UNIQUE  Cost=321,41917  bytes=149562 ,
     UNION-ALL   Cost=,  bytes= ,
       INDEX FULL SCAN PA_COST_DISTRIBUTION_LINES_N12
         Cost=126,32864  bytes=131456 ,
       TABLE ACCESS FULL PA_EXPENDITURE_ITEMS_ALL Cost=105,9053
         bytes=18106 ,
```

The execution plan illustrates that in-line view is not merged due to the UNION operator. In this particular case, the query equi-joins to the view in the base query; however, the set operator prevents the view from being merged. Hence, a full-table scan on PA_EXPENDITURE_ITEMS_ALL is performed.

Views which contain PL/SQL functions invoked via constants as opposed to column name arguments are not merged when they are part of an outer join. Outer joins to views containing OR expressions are not merged because Oracle does not currently support outer-joined OR expressions on the same table. Outer joins to views containing correlated sub-queries are also not currently mergable.

In summary, you can determine whether or not a view is being merged via the execution plan. If the execution plan contains a row source with the keyword VIEW followed by the view name, then the view is not being merged. It is important that you understand the fundamentals of view merging if your application makes extensive use of views. If, for example, view merging is not possible for a given view, you may need to optimize the SQL statement to avoid the view or rewrite the view so that it is mergable.

4.6 THE OPTIMIZER

The Oracle server provides two methods of optimization: rule-based and cost-based. The rule-based optimizer (RBO) uses a fixed ranking of access paths to determine the most efficient execution plan. The cost-based optimizer (CBO) uses dictionary statistics on the objects to generate the most efficient execution plan. The CBO considers different plans by examining the possible access paths, and chooses the execution plan with the best cost. The CBO was introduced in Oracle7, and Oracle plans to obsolete the RBO in a future release. Many new database features, such as partitioning and materialized views, work only with the CBO. If your application still uses the RBO, you should develop a project plan to migrate to the CBO.

4.6.1 RULE-BASED OPTIMIZER

The RBO chooses the execution plan of an SQL statement with the lowest rank—the idea being that the lowest ranking execution plan should be faster than a higher ranking execution plan. The rule-based optimizer selects execution plans based on a heuristic ranking. The rule-based approach, as the term suggests, uses rules (or ranks) to determine the optimal execution plan for a SQL statement. Table 4.1 summarizes the different ranks.[1]

The rule-based approach uses the ranks of the access paths listed in Table 4.1 to determine the optimal execution plan for a SQL statement. As can be seen from the table, a full-table scan has the highest rank. This means that Oracle will always consider index scans over full-table scans, even if a full-table scan may be faster than the index scan. To choose rule-based optimization, you can set the `init.ora` parameter `optimizer_mode=RULE`, or use the alter session command to set `optimizer_goal=RULE`. You can also use the RULE hint as part of the query. A discussion on hints will follow later in section 4.6.3.

In contrast with the cost-based optimizer, the RBO does not consider object statistics. Execution plans are determined by order of rank. The RBO takes a "one plan fits all" approach in the sense that data distribution does not effect the plan. The cost-based optimizer may use different execution plans based on the statistics, and therefore you may not always obtain the same execution plan with the cost-based optimizer. The RBO has been traditionally used by mostly OLTP applications such as SAP or Oracle Applications. However, Oracle Applications release 11i has migrated fully to the CBO, and many other application vendors have followed suit. Oracle is planning to obsolete the RBO in a future release. Many of the new database features and enhancements work only with the cost-based optimizer.

---

1. *Oracle8i Designing and Tuning for Performance Manual*, Chapter 4.

TABLE 4.1   Rule-based optimizer access path rank

RANK	ACCESS PATH
1	single row by ROWID
2	single row by cluster join
3	single row by hash cluster key with unique or primary key
4	single row by unique or primary key
5	cluster join
6	hash cluster key
7	indexed cluster key
8	composite key
9	single-column indexes
10	bounded range search on indexed columns
11	unbounded ranges search on indexed columns
12	sort-merge join
13	MAX or MIN of indexed function
14	ORDERBY on indexed columns
15	full-table scan

4.6.2   COST-BASED OPTIMIZER

The cost-based optimizer was introduced in Oracle7 and is an alternative to the rule-based optimizer. The CBO employs an advanced cost model to determine the most efficient plan. The basic premise is that the plan with the lowest cost will result in the best performance. The cost of the plan is determined by object statistics which are stored in the data dictionary. In general, statistics are generated by using the ANALYZE command or the new DBMS_STATS package in Oracle8i. However, for Oracle Applications 11i, you must use the FND_STATS package or the Gather Schema Statistics Concurrent Program to gather statistics. The CBO uses table, index, and column level statistics to determine the selectivity and cardinality of expressions. The CBO also permutes the join orders for the tables in the FROM clause of the query and chooses the join order with the best cost. The RBO uses a fixed ranking, hence it is essential to order the tables in the FROM clause correctly when using the RBO. The CBO eliminates the need to manually order the FROM clause because it uses a cost model to determine the optimal join order.

The CBO attempts to perform the different possible query transformations, and costs each transformation in accordance with the current best plan. The CBO may consider several different plans before choosing the execution plan with the best cost. Figure 4.3 illustrates the high level flow of the CBO.

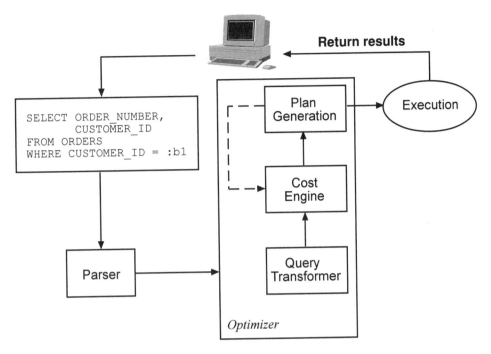

FIGURE 4.3 CBO high-level flow.

In Figure 4.3, the client program submits an SQL statement to the database server. The database server first parses the SQL statement. If the parse completes successfully, the optimizer attempts to transform the query, such as transforming a subquery into a regular join. Following the different transformations, the CBO generates several plans and chooses the plan with the lowest cost. The CBO continues this recursive process until it determines that further plan generation would not improve on the current best plan. This is referred to as the *internal cut-off* point. The CBO also attempts to balance parse time with execution time. For example, it does not make sense to spend several minutes optimizing a query which executes in less than one second.

4.6.2.1 Optimizer Modes

The CBO provides two methods of cost-based optimization: first rows (FIRST_ ROWS) and all rows (ALL_ROWS). The first rows optimization method optimizes for response time. The all rows optimization method optimizes for overall throughput. In order to optimize for response time, first rows attempts to eliminate nonblocking operators such as hash joins or sort-merge joins. If the optimizer mode is set to FIRST_ROWS, then the CBO will tend to favor index probes and nested loops joins. The rationale behind this logic is that index probes and nested loops joins allow rows to be returned to the client immediately without having to block until completion of the SQL statement. An example of a first rows optimization is when the CBO uses an index to perform the ORDER BY rather than sorting the answer set, which is a blocking operator.

The ALL_ROWS optimization method is useful for concurrent requests or SQL statements which should be optimized for the best overall throughput. Oracle Applications 11i uses only the ALL_ROWS optimization method because ALL_ROWS is fully cost-based. The FIRST_ROWS optimization method utilizes a combination of cost and rules to determine the execution plan. Since FIRST_ROWS is not fully cost-based, it is possible to get suboptimal plans in certain cases.

When the init.ora parameter optimizer_mode is set to CHOOSE, Oracle chooses between the CBO and the RBO depending on the presence of statistics. If any one of the tables in an SQL statement contains statistics, and the optimizer mode is set to CHOOSE, Oracle will use the CBO and the ALL_ROWS optimization method. If statistics are not present, then the RBO will be used. In addition, there are certain features which force the use of the CBO, such as partitioned tables or the use of parallel query. For example, if you have some custom code which joins to a partitioned table, the CBO will be used regardless of any RULE hint or optimizer mode settings.

4.6.2.2 Cost-Based Optimizer Architecture

The CBO uses a sophisticated set of costing algorithms to determine the most efficient execution plan. There are several cost components which the CBO uses to determine the cost of an individual operation. The cost components are I/Os, CPU, and network.

The I/O cost determines how many I/Os are needed to source the data. The CBO costs a full-table scan as well as an index probe for the indexes available for access paths. If the cost of the index probe is more expensive than the cost of a full-table scan, then the CBO will choose the full-table scan. When costing full-table scans, the CBO considers multiblock I/Os. For a full-table scan, Oracle is able to read multiple blocks in a single I/O. The init.ora parameter db_file_multiblock_read_count specifies the multiblock I/O factor. For example, if db_file_multiblock_read_count=8, this means that Oracle will read 8 blocks per I/O when performing a full-table scan. A larger value for db_file_multiblock_read_count decreases the cost of a full-table scan. For example, if you increase this parameter from 8 to 32, the cost of a full-table scan is reduced by a factor of 4. Hence, the CBO may use a full-table scan instead of an index as an access method because the cost of the full-table scan is cheaper than the index access due to the high multiblock I/O factor.

The CPU cost is used in conjunction with parallel query. In the case of parallel query, the optimizer will cost a serial plan and compare the cost to a parallel plan. If the serial plan consisted of a full-table scan on a very large table, the cost of a parallel plan will likely be less than the serial plan. The default degree of parallelism is a multiplier of the number of CPUs (cpu_count) and the init.ora parameter parallel_threads_per_cpu. Parallel query should never be used for OLTP or on-line queries. Parallel query is mostly useful for data warehousing or batch queries which perform full-table scans on large tables. Parallel query is also useful for creating large indexes or gathering statistics (DBMS_STATS).

The network cost applies to distributed queries or queries which refer to remote objects via a database link. In such a case, the CBO will determine the optimal driving site for the query. The driving site controls whether Oracle should push the rows from the local database to the remote database, or whether Oracle should pull the rows from the remote site over to the local database. For example, consider the following query:

```
select  c.customer_id,c.customer_name,
        a.street_no,a.street_name,a.city
from    customer c,
        addresses@mydblink a
where   c.customer_id = a.customer_id and
        c.customer_id = :b1
```

In the above example, the optimizer could either take the single customer record and push the row over to the remote site and join to the address table based on the customer id, or pull the address rows over to the local database and join to the customer table. The latter approach would obviously be less efficient because more rows would be processed. In such a case, the optimizer would determine that the driving site for this query should be the local database (where the customer table resides).

4.6.2.3 CBO Terminology

Terms such as cardinality, cost, and selectivity are an integral part of the CBO architecture. Therefore, it is important that you understand these terms and their respective meanings.

4.6.2.3.1 Cost. Cost is the metric that the CBO assigns to each operation such as access methods, joins, and sorts. For each index access or table access, the CBO will assign a cost to this operation which is largely based on the number of I/Os needed for a particular access method. Full-table scan costs are based on the multiblock I/O factor, which is specified via the `init.ora` parameter `db_file_multiblock_read_count`.

4.6.2.3.2 Cardinality. Cardinality refers to the number of rows in a table. The estimated or computed cardinality refers to the number of rows which the CBO expects to return for a given operation. For example, for a specific index access, the computed cardinality may be reported as 100, meaning that the optimizer estimates that 100 rows will be returned after probing on this index. The cardinality is a critical component of the execution plan as it affects the access methods and join methods. The access method refers to the method used to access the data, such as a full-table scan access method or an index access method. The join methods refer to the type of join that the optimizer selected, such as a hash join, nested loops join, or sort merge join. Join methods are discussed in more detail in the Join Methods section. If the cardinality is very large (millions of rows or hundreds of thousands of rows), the CBO may choose to perform a full-table scan as the access method or use a hash join for the join method.

The estimated or computed cardinality can be expressed as follows.

$$Ec = (\text{selectivity}) \times (\text{number of rows})$$

4.6.2.3.3 Selectivity. Selectivity is a value between 0 and 1 which represents the proportion or ratio of rows to be returned for a table based on a filter or join expression.

Selectivity can be expressed as a percentage or ratio of the number of rows divided by the total number of rows. For example, a 50 percent selectivity is also equivalent to a selectivity of 0.5, which means that 50 percent of the rows will be selected.

$$Se = \frac{\text{number of rows returned}}{\text{total number of rows}}$$

If literal values are used in SQL statements, the CBO is able to compare the literal value against the high value and low value for that column using the column statistics from the data dictionary. However, for bind variables, the CBO uses default selectivity estimates since the value of the bind is not examined at plan generation time. For equality expressions of the form [col = :b1], the default selectivity is 1/NDV. For range predicates such as <= or >=, the default selectivity is 5 percent. Predicates involving the BETWEEN operator are converted to the equivalent <= and >=.

When analyzing an execution plan for a particular query, it is important to generate the execution plan based on the original SQL statement. For example, if the SQL statement uses bind variables, you should evaluate the execution plan with the bind variables, and not with the substituted literal values. The optimizer uses different selectivity and cardinality estimates for queries which use bind variables than it uses for queries which use literal scalar values.

The selectivity of an AND expression is defined as:

$$((\text{selectivity of expression 1}) \times (\text{selectivity of expression 2}))$$

The selectivity of an OR expression is defined as:

$$((\text{selectivity of expression 1} + \text{selectivity of expression 2})$$
$$- (\text{selectivity of expression 1} \times \text{selectivity of expression 2}))$$

For example, consider the following query.

```
select ei.expenditure_item_id,ei.task_id,
    ei.project_rate_type
from  pa_expenditure_items_all ei
where ei.task_id between :b1 and :b2
```

```
Execution Plan
-----------------------------------------------------------------

SELECT STATEMENT   Cost=33193,58453  bytes=1636684 ,
FILTER   Cost=, bytes= ,
 TABLE ACCESS BY INDEX ROWID PA_EXPENDITURE_ITEMS_ALL
   Cost=33193,58453  bytes=1636684 ,
   INDEX RANGE SCAN PA_EXPENDITURE_ITEMS_N2 Cost=127,58453  bytes= ,
```

Since the query contains a BETWEEN operator and bind variables, the default selectivity of 5 percent is used. The cost of the index probe on PA_EXPENDITURE_ITEMS_N2 is 127, and the computed cardinality is 58,453. The number of distinct values for the column TASK_ID on PA_EXPENDITURE_ITEMS_ALL is 148,225. The total number of rows in the PA_EXPENDITURE_ITEMS_ALL table is 23,380,831. Using the default selectivity of 5 percent, the computed cardinality is as follows:

$$Ec = (0.05) \times (0.05) \times (23380831) = 58452.0775$$

The BETWEEN operator results in two range predicates when expanded (one for <= and one for >=). Thus, the estimated cardinality is $(0.05) \times (0.05) \times$ (number of rows). The execution plan for the above query reports the estimated cardinality is 58,453, which matches the calculation above using the default selectivity.

4.6.2.3.4 Transitivity. Transitivity is a relational algebraic property whereby an equality expression is implicitly inferred. For example, if A=B and B=C, then A=C via transitivity. The CBO uses transitivity on filters to promote indexes on the transitive table. Transitivity opens up additional access paths and possibly more efficient join orders. Transitivity is used only by the CBO, and not by the RBO. The following is an example of join transitivity.

```
SELECT CWIAS.BEGIN_DATE, CWIAS.END_DATE
FROM WF_ITEM_ACTIVITY_STATUSES CWIAS,
     WF_ITEMS WI
where CWIAS.ACTIVITY_STATUS = 'DEFERRED'
      and CWIAS.BEGIN_DATE <= SYSDATE
      and CWIAS.ITEM_TYPE = WI.ITEM_TYPE
      and CWIAS.ITEM_KEY = WI.ITEM_KEY
      and CWIAS.ITEM_TYPE = :itemtype
      and CWIAS.ITEM_KEY = :itemkey
      and CWIAS.PROCESS_ACTIVITY = :actid
```

```
Execution Plan
----------------------------------------------------------------
SELECT STATEMENT   Cost=4,1  bytes=66 ,
  NESTED LOOPS   Cost=4,1  bytes=66 ,
    INDEX UNIQUE SCAN WF_ITEMS_PK Cost=2,1  bytes=18 ,
    TABLE ACCESS BY INDEX ROWID WF_ITEM_ACTIVITY_STATUSES Cost=2,1
      bytes=48 ,
      INDEX UNIQUE SCAN WF_ITEM_ACTIVITY_STATUSES_PK Cost=1,1  bytes= ,
```

In the example above, the query specifies all of the columns of the unique index on the table WF_ITEM_ACTIVITY_STATUSES. There are filters for ITEM_TYPE, ITEM_KEY, and PROCESS_ACTIVITY. There is a join between WF_ITEM_ACTIVITY_STATUSES and WF_ITEMS based on ITEM_TYPE and ITEM_KEY. Since the query specifies equality filters via bind variables for ITEM_TYPE and ITEM_KEY, transitivity is applied, and the filters are propagated to the WF_ITEMS table. This allows the optimizer to start with the WF_ITEMS table and utilize the unique index on (ITEM_TYPE, ITEM_KEY).

4.6.2.4　Join Methods

The CBO provides four join methods which can be used to join tables.

❏ Merge join Cartesian
❏ Hash join
❏ Sort merge join
❏ Nested loops join

A merge join Cartesian is used when two tables are joined, and no explicit join expression exists between these two tables. In certain cases, the CBO may consider a Cartesian join when one of the tables is relatively small, such as a lookup table or a table which returns a few rows after applying local filters. Utilizing a Cartesian join may open up new access paths and may reduce the answer set early on rather than later in the join graph.

A hash join is one of the new join methods that was added in Oracle7 release 7.3. Hash joins are used only with the CBO. In a hash join, the smaller table is scanned, and an in-memory hash table is built using this smaller table. The hash table is then used to probe the larger table in order to identify the matching tuples. This process of the hash join is known as the build and probe cycle. Hash joins are extremely efficient for large table joins and are typically chosen by the CBO when the computed cardinality of one side of the join input is large. The cost of a hash join is influenced by the init.ora parameter hash_area_size. The init.ora parameter hash_area_size specifies the maximum amount of process memory that can be used for a hash join. A larger value for hash_area_size reduces the cost of an in-memory hash join. Hash joins use memory and temporary segments (if needed) to perform the join, whereas nested loops joins, for example, do not.

In a sort merge join, if joining tables A and B, table A and B are both individually sorted, and the results of each table sort are then merged into a final answer set in which nonmatching tuples are discarded. Sort merge joins can be expensive when both tables are large and the local filters on each table are not selective. When costing a sort merge join, the optimizer costs the sort for each table as well as for the final merge phase.

The nested loops join method is probably the most popular join method. In a nested loops join, for each outer row of the driving table, the inner table is scanned for a corresponding match. Nested loops joins are efficient when the outer table filters are very selective and only a small percentage of the inner table is visited. If the outer query returns a large number of rows or the criteria in the outer query causes a large portion of the inner table to be scanned, then the nested loops join method may not be optimal.

The following query demonstrates the different join methods.

Hash Join:

```
select oeh.order_number,oeh.header_id,oel.line_id
from   oe_order_headers_all oeh,
         oe_order_lines_all oel
  where  oeh.header_id=oel.header_id
```

```
Execution Plan
-----------------------------------------------------------------
SELECT STATEMENT   Cost=160,14835  bytes=267030 ,
HASH JOIN   Cost=160,14835  bytes=267030 ,
 TABLE ACCESS FULL OE_ORDER_HEADERS_ALL Cost=82,8952  bytes=89520 ,
 INDEX FULL SCAN OE_ORDER_LINES_N8 Cost=60,14833  bytes=118664 ,
```

The CBO chose a hash join because there are no selective filters in this query. The query only specifies a join condition which means that all the lines for all the orders will be retrieved. In such a case, the optimizer determined that a hash join with a full-table scan on the OE_ORDER_HEADERS_ALL table would be more efficient.

Nested Loops Join:

For the same query, if we forced a nested loops join via the USE_NL hint, the cost is much higher than that of the plan for the hash join. The cost of the plan with the nested loops join is 9,034 versus a cost of 160 for the hash join plan.

```
Execution Plan
-----------------------------------------------------------------
SELECT STATEMENT   Cost=9034,14835  bytes=267030 ,
NESTED LOOPS   Cost=9034,14835  bytes=267030 ,
 TABLE ACCESS FULL OE_ORDER_HEADERS_ALL Cost=82,8952  bytes=89520 ,
 INDEX RANGE SCAN OE_ORDER_LINES_N8 Cost=1,14833  bytes=118664 ,
```

Again, if we forced a sort merge join via the USE_MERGE hint, the cost is much less than that of the plan for the nested loops join. The cost of the plan with the nested loops join is 9,034 versus a cost of 170 for the merge join plan. However, the cost of the hash join (cost=160) is still less than that of the plan which uses the sort merge join method (cost=170). Given that a full-table scan is being performed on OE_ORDER_HEADERS_ALL, a hash join is more efficient than a nested loops join. The cost differential between the hash join plan and the nested loops join plan is quite significant. This is mostly due to the fact that a nested loops join becomes very expensive when the number of rows scanned is very large. In this particular case, the computed cardinality reported in the execution plan for the OE_ORDER_HEADERS_ALL table scan is 8,952. Hence, using a nested loops join to join 8,952 rows with the OE_ORDER_LINES table will be slower than performing a hash join.

Sort Merge Join:

```
Execution Plan
-----------------------------------------------------------------
SELECT STATEMENT   Cost=170,14835  bytes=267030 ,
MERGE JOIN   Cost=170,14835  bytes=267030 ,
 INDEX FULL SCAN OE_ORDER_LINES_N8 Cost=60,14833  bytes=118664 ,
 SORT JOIN  Cost=110,8952  bytes=89520 ,
   TABLE ACCESS FULL OE_ORDER_HEADERS_ALL Cost=82,8952  bytes=89520 ,
```

Cartesian Join:

Removing the explicit join expression from the above query, a Cartesian join will occur between the order headers table and the order lines table.

```
select oeh.order_number,oeh.header_id,oel.line_id
from oe_order_headers_all oeh,
     oe_order_lines_all oel
```

```
Execution Plan
-----------------------------------------------------------------
SELECT STATEMENT   Cost=420826,132785016  bytes=1858990224 ,
MERGE JOIN CARTESIAN  Cost=420826,132785016  bytes=1858990224 ,
  TABLE ACCESS FULL OE_ORDER_HEADERS_ALL Cost=82,8952  bytes=89520 ,
  SORT JOIN  Cost=420744,14833  bytes=59332 ,
    INDEX FULL SCAN OE_ORDER_LINES_U1 Cost=47,14833  bytes=59332 ,
```

The CBO will cost the different join methods and choose the join method with the least cost. The selection of join methods also typically depends on the access methods, such as whether an index or a full-table scan access method is used.

4.6.2.5 Join Permutations

In order to determine the most efficient join order, the CBO generates the different join permutations and chooses the join permutation with the best cost. Permutations are pruned if they exceed the current best permutation. The CBO uses a heuristic pruning approach which attempts to limit the amount of permutations that the optimizer will consider. For example, if a query joins 3 tables, the number of possible join permutations is 3! = 6. For a query which joins 7 tables, the number of possible join permutations increases to 5,040. For a query which consists of 15 table joins, the number of possible join permutations is 1,307,674,368,000. Hence, it is crucial that the optimizer cap the number of permutations to a reasonable limit in order to maintain a reasonable parse time. The maximum number of permutations that the optimizer will consider is controlled via the `init.ora` parameter `optimizer_max_permutations`. It is recommended that you set `optimizer_max_permutations` to a value less than that of the default for several reasons. First, such a high setting may result in large parse times. Second, values less than 80,000 cause the CBO to consider multiple starting tables. This results in the CBO's ability to generate a better plan for queries which consist of a large number of table joins.

The CBO uses a depth-first pruning of alternates to limit the amount of permutations considered. In addition, the CBO ranks single row tables higher than nonsingle row tables. A single row table is defined as a table which returns only one row through local filters. The following query is an example of a single row table.

```
select  rc.customer_number,rc.customer_name,
        ra.address1,ra.address2,ra.city, ra.state
from    ra_customers rc,
        ra_addresses_all ra
where   rc.customer_id = ra.customer_id and
        rc.customer_id = :b1
```

```
SELECT STATEMENT    Cost=4,3  bytes=678 ,
NESTED LOOPS    Cost=4,3  bytes=678 ,
  TABLE ACCESS BY INDEX ROWID RA_CUSTOMERS Cost=3,1  bytes=57 ,
    INDEX UNIQUE SCAN RA_CUSTOMERS_U1 Cost=2,1  bytes= ,
  TABLE ACCESS BY INDEX ROWID RA_ADDRESSES_ALL Cost=1,3  bytes=507 ,
    INDEX RANGE SCAN RA_ADDRESSES_N3 Cost=,3  bytes= ,
```

In this example, RA_CUSTOMERS is a single row table because the filter (`rc.customer_id = :b1`) uniquely identifies a customer via the unique index on RA_CUSTOMERS (RA_CUSTOMERS_U1). The execution plan also confirms that the estimated cardinality is 1 for the index row source RA_CUSTOMERS_U1. Since RA_CUSTOMERS is a single row table, it precedes RA_ADDRESSES in the join order.

4.6.2.6 Statistics

The CBO uses object statistics including table, index, and column statistics to generate the most optimal execution plan. Hence, it is crucial that statistics be gathered on all the objects and that the statistics be reflective of the data set. For example, the presence of statistics which are several months old may result in suboptimal plans due to the fact that the plans being generated do not reflect the current data distribution.

4.6.2.6.1 Table Statistics. The CBO uses table statistics to determine the selectivity and cardinality of filters and joins. Statistics such as the number of rows, number of blocks, and average row length allow the optimizer to compute the cardinality and choose the optimal join order. The number of blocks statistic is used to cost a full-table scan. Table statistics are available via the dictionary view DBA_TABLES. The table statistics are stored in the tab$ dictionary table.

The following is a sample query which can be used to query table statistics via the view DBA_TABLES.

```
select table_name,num_rows,blocks,avg_row_len,
       to_char(last_analyzed,'MM/DD/YYYY HH24:MI:SS')
LAST_ANALYZED
from dba_tables
where table_name in ('AP_INVOICES_ALL','AP_HOLDS_ALL') and
      owner='AP'
```

TABLE_NAME	NUM_ROWS	BLOCKS	AVG_ROW_LEN	LAST_ANALYZED
AP_HOLDS_ALL	1,817,472	37,273	158	01/15/2000 22:46:46
AP_INVOICES_ALL	3,507,324	138,579	294	01/15/2000 22:47:22

In the above output, the AP_HOLDS_TABLE has 1,817,472 rows (invoices on hold) and consumes 37,273 blocks on disk. If the db_file_multiblock_read_count=8, the cost of a full-table scan on AP_HOLDS_ALL is approximately 4,659.

You can also query DBA_TABLES to determine the last time that statistics were gathered on a particular table.

4.6.2.6.2 Column Statistics. Column statistics are an essential part of the CBO's cost estimation. Statistics such as the number of distinct keys, number of nulls, density, high values, and low values are used to determine the selectivity of filters and expressions involving columns. Column statistics are stored in the data dictionary tables col$ and hist_head$. The dictionary view DBA_TAB_COLUMNS can be used to report the column statistics for tables.

Consider the following set of table statistics for the tables PA_PROJECTS_ALL and PA_TASKS.

```
TABLE_NAME        NUM_ROWS    BLOCKS   AVG_ROW_LEN  LAST_ANALYZED
---------------   --------    ------   -----------  -------------------
PA_PROJECTS_ALL    41,236        935       350       02/10/2000 14:10:03
PA_TASKS          425,799      6,805       254       02/10/2000 11:54:50
```

The following query can be used to query the column statistics for a particular table or set of tables.

```
select table_name,column_name,num_distinct,num_nulls,density
from dba_tab_columns
where table_name in ('PA_TASKS','PA_PROJECTS_ALL') and
      column_name in ('PROJECT_ID','TOP_TASK_ID') and
          owner='PA'
order by column_name
```

```
TABLE_NAME        COLUMN_NAME    NUM_DISTINCT   NUM_NULLS     DENSITY
---------------   -----------    ------------   ---------   -----------
PA_PROJECTS_ALL   PROJECT_ID         41236           0      0.000024251
PA_TASKS          PROJECT_ID         41236           0      0.000024251
PA_TASKS          TOP_TASK_ID        86494           0      0.000011561
```

Given the above statistics, consider the following query.

```
select p.project_id,p.name,p.segment1,t.task_id,t.task_name
from  pa_projects_all p,
      pa_tasks t
where p.project_id = t.project_id and
      t.top_task_id = :b1
```

```
Execution Plan
-------------------------------------------------------------------
SELECT STATEMENT   Cost=8,5  bytes=320 ,
NESTED LOOPS   Cost=8,5  bytes=320 ,
  TABLE ACCESS BY INDEX ROWID PA_TASKS Cost=3,5  bytes=135 ,
    INDEX RANGE SCAN PA_TASKS_N7 Cost=1,5  bytes= ,
  TABLE ACCESS BY INDEX ROWID PA_PROJECTS_ALL Cost=1,41236
      bytes=1525732 ,
    INDEX UNIQUE SCAN PA_PROJECTS_U1 Cost=,41236  bytes= ,
```

In this case, the optimizer uses the column statistics on the TOP_TASK_ID column to determine the selectivity of the predicate [t.top_task_id = :b1]. The number of distinct values for TOP_TASK_ID is 86,494. The selectivity of this filter is (1/NDV) = (1/86494) = 0.000011561. The computed cardinality for the table is Ec = (selectivity) × (number of rows) = (0.000011561) × (425,799) = 4.9 (rounded to 5). The estimated cardinality is reported as 5 in the execution plan along with the cost of 3 for the table access via the index PA_TASKS_N7.

By analyzing the execution plan for a given query in conjunction with the column statistics, you can identify whether or not a particular query is selective. For example, if a particular custom code query is not selective or is very expensive, you may need to investigate the possibilities of optimizing the SQL statement.

4.6.2.6.3 Index Statistics. The CBO uses index statistics to compute the selectivity and cost of an index access path for a particular index. This allows the CBO to eliminate nonselective indexes and choose the most selective index (if possible). If the index access path for a particular table is more expensive than a full-table scan, the optimizer will choose a full-table scan as the access method. The main statistics for an index are the number of distinct keys, number of nulls, the depth of the index, and the clustering factor. The clustering factor is the degree of colocation of index leaf blocks to data blocks. The clustering factor is considered by the CBO when an index access path cannot alone satisfy the table filters. In this case, the table access via rowid from the index will be costed. The clustering factor is used to determine the cost of this extra table-rowid access. If the clustering factor is high, then the optimizer may choose to use another access method in order to minimize the cost of too many random I/Os. The clustering factor of an index should not be confused with clustered tables.

Index statistics are stored in the data dictionary table ind$ and are available via the dictionary view DBA_INDEXES. The following query can be used to report index statistics for a given table.

```
select index_name "NAME",num_rows,distinct_keys "DISTINCT",
       leaf_blocks,clustering_factor "CF",
          avg_leaf_blocks_per_key "ALFBPKEY" ,
       to_char(last_analyzed,'MM/DD/YYYY HH24:MI:SS') LAST_ANALYZED
from dba_indexes
where table_name='PA_EXPENDITURE_ITEMS_ALL' and
       owner='PA'
order by index_name
```

NAME	NUM_ROWS	DISTINCT	BLEVEL	LEAF_BLOCKS	CF	ALFBPKEY
PA_EXPENDITURE_ITEMS_N1	23,266,118	5724125	2	38405	8715453	1
PA_EXPENDITURE_ITEMS_N2	23,410,728	211765	2	27629	7347996	1
PA_EXPENDITURE_ITEMS_N3	23,360,506	2	2	19955	358927	9977
PA_EXPENDITURE_ITEMS_N4	23,375,317	3	2	20216	574132	6738
PA_EXPENDITURE_ITEMS_N5	1,713,442	1695778	2	2125	1054836	1
PA_EXPENDITURE_ITEMS_N6	1,101,342	952598	2	1232	782136	1
PA_EXPENDITURE_ITEMS_N7	23,266,887	146826	2	30275	4434131	1
PA_EXPENDITURE_ITEMS_N8	23,359,462	4102441	2	38698	8500753	1
PA_EXPENDITURE_ITEMS_U1	23,390,902	23390901	2	24452	6289844	1

The `NUM_ROWS` statistic reports the number of rows in the index (not the table). The `DISTINCT` column reports the number of distinct values for that index, which is used to compute the selectivity for the index. The `BLEVEL` column statistics represents the depth of the index. A larger index depth translates into more I/Os during index traversal. This increases the cost of the index access since cost is proportional to the number of I/Os needed to source the data. The clustering factor statistic (`CF`) depicts the degree of colocation of index leaf blocks to data blocks. The clustering factor is included in the cost of an index access when a table access via index `rowid` is required.

4.6.2.6.4 Histograms. Histograms are another level of column statistics which record the low value and high value for a column. When statistics are gathered on columns, a default histogram is built with endpoints 0 and 1. This represents the default uniform distribution. For columns which are skewed, a histogram is needed in order to properly estimate the selectivity of expressions on this column. If only the default histogram exists, a uniform distribution is assumed. This can adversely affect execution plans for indexed columns with data skew. There are two types of histograms: frequency-based and height-based. A frequency-based histogram creates a bucket for each distinct value. A height-based histogram groups repeatable values into buckets whereby the number of buckets is less than the number of distinct values.

Histograms are used to record column data skew which allows the optimizer to better estimate the selectivity for filters. For example, consider the following column data distribution.

```
COLUMN DISTRIBUTION:

ACCRUAL_POSTED_FLAG  COUNT(*)
-------------------- ----------
    N                   1,225
    Y                  28,198
```

Now consider the following query.

```
select aid.invoice_id,aid.ACCRUAL_POSTED_FLAG,
       aid.accounting_date,aid.vat_code
from ap_invoice_distributions_all aid
where ACCRUAL_POSTED_FLAG='N'
```

Since there are only two distinct values for `ACCRUAL_POSTED_FLAG` (Y and N), the default selectivity is 50 percent. Without a histogram, the optimizer would not utilize the index on `ACCRUAL_POSTED_FLAG` on the `AP_INVOICE_DISTRIBUTIONS_ALL` table since the index probe would result in fetching 50 percent of the rows. However, given the above distribution, only 1,225 rows have the value of N, while 28,198 rows have the value of Y for `ACCRUAL_POSTED_FLAG`. Given this skew, a histogram is needed in order for the optimizer to compute the correct selectivity.

The following is the execution plan for the above query without the histogram on ACCRUAL_POSTED_FLAG. The estimated cardinality is 14,712 which reflects 50 percent of the rows of the table AP_INVOICE_DISTRIBUTIONS_ALL because there are only two distinct values. Since only the default histogram is present, the optimizer assumes a uniform distribution. With a selectivity of 50 percent, the optimizer chooses a full-table scan as the optimal access method since an index probe would be too costly to fetch half of the table data.

```
Execution Plan
----------------------------------------------------------------------
SELECT STATEMENT   Cost=190,14712  bytes=250104 ,
  TABLE ACCESS FULL AP_INVOICE_DISTRIBUTIONS_ALL Cost=190,14712
      bytes=250104 ,
```

However, given that there is data skew, and the rows containing N for the value of ACCRUAL_POSTED_FLAG actually represent 4 percent of the rows (1,225/29,423), after creating the histogram using FND_STATS.GATHER_COLUMN_STATS, the execution plan now uses the index on ACCRUAL_POSTED_FLAG (AP_INVOICE_DISTRIBUTIONS_N8).

```
Execution Plan
----------------------------------------------------------------------
SELECT STATEMENT   Cost=48,1212  bytes=23028 ,
  TABLE ACCESS BY INDEX ROWID AP_INVOICE_DISTRIBUTIONS_ALL Cost=48,1212
      bytes=23028 ,
    INDEX RANGE SCAN AP_INVOICE_DISTRIBUTIONS_N8 Cost=3,1212  bytes= ,
```

Histograms can be generated by either using the ANALYZE command or using the new Oracle8*i* DBMS_STATS PL/SQL package. The following example illustrates the use of DBMS_STATS to generate a histogram on the column POSTED_FLAG.

```
SQL> execute DBMS_STATS.GATHER_TABLE_STATS ('PRODS','ORDERS',
        METHOD_OPT => 'FOR COLUMNS SIZE 10 ORDER_STATUS');
```

Column histogram information is available via the data dictionary view DBA_HISTOGRAMS or USER_HISTOGRAMS. The following is sample query which lists the endpoints for the buckets of the histogram on the column TRANSLATED_FLAG on the GL_BALANCES table.

```
select endpoint_number,endpoint_value
from dba_histograms
where table_name='GL_BALANCES' and
      column_name='TRANSLATED_FLAG' and
      owner='GL'
```

```
ENDPOINT_NUMBER  ENDPOINT_VALUE
---------------  --------------
            243  4.2577E+35
            282  4.6211E+35
              6  4.0500E+35
```

In this example, there are three buckets for the histogram on the TRANSLATED_FLAG column. Since the default endpoints of 0 and 1 do not appear, this confirms that a user-requested histogram exists on the TRANSLATED_FLAG column. The endpoint values are normalized. The optimizer uses these endpoint ranges to compute the selectivity by determining the repeatability of the value, or the popularity of a certain value.

4.6.2.6.5 Gathering Statistics. Gathering statistics can be done via the ANALYZE command or the DBMS_STATS package. If you are running Oracle8*i*, I recommend that you utilize the new DBMS_STATS package, which is much more efficient than the ANALYZE command. In addition, the DBMS_STATS package allows statistics gathering to be parallelized. The DBMS_STATS package provides the ability to gather statistics in parallel. The DBMS_STATS package provides the gather_table_stats procedure which allows a degree of parallelization to be specified in order to parallelize the gathering of the statistics. The following example illustrates the use of the DBMS_STATS package to generate table statistics.

```
dbms_stats.gather_table_stats (ownname=>'PRODO',       *** Schema name
                tabname=>'ORDERS',                      *** Table name
                estimate_percent=>10,                   *** Sample Size (%)
                method_opt=>'FOR ALL COLUMNS',  *** Columns
                degree=> 10,                            *** Parallelism
                cascade=>TRUE);                         *** Cascade to indexes
```

You can also gather statistics in parallel at the schema level by using the DBMS_STATS.gather_schema_stats procedure. The gather_schema_stats procedure also accepts a degree of parallelism. The following example illustrates the use of gather_schema_stats and specifies a degree of parallelism of 10.

```
dbms_stats.gather_schema_stats (ownname=>'PRODO',      *** Schema name
                estimate_percent=>10,                   *** Sample Size (%)
                method_opt=>'FOR ALL COLUMNS',  *** Columns
                degree=> 10,                            *** Parallelism
                cascade=>TRUE);                         *** Cascade to indexes
```

The ability to generate statistics in parallel significantly reduces the time needed to refresh object statistics. Maintaining current object statistics helps improve the optimizer's ability to choose the most optimal execution plans. Index statistics can also be generated during the index creation by specifying the COMPUTE STATISTICS clause in the CREATE INDEX or ALTER INDEX command. The DBMS_STATS package also allows statistics to be exported by using the procedure `DBMS_STATS.export_table_stats`. The statistics can then be imported using the `DBMS_STATS.import_table_stats` procedure. This is extremely useful because it allows object statistics to be copied to other databases where the distribution is identical (i.e., standby database) or very similar. The ability to export and import statistics can be useful for plan analysis. For example, you can import the production database statistics into the development database, and use these statistics to review the execution plans.

The `DBMS_STATS` package provides the following procedures.

- ❏ `CREATE_STAT_TABLE`
- ❏ `DELETE_COLUMN_STATS`
- ❏ `DELETE_DATABASE_STATS`
- ❏ `DELETE_INDEX_STATS`
- ❏ `DELETE_SCHEMA_STATS`
- ❏ `DELETE_TABLE_STATS`
- ❏ `DROP_STAT_TABLE`
- ❏ `EXPORT_COLUMN_STATS`
- ❏ `EXPORT_DATABASE_STATS`
- ❏ `EXPORT_INDEX_STATS`
- ❏ `EXPORT_SCHEMA_STATS`
- ❏ `EXPORT_TABLE_STATS`
- ❏ `GATHER_DATABASE_STATS`
- ❏ `GATHER_INDEX_STATS`
- ❏ `GATHER_SCHEMA_STATS`
- ❏ `GATHER_TABLE_STATS`
- ❏ `GET_COLUMN_STATS`
- ❏ `GET_INDEX_STATS`
- ❏ `GET_TABLE_STATS`
- ❏ `IMPORT_COLUMN_STATS`
- ❏ `IMPORT_DATABASE_STATS`
- ❏ `IMPORT_INDEX_STATS`
- ❏ `IMPORT_SCHEMA_STATS`
- ❏ `IMPORT_TABLE_STATS`

For more information on the `DBMS_STATS` package, refer to *Oracle8i Supplied PL/SQL Packages Reference* manual.

4.6.2.7 Oracle8*i* Optimizer Enhancements

Oracle8*i* greatly enhanced the cost-based optimizer by providing many new features which improve execution plans, resulting in improved execution times. The `optimizer_features_enable` init.ora parameter controls which release and which features are used by the CBO. Setting `optimizer_features_enable=8.1.6` enables the new

Oracle8*i* release 2 CBO features, such as extended view merging and the pushing of join predicates inside UNION ALL views.

In 8.1.6, the CBO improves plan generation by considering more tables as the starting table. In order to enable the new multiple starting table optimization, set the init.ora parameter optimizer_max_permutations to a value less than the default of 80,000. For example, setting optimizer_max_permutations=79000 enables the new multiple starting table optimization.

In Oracle8*i*, complex view merging is disabled by default. In Oracle8, complex view merging was enabled if optimizer_features_enable=8.0.4, and complex view merging could be disabled by setting the init.ora parameter complex_view _merging=FALSE. In Oracle8*i*, complex view merging can be enabled by setting the init.ora parameter _complex_view_merging=TRUE. This parameter enables the complex view merging feature, which allows certain types of complex views, such as views with aggregates or column concatenations, to be merged. This parameter is disabled by default, so it must be explicitly set. For more details on view merging, refer to section 4.5.2 on view merging.

Another optimizer feature which was introduced in Oracle8 release 8.0.4, and further expanded in Oracle8*i*, is known as the push join predicate feature. The push join predicate feature allows the optimizer to push join predicates inside nonmergable views. This helps eliminate full-table scans against the adjoining table of a nonmergable view. Pushing the join predicate allows the optimizer to promote an index on the table inside the view and utilize a nested loops join to the outer referencing table. In Oracle8*i*, the push join predicate feature is disabled by default, so it must be explicitly enabled via the init.ora parameter _push_join_predicate=TRUE. The following is an example of the push join predicate feature.

```
Select ai.invoice_num, ai.invoice_id
from   ap_invoices_all ai,
       ap_holds_v ahv
where ai.invoice_id = ahv.invoice_id(+) and
      ai.invoice_num = :b1
```

```
Execution Plan
-------------------------------------------------------------------
SELECT STATEMENT   Cost=5948,125  bytes=11625 ,
  HASH JOIN OUTER  Cost=5948,125  bytes=11625 ,
    TABLE ACCESS BY INDEX ROWID AP_INVOICES_ALL Cost=109,125  bytes=10000 ,
      INDEX RANGE SCAN AP_INVOICES_N6 Cost=3,125  bytes= ,
    VIEW AP_HOLDS_V   Cost=5817,1867714  bytes=24280282 ,
      NESTED LOOPS OUTER  Cost=5817,1867714  bytes=76576274 ,
        TABLE ACCESS FULL AP_HOLDS_ALL Cost=5817,1867714  bytes=50428278 ,
        INDEX UNIQUE SCAN AP_HOLD_CODES_U1 Cost=,111  bytes=1554 ,
```

```
SQL> alter session set "_push_join_predicate"=TRUE;
```

Execution Plan

```
SELECT STATEMENT   Cost=3,2  bytes=44 ,
  NESTED LOOPS OUTER  Cost=3,2  bytes=44 ,
    TABLE ACCESS BY INDEX ROWID AP_INVOICES_ALL Cost=2,1  bytes=17 ,
      INDEX RANGE SCAN AP_INVOICES_N6 Cost=1,1  bytes= ,
    VIEW AP_HOLDS_V PUSHED PREDICATE   Cost=,9792  bytes=48960 ,
      NESTED LOOPS OUTER  Cost=2,2  bytes=68 ,
        TABLE ACCESS BY INDEX ROWID AP_HOLDS_ALL Cost=2,2  bytes=36 ,
          INDEX RANGE SCAN AP_HOLDS_N1 Cost=1,2  bytes= ,
        INDEX UNIQUE SCAN AP_HOLD_CODES_U1 Cost=,61  bytes=976 ,
```

In the example above, without the push join predicate feature, a full-table scan is performed on the AP_HOLDS_ALL table since the query outer-joins to a complex view, which results in the inability to merge the view. Since the AP_HOLDS_ALL table is a rather large table (Cost=5817), the performance of this query will be poor. By enabling the push join predicate feature, the optimizer pushes the join predicate, in this case the invoice_id join predicate. This allows the optimizer to utilize an index on AP_HOLDS_ALL, and improves the performance of the query by orders of magnitude since invoice_id is selective on the AP_HOLDS_ALL table.

In 8.1.6, the CBO was enhanced to allow the optimizer to utilize dictionary statistics for columns that are involved in no-op expressions such as [col + 0] and [col || '']. This improves the ability of the CBO to apply the dictionary column statistics rather than the internal default statistics for complex expressions. This enhancement improves the execution plans for queries which contain expressions of the form [col + 0], [col || ''], to_char(col), and nvl(col,:b1). This also helps reduce the parse time of queries since the optimizer is able to apply the actual column statistics rather than internal defaults which may result in initial expensive plans, forcing the optimizer to consider additional permutations. This feature can be enabled by setting the init.ora parameter _use_column _stats_for_function=TRUE. Consider the following query.

```
select *
from GL_BALANCES GBAL,
     GL_CODE_COMBINATIONS GCC
where GBAL.code_combination_id+0 = GCC.code_combination_id and
      GBAL.code_combination_id >= :b1 and
      GBAL.TRANSLATED_FLAG ||'' = 'N'
```

Execution Plan

```
SELECT STATEMENT   Cost=29012,5402667  bytes=1707242772 ,
  HASH JOIN    Cost=29012,5402667  bytes=1707242772 ,
    TABLE ACCESS BY INDEX ROWID GL_BALANCES Cost=26198,4213  bytes=383383 ,
      INDEX RANGE SCAN GL_BALANCES_N1 Cost=497,4213  bytes= ,
    TABLE ACCESS FULL GL_CODE_COMBINATIONS Cost=1009,128238  bytes=28853550 ,
```

In this example, the dictionary column statistics for `GBAL.code_combination_id` and `GBAL.translated_flag` are not applied due to the presence of the expressions `+0` and `||''`, respectively. Therefore, the CBO applies the internal default statistics and estimates the computed cardinality for the GL_BALANCES table to be 4,213 rows. The CBO chooses a hash join method between the two tables GL_BALANCES and GL_CODE_COMBINATIONS and performs a full-table scan on the GL_CODE_COMBINATIONS table, which consists of 128,238 rows. If the `use_column_statistics_for_function` feature is enabled, then the resulting execution plan is much more efficient as well as more accurate in terms of cardinality.

```
SQL> alter session set "_use_column_stats_for_function"=TRUE;
```

```
Execution Plan
-----------------------------------------------------------------------
SELECT STATEMENT    Cost=27287,1089  bytes=344124 ,
 NESTED LOOPS    Cost=27287,1089  bytes=344124 ,
   TABLE ACCESS BY INDEX ROWID GL_BALANCES Cost=26198,1089  bytes=99099 ,
    INDEX RANGE SCAN GL_BALANCES_N1 Cost=497,1089  bytes= ,
   TABLE ACCESS BY INDEX ROWID GL_CODE_COMBINATIONS Cost=1,128238
      bytes=28853550 ,
    INDEX UNIQUE SCAN GL_CODE_COMBINATIONS_U1 Cost=,128238  bytes= ,
```

The execution plan now shows an estimated cardinality of 1,089 for the GL_BALANCES table which is almost one-fourth of the previous cardinality estimate. The CBO subsequently chose a nested loops join between GL_BALANCES and GL_CODE_COMBINATIONS and used the unique index on CODE_COMBINATION_ID on the GL_CODE_COMBINATIONS table as opposed to the previous execution plan, which used a full-table scan access method. This feature is extremely useful for those applications which previously used the RBO and migrated to the CBO. In the RBO, many developers would typically use the `+0` or `||''` to disable nonselective indexes or to force a particular join order. If the application was previously based entirely on the RBO, there may be a large amount of SQL statements which use this classic RBO technique to control the access methods. This feature reduces the impact of the migration to the CBO by not requiring that the `+0` and `||''` constructs be manually removed from all of the SQL statements.

Another CBO feature, which was added in 8.1.6, allows the optimizer to push join predicates inside UNION ALL views. Since views containing set operators such as the UNION or UNION ALL operator are not mergable, this feature allows the optimizer to push join predicates inside nonmergable views which contain the UNION ALL set operator. This improves query execution performance for queries joining to views which contain the UNION ALL operator. The push join union view feature can be enabled by setting the `init.ora` parameter `_push_join_union_view=TRUE`. The following example illustrates the use of push join union view feature.

```
select p.project_id,p.name ,p.segment1
from pa_projects_all p,
    (select pcdl.project_id
     from PA_COST_DISTRIBUTION_LINES_ALL pcdl
     UNION
     select pei.project_id
     from pa_expenditure_items_all pei) pv
where (p.project_id = pv.project_id) and
      (p.segment1 = :b1)
```

```
Execution Plan
-------------------------------------------------------------------------------
SELECT STATEMENT   Cost=323,61  bytes=2745 ,
  NESTED LOOPS    Cost=323,61  bytes=2745 ,
    TABLE ACCESS BY INDEX ROWID PA_PROJECTS_ALL Cost=2,1  bytes=32 ,
      INDEX UNIQUE SCAN PA_PROJECTS_U2 Cost=1,1  bytes= ,
    VIEW   Cost=,41917  bytes=544921 ,
      SORT UNIQUE   Cost=321,41917  bytes=149562 ,
        UNION-ALL   Cost=,  bytes= ,
          INDEX FULL SCAN PA_COST_DISTRIBUTION_LINES_N12 Cost=126,32864
              bytes=131456 ,
        TABLE ACCESS FULL PA_EXPENDITURE_ITEMS_ALL Cost=105,9053  bytes=18106 ,
```

In the above example, the in-line view is nonmergable due to the presence of the UNION operator; hence, a full-table scan is performed on the adjoining table PA_EXPENDITURE_ITEMS_ALL. However, if the view can be rewritten to use the UNION ALL operator as opposed to the UNION operator, then the push join union view feature can be used to promote an index as follows.

```
select p.project_id,p.name ,p.segment1
from pa_projects_all p,
    (select pcdl.project_id
     from PA_COST_DISTRIBUTION_LINES_ALL pcdl
     UNION ALL
     select pei.project_id
     from pa_expenditure_items_all pei) pv
where (p.project_id = pv.project_id) and
      (p.segment1 = :b1)
```

```
Execution Plan
-------------------------------------------------------------------------------
SELECT STATEMENT   Cost=3,419  bytes=15084 ,
  NESTED LOOPS    Cost=3,419  bytes=15084 ,
    TABLE ACCESS BY INDEX ROWID PA_PROJECTS_ALL Cost=2,1  bytes=32 ,
      INDEX UNIQUE SCAN PA_PROJECTS_U2 Cost=1,1  bytes= ,
    VIEW   Cost=,41917  bytes=167668 ,
      UNION-ALL PARTITION  Cost=,  bytes= ,
        INDEX RANGE SCAN PA_COST_DISTRIBUTION_LINES_N12 Cost=2,115  bytes=460 ,
        INDEX RANGE SCAN PA_EXPENDITURE_ITEMS_N8 Cost=1,906  bytes=1812 ,
```

The execution plan illustrates that the index `PA_EXPENDITURE_ITEMS_N8` which is based on the `PROJECT_ID` column is being used because the push join union view feature is pushing the `project_id` join predicate inside each branch of then `UNION ALL`. If your application consists of views which contain `UNION` operators and you have SQL statements which join to the view, you can utilize this feature to improve the execution plan.

In Oracle8 and Oracle8*i*, the ordered nested loops optimization can be enabled to improve the cost metric for queries which prefer nested loops joins over sort merge joins. In cases where the CBO may conclude that a nested loops join may be more expensive than a sort merge join, such as when the join results in a large answer set, the nested loops join cost can be discounted by the fact that the join input is effectively ordered in the nested loops join case. The ordered nested loops optimization discounts the cost of a nested loops join and index probe when the left side of the join input is being satisfied via an index or sort row source. You can enable this optimization by setting the `init.ora` parameter `_ordered_nested_loop=TRUE`. This optimization is useful for cases where a nested loops join and an index probe is more efficient than a sort merge join and a full-table scan.

4.6.2.8 Extensible Optimizer

Oracle8*i* allows you to extend the optimizer by defining user-defined cost functions and selectivity estimates using the Extensible Optimizer. User-defined cost functions are extremely useful for user-defined PL/SQL functions which are referenced in SQL statements. The CBO uses a default statistic to estimate the selectivity of a filter containing a reference to a PL/SQL function or procedure. The default estimate may not be representative of the actual selectivity of the user-defined function. For example, consider the following query which references a user-defined PL/SQL package.

```
select PERSON_ID, EFFECTIVE_START_DATE
from per_all_people_f PAP
where pap.full_name LIKE :b1
```

The execution plan for the SQL statement is as follows.

```
SELECT STATEMENT   Cost=1410,14566  bytes=2097504 ,
  TABLE ACCESS BY INDEX ROWID PER_ALL_PEOPLE_F Cost=1410,14566
    bytes=2097504 ,
   INDEX RANGE SCAN PER_PEOPLE_F_N54 Cost=22,14566  bytes= ,
```

Now consider a modified version of the query, which uses a PL/SQL function to limit the rows which can be seen.

```
select PERSON_ID, EFFECTIVE_START_DATE
from per_all_people_f PAP
where pap.full_name LIKE :b1 and
    HR_SECURITY.SHOW_RECORD('PER_ALL_PEOPLE_F', PAP.PERSON_ID,
              PAP.PERSON_TYPE_ID, PAP.EMPLOYEE_NUMBER,
              PAP.APPLICANT_NUMBER ) = 'TRUE'
```

The execution plan is as follows.

```
SELECT STATEMENT    Cost=1410,146  bytes=29784 ,
   TABLE ACCESS BY INDEX ROWID PER_ALL_PEOPLE_F Cost=1410,146  bytes=29784 ,
      INDEX RANGE SCAN PER_PEOPLE_F_N54 Cost=22,146  bytes= ,
```

In the first query, the estimated cardinality is 14,566 while the estimated cardinality for the second query is 146. This is 1 percent of the first query. This is the default statistic which the CBO uses to assign selectivity for a user-defined PL/SQL function since it has no real way of knowing the actual selectivity. However, in the original query the optimizer expects that approximately 14,566 rows will be returned while the optimizer expects only 146 rows from the query which references the PL/SQL function. If the function HR_SECURITY.SHOW_RECORD had an actual selectivity of 90 percent, then the CBO estimate may lead to a suboptimal plan in cases where there are numerous table joins. The Extensible Optimizer can be used to register a user-defined cost function or a default selectivity estimate for the package HR_SECURITY. For example, using the ASSOCIATE STATISTICS clause of the Extensible Optimizer, the default selectivity of the HR_SECURITY package can be set to 90 percent.

```
SQL> associate statistics with packages HR_SECURITY DEFAULT SELECTIVITY 90;
```

You can also write a user-defined cost function or a user-defined function to assign the selectivity for a function or procedure. For more information on the use of the Extensible Optimizer, refer to the *Oracle8i Data Cartridge Developer's Guide*.

4.7   CURSOR SHARING

In general, there are two types of cursors: sharable and nonsharable. Nonsharable cursors are cursors that are not stored in the shared cursor cache, which is part of the shared pool. DDL cursors, such as create table, alter table, create index, and alter index are not sharable and are not stored in the shared cursor cache. In some cases, DDL cursors are shared, such as the DDL cursors used by parallel query when creating an index in parallel. DDL cursors are executed as part of the parse call.

Sharable cursors are those cursors which are stored in the shared cursor cache and are available for reuse. For example, a user session may execute the same set of SQL statements which another session executed; hence the user would reuse the cursors as opposed to creating a new set of cursors. The shared cursor model was introduced in Oracle7 in order to facilitate cursor reuse and significantly reduce the memory requirements. Prior to Oracle7, each user that executed a cursor would build a parsed representation of the SQL statement and generate an execution plan. The cursor would be stored in the private process area. For an application with a large number of users, each issuing the same set of SQL statements, scalability would be limited since more private memory is required. In the shared cursor model, the idea is that SQL statements are reusable or shared amongst users of the application. Hence, it is not necessary for each user to build a private instance of a cursor. This increases application scalability by reducing the memory requirements and reducing the cycles associated with SQL parsing and plan generation.

There are several rules for sharing cursors such as the SQL text, optimizer mode, NLS environment, bind variables, and security. In order for a cursor to be shared, application developers must ensure that the SQL statement is exactly the same, including white space and hints. This is especially important if the application uses dynamic SQL to construct the SQL statement. If you are using dynamic SQL, you should use bind variables to ensure that the SQL statement which is constructed is the same across all instances. Generating a different SQL statement with literals in place of bind variables prevents cursor sharing. The optimizer mode is also part of the cursor sharing criteria. For example, running the same SQL statement under the RBO and then switching the optimizer mode to use the CBO for the same SQL statement will result in the inability to share the cursor that is based on the RBO. Since the execution plan is part of the shared cursor, optimizer environments are part of the rules for cursor sharing. The cursor sharing criteria also includes the NLS environment such as the character set, NLS format mask, and the NLS language environment used to build the cursor. Security is also part of the criteria to share cursors. For example, user 1 connects to the PROD1 schema and issues an SQL statement to access the tables in the PROD1 schema. User 2 connects to the PROD2 schema and issues the same exact SQL as user 1; however, the objects are now owned by the PROD2 schema as opposed to the PROD1 schema. Hence, in this case, even though the SQL statement is the same, the referencing objects point to different schemas which will each have a set of privileges.

There were several known bugs in Oracle8*i* release 8.1.5 which prevented cursors from being shared when `SQL_TRACE` or `TIMED_STATISTICS` were enabled. These were fixed in Oracle8*i* release 8.1.6. If you are running release 8.1.5, you should set `sql_trace=FALSE` and `timed_statistics=FALSE` in order to improve cursor sharing.

4.7.1 CHILD CURSOR

The library cache uses an object hierarchy to manage its objects. In terms of cursor objects, there is the concept of a parent cursor and a child cursor. The parent cursor maintains basic information on the SQL statement making up the cursor and the child cursors. The child cursor is used for execution, and statistics such as the number of executions, buffer gets, and disk reads are maintained on a child cursor basis. The same SQL statement may result in several child cursors in the library cache due to changes in the optimizer environment, NLS environment, or bind metadata. Figure 4.4 illustrates the concept of a parent cursor and a child cursor.

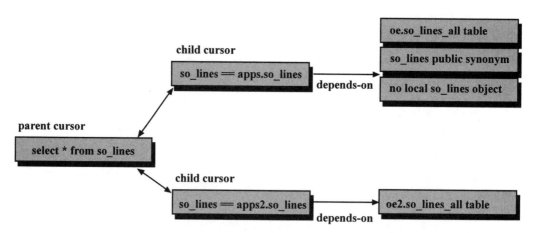

FIGURE 4.4   Parent cursor and child cursor concept.

In Figure 4.4, the parent cursor, which consists of the SQL statement (select *
from so_lines), has two child cursors. The first child points to the so_lines object
in the APPS schema, which then points to a public synonym, which finally expands to the
table SO_LINES_ALL in the OE schema. The second child points to the SO_LINES object
in the APPS2 schema, which points to the SO_LINES_ALL table in the OE2 schema. Even
though the SQL statement is the same, the underlying objects reside in different schemas.

You can determine the number of child cursors for a given SQL statement by querying the V$SQL or V$SQLAREA views. The column CHILD_NUMBER of the V$SQL view
reports the child number for each child cursor, starting with 0. The V$SQLAREA view pro-
vides the VERSION_COUNT column, which can be used to determine the number of child
cursors. The following query reports the hash value and the number of child cursors for the
SQL statements which have five child cursors or more.

```
SQL> select hash_value,count(*)
     from v$sql
     group by hash_value
     having count(*) > 4
     order by 2

HASH_VALUE   COUNT(*)
----------   ----------
 733837468          5
2182723903          5
2406268673          5
3701089004          7
2712563562         10
3493394246         11
 229242746         13
4240583291         15
1717947707        267
```

The hash value 1717947707 consists of 267 child cursors. You can then select the SQL text for this hash value by querying either the V$SQL view or the V$SQLTEXT view. The V$SQL view contains only the first 1,000 characters of the SQL statement. The V$SQLTEXT view contains the full SQL text in chunks of 64 bytes. The following query can be used to extract the full SQL text for the cursor which has 267 child cursors.

```
SQL> select sql_text
     from v$sqltext
     where hash_value=1717947707
     order by piece
```

The SQL statement can then be examined to determine why so many child cursors exist for this SQL statement. It could be due to many factors such as the application's use of bind variables, or optimizer or NLS environment changes in between each execution of the SQL statement. In this particular case, it was determined that the application was changing the NLS environment in between each execution via alter session. Changing the application code to eliminate the alter session statements for the NLS environment reduced the number of child cursors to five.

4.7.2 BIND GRADUATION

Bind graduation is the process of graduating the lengths of the bind variables so as to improve cursor sharing. For example, if you submit an SQL statement which uses a bind variable of type VARCHAR, and the first execution uses a value of "HILL" which will result in a bind length of 4, and the second execution uses a value of "JOHNSON" which will result in a bind length of 7, the bind variable is first graduated to a length of 32 so that all values of the bind variable with length less than or equal to 32 can share the same cursor. This avoids having to build a cursor with a bind length of 4, and another with a bind length of 7. If the length of the value for the VARCHAR bind variable exceeds 32, then the bind variable is then graduated to a value of 64. Bind graduation for VARCHAR bind types occurs in powers of 2 (32, 64, 128, etc.). Bind variables of type NUMBER are always graduated to the maximum length of a number which is 22 bytes.

Since bind graduation builds a new child cursor with the extended bind length, the existing child cursors with the smaller length are invalidated so that the new graduated cursor is used.

4.7.3 BIND METADATA

The view V$SQL_BIND_METADATA can be used to report bind metadata information for a cursor. The bind metadata contains information such as the bind variable name, maximum length, and bind variable data type. The bind metadata information is useful in situations when it is determined that certain SQL statements which use bind variables are not being shared. Examining the bind lengths and the bind data types for the particular cursor can help identify why a cursor is not being shared. Consider the following SQL statement which has two child cursors (VERSION_COUNT = 2 from the V$SQLAREA view).

```
SELECT HZ.PARTY_NUMBER,HZ.PARTY_TYPE
FROM HZ_PARTIES HZ
WHERE HZ.PARTY_ID = :b1  AND
     HZ.PARTY_NAME = :b2
```

The following query reports the bind metadata for the above SQL statement.

```
SQL>  select address,  BIND_NAME, DATATYPE, MAX_LENGTH, POSITION
      from v$sql_bind_metadata
      where address in (select kglhdadr
                        from  sys.x$kglcursor
                        where KGLHDPAR = (select address
                                          from v$sqlarea
                                          where hash_value=2043943952))
order by ADDRESS,POSITION;
```

ADDRESS	BIND_NAME	DATATYPE	MAX_LENGTH	POSITION
D0388FC0	B1	2	22	1
D0388FC0	B2	1	128	2
D03978B8	B1	2	22	1
D03978B8	B2	1	32	2

The above SQL statement shows that two child cursors exist. The SQL statement consists of two bind variables: B1 and B2. The bind variable B1 is of type NUMBER (DATATYPE = 2), and the maximum length is 22 bytes, which reflects the maximum size of an Oracle NUMBER. The bind variable B2 is of type VARCHAR (DATATYPE = 1), and the maximum length for the first child cursor listed is 128 while the second cursor listed has a maximum length of 32. This indicates that bind graduation on the VARCHAR bind variable occurred, which is one of the reasons a second child cursor was created.

By examining the bind metadata for your cursors, you can determine if the bind lengths are increasing, or if the bind datatypes are changing. This information will help you correlate the existence of multiple child cursors for the same SQL statement. The V$SQL_BIND_METADATA view can also be used to ensure that the bind data types match that of the corresponding column types. For example, a SQL statement may consist of the filter [customer_id = :b1], and the bind variable B1 may have been declared as a VARCHAR2 while the database column CUSTOMER_ID is defined as a NUMBER.

4.8   TUNING SQL

The beauty of the SQL language is that the same SQL statement can semantically be represented syntactically in numerous different ways. In other words, the statement can be rewritten in many different ways but still produce the same results. The key to tuning SQL is to maximize on this principal of the SQL language. Increasing the performance of SQL statements is often done by rewriting the SQL statement more efficiently. Understanding the Oracle optimizer and the execution plan can help you tune SQL effectively.

4.8.1   THE EXPLAIN PLAN

I cannot emphasize enough the importance of the execution plan. Explain plans are crucial to tuning SQL. The explain plan lists the sequence of execution steps that the Oracle optimizer will use for a given query. This allows you to observe the execution plan before actually submitting the query. You can use the explain plan to analyze your queries, and tune the query before executing it. I am amazed at how often people submit queries (or other SQL statements) that run for hours and days and never run an explain plan on the query until after the fact. Always run an explain plan on every SQL statement you intend to use in a production application. This accomplishes two goals. First, it verifies that the query is correct by examining it in detail to ensure that the query returns the desired results. Second, it shows the execution plan of the query. If you feel the execution plan is optimal, then this is simply a confirmation. If the explain plan shows a poor execution plan, then you can optimize the SQL statement using the various different SQL tuning techniques in order to improve the execution plan. To use the explain plan utility, you must have select permissions on the tables you are attempting to explain, as well as select and insert permissions on the PLAN_TABLE. You can create the explain plan table by running the $ORACLE_HOME/rdbms/admin/utlxplan.sql script. This creates an explain plan table. The following is an example of an explain plan.

```
SQL> explain plan
     set statement_id = 'call pattern'
     into plan_table
     FOR SELECT *
         from account a,
              branch b,
              teller t
     where (a.branch_id=b.branch_id) AND
           (b.branch_id=t.branch_id);
```

ID	EXPLAIN_PLAN	POSITION
0	SELECT STATEMENT	
1	MERGE JOIN	1
2	SORT JOIN	1
3	NESTED LOOPS	1
4	TABLE ACCESS FULL TELLER	1
5	TABLE ACCESS BY ROWID BRANCH	2
6	INDEX UNIQUE SCAN IBRANCH	1
7	SORT JOIN	2
8	TABLE ACCESS FULL ACCOUNT	1

The execution path for the preceding query is shown in Figure 4.5. The execution plan shows the individual paths of the execution plan that are needed to execute the query. I strongly urge you to become familiar with the explain plan command, if you are not

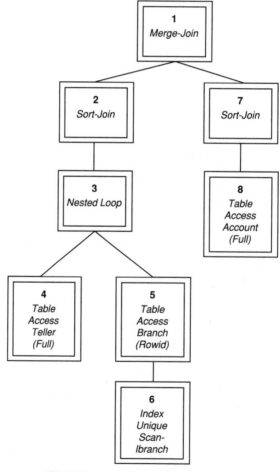

FIGURE 4.5   Query execution path.

already. You should also get into the habit of running explain plans on queries to ensure that the queries are correct and optimally tuned. I have witnessed cases where an explain plan on a query that ran for several hours was used to help tune the query immediately following the explain plan. The explain plan helped to determine the main bottleneck of the query, and the tuning of the query reduced the execution time from hours to seconds. You should not underestimate the power of tuning SQL. Poorly tuned queries that run for hours and days can be made to run in seconds or minutes. Familiarizing yourself with the optimizer execution plan and the explain plan utility will help you analyze and tune SQL statements more effectively.

4.8.2 SQL TRACE

The SQL trace facility provides numerous useful statistics regarding application SQL statements. The SQL trace output can be used to determine the execution plans for a given SQL statement as well as the execution statistics, such as buffer gets, disk reads, number of parses, and elapsed times. You can enable SQL trace via the `alter session` command by setting `sql_trace=true`:

```
SQL> alter session set sql_trace=true;
```

Once an SQL trace file has been generated, you can use the `tkprof` utility to examine the SQL trace file. SQL trace files are placed in the directory specified by the `init.ora` paramater `user_dump_dest`. The `tkprof` utility reads the raw SQL trace file and produces a formatted output file which summarizes the raw SQL trace file. The following is a section from a sample output file from `tkprof` run on a SQL trace file.

```
* * * * * * * * * * * * * * * * * * * * * * * * * * * * * * * * * * * * * * * * * * * * * * * * * * * * * * * *

SELECT 'Y'
FROM
  WF_ITEM_ACTIVITY_STATUSES WIAS,WF_PROCESS_ACTIVITIES WPA   WHERE
    WIAS.ITEM_TYPE = 'OEOL'  AND WIAS.ITEM_KEY = :b1   AND
      WIAS.ACTIVITY_STATUS =
    'NOTIFIED'  AND WPA.ACTIVITY_NAME = 'SHIP_AUTHORIZATION_WAIT'  AND
  WPA.INSTANCE_ID = WIAS.PROCESS_ACTIVITY
```

call	count	cpu	elapsed	disk	query	current	rows
Parse	1	0.01	0.00	0	0	0	0
Execute	200	0.01	0.04	0	0	0	0
Fetch	200	43.07	43.14	0	391040	0	0
total	401	43.09	43.18	0	391040	0	0

```
Misses in library cache during parse: 1
Optimizer goal: CHOOSE
Parsing user id: 52   (APPS)    (recursive depth: 1)

Rows      Row Source Operation
-------   -------------------------------------------------------
      0   NESTED LOOPS
    400   TABLE ACCESS BY INDEX ROWID WF_ITEM_ACTIVITY_STATUSES
4438750   INDEX RANGE SCAN (object id 6656)
      0   TABLE ACCESS BY INDEX ROWID WF_PROCESS_ACTIVITIES
    400   INDEX UNIQUE SCAN (object id 253408)


Rows      Execution Plan
-------   -------------------------------------------------------
      0   SELECT STATEMENT    GOAL: CHOOSE
      0    NESTED LOOPS
    400     TABLE ACCESS    GOAL: ANALYZED (BY INDEX ROWID) OF
                'WF_ITEM_ACTIVITY_STATUSES'
4438750      INDEX   GOAL: ANALYZED (RANGE SCAN) OF
                'WF_ITEM_ACTIVITY_STATUSES_PK' (UNIQUE)
      0     TABLE ACCESS    GOAL: ANALYZED (BY INDEX ROWID) OF
                'WF_PROCESS_ACTIVITIES'
    400      INDEX   GOAL: ANALYZED (UNIQUE SCAN) OF
                'WF_PROCESS_ACTIVITIES_PK' (UNIQUE)
```

* *

In the above `tkprof` output, the SQL statement performed 391,040 buffer gets (i.e., logical reads), and 0 disk reads (i.e., physical reads). The SQL statement was also executed 200 times and parsed only once. The `Misses in the library cache during parse` statistic indicates whether or not the SQL statement was hard-parsed or soft-parsed. In this case, the value for `Misses in library cache during parse` is one, which means that the SQL statement was hard-parsed because the SQL statement was not found in the shared cursor cache. The total elapsed time for the SQL statement is 43.18 seconds over 200 executions. This translates into an average of 0.22 seconds per execution and 1,955 logical reads per execution. In addition, the rows column of the `tkprof` output lists the number of rows returned or processed by the SQL statement. In this case, in 200 executions, the SQL statement never returned any rows.

A new feature of `tkprof` in Oracle8*i* is that `tkprof` prints the run-time execution plan which was used to execute the SQL statement and the execution plan generated at the time of running `tkprof`. The `tkprof` utility provides an explain option which can be used to generate an execution plan for the SQL statements in the raw SQL trace file. However, prior to Oracle8*i*, the execution plan was generated at the time of running `tkprof`. The execution plan that was generated resulted from `tkprof` logging into the database and generating the execution plan. However, this may not be representative of the actual plan that was used at the time the SQL trace file was generated. Hence, in Oracle8*i*, `tkprof` reports the original execution plan which was used at the time when the raw SQL trace file was generated, as well as the execution plan generated by `tkprof` at the time of running `tkprof`. This allows you to compare the plans to determine discrepancies.

Using the `tkprof` utility with the explain plan option, you can analyze the activity and workload required by each SQL statement. In the above example, the SQL statement was not detected in the library cache, and hence a parse and execute was required. Notice that the `cpu` and `elapsed` time-based statistics are being reported. This is because of the `init.ora` parameter `timed_statistics=TRUE`. In the above example, the `disk` column statistics are zero. This means that the data was found in the buffer cache, and physical disk I/O was not needed to satisfy the statement. By reviewing the `disk` (physical I/Os) and `query` (logical I/Os or buffer gets) column statistics and the elapsed times thereof, you can determine where the majority of the time for execution of the SQL statement is being spent. Also, the elapsed times can help identify disk I/O contention by analyzing the elapsed times for the `disk` column. For example, if the `disk` I/O column reports that two disk I/Os have been performed for a particular SQL statement which resulted in an elapsed time of 2 seconds to read these two blocks, then the disk I/O subsystem containing these blocks should be investigated because 2 seconds to read two blocks is indicative of an I/O bottleneck. `tkprof` is an extremely useful tool and can help you pinpoint SQL bottlenecks in an application. If `timed_statistics=TRUE`, the SQL trace will contain CPU and elapsed times for the parsing, execution, and fetching phases, as well as total CPU and total elapsed timings. Use `tkprof` and the explain plan to monitor the application periodically. `tkprof` and the explain plan may help you catch potential performance problems by examining the SQL workload from the trace file. There are numerous ways in which SQL trace can be enabled: via the `alter session set sql_trace=TRUE` command, via PL/SQL by using the `DBMS_SESSION.SET_SQL_TRACE` procedure, or through `oradebug` in the event that you need to enable SQL trace for an existing process.

4.8.2.1 The 10046 Event

The regular SQL trace can be used to identify high load SQL and aggregate SQL execution statistics for the application. However, the default SQL trace, which is generated by setting the `init.ora` parameter `sql_trace=TRUE`, does not report bind variable values or wait event information. The 10046 event can be used to provide this set of extended information. The 10046 event is the event which enables SQL trace. The default SQL trace represents level 1 of the 10046 event. There are several levels of the 10046 event which can be used to provide more detailed information on the SQL statement and the SQL execution statistics. Table 4.2 summarizes the levels and their corresponding functionality.

TABLE 4.2 Levels of the 10046 event

Level 1	Default SQL Trace
Level 4	Bind Variable information
Level 8	Wait Event Information
Level 12	Bind Variable and Wait Event Information

The following SQL statement can be used to enable the 10046 event with the different levels.

```
alter session set events = '10046 trace name context forever, level 1';

alter session set events = '10046 trace name context forever, level 4';

alter session set events = '10046 trace name context forever, level 8';

alter session set events = '10046 trace name context forever, level 12';
```

You can also enable the 10046 event for a given process by using the oradebug command. For example, once you have identified the system process id (i.e., SPID from V$PROCESS) of the database server process for a given session, you can use the oradebug utility to enable the 10046 event for the particular process.

```
SVRMGR> oradebug setospid 20931
Oracle pid: 12, Unix process pid: 20931, image: oracle@myhost (TNS V1-V3)

SVRMGR> oradebug event 10046 trace name context forever, level 12
Statement processed.
```

In general, level 1 and level 8 are the most useful in terms of SQL execution statistics. Level 8 helps identify the wait events that the session is waiting on. For example, the session may be waiting on an I/O event or waiting for a particular latch. The wait event information is particularly useful when the elapsed time of an SQL statement is suspicious in terms of actual work versus elapsed time, for example, an SQL statement which takes 11 seconds to execute and performed eight buffer gets and one disk read. The wait events can be used to determine where the majority of the time (11 seconds) is being spent. The session may be waiting on I/O events which may be causing abnormal elapsed times.

In order to analyze the bind variable information or wait event information, you will need to examine the raw SQL trace file (not the tkprof report). The raw SQL trace file will contain the data which tkprof uses to aggregate into an easy-to-read format. The following is sample output from the raw SQL trace when level 8 of the 10046 event was enabled.

```
10046 Raw Trace Output:
=====================================================================
PARSING IN CURSOR #112
select order_number from orders where order_id = :b1
END OF STMT
PARSE #112:c=0,e=0,p=0,cr=0,cu=0,mis=0,r=0,dep=1,og=4,tim=1024308352
EXEC #112:c=0,e=0,p=0,cr=0,cu=0,mis=0,r=0,dep=1,og=4,tim=1024308352
WAIT #112: nam='db file sequential read' ela= 3 p1=18 p2=62059 p3=1
FETCH #112:c=0,e=3,p=1,cr=4,cu=0,mis=0,r=1,dep=1,og=4,tim=1024308355
FETCH #112:c=0,e=0,p=0,cr=1,cu=0,mis=0,r=0,dep=1,og=4,tim=1024308355
=====================================================================
```

In the above example, the `cursor #112` was executed and then waited on an I/O event (`db file sequential read`). The elapsed time (`ela` column) for the wait was 3 centiseconds. The wait event parameters `p1`, `p2`, and `p3` refer to the file#, block#, and the number of blocks being read, respectively. In this case, one block from file# 18 and block# 62059 was read, which took 3 centiseconds. Three centiseconds is higher than the expected amount of time to read one block. The I/O event `db file sequential read` typically refers to an index read. The I/O event `db file scattered read` typically refers to a full-table scan. The following is another example of the 10046 output which shows that the cursor is waiting on a full-table scan I/O event.

```
PARSING IN CURSOR #50
SELECT COUNT(*) FROM MSC_ST_BOM_COMPONENTS WHERE SR_INSTANCE_ID=
   :p_instance_id
END OF STMT
PARSE #50:c=0,e=1,p=0,cr=0,cu=0,mis=1,r=0,dep=1,og=0,tim=1025819693
EXEC #50:c=0,e=0,p=0,cr=0,cu=0,mis=0,r=0,dep=1,og=4,tim=1025819693
WAIT #50: nam='file open' ela= 0 p1=0 p2=0 p3=0
WAIT #50: nam='db file scattered read' ela= 1 p1=30 p2=49471 p3=4
WAIT #50: nam='db file scattered read' ela= 0 p1=30 p2=49475 p3=4
WAIT #50: nam='db file scattered read' ela= 0 p1=30 p2=49479 p3=4
WAIT #50: nam='db file scattered read' ela= 0 p1=30 p2=49483 p3=4
WAIT #50: nam='db file scattered read' ela= 0 p1=30 p2=49487 p3=4
WAIT #50: nam='db file scattered read' ela= 0 p1=30 p2=49491 p3=4
WAIT #50: nam='db file scattered read' ela= 0 p1=30 p2=49495 p3=4
WAIT #50: nam='db file scattered read' ela= 0 p1=30 p2=49499 p3=4
WAIT #50: nam='db file scattered read' ela= 0 p1=30 p2=49503 p3=4
WAIT #50: nam='db file scattered read' ela= 0 p1=30 p2=49507 p3=4
```

In the example above, the cursor is waiting on the full-table scan I/O event `db file scattered read`. The file # is 30 (`p1=30`), the block numbers continue to change per request, and the number of blocks being read is 4 (`p3=4`). This means that the `init.ora` parameter `db_file_multiblock_read_count=4`. The first wait shows an elapsed time of 1 centisecond for an I/O request of four blocks. The subsequent waits show an elapsed time of zero, which means that the time to read the four blocks took less than 1 centisecond.

The wait event information is extremely useful in identifying bottlenecks and areas of contention. You can also scan through the raw SQL trace file using a utility such as `grep` or `awk` in order to look for the `WAIT` event lines in the trace. This can help quickly identify the lines in the trace with large wait times.

The 10046 event can also be used to report bind variable information, which is helpful when tuning SQL statements. If level 4 or level 12 of the 10046 event is enabled, then Oracle will report bind variable information such as the bind variable data types and the actual bind variable data. The following sample output illustrates the bind variable information that is reported by the 10046 event.

```
==================================================================
PARSING IN CURSOR #33
select 'Transaction type is valid'
from po_lookup_codes plc
where (plc.lookup_type='RCV TRANSACTION TYPE' and
    plc.lookup_code=:b1)
END OF STMT
PARSE #33:c=0,e=1,p=0,cr=2,cu=0,mis=1,r=0,dep=0,og=0,tim=1024307979
BINDS #33:
  bind 0: dty=1 mxl=128(78) mal=00 scl=00 pre=00 oacflg=00 oacfl2=0
      size=128 offset=0
    bfp=01931330 bln=128 avl=07 flg=05
    value="RECEIVE"
EXEC #33:c=1,e=0,p=0,cr=0,cu=0,mis=0,r=0,dep=0,og=1,tim=1024307979
==================================================================
```

In the output above, the bind variable information for :b1 is reported in the BINDS section of the trace. The bind variable information starts with bind 0 as the first bind variable in an SQL statement. In this case, bind 0 refers to the :b1 bind variable in the SQL statement, which is used as part of the predicate [plc.lookup_code]. The bind variable information contains the data type of the bind variable (dty). In this case, dty=1, which refers to the VARCHAR data type. The actual length of the string is 7 (avl=07). The value of the bind variable is "RECEIVE" (value="RECEIVE"). Enabling bind variable information for the 10046 event can lead to a rather large trace file, hence, you should enable this event only if you need bind variable information such as the values of the bind variables for a particular SQL statement or series of SQL statements. The values of the bind variables can be useful in cases where you are trying to tune an SQL statement which uses bind variables, but you are not sure which values are being used by the application. For example, in cases of data skew, one value may result in a large number of buffer gets and disk reads, while another value may be very selective.

4.8.3 TUNING BY SELECTIVITY

The goal of tuning SQL is first to examine what is being done, how it is being done, and what the selectivity of the query is. For example, consider the following query.

```
SQL> SELECT
        count(*)
     FROM CUSTOMER C,
          ADDRESS A,
          ZIP Z
     WHERE (C.ADDRESS_ID=A.ADDRESS_ID) AND
           (A.ZIP_ID = Z.ZIP_ID) AND
           (Z.ZIP_CODE = '10016');
```

This query counts the number of customers who live in the zip code 10016 (New York). However, without statistics, it would be difficult to determine the proper execution order of the query. Common sense tells us that starting with the ZIP table is more efficient, followed by the addresses which exist in the specified zip code, and then followed by the join to the customer table. For example, if you joined the tables in the order listed in the FROM clause, you would scan every customer row and join it with its corresponding address row to determine if the customer's address was in the zip code specified. If the customer and address tables were large tables, this query could take a long time to run. In addition, even if no customers existed in the New York zip code 10016, a large majority of the rows would be scanned before this could be determined. On the other hand, if we started with the ZIP table first, the query would return fairly quick once it was determined that the zip code 10016 does not exist in the ZIP table. Although this may seem like an easy example, all queries (even complex) can be broken down into the individual join layers. Once broken down, you can determine the selectivity of the query by analyzing each join and each subquery layer. The goal is to start with the layer that reduces the selectivity the most. This way you avoid scanning unnecessary rows.

4.8.4 ONE SQL FITS ALL

Developers sometimes code a single SQL statement to handle all the possible cases of user input. In this case, the nvl() or the decode() function may be used in the SQL statement to test for the presence of certain values. However, this may not be the optimal approach since the optimizer will only produce one plan for the same SQL statement. For example, consider the following SQL statement which uses the nvl() function to test for the presence of the bind variable. In this query, whether or not the user supplied an invoice number for this query, the execution plan will remain the same.

```
select ai.invoice_num,ai.amount_paid,ai.posting_status
from   ap_invoices ai
where ai.invoice_num = nvl(:b1,ai.invoice_num)
```

Although you may think that the optimizer can use the index on AI.INVOICE_NUM because the nvl() is on the right-hand side, it will not. In this case, the nvl() function is considered index-unsafe for the simple reason that the ability to utilize an index depends on the bind variable value. In the example above, if the bind variable :b1 is null, then the expression will result in the following: (ai.invoice_num = ai.invoice_num). Obviously, in this case, the index on AI.INVOICE_NUM cannot be used because this expression is semantically equivalent to a self-identity predicate (e.g., 1=1). The optimizer has no way of knowing whether or not a bind variable value is supplied or if it is null. This means that users of this query will obtain the same performance if they provide an invoice number or if they performed a blind query. You should test for the value of null in the application code as opposed to in the SQL statement. For users who provide an invoice number, they will experience much faster response times than will users who perform blind queries (no invoice number was specified).

4.8.5 `nvl()` **AND OPTIMIZER STATISTICS**

Another example of an `nvl()` construct which should not be used is as follows.

```
update GL_BALANCES GBAL
set PERIOD_NET_DR = :b1
where (GBAL.CODE_COMBINATION_ID,GBAL.PERIOD_NAME,
       GBAL.SET_OF_BOOKS_ID,GBAL.CURRENCY_CODE,GBAL.ACTUAL_FLAG)
     in (select CODE_COMBINATION_ID , PERIOD_NAME ,
                SET_OF_BOOKS_ID , CURRENCY_CODE ,
                ACTUAL_FLAG
          from POSTING_INTERIM )
and NVL(GBAL.TRANSLATED_FLAG,'X') <>'R'
```

In the above example, although `TRANSLATED_FLAG` is not indexed and is not the main driving filter, it does have a histogram because it is a skewed column. However, the `nvl()` construct prevents the optimizer from accurately estimating the selectivity of the filter. Hence, a suboptimal execution plan is generated. In Oracle8*i* release 8.1.6, you can set the `init.ora` parameter `_use_column_stats_for_function`, which allows the CBO to probe inside the `nvl()` function in order to assign the correct selectivity estimates for the `TRANSLATED_FLAG` filter.

4.8.6 **DYNAMIC JOIN-KEY RESOLUTION VIA** `decode()`

You should also not use `decode()` or `nvl()` as a run-time join filter. This prevents the optimizer from assigning the correct join cardinality estimates. Doing so often leads to poor execution plans. You should join directly to the tables, and the join keys should be explicitly provided. For example,

```
select ae.source_table,  d.invoice_distribution_id,
       ap.invoice_payment_id
from ap_ae_lines_all ae,
     ap_invoice_distributions_all d,
     po_distributions_all pd,
     ap_invoice_payments_all ap
where decode(ae.source_table, 'AP_INVOICE_DISTRIBUTIONS',ae.source_id,null)
     = d.invoice_distribution_id (+)
  and ae.source_id = 21628
  and ae.source_table = 'AP_INVOICE_DISTRIBUTIONS'
  and pd.po_distribution_id(+) = d.po_distribution_id
  and decode(ae.source_table, 'AP_INVOICE_PAYMENTS',ae.source_id,null)
     = ap.invoice_payment_id (+)
```

In the above example, the join between the tables `AP_AE_LINES_ALL` and `AP_INVOICE_PAYMENTS_ALL` depends on the runtime value of the `AE.SOURCE_TABLE` column. Hence, the optimizer will not be able to accurately estimate the join cardinality between these two tables at plan generation time. The optimizer will use internal defaults, and it may result in a suboptimal plan.

4.8.7 `nvl()` AND THE NEGATION CASE

Another common use of `nvl()` which I have seen is the negation case, whereby you want to retrieve rows given a certain criteria. Consider the following query.

```
select max(poll2.creation_date)
from po_line_locations_archive poll2,
     po_headers_archive poh,
     po_lines_archive poll
where  poll.po_line_id=poll2.po_line_id and
       poh.po_header_id=poll.po_header_id and
       NVL(POL1.LATEST_EXTERNAL_FLAG ,'N')='Y' and
       poll.item_id=:b1
```

In the previous example, the predicate [`NVL(POH.LATEST_EXTERNAL_FLAG , 'N')='Y'`] can be semantically rewritten as [`POH.LATEST_EXTERNAL_FLAG='Y'`] since the query wants to discard the null rows. If the `LATEST_EXTERNAL_FLAG` is null, then the filter will effectively result in 'N' = 'Y'. In this case, the `nvl()` can be eliminated, which eliminates the unnecessary overhead of invoking the `nvl()` SQL function. Do not use `nvl()` on a column in which you are after the nonnull rows and the predicate is an equality predicate.

4.8.8 CURSOR MEMORY

SQL statements which consume a large amount of sharable memory place a large burden on the shared pool. The larger the SQL statement, the more memory allocations and latch gets will be needed in order to build a sharable cursor in the cursor cache. SQL statements which require a large amount of memory (i.e., several megabytes) pose a scalability problem since this limits the amount of sharable cursors that can be active in the shared pool. Suppose, for example, that a query Q1 against a view V1 consumes 1.5 MB of sharable memory. Suppose that query Q2 is a slight variant of Q1 in that it specifies an additional filter or a different filter. This results in 3 MB of shared memory allocated for only two cursors. Shared pool operations are also slightly more expensive in an OPS environment due to the need to acquire global cache locks. Hence, it is important that your application's SQL statements are kept to a reasonable minimum in terms of the sharable memory required.

You should set a reasonable threshold for cursor sizes so that SQL statements which are developed do not exceed the standard. Also, some SQL statements may be small in text size because the SQL statement may be referring to a complex view. However, the view will be expanded, which may result in a large cursor even though the text may appear to be small. The amount of sharable memory for an SQL statement can be measured by querying the `V$SQL` view and examining the `SHARABLE_MEM` column. The following is an example query which reports the amount of sharable memory consumed for a given SQL statement.

```
select sql_text,sharable_mem
from v$sql
where sql_text like '%OE_TAX_LINES_SUMMARY_V%'


SHARABLE_MEM (bytes)
================================================================
1,228,548

SQL_TEXT
================================================================
select SHIP_TO_CUSTOMER_ID, BILL_TO_CUSTOMER_ID, TRX_CHARGE_LINE_ID,
     TRX_LINE_ID, TRX_HEADER_ID , TRX_LINK_TO_CUST_TRX_LINE_ID,
     TRX_DATE, GL_DATE, TAX_CODE , TAX_RATE, TAX_AMOUNT,
     SHIP_TO_SITE_USE_ID, BILL_TO_SITE_USE_ID,  SHIP_TO_POSTAL_CODE,
     BILL_TO_POSTAL_CODE
from OE_TAX_LINES_SUMMARY_V
where trx_line_id = :b1
order by trx_header_id, trx_line_id
```

In the above example, the SQL statement consumed almost 1.2 MB of shared memory for the cursor. It is important that you monitor the amount of sharable memory consumed for your SQL statements to ensure that it is a reasonable amount. If your query references a view, you may need to optimize the view or simplify the query in order to reduce the amount of sharable memory consumed.

4.8.9 SQL BALLOONING

SQL is not a procedural language, hence it should not be used to incorporate complex business logic. Often developers code an extremely complex SQL statement or code a simple SQL statement which references a complex view. While this may make programming easy, it typically results in SQL execution performance problems. Complex business logic should be handled in the application code rather than via SQL. Coding a very complex SQL statement will make maintenance difficult and limit the optimizer's ability in terms of plan generation. For example, if you code an SQL statement which joins 20 tables or code a SQL statement which references a view which in turn joins 20 tables, the optimizer will obviously not consider 20 (2.432902008177e+18) permutations! Hence, the optimizer may miss an optimal permutation since there are so many table joins.

In terms of maintainability and scalability, it is much better to write application code which implements the business logic rather than coding a 2-page SQL statement in which the execution plan is over 200 lines long. For certain SQL statements which are frequently executed (*hot cursors*), the SQL statements need to be highly optimized in terms of the number of joins and the number of buffer gets that the SQL performs.

4.8.10   WHEN TO USE EXISTS AND WHEN TO USE IN

The EXISTS operator is typically used to validate a set of records via a correlated subquery. The IN operator is usually used to feed another query from the results of the IN subquery. In the case of a correlated join with the EXISTS operator, the parent query becomes the driving query while the EXISTS subquery becomes the child query. For each parent row, the EXISTS subquery is executed in order to determine if a matching child row exists. This is known as *Tuple Iteration Semantics* (TIS). In the TIS mode, each parent row, or tuple, is used as the join input of the EXISTS child subquery in order to determine if a match exists. Upon the first match, the subquery returns TRUE and continues processing the next parent tuple until all parent tuples have been processed. The EXISTS operator is best used when the parent query is selective and you want to validate some additional conditions.

The IN operator causes the subquery to be executed first, assuming that the subquery is not correlated, and the results of the subquery are used to drive the parent query. The IN operator should be used when the child subquery is more selective than the parent query conditions; hence it can be used to drive the parent query. Consider the following query which utilizes an EXISTS operator.

```
SELECT AI.INVOICE_ID,
       AI.INVOICE_NUM
FROM  AP_INVOICES  AI
WHERE
      EXISTS (SELECT 1
              FROM AP_BATCHES_ALL AB
              WHERE AI.BATCH_ID = AB.BATCH_ID AND
                    AB.BATCH_NAME = :b1)
```

The execution plan is as follows.

```
SELECT STATEMENT    Cost=21706,1803  bytes=118998 ,
  FILTER   Cost=, bytes= ,
    TABLE ACCESS FULL AP_INVOICES_ALL Cost=21706,1803  bytes=118998 ,
    TABLE ACCESS BY INDEX ROWID AP_BATCHES_ALL Cost=2,1  bytes=40 ,
     INDEX UNIQUE SCAN AP_BATCHES_U1 Cost=1,1  bytes= ,
```

The above query selects all invoices of a particular batch. However, because the query uses an EXISTS and there are no other selective filters in the parent query, the execution plan results in a full-table scan on the AP_INVOICES_ALL table and then performs the EXISTS subquery check for each invoice row. This will be extremely inefficient since all invoices will be scanned. Since the subquery is more selective because a particular batch name is being specified, the IN operator is more appropriate than the EXISTS approach. The following SQL rewrite illustrates the improvement.

```
SELECT AI.INVOICE_ID,
       AI.INVOICE_NUM
FROM   AP_INVOICES   AI
WHERE AI.BATCH_ID    IN
       (SELECT AB.BATCH_ID
        FROM AP_BATCHES_ALL AB
        WHERE AB.BATCH_NAME = :b1)

SELECT STATEMENT     Cost=16,4  bytes=316 ,
  NESTED LOOPS     Cost=16,4  bytes=316 ,
    VIEW    Cost=10,1  bytes=13 ,
      SORT UNIQUE  Cost=10,1  bytes=40 ,
        TABLE ACCESS BY INDEX ROWID AP_BATCHES_ALL Cost=4,1  bytes=40 ,
          INDEX RANGE SCAN AP_BATCHES_U2 Cost=3,1  bytes= ,
      TABLE ACCESS BY INDEX ROWID AP_INVOICES_ALL Cost=6,36056
          bytes=2379696 ,
        INDEX RANGE SCAN AP_INVOICES_N1 Cost=2,36056  bytes= ,
```

The execution plan shows that the subquery is executed first, which allows the optimizer to utilize the index on the BATCH_NAME filter and then join back to the AP_INVOICES_ALL table via the BATCH_ID index. The cost of the plan with the EXISTS operator is 21,706, while the cost of the plan with the IN operator is only 16. This represents an order of magnitude improvement in the execution plan.

The EXISTS operator can also be used to convert a full join into a semi-join. This improves performance when the cardinality of the join is greater than 1. For example, consider the following query.

```
SELECT DISTINCT HRE.FULL_NAME,
       HRE.EMPLOYEE_NUM,
       HRE.EMPLOYEE_ID
FROM   PO_REQUISITION_LINES PRL,
       HR_EMPLOYEES HRE
WHERE FULL_NAME = :b1 AND
       PRL.SUGGESTED_BUYER_ID = HRE.EMPLOYEE_ID
ORDER BY HRE.FULL_NAME
```

This query displays employee information for a particular employee if the employee has created at least one purchase order requisition. However, if the specified person created a large number of purchase order requisitions, the query will need to fetch all of those rows even though the query does not explicitly reference any columns from the PO_REQUISITION_LINES table. Hence, the SQL statement can be rewritten to avoid the full join and the DISTINCT operator as follows.

```
SELECT HRE.FULL_NAME,
       HRE.EMPLOYEE_NUM,
       HRE.EMPLOYEE_ID
FROM  HR_EMPLOYEES HRE
WHERE FULL_NAME = :b1 AND
      EXISTS (SELECT 1
                FROM PO_REQUISITION_LINES PRL
                WHERE PRL.SUGGESTED_BUYER_ID = HRE.EMPLOYEE_ID)
ORDER BY UPPER(HRE.FULL_NAME)
```

The above query is more efficient than the original query because the subquery will return TRUE upon the first match, meaning as soon as the first requisition line is found for that employee. In addition, since EXISTS returns either TRUE or FALSE for a particular row, the DISTINCT can be eliminated since the query does not produce duplicates. The DISTINCT was needed earlier because the query explicitly joined to the PO_REQUISITION_LINES table. Hence the same employee record would be repeated for each requisition line.

4.8.11 REVERSE THE LOGIC

Another SQL tuning technique which can be used with SQL statements using the NOT IN clause is to reverse the logic such that instead of returning the rows NOT IN 'X', you return the rows that are IN 'Y'. This can be done when the negation set can be reversed to include the remaining values. For example, consider the following query.

```
DELETE FROM ap_temp_trial_balance attb
  WHERE  attb.invoice_id in
    (SELECT ai.invoice_id
      FROM  ap_invoices ai
      WHERE  ai.cancelled_date is not null
      AND    ai.invoice_id not in
              (SELECT  aid.invoice_id
               FROM    ap_invoice_distributions aid
               WHERE   aid.accrual_posted_flag = 'Y'
               AND     aid.invoice_id = ai.invoice_id
               AND     accounting_date > sysdate))
```

The execution plan is as follows.

```
DELETE STATEMENT
  DELETE   AP_TEMP_TRIAL_BALANCE
    MERGE JOIN
      SORT JOIN
        TABLE ACCESS FULL AP_TEMP_TRIAL_BALANCE
      SORT JOIN
        VIEW
          SORT UNIQUE
            FILTER
              TABLE ACCESS FULL AP_INVOICES_ALL
              TABLE ACCESS BY INDEX ROWID AP_INVOICE_DISTRIBUTIONS_ALL
                INDEX RANGE SCAN AP_INVOICE_DISTRIBUTIONS_N8
```

The above SQL statement deletes the rows from the AP_TEMP_TRIAL_BALANCE table for those invoices which do not have the accrual_posted_flag = 'Y'. The execution plan shows that a full-table scan on the AP_INVOICES_ALL table is occurring and that the index on ACCRUAL_POSTED_FLAG on the AP_INVOICE_DISTRIBUTIONS_ALL table is being used. However, since the majority of the rows in the AP_INVOICE_DISTRIBUTIONS_ALL table will have a value of 'Y' for the accrual_posted_flag, the index on the accrual_posted_flag is not very selective. Since the accrual_posted_flag can either be 'Y', 'N', or null, we can reverse the logic to improve the selectivity of the query as follows.

```
DELETE FROM ap_temp_trial_balance attb
 WHERE  attb.invoice_id in
 (SELECT ai.invoice_id
    FROM  ap_invoices_all ai
    WHERE  ai.cancelled_date is not null
    AND    ai.invoice_id in
            (SELECT  aid.invoice_id
            FROM    ap_invoice_distributions_all aid
            WHERE   aid.accrual_posted_flag = 'N'
            AND     aid.invoice_id = ai.invoice_id
            AND     accounting_date <= sysdate) AND
            NOT EXISTS
            (SELECT 1
             from ap_invoice_distributions_all aid2
             where aid2.invoice_id = ai.invoice_id and
                   aid2.accrual_posted_flag||'' = 'Y'))
```

The execution plan is as follows.

```
DELETE STATEMENT
  DELETE   AP_TEMP_TRIAL_BALANCE
    MERGE JOIN
      SORT JOIN
        TABLE ACCESS FULL AP_TEMP_TRIAL_BALANCE
      SORT JOIN
        VIEW
          SORT UNIQUE
            FILTER
              NESTED LOOPS
              TABLE ACCESS BY INDEX ROWID AP_INVOICE_DISTRIBUTIONS_ALL
                  INDEX RANGE SCAN AP_INVOICE_DISTRIBUTIONS_N8
                TABLE ACCESS BY INDEX ROWID AP_INVOICES_ALL
                    INDEX UNIQUE SCAN AP_INVOICES_U1
                TABLE ACCESS BY INDEX ROWID AP_INVOICE_DISTRIBUTIONS_ALL
                  INDEX RANGE SCAN AP_INVOICE_DISTRIBUTIONS_U1
```

The rewrite is more efficient because the number of rows with the value of `'N'` for `accrual_posted_flag` will be significantly less than with the value of `'Y'`. In addition, by converting the `NOT IN` into an `IN`, the optimizer is able to probe on the `INVOICE_ID` index on the `AP_INVOICES_ALL` table.

4.8.12 USING HINTS

Hints are useful in situations where the optimizer did not choose the most optimal plan, such as in cases where bind variables are used in SQL statements and the data is largely skewed. In such a case, you may need to use optimizer hints to force a particular execution plan. Coupling your intimate knowledge of the data with your knowledge of the Oracle Server, you can use hints to tune your SQL statements. In order to use hints, you must embed the hint string explicitly following the keywords select, update, or delete using either the `/*+ HINT */` syntax or `--+ HINT` syntax.

4.8.12.1 `ALL_ROWS`

The `ALL_ROWS` hint tells the CBO to optimize the statement with the goal of best throughput. The best throughput means that the statement should be executed such that total resource consumption is minimized. For example,

```
SQL> SELECT /*+ ALL_ROWS */
            count(*) from orders;
```

or

```
SQL> SELECT --+ ALL_ROWS
            count(*) from orders;
```

The ALL_ROWS hint is often used to tune an SQL statement by optimizing the processing of all the rows.

4.8.12.2 FIRST_ROWS

The FIRST_ROWS hint tells the CBO to optimize the statement with the goal of best response time. The best response means that the statement should be executed such that the minimum amount of resources are used to return the first set of rows. The FIRST_ROWS hint will always choose an index, if available, over a full-table scan, even if the full-table scan is faster. The FIRST_ROWS hint also causes the CBO to use a nested loops join over a sort-merge join whenever the associated table is the inner table of the nested loop. This avoids the overhead of the sort-merge operation. Remember, the goal here is to return the first set of rows the quickest way possible. Therefore, index scans and nested loops joins will be the fastest way to return the first set of rows. For statements using group by, set operators (UNION, INTERSECT, MINUS, UNION ALL), distinct operator, group functions, or FOR UPDATE clause, the CBO ignores the FIRST_ROWS hint because these operations require all the rows to be processed before returning the first row. FIRST_ROWS can be used for applications that need to see the first set of rows immediately and can wait to fetch the remaining set of rows. Prior to Oracle 7.2, the FIRST_ROWS implementation was faulty. Therefore, do not rely on this hint unless running Oracle 7.2 or higher.

4.8.12.3 CHOOSE

The CHOOSE hint tells the optimizer to choose either the CBO or the RBO depending on the availability of statistics. If no statistics are available for any of the tables involved in the statement, the RBO is used. If at least one table has statistics, the CBO is used.

4.8.12.4 RULE

The RULE hint causes the RBO to be used to optimize the statement. The RBO will use the 15-rank access path listed in Table 4.1. The RBO will choose the plan with the lowest ranking. You can use the RULE hint for OLTP applications to guarantee plan consistency. However, keep in mind that Oracle will be phasing out the RBO in future releases in favor of the CBO.

4.8.12.5 FULL

The FULL hint forces a full-table scan on the table specified. The syntax of the FULL hint is FULL (table name), or FULL (table alias name). Even if there is an index on the table, the FULL hint causes a full-table scan to be performed. This hint typically is used in DSS applications in conjunction with the PARALLEL hint.

4.8.12.6 ROWID

The ROWID hint uses ROWID to scan the table. The syntax of the ROWID hint is ROWID (table name), or ROWID (table alias name). You can use this hint in applications where the rowid is available. For example, suppose you fetch some rows from the database and now you want to update those rows. Instead of updating the rows with the standard where clause (selecting those rows of interest), update the rows using the rowids as part of the where clause and use the ROWID hint. When using this technique, you will also need to fetch the rowid values as part of the fetch statement, as well as lock the corresponding rows (to ensure the consistency of the rowids fetched).

4.8.12.7 CLUSTER or HASH

The CLUSTER hint causes a cluster key scan to be performed on the table. The syntax of the CLUSTER hint is CLUSTER (table name). The HASH hint causes a hash key scan to be used. The syntax of the HASH hint is HASH (table name).

4.8.12.8 INDEX or INDEX_COMBINE

The INDEX hint causes the specified index to be used. The INDEX hint forces the optimizer to not consider a full-table scan. The syntax of the INDEX hint is INDEX (table name, index name). This hint is very useful when multiple indexes are used in a query. You can use this hint to specify which index is used. The INDEX hint also works on bitmap indexes (provided in Oracle 7.3). You can also use the new hint provided with Oracle 7.3, INDEX_COMBINE, which has the same syntax as the INDEX hint. The INDEX_COMBINE hint causes the optimizer to use a Boolean combination of the bitmapped indexes specified in the hint.

4.8.12.9 AND_EQUAL

The AND_EQUAL hint causes multiple single-column indexes to be merged. The limit to the number of single-column indexes specified is currently five. The syntax of the AND_EQUAL hint is AND_EQUAL (table index index ...). This hint is very useful when multiple indexes on the same table are used within a query. You can use this hint to specify which indexes to merge. The AND_EQUAL hint is useful when many single-column indexes can be used together to reduce the selectivity of the query as opposed to scanning one index only.

4.8.12.10 USE_CONCAT

The USE_CONCAT hint, introduced in Oracle 7.2, forces combined OR predicates specified in the WHERE clause of the query to be transformed into a compound query via the UNION ALL operator. Without this hint, the transformation would occur only if the cost of the transformation is less than the cost without the transformation. The USE_CONCAT hint can be used with large table queries to help subdivide the larger query into multiple UNION ALL queries. This allows the multiple UNION ALL subqueries to proceed in parallel, which can increase performance over a single large query.

4.8.12.11 ORDERED

The ORDERED hint causes Oracle to join tables in the order the tables are listed in the FROM clause. For example,

```
SQL> SELECT /*+ ORDERED */
     count(*)
     FROM CUSTOMER C,
          ORDERS O,
          PARTS P
     WHERE (C.customer_id=O.customer_id) AND
          (O.partno=P.partno);
```

This causes Oracle first to join the customer table with the orders table and then to join the result of the first join with the parts table. The ORDERED hint can increase performance substantially by specifying small tables first, hopefully causing a reduction in the selectivity when later joined against the larger tables.

4.8.12.12 USE_NL or USE_MERGE or USE_HASH or USE_ANTI or USE_SEMI

The USE_NL hint causes a nested loops join to be used when joining tables. The table specified in the USE_NL hint is the table to be used as the inner table in the nested loops join. The USE_MERGE hint causes a sort-merge join to be used when joining tables. The table specified in the USE_MERGE hint is used to join with the previous resultant sets of a sort-merge join. The USE_HASH hint, introduced in Oracle 7.3, causes a hash join to be used when joining tables. For very large tables that have a good data distribution, hash joins can increase performance significantly. The USE_ANTI hint causes an anti-join to be used for NOT IN subqueries. The USE_SEMI hint causes a semi-join to be used. The syntax for the USE_NL, USE_MERGE, USE_HASH, USE_ANTI, and USE_SEMI hints are as follows: USE_NL (table1 table2 ...), USE_MERGE (table1 table2 ...), USE_HASH (table1 table2), USE_ANTI (table1 table2), and USE_SEMI (table1 table2).

4.8.12.13 PARALLEL or NOPARALLEL

The PARALLEL hint causes Oracle to parallelize a full-table scan or join operation by the degree of parallelization specified in the PARALLEL clause. The syntax for the PARALLEL hint is PARALLEL (table, degree). The NOPARALLEL hint causes the optimizer to disable parallel scanning of the table, even if the table was created with the PARALLEL clause. The syntax of the NOPARALLEL hint is NOPARALLEL (table). The NOPARALLEL hint can be used on small tables where the overhead of using a parallel query increases the time needed to scan the table. The hint can also be used in cases where the table's data is located on one or a few disks and parallelizing the query may have a negative effect.

4.8.12.14   CACHE **or** NOCACHE

The CACHE hint specifies that the blocks retrieved during a full-table scan for the table specified in the hint are to be placed at the most recently used end of the least recently used (LRU) list in the buffer cache. The CACHE hint can increase the performance of full-table scans for lookup tables that are relatively small by maintaining the table data blocks in the cache. The syntax of the CACHE hint is CACHE (table). The NOCACHE specifies that the blocks retrieved during a full-table scan for the table specified in the hint are to be placed at the least recently used end of the LRU list in the buffer cache. The NOCACHE hint can be used for large tables during a full-table scan so that the overhead of bringing the data blocks into the most recently used section of the buffer cache is reduced. The syntax of the NOCACHE hint is NOCACHE (table).

4.8.12.15   PUSH_SUBQ

The PUSH_SUBQ hint causes the evaluation of nonmerged subqueries to be done at the earliest possible place in the execution plan. This can improve performance by allowing subqueries that reduce the selectivity to be executed first, thereby reducing the number of rows processed upfront rather than near the end.

4.8.12.16   HASH_AJ **or** MERGE_AJ

The HASH_AJ or MERGE_AJ hints specify the use of an anti-join. An anti-join returns the rows that do not satisfy the predicate, as opposed to a standard join which would return those rows that match the right side and the left side of the join predicate. The anti-join is equivalent to the NOT IN subselect query. However, the NOT IN subselect typically uses a nested loops join to join the subselect with the parent query. The HASH_AJ and MERGE_AJ (introduced in Oracle 7.3) allow you to use a hash or merge-join for a nested subselect query using the NOT IN clause. The HASH_AJ or MERGE_AJ hints need to be specified in the nested subselect following the NOT IN clause to cause Oracle to use a hash or merge-join, respectively. The anti-join feature can increase performance for large subselects.

4.8.12.17   HASH_SJ **or** MERGE_SJ

Oracle 8.0.4 provides the HASH_SJ or MERGE_SJ hints in order to specify the use of a hash or merge semi-join. A semi-join improves the performance of certain EXISTS subqueries. A semi-join returns the rows that satisfy an EXISTS subquery and avoids the duplication of rows from the left side of the predicate when the subquery criteria can be satisfied by multiple rows on the right side. You can specify the HASH_SJ or MERGE_SJ hints in your query to use a hash or merge semi-join as opposed to using a nested-loop join which is the default for EXISTS subqueries. In order to enable the optimizer to consider semi-join access paths, set the init.ora parameter always_semi_join=HASH or always_semi_join=MERGE.

4.8.12.18 INDEX_FFS

Oracle 7.3.3 and Oracle8 provide a feature known as a fast full scan. The fast full scan feature allows you to perform a full index range scan in parallel. This is useful for data warehousing applications where queries often require scanning the entire table. Using the fast full scan feature, you can scan the index in parallel assuming the index columns satisfy your predicates. A fast full parallel index range scan will likely be faster than scanning the entire table since the index blocks make up less data than the entire data blocks. For example, if your table is 100 GB in size, and your index is 10 GB, performing a full scan on the index as opposed to the entire table will significantly reduce the amount of I/O needed to complete the query since you will be scanning a 10-GB index versus a 100-GB table. The syntax of the INDEX_FFS hint is INDEX_FFS (table index). To enable the optimizer to consider fast full scans, set the init.ora parameter fast_full _scan_enabled=TRUE.

4.8.12.19 PARALLEL_INDEX or NOPARALLEL_INDEX

Oracle8 provides the PARALLEL_INDEX or NOPARALLEL_INDEX hints that allow you to specify the degree of parallelism for index range scans for partitioned indexes. The syntax for the PARALLEL_INDEX hint is PARALLEL_INDEX (table index degree). The NO_PARALLEL_INDEX hint overrides any parallel settings for the index and its syntax is NO_PARALLEL_INDEX (table index).

4.8.12.20 DRIVING_SITE

Oracle8 provides a way to speed up distributed join queries by specifying the driving site for the join. The syntax for the DRIVING_SITE hint is DRIVING_SITE (table). For example, consider the following query.

```
SELECT /*+ DRIVING_SITE (o) */
            o.cust_no
            o.ord_no
FROM customer c,
        orders@reodb o
WHERE (c.cust_no = o.cust_no);
```

Without the DRIVING_SITE hint, the rows from the orders table from the remote database will be brought into the local database with the join being executed locally. Using the DRIVING_SITE hint, the customer rows will be sent to the remote database and joined with the orders table on the remote database. This will improve distributed query performance since it is likely that there will be fewer customer rows than orders rows. The DRIVING_SITE hint is useful for tuning distributed join queries that often join local tables with large-size remote database tables. Using the DRIVING_SITE hint, you can choose the driving table that makes the most sense, thereby reducing the data transmission and join workload.

4.8.12.21 `PUSH_PRED` or `NO_PUSH_PRED`

Oracle 8.0.4 provides the `PUSH_PRED` and `NO_PUSH_PRED` hints which allows the optimizer to push the individual join predicates down into the view when the query involves a view with multiple base tables on the right side of an outer join. This enables more efficient execution plans by transforming hash joins into nested loops and full-table scans into index scans. The `NO_PUSH_PRED` hint prevents the join predicates from being pushed into the view. To enable the optimizer to consider pushing the join predicates, set the `init.ora` parameter `push_join_predicate=TRUE` or `_push_join_predicate=TRUE` in Oracle8*i*. The syntax for these hints are `PUSH_PRED` (table) and `NO_PUSH_PRED` (table).

4.8.12.22 `MERGE` or `NO_MERGE`

Oracle 8.0.4 provides the `MERGE` and `NO_MERGE` hints which control whether or not a complex view or subquery within a query is evaluated prior to the surrounding query. The `NO_MERGE` hint causes the optimizer not to merge the view. The syntax for these hints are `MERGE` (table) and `NO_MERGE` (table). Set the `init.ora` parameter `complex_view_merging=TRUE` or `_complex_view_merging=TRUE` in Oracle8*i* to enable the optimizer to consider merging the views.

4.8.12.23 `APPEND` or `NO_APPEND`

The Oracle8 hints `APPEND` and `NO_APPEND` specify for an insert statement whether or not data is appended to the table and the existing free space in the blocks is used. The `APPEND` hint causes the data to be appended to the table in the similar fashion as a direct load, and the existing free space in the blocks to not be used. The `NO_APPEND` hint can be used to override the `APPEND` mode.

4.8.12.24 `STAR` or `STAR_TRANSFORMATION`

The `STAR` hint causes the optimizer to choose a star diagram execution plan. The star plan places the largest table, usually the fact table, as the last table in the join order and uses a nested loops join on the concatenated index on the fact table to join with the smaller dimension tables. In Oracle8, the `STAR_TRANSFORMATION` hint provides an alternative method to executing star queries efficiently. The typical method is to perform a Cartesian product on the dimension tables and then join the result via a nested loops index join to the fact table. The Cartesian method works well for a schema with a dense fact table and a small number of dimensions. When there are a large number of dimensions and the fact table is sparse, the star transformation method is a more optimal method. Essentially, the star transformation method transforms the star query into subqueries using bitmap index access paths on the individual constraints without the need of performing a Cartesian product and requiring a concatenated index on the fact table. The various bitmap indexes can then be merged together to complete the query. To enable star transformations you can use the `STAR_TRANSFORMATION` hint or set the Oracle8 `init.ora` parameter `star_transformation_enabled=TRUE`.

4.8.12.25 UNNEST or NO_UNNEST

The UNNEST hint allows the optimizer consider unnesting the subquery so that the subquery is merged with the parent query. This may foster additional access paths and additional query optimizations that may not be possible as a standalone subquery. The NO_UNNEST hint can be used to disable subquery unnesting. Subquery unnesting is a new feature in Oracle8i release 8.1.6 You can also set the init.ora parameter _unnest_subquery=TRUE in order to enable subquery unnesting.

4.8.12.26 ORDERED_PREDICATES

The ORDERED_PREDICATES hint is a new feature of Oracle8i which allows you to control the order of predicate evaluation or non-index filter evaluation. This hint can be useful for preserving the order of filter evaluation when the order of filter evaluation greatly reduces the answer set. For example, if you have several predicates or filters in the query, and one of the filters involves a PL/SQL function call, then you may want to order the predicates such that the most selective filters are executed before the PL/SQL function.

4.8.12.27 LEADING

The LEADING hint is a new feature of Oracle8i release 8.1.6 which allows you to specify the join order without manually ordering the FROM clause as is the case with the use of the ORDERED hint. The following example demonstrates the use of the LEADING hint to force the starting table.

```
SELECT /*+ LEADING (AB) */
        AI.INVOICE_ID,
        AI.INVOICE_NUM,
        AH.HOLD_REASON
FROM   AP_INVOICES  AI,
        AP_HOLDS AH,
        AP_BATCHES AB
WHERE AI.BATCH_ID = AB.BATCH_ID AND
        AI.INVOICE_ID = AH.INVOICE_ID AND
        AH.HOLD_LOOKUP_CODE = :b1
```

In the above example, the leading hint is used to tell the optimizer to use the AP_BATCHES table as the starting table in the join order. The LEADING hint is useful for when you want to specify the main driving table without having to manually reorder the FROM clause.

4.8.12.28 REWRITE or NOREWRITE

The REWRITE and NOREWRITE hints are used in conjunction with Materialized views which is a new feature of Oracle8i. The REWRITE hint is used to force query rewrite irrespective of cost. The REWRITE hint can be used to specify a Materialized view which to use for rewrite. If no Materialized view is specified with the REWRITE hint, the optimizer determines an eligible Materialized view and rewrites the query. The NOREWRITE can be used to disable query rewrite. You can also use the init.ora parameter query_rewrite_enabled to enable or disable query rewrite.

4.8.12.29 Global Hints

Global hints are yet another optimizer enhancement introduced in Oracle8*i* release 8.1.6. Table access hints, such as the INDEX, FULL, or USE_NL hints, typically apply directly to a table name or table alias. However, if your SQL statement references mostly views which consist of numerous table joins or set operators, such as UNION or MINUS, the use of hints in the base query may be limited by the fact that the optimizer ignores certain hints when used against a view. For example, if you have a query which references a view which consists of several joins, and you use an INDEX hint in the referencing query. The INDEX hint will be ignored because the optimizer does not push the hint inside the view query block. Global hints allow hints to be used against views by extending the current hint syntax via a dot notation. The dot notation allows the developer to specify the namespace of the hint in terms of which objects the hint should apply to. The following example query uses global hints to force a particular access method while accessing a complex and nested view.

```
select /*+ FULL (v1.T)
           LEADING (v1.BDB.CB)
           INDEX_FFS (v1.BDB.CB)
           FULL (v2.T) */
       v1.burden_cost_code,
       sum(v1.raw_cost),
       sum(v1.burden_cost)
from pa_cost_burden_details_v v1,
     pa_cost_burden_details_v v2
where v1.project_id=v2.project_id
group by v1.burden_cost_code
```

VIEW DEFINITION: pa cost burden details v

```
SELECT p.segment1,p.name,p.project_id,t.task_number,
       t.task_name, t.task_id, bdb.expenditure_organization,
       bdb.expenditure_organization_id, ei.expenditure_type,
       ei.expenditure_item_date, cdl.pa_date, cdl.gl_date,
       cdl.amount, cdl.burdened_cost
FROM pa_burden_details_base_v bdb,
     pa_projects_all p,
     pa_tasks t,
```

```
        pa_expenditures e,
        pa_expenditure_items ei,
        pa_cost_distribution_lines cdl
WHERE bdb.compiled_set_id = cdl.ind_compiled_set_id AND
        bdb.expenditure_type = ei.expenditure_type AND
        bdb.expenditure_organization_id=nvl(ei.override_to_organization_id,
                              e.incurred_by_organization_id) AND
        ei.expenditure_item_id = cdl.expenditure_item_id AND
                              cdl.line_type = 'R' AND
        e.expenditure_id = ei.expenditure_id AND t.task_id = ei.task_id AND
        p.project_id = t.project_id
```

VIEW DEFINITION: PA BURDEN DETAILS BASE V

```
SELECT ics.ind_compiled_set_id ,o.name ,ics.organization_id ,
        cbet.expenditure_type ,cb.cost_base ,cb.report_sort_order ,
        cm.ind_cost_code ,cm.precedence ,cm.multiplier ,
        cm.compiled_multiplier ,
        irs.ind_rate_sch_name ,irs.ind_rate_sch_id ,
        irsr.ind_rate_sch_revision ,
        irsr.ind_rate_sch_revision_id ,cbet.cost_plus_structure
FROM HR_ALL_ORGANIZATION_UNITS O,
        PA_COMPILED_MULTIPLIERS CM,
        PA_COST_BASE_EXP_TYPES CBET,
        PA_COST_BASES CB,
        PA_IND_COMPILED_SETS ICS,
        PA_IND_RATE_SCH_REVISIONS IRSR,
        PA_IND_RATE_SCHEDULES_ALL_BG IRS
WHERE cm.ind_compiled_set_id = ics.ind_compiled_set_id AND
        ics.ind_rate_sch_revision_id = irsr.ind_rate_sch_revision_id AND
        irsr.cost_plus_structure = cbet.cost_plus_structure AND
        cm.cost_base = cbet.cost_base AND
        cbet.cost_base_type = 'INDIRECT COST' AND
        irs.ind_rate_sch_id = irsr.ind_rate_sch_id AND
        ics.organization_id = o.organization_id AND
        cb.cost_base = cbet.cost_base AND
        cb.cost_base_type = cbet.cost_base_type
```

The following is a subsection of the full execution plan which demonstrates that the global hints have been applied.

```
NESTED LOOPS    Cost=1,1
    INDEX FAST FULL SCAN PA_COST_BASES_U1 Cost=1,1
        INDEX FULL SCAN PA_COST_BASE_EXP_TYPES_U1 Cost=,1
    TABLE ACCESS BY INDEX ROWID PA_EXPENDITURE_ITEMS_ALL Cost=,1
        INDEX RANGE SCAN PA_EXPENDITURE_ITEMS_N18 Cost=,1
    TABLE ACCESS BY INDEX ROWID PA_EXPENDITURES_ALL Cost=,1
        INDEX UNIQUE SCAN PA_EXPENDITURES_U1 Cost=,1
    TABLE ACCESS BY INDEX ROWID PA_COST_DISTRIBUTION_LINES_ALL
        Cost=,1
        INDEX RANGE SCAN PA_COST_DISTRIBUTION_LINES_U1 Cost=,1
    TABLE ACCESS FULL PA_COMPILED_MULTIPLIERS Cost=2,82
    TABLE ACCESS BY INDEX ROWID PA_IND_COMPILED_SETS Cost=,82
        INDEX RANGE SCAN PA_IND_COMPILED_SETS_N3 Cost=,82
    INDEX UNIQUE SCAN HR_ORGANIZATION_UNITS_PK Cost=,82
    TABLE ACCESS BY INDEX ROWID PA_IND_RATE_SCH_REVISIONS Cost=,82
        INDEX UNIQUE SCAN PA_IND_RATE_SCH_REVISIONS_U1 Cost=,82
    INDEX UNIQUE SCAN PA_IND_RATE_SCHEDULES_U1 Cost=,82
TABLE ACCESS FULL PA_TASKS Cost=2,82
    INDEX UNIQUE SCAN PA_PROJECTS_U1 Cost=,82
  INDEX UNIQUE SCAN PA_PROJECTS_U1 Cost=,82
TABLE ACCESS FULL PA_TASKS Cost=2,82
```

In the above example, the query references the complex view PA_COST_BURDEN_DETAILS_V and specifies that a full-table scan should be performed on the alias V1.T and V2.T. The alias T maps to the table PA_TASKS inside the view PA_COST_BURDEN_DETAILS_V. The query uses the aliases V1 and V2, one for each instance of the view PA_COST_BURDEN_DETAILS_V. The dot notation used in the hint [FULL (V1.T)] represents the new syntax for global hints, which allows a developer to provide a hint to the optimizer as to which object the hint should be applied. The global hints feature also allows hints to be used against deeply nested views by continuing the dot notation until final object resolution. In the example above, the LEADING hint is used to request that the optimizer start with the table PA_COST_BASES as specified via the hint dot syntax V1.BDB.CB. The reference to V1 refers to the first instance of the view PA_COST_BURDEN_DETAILS_V, and the BDB alias refers to the view PA_BURDEN_DETAILS_BASE_V, which is yet another view referenced by the view PA_COST_BURDEN_DETAILS_V. The view PA_BURDEN_DETAILS_BASE_V then directly references the table PA_COST_BASES via the table alias CB.

Global hints are an extremely useful feature for applications which are largely based on views. Global hints allow developers to tune SQL statements which reference complex views without having to directly insert the hints in the view or manually expand the referencing query to include the view definitions.

4.8.13 STORED OUTLINES

Stored outlines are a new feature of Oracle8*i* which can be used to provide execution plan stability. Stored outlines can also be used in place of hints. One of the main issues with using optimizer hints is that manual code changes may be needed in order to introduce the hint in the SQL statement. For example, if a particular SQL statement is resulting in a sub-optimal execution plan in the production environment and a quick turnaround is needed to resolve the issue, then outlines can be used to tune the SQL statement without the need to change the application code. Stored outlines can also be used to facilitate plan stability from environmental changes. Gathering statistics or configuration changes, including modifications to the `init.ora` parameters such as the hash area size or sort area size, may result in execution plan changes. Stored outlines can be used to maintain plan stability across such environmental changes.

Stored outlines can also be used to migrate applications from the rule-based optimizer to the cost-based optimizer. Stored outlines can be organized into different categories based on application criteria, such as by module. Stored outlines use optimizer hints to enforce plan stability. When a stored outline is created, a series of optimizer hints for the SQL statement is generated and stored in the data dictionary. The hints that are generated are based on the execution plans from the environment where the outlines were created. For example, if the outlines were created when the optimizer mode was set to RULE, the stored outlines would reflect the equivalent set of optimizer hints.

You can create stored outlines by setting the `init.ora` parameter `create_stored_outlines=<outline category name>`. You can also store the outlines in the default category by setting the `init.ora` parameter `create_stored_outlines=TRUE`. In order to create the stored outlines, you can issue an `alter session set create_stored_outlines=TRUE`, and then execute the application or series of SQL statements for which you would like to generate stored outlines. Stored outlines use SQL text matching, which is white space sensitive; hence it is important that you execute the SQL statements from the application or ensure that the SQL statements being executed while the stored outlines are being created exactly match those of the application. If you plan to create stored outlines, you should enable the `create_stored_outlines` parameter, and then run the application or the portion of the application for which you would like to create stored outlines. You can also create stored outlines using the CREATE OUTLINE command. The following example illustrates the use of the CREATE OUTLINE command.

```
create or replace outline ol1
for category P_ORDERS on
select order_number
from oe_order_headers_v
where order_number=:b1;
```

Outlines are stored in the tables OL$ and OL$HINTS in the OUTLN schema. The dictionary view DBA_OUTLINES can be used to report information on the existing outlines including whether the outline has been used. The V$SQL view also contains the

OUTLINE_CATEGORY column, which lists the name of the outline category for the SQL statement if the cursor used an outline.

Once the outlines have been created, you can enable the usage of the outlines by setting the init.ora parameter use_stored_outlines=TRUE or use_stored_outlines=<outline_category_name>. If the session has enabled stored outline usage (e.g., alter session set use_stored_outlines), then the optimizer will find a matching outline for the particular SQL statement, and bind the cursor to the outline as opposed to generating a new execution plan. In 8.1.6, the algorithm for caching outlines was improved, which reduced the overhead of loading and accessing outline information.

4.8.14 USING PARALLEL QUERY

In some cases, further optimization of an SQL statement may not be possible due to the nature of the query. The query may be used in a complex report which aggregates a lot of information and effectively passes across most of the data set. This is very common with data warehousing applications which perform full scans and aggregate large amounts of data for the sake of analysis. In such cases, parallel query can be used to reduce the overall elapsed time of the query. The parallel query option, introduced in Oracle 7.1, causes query slave processes to be created, and the base connection is transformed into the query coordinator. The query coordinator is then responsible for dividing the work across the query slaves. Once the query slaves complete their scans, the query coordinator is signaled, and a final merge is done merging the individual slaves. Figure 4.6 illustrates the parallel query option.

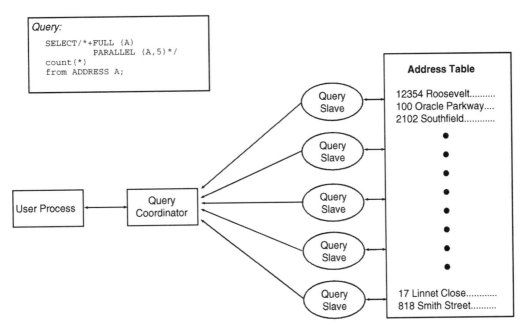

FIGURE 4.6   Parallel query option.

In Figure 4.6, the query uses the parallel query option. In this example, five query slaves (as specified by the degree of parallelism of five in the parallel hint) are spawned by the query coordinator. The query slaves each scan a section of the table and signal the query coordinator when complete. Once all the slaves have completed their scans, the query coordinator merges the results from the query slaves and returns the result to the user process. Parallel query can be used to significantly reduce the time needed to scan a table.

The parallel query option can also be used to parallelize a join. For example, suppose you want to determine the total count of customers broken down by geographic region. The query might look something like this:

```
SQL> SELECT /*+ ORDERED
                FULL ( C)
                FULL (A)
                PARALLEL (C,10)
                PARALLEL (A,10)
                USE_HASH (A C)
                USE_HASH (Z A) */
        Z.ZIP_CODE, count(*)
        FROM ZIP Z,
             ADDRESS A,
             CUSTOMER C
        WHERE (C.ADDRESS_ID=A.ADDRESS_ID) AND
              (A.ZIP_ID = Z.ZIP_ID)
        GROUP BY Z.ZIP_CODE
        ORDER BY Z.ZIP_CODE
```

There are two types of parallelism when the parallel query option is used: *intraparallelism* and *interparallelism*. The intraoperation parallelism is the degree of parallelism used for a single operation, such as a full-table scan in parallel without any joins or sorts. The interoperation parallelism is the degree of parallelism used between operations, such as a full-table scan and a join. The preceding query demonstrates an example of the interoperation parallelism. The query specifies a degree of parallelism of 10 for the full-table scan. However, once this query is executed, 20 query slaves will be created. Ten of the query slaves will be used to scan the objects, and ten of the slaves will be used to perform the sort and hash join. This not only allows the scan to be parallelized, it also parallelizes the hash join, which can reduce the time of the scan and the join significantly. The parallel query option provides tremendous flexibility and functionality by allowing single scans and joins to be parallelized, thus reducing the elapsed time by an almost linear factor.

The parallel query option uses slave processes to parallelize the query. Each slave process scans a different section of the table. Therefore, it is important that your data be distributed (or striped) across multiple disk drives and controllers. If your data is not distributed properly, using parallel query can have a negative effect by saturating one or a few disks. Distributing your data using the guidelines presented in Chapter 3 can help the query slaves achieve near linear performance by minimizing I/O contention. For more information on the parallel query option, refer to the *Oracle8i Designing and Tuning for Performance* guide. Use an explain plan on your query to verify that your hints are being accepted and the query is being executed in parallel. The OBJECT_NODE column of the explain plan table describes the degree of parallelism used for a given query. The OTHER column of the explain plan table shows the text of the query being distributed to each query slave.

The OTHER_TAG column of the explain plan table can be used to determine whether or not a query is being parallelized. If a query is being parallelized, the OTHER_TAG also indicates the stage or event of the parallel query for each operation. The following are the different types of parallel query events.

- ❑ PARALLEL_TO_PARALLEL
- ❑ PARALLEL_TO_SERIAL
- ❑ SERIAL_TO_PARALLEL
- ❑ PARALLEL_COMBINED_WITH_PARENT
- ❑ PARALELL_COMBINED_WITH_CHILD

The PARALLEL_TO_PARALLEL event indicates that interparallelism is being used and the output of the parallel operation is being sent to another set of parallel slaves for further parallelization. This is usually the case for sorts, hash joins, and merge-joins. The PARALLEL_TO_SERIAL event indicates that the results of the parallel query execution will be returned to the Query Coordinator (QC) process. The SERIAL_TO_PARALLEL event refers to the step whereby the QC is partitioning the work to the parallel slaves. In the PARALLEL_COMBINED_WITH_PARENT and PARALLEL_COMBINED_WITH_CHILD phases, output from the parallel operation proceeds to the next step within the same parallel process. In this case, no interprocess communication to the parent is required. Using the OTHER_TAG column in addition to the other information from the explain plan allows you to examine the individual steps of your parallel query. The information provided in the explain plan is extremely useful when analyzing complex parallel queries with multiple joins. It is crucial that you become familiar with the explain plan utility in order to understand query execution behavior and tune your queries effectively. More uses of the parallel query option follow in Chapter 6.

4.9   USING PL/SQL

PL/SQL is Oracle's procedural language extension to SQL. PL/SQL has many features above and beyond SQL's capabilities. Using PL/SQL, you can create stored procedures and packages that maximize the power of the server. For example, you can use PL/SQL to invoke stored procedures and packages on the database server. This can help reduce the workload on the client by moving *heavy* processing from the client to the server, where it belongs. This not only reduces network traffic between the client and the server, it also maximizes the use of the server. Database servers tend to be multiprocessor machines with large amounts of memory. Running stored procedures and PL/SQL on the server is much more efficient than duplicating the same code on the client using SQL or some 4GL language. PL/SQL provides a tremendous amount of functionality and can drastically increase performance over the traditional client SQL calls.

Use PL/SQL to process long-running SQL operations such as inserts, updates, or deletes that operate on a large number of rows. This avoids the excessive network traffic caused by traditional SQL calls to first fetch the data and then send the data back with its updates. You can accomplish the same task by invoking PL/SQL stored procedures and packages, thereby reducing the network traffic massively. You can call PL/SQL stored procedures and packages from PRO*C and Oracle Developer. When you design the application, try to make as much use of server PL/SQL where appropriate. Using PL/SQL server side units where appropriate not only increases overall application performance, but it also maintains business rules and application logic in one central location. If the business rules change, you have to make the change in only one place: the database server. This is a far superior approach over having to change the client application code and redeploy the application to accommodate the change in business rules or logic.

4.9.1 PL/SQL TYPES

PL/SQL 2.3 also provides the ability to create PL/SQL tables (not to be confused with database tables). PL/SQL tables are basically an array of like elements, with the exception that indexing into the array is not done through a consecutive sequential counter as is done with traditional arrays. With PL/SQL tables, you build a table that specifies the data type of the table as well as the index of the table. The index of the table is a binary integer ranging from –2147483647 to +2147483647. This table index option is known as sparsity and allows meaningful index numbers such as customer numbers, employee numbers, or other useful index keys. PL/SQL tables provide an ideal method to process large amounts of data. The PL/SQL tables can be used in PRO*C as well as OCI. This allows you to pass in arrays from PRO*C into PL/SQL stored procedures in order to process large batches of data. PL/SQL tables can increase performance by operating on tables rather than single rows.

If your application makes extensive use of PL/SQL tables, you should ensure that the tables are indexed by binary integer, and that the index is based on the application key. For example, if you build a PL/SQL table containing customer information, you may want use the `customer_id` as the index to facilitate quick searches of the PL/SQL table. When using PL/SQL tables in your application, try to avoid coding FOR loops, which effectively scan the PL/SQL table until a match is found. Even though PL/SQL tables are in-memory structures, this type of scan is inefficient and a database lookup via an index would probably be faster than scanning through a large PL/SQL table sequentially.

Oracle8 expanded PL/SQL to provide the TABLE and VARRAY (variable-size array) collection types. The TABLE collection type is referred to as a nested table. Nested tables are unlimited in size and can be sparse, meaning that elements within the nested table can be deleted using the DELETE procedure. Variable size arrays have a maximum size and maintain their order and subscript when stored in the database. Nested table data is stored in a system table that is associated with the nested table. Variable size arrays are suited for batch operations in which the application processes the data in batch array style. Nested tables make for efficient queries by storing the nested table in a storage table in which each element maps to a row in the storage table. For more information on collection types, refer to the *PL/SQL User's Guide and Reference*.

Numerous performance enhancements which increase the performance of collection types by orders of magnitude were made to collection types in Oracle*8i*.

4.9.2 EXTERNAL PROCEDURES

PL/SQL 8.0 provides a new feature known as external procedures which allows you to call an external host language procedure from PL/SQL. This allows you to utilize the power of the C host language to accomplish certain tasks better suited in a host language like C than in PL/SQL. For example, you may want to have a PL/SQL procedure invoke an external procedure that performs intense and complex mathematical calculations. The external program is in the form of a dynamic-link library (DLL) which needs to be registered with PL/SQL. The PL/SQL interface then loads the DLL at run-time and calls the routine as if it were a PL/SQL routine. The external procedure feature can be extremely useful for scientific or engineering applications that need the power of the host language.

There are a few steps needed to configure an external procedure. You must identify the DLL, and then register the DLL with PL/SQL. For example, to identify the DLL you would use the following command.

```
SQL> create library banklib as '/apps/lib/banklib.so';

SQL> CREATE FUNCTION getlpaym (
        - Determine the optimal payment
        - plan for a customer loan
        - using a complex financial model.
          irat FLOAT,
          mperd BINARY_INTEGER,
          crsks BINARY_INTEGER,
          lamount FLOAT)
     RETURN BINARY_INTEGER AS EXTERNAL
     LIBRARY banklib
     NAME "getlpaym"   - quotes preserve lower case
     LANGUAGE C;
```

External procedures are ideal for applications performing complex data analysis or modeling allowing the application to benefit from the power of the host language. External procedures should not be used for short-lived functions that are frequently called by the PL/SQL application. For example, using an external procedure to perform simple operations such as adding two numbers and then return the result to PL/SQL is not an optimal use of external procedures. The overhead of performing frequent call-outs to external procedures that are short-lived may have a negative effect on overall application performance.

Therefore, it is important that you carefully review the application architecture and process flow before deciding to implement application modules as external procedures. When used appropriately, external procedures can provide tangible benefits to certain applications.

4.9.3 NATIVE DYNAMIC SQL

Oracle8*i* provides a new native interface to execute dynamic SQL directly within PL/SQL. Prior to Oracle8*i*, the DBMS_SQL package was needed in order to perform dynamic SQL from PL/SQL. The new dynamic SQL interface is much easier to use than the DBMS_SQL equivalent, and offers improved performance over DBMS_SQL. The new interface is via the EXECUTE IMMEDIATE statement. The following is an example of the new interface.

```
declare

  l_horders_rec oe_order_headers_all%ROWTYPE;
  l_order_num number(10):=10;
  l_sql_str varchar2(32000);

begin

        l_sql_str :='select * from OE_ORDER_HEADERS_ALL
            where ORDER_NUMBER = :b1';

        EXECUTE IMMEDIATE l_sql_str INTO l_horders_rec USING
l_order_num;

end;
```

The new dynamic SQL interface is much easier to use than the DBMS_SQL package. In addition, EXECUTE IMMEDIATE is faster than DBMS_SQL in cases where the application builds a dynamic SQL statement, opens the cursor, executes the cursor, and closes the cursor. The performance improvement between EXECUTE IMMEDIATE and DBMS_SQL varies depending on the application usage of dynamic SQL. In internal tests using Oracle Applications, a 25 percent performance improvement was observed after converting the code from DBMS_SQL to use the new EXECUTE IMMEDIATE interface. Each execution of EXECUTE IMMEDIATE results in a soft parse; hence it is important to keep this in mind when deciding whether or not to convert to the new interface. The new interface increases dynamic SQL execution performance; however, the soft parse overhead introduced by EXECUTE IMMEDIATE may actually diminish the gains. DBMS_SQL is useful for situations where the same cursor is being reexecuted, and only the bind values are changing. In such a case, DBMS_SQL will outperform EXECUTE IMMEDIATE because DBMS_SQL allows the application to open the cursor once, and then execute the cursor repeatedly, whereas EXECUTE IMMEDIATE would incur a soft parse for each execution.

4.9.4 BULK OPERATIONS

Oracle8 offered the ability to perform bulk binds in OCI8. Oracle8*i* extends this functionality to PL/SQL. Using this feature, an array of bind variables can be sent to the SQL engine in a single SQL statement. This avoids having to resend the same statement multiple times, each with different bindings. This is similar to the array interface provided in OCI and PRO*C. Using this feature helps reduce communication overhead and can improve performance considerably. Using the FORALL keyword in the PL/SQL block, bulk binds can be performed for DML statements as well as DML returns. The return values can be sent as a group once the bulk bind DML has completed. The following is an example of using bulk binds in PL/SQL.

```
declare

  TYPE t_order_rec is TABLE OF NUMBER(15);

  l_order_rec t_order_rec:=t_order_rec(100,101,1500,2000,2100);
  l_order_num number(10):=10;
  l_batch_size number(10):=100;

begin

      FORALL i in l_order_rec.first..l_order_rec.last
        UPDATE OE_ORDER_HEADERS_ALL
          SET OPEN_FLAG = 'N'
        WHERE ORDER_NUMBER = l_order_rec(i);

end;

/
```

You can also perform bulk inserts, fetches, deletes, and updates. The following example illustrates the bulk fetch operation using the LIMIT clause to control the fetch batch size.

```
declare

  TYPE t_num_arr is TABLE OF NUMBER(15);

  l_ordernum_arr t_num_arr;
  l_headerid_arr t_num_arr;
  l_num_fetches pls_integer:=0;
  l_batch_size number(10):=100;
```

```
    CURSOR order_cur IS SELECT ORDER_NUMBER,HEADER_ID
                    FROM OE_ORDER_HEADERS_ALL WHERE OPEN_FLAG='Y';

begin

    OPEN order_cur;

    LOOP

      FETCH order_cur
          BULK COLLECT INTO l_ordernum_arr, l_headerid_arr
          LIMIT l_batch_size;
      EXIT WHEN order_cur%NOTFOUND;
      l_num_fetches:=l_num_fetches+1;

    END LOOP;

    CLOSE order_cur;

    dbms_output.put_line ('Number of Fetches = '|||l_num_fetches);

end;

/
```

The BULK operations are significantly faster than the traditional looping construct which executes an SQL statement per iteration. The BULK operation reduces the number of SQL calls and reduces the communication overhead between the SQL layer and the PL/SQL engine. Using collection types in conjunction with the bulk operations can increase the performance of your application.

4.9.5 PASSING BY REFERENCE

Oracle8*i* allows PL/SQL parameters to be passed by reference. The default is that IN parameters are passed by reference, but IN-OUT and OUT parameters are passed by value. For large parameters such as PL/SQL tables or RECORD types, passing by value results in additional overhead in copying the values, which involves setting up PL/SQL stack frames for the data to be copied. In Oracle8*i*, OUT and IN-OUT parameters may be passed by reference or by value. In Oracle8 release 8.0, only IN parameters could be passed by reference. The OUT and IN-OUT parameters are copied by default. Oracle8*i* allows certain parameters to be passed by reference, thus improving efficiency when dealing with large-size variables. The NOCOPY PL/SQL compiler hint can be used to instruct the PL/SQL compiler to pass the parameter by reference (if possible). The NOCOPY hint should be used for passing parameters such as PL/SQL tables, collection types, or large-size parameters. The performance increase associated with using the NOCOPY hint is extremely visible for procedures which are frequently called and for which the parameters are either IN-OUT or OUT consisting of PL/SQL tables or collection types. Internal tests using Oracle Applications have resulted in gains of approximately 40 percent in application throughput. The overhead of copying the parameters was eliminated, and for procedures which are frequently called, this can translate into a massive savings. The NOCOPY hint should be placed following the IN-OUT or OUT declaration, such as:

```
PROCEDURE myproc1 (l_mfg_rec IN OUT NOCOPY t_mfg_rec)
```

4.9.6 USING VARIABLE ASSIGNMENT IN PLACE OF SQL

PL/SQL allows direct variable assignment of variables such as SYSDATE or complex expressions. You should use native PL/SQL assignment as opposed to the classic approach of selecting a value from DUAL. For example, instead of SELECT SYSDATE INTO l_sdate FROM DUAL, you can assign the value of SYSDATE directly to l_sdate using l_sdate := SYSDATE. On the average, SQL queries which reference only the DUAL table result in five buffer gets per execution. Hence, for frequently executed code which accesses the DUAL table, it can result in a large number of buffer gets. Try to avoid using SQL to compute the value of an expression such as "select (l_var1 * l_var2) / (l_var3) from DUAL." Instead, you can use direct PL/SQL variable assignment in place of selecting from the DUAL table.

4.9.7 REF CURSORS

PL/SQL supports the use of cursors which can be based on dynamic SQL. Such cursors are known as REF cursors. REF cursors are typically used as an interface medium between PL/SQL programs and host programming languages. The syntax for opening a REF cursor is OPEN <cursorname> FOR <sql statement>. REF cursors are always soft parsed since they are essentially similar to dynamic SQL. Therefore, if you do not need the functionality of a REF cursor, and the SQL statement is mostly static, you should use a regular cursor in order to avoid the additional overhead of a soft parse for each execution.

4.9.8 INVOKERS RIGHTS

PL/SQL 8*i* introduces a new feature, known as invokers rights, which allows a PL/SQL package or procedure to be invoked as the executing user or the owning user of the PL/SQL unit. By default, PL/SQL units are executed as the owner. For example, if USER1 calls a package P1 which is owned by the USER2 schema, then the P1 package is executed under the USER2 schema. However, in Oracle8*i*, you can specify that the procedure or package should be executed as the caller rather than the owner. The new AUTHID clause can be used to specify whether the package or procedure should use an invokers rights model (AUTHID CURRENT_USER) or the default behavior of definers rights (AUTHID DEFINER). The AUTHID clause should be used in the header for a standalone PL/SQL unit, or in the package specification for a package. For example, `CREATE OR REPLACE PACKAGE OPROD.PROCESS_MFG_REQ AUTHID {CURRENT_USER | DEFINER}] {IS | AS}`.

In Oracle8*i* release 8.1.5, SQL statements issued from within PL/SQL units which have invokers rights enabled result in a soft parse for each execution. This is different than the normal behavior of static SQL statements within PL/SQL units which parses the SQL once and does not subsequently soft parse the SQL for repeated executions within the same session. However, for invokers rights packages, the static SQL will be soft parsed for each execution within the same session. In Oracle8*i* release 8.1.6, an optimization was made to avoid the soft parse for static SQL statements within invokers rights PL/SQL units, provided that the user remains the same across executions, which is typically the case.

4.9.9 PL/SQL PROFILER

The PL/SQL profiler is another feature of PL/SQL 8i which allows PL/SQL code to be profiled. The profiler is extremely useful for PL/SQL based applications. The profiler data helps you identify the frequently executed code segments, and the hot spots in the code. The information can then be used to investigate further optimization possibilities. Prior to 8i, it was difficult for developers to identify specific performance problems in PL/SQL code. In most cases, developers would focus more on the SQL statements which were executed from the PL/SQL package or procedure rather than on the other PL/SQL code such as loops, parameter passing, or use of PL/SQL data structures. The PL/SQL profiler reports timings and number of executions for each line of code in the PL/SQL unit. Lines which were not executed will have a zero execution count, which can be useful to help identify possible *"dead code"* segments.

The PL/SQL Profiler package `DBMS_PROFILER` allows you to enable and disable profiling. The `profload.sql` script located in the `$ORACLE_HOME/rdbms/admin` directory creates the `DBMS_PROFILER` package. You should run the `profload.sql` script via `svrmgrl` (connect internal). The `proftab.sql` script, located in the `$ORACLE_HOME/rdbms/admin` directory, creates the run-time PL/SQL profiler tables which are used to store the profile output following a completed run. You should create these tables in your private schema or in the schema from which your application executes. The tables `PLSQL_PROFILER_DATA`, `PLSQL_PROFILER_UNITS`, and `PLSQL_PROFILER_RUNS` store the line level profile information, unit level profile information, and run level profile information, respectively.

The `START_PROFILER` procedure or function starts PL/SQL profile collection, and the `STOP_PROFILER` procedure flushes the PL/SQL profiler information collected during the run to the PL/SQL profiler tables. The PL/SQL profiler run-time information is stored in memory so as not to incur the expense of constantly flushing the profiler data to the PL/SQL profiler tables. The following example shows how the PL/SQL profiler can be used to collect profile information for the application.

```
SQL>select dbms_profiler.start_profiler('MY_TEST_PROFILER') from dual;
SQL>@run_my_plsql_code_script
SQL>select dbms_profiler.stop_profiler from dual;
SQL>@profsum
```

The `profsum.sql` script summarizes the PL/SQL profiler data by unit and then provides line level details for each line of each PL/SQL unit. The `profsum.sql` script is located in the `$ORACLE_HOME/plsql/demo` directory. The following is sample output from `profsum.sql`.

```
RUNID   RUN_COMMENT        SECONDS
-----   ----------------   --------
   13   MY_TEST_PROFILER   1194.31
```

RUNID	RUN_COMMENT	OWNER	UNIT_NAME	SECONDS	PRCNT
13	MY_TEST_PROF	APPS	OE_LINE_UTIL	78.52	6.6
13	MY_TEST_PROF	APPS	OE_LINE_PCFWK	51.05	4.3
13	MY_TEST_PROF	APPS	OE_DELAYED_REQUESTS_	43.35	3.6
13	MY_TEST_PROF	APPS	OE_ORDER_PVT	41.64	3.5
13	MY_TEST_PROF	SYS	STANDARD	40.30	3.4
13	MY_TEST_PROF	APPS	OE_DELAYED_REQUESTS_	40.19	3.4
13	MY_TEST_PROF	APPS	OE_LINE_UTIL_EXT	37.81	3.2
13	MY_TEST_PROF	APPS	OE_DEBUG_PUB	36.44	3.1
13	MY_TEST_PROF	APPS	ONT_LINE_DEF_UTIL	28.95	2.4
13	MY_TEST_PROF	APPS	ONT_LINE_DEF_HDLR	26.78	2.2
13	MY_TEST_PROF	APPS	OE_ORDER_IMPORT_PVT	23.42	2.0
13	MY_TEST_PROF	APPS	OE_ORDER_SCH_UTIL	20.17	1.7
13	MY_TEST_PROF	SYS	DBMS_SYS_SQL	19.92	1.7
13	MY_TEST_PROF	APPS	INV_RESERVATION_PVT	19.06	1.6
13	MY_TEST_PROF	APPS	WF_ITEM	18.89	1.6
13	MY_TEST_PROF	APPS	OE_DEFAULT_LINE	18.61	1.6
13	MY_TEST_PROF	APPS	ARP_PROCESS_TAX	15.72	1.3
13	MY_TEST_PROF	APPS	FND_PROFILE	15.71	1.3
13	MY_TEST_PROF	APPS	QP_PRICING_ENGINE_PV	15.64	1.3
13	MY_TEST_PROF	APPS	WF_ENGINE	14.31	1.2
13	MY_TEST_PROF	APPS	WF_CORE	13.79	1.2
13	MY_TEST_PROF	APPS	OE_DEPENDENCIES	13.55	1.1
13	MY_TEST_PROF	APPS	QP_PRC_UTIL	12.68	1.1

The PL/SQL profiler collects times in units of nanoseconds, using a high-resolution timer. The `profsum.sql` script converts nanoseconds to seconds for reporting purposes. If your application consists of numerous PL/SQL units, scanning through the detail reports may be cumbersome. You can use the following SQL script, which reports the line level detail information on a per-unit and per-run basis.

SCRIPT: profdetail.sql

```
col seconds format 9999.99
col text format a50 trunc
col total_occur format 99999 heading '#Occ'
col line format 99999 heading 'Line#'

break on report
compute sum of seconds on report

select d.line# line, d.total_occur, d.total_time as nanoseconds,
       p.text
  from plsql_profiler_data d,
       plsql_profiler_units u,
       plsql_source p
 where p.line = d.line#
   and p.type in ('PACKAGE BODY','PROCEDURE')
   and p.name = upper('&unit_name')
   and p.owner = &schema_owner
   and d.unit_number = u.unit_number
   and d.runid = u.runid
   and p.name = u.unit_name
   and p.type = u.unit_type
   and p.owner = u.unit_owner
   and u.runid = &run_id
 order by p.line;
```

The following sample output shows the line level detail for the PL/SQL unit WF_ENGINE.

```
Line# #Occ NANOSECONDS   TEXT
----- ---- -----------   ------------------------------------------------
   33  440     1880191    if (not Wf_Item.Item_Exist(itemtype, itemkey)) t
   34    0           0      Wf_Core.Token('TYPE', itemtype);
   35    0           0      Wf_Core.Token('KEY', itemkey);
   36    0           0      Wf_Core.Raise('WFENG_ITEM');
   39  220      856117    if (itemkey = wf_engine.eng_synch) then
   41    0           0      wf_engine.synch_attr_count := wf_engine.synch_
   42    0           0      wf_engine.synch_attr_arr(wf_engine.synch_attr_
   43    0           0      wf_engine.synch_attr_arr(wf_engine.synch_attr_
   45    0           0      wf_engine.synch_attr_arr(wf_engine.synch_attr_
   47    0           0      wf_engine.synch_attr_arr(wf_engine.synch_attr_
   50  220    78911105      insert into WF_ITEM_ATTRIBUTE_VALUES (
   69    0           0      Wf_Core.Context('Wf_Engine', 'AddItemAttr', it
   70    0           0      Wf_Core.Token('TYPE', itemtype);
```

```
 71     0           0    Wf_Core.Token('KEY', itemkey);
 72     0           0    Wf_Core.Token('ATTRIBUTE', aname);
 73     0           0    Wf_Core.Raise('WFENG_ITEM_ATTR_UNIQUE');
 75     0           0    Wf_Core.Context('Wf_Engine', 'AddItemAttr', it
 76   220      871931    raise;
103     0           0    if (not Wf_Item.Item_Exist(itemtype, itemkey)) t
104     0           0    Wf_Core.Token('TYPE', itemtype);
```

The line level timings do not include the overhead of the PL/SQL profiler, while the total run time reported by PROFSUM does include the overhead of the profiler. The percentages reported by profsum.sql are percentages based on the total elapsed time, hence the percentages reported by profsum.sql are lower than the actual percentages. However, you should focus on the times reported for each unit. You can then identify the units which account for the majority of the time, and then use the detail script (profdetail.sql) to report the line level detail for the particular units.

When generating PL/SQL profiler data, it is good idea to compile your packages in debug mode so that the line timing attribution is as accurate as possible. To compile your package in debug mode, use the ALTER PACKAGE command, such as ALTER PACKAGE <package name> COMPILE DEBUG BODY.

In addition, you may observe that the PL/SQL profiler is attributing a large amount of time to the first line of the package and/or the last line of the package. This indicates that the cost of package initialization and package exit (i.e., tear down) is a reasonable portion of the total execution time. In such a case, this usually means that the package has a lot of large-size package variables, such as large PL/SQL tables or records. You will need to optimize these structures and try to reduce the number and size of the package data structures. In addition, if you are passing records or PL/SQL tables, make sure that you pass them by reference using the new NOCOPY compiler hint. This should reduce the package initialization and termination costs. Another possible cause of time attribution to the last or first line of packages is due to variable initialization. For example, in one case, we observed a variable which was based on a record type consisting of over 300 fields. The record was declared such that each field had a default value. This means that each time the package was called, the PL/SQL engine had to initialize each and every member of the record with the default value being specified. This is extremely expensive, and it is best not to initialize every field with default values. You should initialize only those fields which absolutely require default values.

The PL/SQL profiler is an extremely useful feature which allows PL/SQL developers to profile their PL/SQL code and identify the hot and expensive code segments. As with any profiling tool, the overhead of the PL/SQL profiler is quite substantial. However, since the line level times do not account for the overhead of the profiler, you can easily identify the overhead of the profiler by comparing the wall clock time (i.e., total elapsed time) with the total line level times. You should use the PL/SQL profiler to profile your PL/SQL code so that you can investigate the possibilities of additional code optimizations.

4.10   NATIONAL LANGUAGE SUPPORT

Oracle8 also extended National Language Support (NLS) for applications by providing the new NLS data types NCHAR and NVARCHAR2. National Language support allows number and date formats to automatically adapt to the language conventions specified by a user's session. This allows native language interaction between Oracle and the application. PL/SQL also supports a national character set that is used for NLS data. The NCHAR and NVARCHAR2 PL/SQL data types enable you to store character strings that are formed from the national character set.

Oracle8 also provides the ability to create a database using the UTF8 character set. The UTF8 character set is based on the variable width encoding Unicode standard. The UTF8 character set is useful for global-based applications which require a single database. For example, a multinational corporation may want to globalize operations without having a localized database per region. The UTF8 character set allows the corporation to create one database and handle transactions originating from different regions while being able to preserve region semantics such as NLS locale.

Numerous performance enhancements were made to the NLS layer in Oracle8*i* in order to improve the performance of databases using multibyte and UTF8 character sets.

4.11   APPLICATION LOCKING

In a distributed application, locking can cause a high number of waits. You can increase the performance of your application by reducing the number of locks held as well as the length of time the lock is held. For example, if you have an application that needs to update rows in a table, lock only those rows and commit the update once it is complete to release the locks. Do not acquire exclusive locks on objects unless they are absolutely needed, and if needed, avoid holding the lock for an extended period of time. One common technique used to lock rows in a PRO*C application is to SELECT the rows for update. The FOR UPDATE clause locks those rows that satisfy the predicate of the query (if no predicate is given, all rows are selected). The FOR UPDATE clause causes the application to wait until the locks are obtained unless the NOWAIT option was specified in the FOR UPDATE clause. This means that the process or application could experience long wait times if another process holds the locks for a long time, or if a number of other users are waiting on the locks. To minimize the contention, use the NOWAIT option when locking rows. If a lock cannot be obtained on the rows, then control is returned to the user with an error indicating that the lock could not be obtained. This will allow the application to continue processing and try for the lock again later.

Another typical PRO*C implementation is when the programmer fetches some rows with the FOR UPDATE clause and then issues an update to those rows following some local processing. To increase concurrency, do not lock the rows upon FETCH; rather, lock the rows as part of the UPDATE statement. This reduces the time that the row locks are held, allowing other users to get the locks on those rows while the application is doing some local processing. If, however, you do not need to lock the rows upon the fetch, then obtain the rowids as part of the fetch, and use the ROWID hint as part of the update. This increases the performance of the update because the update can use the rowids to update the rows.

The beauty of Oracle is that it is centered around the concept of fine-granular-level locking. To take advantage of this feature, design your application so that exclusive locks are avoided unless they are absolutely needed; and distribute the application processing so that data is operated on in smaller batches and in parallel. This avoids one process operating on a large amount of data and possibly preventing others from obtaining locks. Remember, think in parallel and asynchronously when designing an application.

4.11.1 DEADLOCK AND LOCKING ORDER

SQL statements which lock rows need to be analyzed carefully so that application deadlock or lock ordering issues are avoided. The Oracle database raises an error (ORA-60) when application deadlock occurs; however, it does not resolve the deadlock. The application must be designed in such a way that these scenarios do not occur. Consider the following cursor, which attempts to lock the qualifying rows.

```
CURSOR lock_departure(x_dep_id NUMBER) IS
    SELECT DEP.STATUS_CODE,
           DEL.STATUS_CODE,
           LD.LINE_DETAIL_ID,
           PLD.PICKING_LINE_DETAIL_ID
    FROM WSH_DEPARTURES          DEP,
         WSH_DELIVERIES          DEL,
         SO_LINE_DETAILS         LD,
         SO_PICKING_LINE_DETAILS PLD
    WHERE DEP.DEPARTURE_ID     = x_dep_id
    AND   DEL.ACTUAL_DEPARTURE_ID(+) = DEP.DEPARTURE_ID
    AND   LD.DEPARTURE_ID(+) = DEP.DEPARTURE_ID
    AND   PLD.DEPARTURE_ID(+) = DEP.DEPARTURE_ID
    FOR UPDATE NOWAIT;
```

The problem with this query is that the locking order is largely dependent on the execution plan and the row source order. For example, it is possible that the rows in SO_LINE_DETAILS can be locked before the rows in SO_PICKING_LINE_DETAILS. It is also possible that the rows of SO_PICKING_LINE_DETAILS are locked before the rows in SO_LINE_DETAILS. The locking order is based on the join order (i.e., execution plan). If one user ran this query under the RBO, and another user ran this query under the CBO, locking order issues could arise due to the likelihood of a plan difference.

Another problem with this cursor is that it performs a nonqualified locking via the FOR UPDATE. The FOR UPDATE clause can take additional optional arguments which specify the tables to be locked. For example, FOR UPDATE OF DEP means that only the rows in WSH_DEPARTURES should be locked.

The solution to this query is to specify the tables to be locked in the FOR UPDATE clause via the FOR option, or to break the query into separate cursors such that each cursor locks a single table only. For example, the above cursor can be rewritten as follows.

```
CURSOR lock_departure(x_dep_id NUMBER) IS
    select departure_id
      from WSH_DEPARTURES
      where DEPARTURE_ID = x_dep_id
      FORUPDATE NOWAIT;

CURSOR lock_deliveries(x_dep_id NUMBER) IS
    select  delivery_id
      from WSH_DELIVERIES
      where ACTUAL_DEPARTURE_ID = x_dep_id
      FOR UPDATE NOWAIT;

CURSOR lock_line_details(x_dep_id NUMBER) IS
    select  line_detail_id
      from SO_LINE_DETAILS
      where DEPARTURE_ID = x_dep_id
      FOR UPDATE NOWAIT;

CURSOR lock_picking_details(x_dep_id NUMBER) IS
    select  picking_line_detail_id
      from SO_PICKING_LINE_DETAILS
      where DEPARTURE_ID = x_dep_id
      FOR UPDATE NOWAIT;

Begin

            OPEN   lock_departure(entity_id);
            CLOSE lock_departure;

            OPEN   lock_deliveries(entity_id);
            CLOSE lock_deliveries;

            OPEN   lock_line_details(entity_id);
            CLOSE lock_line_details;

            OPEN   lock_picking_details(entity_id);
            CLOSE lock_picking_details;
End;
```

In summary, do not code an SQL statement which performs an unqualified lock via the `FOR UPDATE` clause. You should either break up the SQL statement into multiple single table cursors or specify the `FOR <table>` option of the `FOR UPDATE` clause.

4.11.2 SKIP LOCKED ROWS

Oracle8*i* allows you to perform a select for update and skip over the locked rows. This improves concurrency by avoiding situations where one session has a lock on a set of rows, and another session is forced to wait for the lock to be released. By using the `SKIP LOCKED` clause of the `SELECT FOR UPDATE` statement, you can skip over the locked rows and lock the remaining rows which satisfy the query. The following is an example of how to use the `SKIP LOCKED` option.

```
select order_id
from porders
where order_status = :b1
for update  skip locked;
```

The skip locked feature is extremely useful for queuing-based applications where multiple dequeue processes may exist whereby each process is looking for outstanding requests. If each dequeue process is issuing a `SELECT FOR UPDATE` statement in order to fetch and lock the rows to be processed, then the skip locked feature can be used to pass over the locked rows and pick up the available set of rows. The `SKIP LOCKED` rows allow multiple dequeue processes to work in parallel because without the `SKIP LOCKED` option, the processes would likely either wait on each other, or fail to obtain locks if the `NOWAIT` clause was specified.

4.12 USING THE SYSTEM PACKAGES

Oracle 7.2 and 7.3 introduced new system packages that allow you to submit jobs, communicate with different sessions, and submit remote procedure calls. The `DBMS_PIPE` package enables multiple sessions within the same instance to communicate with each other. The `DBMS_PIPE` package uses named pipes to communicate between sessions. You can use `DBMS_PIPE` to create public or private pipes. Private pipes allow different sessions of the same user `ID` to communicate with one another. Any user who has execute permission on `DBMS_PIPE` and knows the name of the pipe can use a public pipe. The `DBMS_PIPE` provides a mechanism for communication between sessions on the same instance by using named pipes. This is much faster than communicating via SQL or PL/SQL to send small messages. Database pipes (i.e., `DBMS_PIPES`) use library cache pins and unpins to synchronize access to the pipes. Hence, in certain situations, it is possible that latch contention can occur for the pipes if the application is using a single pipe to send and receive messages. Try to use a pool of pipes so that one particular pipe is not very hot. You should also monitor the session wait events (v$session_wait) and system wait events (v$system_event) for the event 'pipe put'. If sessions are waiting on the 'pipe put' event, this is an indication that the readers of the pipe are not keeping up with the writers. For example, if the pipe is full and a session is trying to write into the pipe, the writing session will wait on the 'pipe put' event until space in the pipe becomes available.

The DBMS_JOB also enables the administrator to schedule jobs, such as database maintenance scripts, analyzing tables, space management, or other typical database functions. The DBMS_JOB.SUBMIT procedure submits a job to the job queue. Oracle uses SNP background processes (SNP0 . . . SNP9). Each SNP process executes a job. You can set the number of SNP background processes by setting the init.ora parameter job_queue _processes.

You can also use the DBMS_ALERT package to register alerts. This allows for asynchronous notification of events. Using the DBMS_ALERT, a process could wait on an alert such as an insert into a table. Once the insert commits, the process waiting on the alert is signaled. The process can then continue processing and wait for the next alert following the completion of the processing. This provides a much better approach than sleeping and waking up every so often only to find that no work needs to be done. The DBMS_ALERT package allows a process to receive notification when specific database values change.

The DBMS_DEFER package is used to submit deferred remote procedure calls. The DBMS_DEFER.CALL procedure submits a deferred call to a remote procedure. The remote procedure call is not executed until the deferred call queue is pushed using either the DBMS_DEFER_SYS.SCHEDULE_EXECUTION procedure or the DBMS_DEFER_SYS.EXECUTE procedure. The deferred remote procedure call functionality is provided by the advanced replication option. For more information on the use of deferred remote procedure calls, refer to the *Oracle8i Replication Management API Reference*.

4.12.1 ADVANCED QUEUING

Oracle8 Advanced Queuing (AQ) integrates message queuing functionality into the Oracle8 kernel. Advanced Queuing offers SQL access to messages by storing the messages in a database table. This allows indexes to be utilized to improve message access times. The AQ queues consist of database tables, thus allowing you to manage queues using standard tools. AQ queues can also be imported and exported using the import and export utilities. Since Oracle8 is an object-relational database, messages can be routed based on the content or type of the message. Message contents can also be queried. The integration of messaging services into the database allows messages to be managed in similar fashion as other database objects. Oracle AQ also maintains history information of each message such as the ENQUEUE/DEQUEUE time. Oracle AQ also allows you to manage event journals which helps correlate related messages. Messages can also be prioritized and grouped. Oracle8 AQ allows you to send and receive messages between applications. AQ is integrated into the Oracle8 Server, and is extremely useful for applications that prior to Oracle8 had to develop a complete messaging system or rely on middleware to provide messaging services.

Oracle8 AQ consists of several basic components including the message, queue, queue table, agents, and the queue monitor. The message is the basic unit of information either inserted into or retrieved from a queue. The enqueue and dequeue calls create a message and consume the message, respectively. User queues are used to store messages and exception queues are used to store messages that incurred problems during processing or retrieval. Queue tables are database tables that consist of one or more queues and a default exception queue. Agents are queue users consisting of either consumers or producers of the messages. The queue monitor manages the messages in the queue via a background process. You can also utilize the AQ message queuing functionality from within your PRO*C and OCI applications. This allows your applications to maintain a high level of throughput by avoiding the overhead introduced when using a third-party middleware package to send messages between your applications.

The `init.ora` parameters `aq_tm_processes` and `job_queue_processes` specify the number of queue monitor processes and number of SNP background processes used for snapshots, DBA jobs, and message propagation, respectively. The `init.ora` parameter `job_queue_interval` specifies the period between wake-ups of the SNP background processes. No queue monitor processes are created if `aq_tm_processes=0`. The AQ system catalog tables `AQ$_MESSAGE_TYPES` (SYS schema), `AQ$_SCHEDULES` (SYSTEM schema), and `AQ$_QUEUE_STATISTICS` (SYS schema) can be used to monitor the message and queue statistics. The `catqueue.sql` (`$ORACLE_HOME/rdbms/admin`) script creates the AQ related objects. Oracle8*i* also provides a set of Java classes which allow Java applications to utilize the Advanced Queue APIs.

The Oracle8 AQ option is extremely useful for applications requiring messaging and queuing services. AQ provides a tremendous amount of functionality and flexibility over traditional middleware messaging packages. AQ can increase the performance of your application by utilizing the messaging services incorporated into the Oracle8 Server. For more information on AQ, please refer to the section on AQ in the *Oracle8i Application Developer's Guide—Advanced Queuing*.

4.13 PROFILING AND OPTIMIZATION

I recommend that you profile your application to determine where the majority of processor time is spent. This will allow you to examine the execution path and call graph in greater detail and possibly to identify any bottlenecks. For instance, you may find that your application is spending 40 percent of its time in a certain module or function. You can then analyze the module and/or function to determine if the module or function can be optimized. Profiling is extremely useful, and you should collect profiling statistics on your application before moving it into production. The profiling will also help you identify the source of an application bottleneck (if any). You may find that the bottleneck is in the application space itself, or the network, or the database server, or a combination thereof.

On Intel platforms, there are additional tools such as VTUNE from Intel that provide a great deal of useful information for application profiling. These tools report application statistics such as call graph profiles and cache utilization. VTUNE can be used to monitor different performance events and can also perform time-based sampling. Coupling these tools with the compiler allows you to study your application flow in detail and optimize accordingly. The statistics gathered from these tools will help you optimize your application in the areas of function flow and data structure design. OptimizeIT is a tool which can be used to profile Java based applications. OptimizeIT provides the capability to profile the Java application based on time and CPU utilization. OptimizeIT can be used to identify the hot classes and hot methods as well as identify where the majority of the execution time is being spent.

Optimization also helps improve the efficiency of object code by optimizing the object code generated. Compiler optimization techniques such as common subexpression elimination, register allocation and utilization, invariant loop hoisting, operation replacement, dead code elimination, loop pipelining, instruction scheduling, code in-lining, code motion frequency, feedback profiling, tail recursion elimination, loop parallelization, cache blocking, and loop inversion are attempts by the compiler to produce high-performance optimized code. Depending on the compiler, you should use the highest level of optimization (-On where n represents the level of optimization) when you compile your application. You should also try different levels of optimization to determine which level offers the best performance for your application. You can specify the optimization level as a compiler option through your application's make file. Optimization often increases the performance of the application, and vendors are constantly enhancing and improving the compilers. On Sun Solaris, I recommend that you upgrade to the latest SPARC C Compiler (currently 5.0). The new compiler provides many new features and performance enhancements. It also provides support for 64-bit application development. In addition, Sun WorkShop Professional C release 5.0 includes numerous performance enhancements which improve application execution. WorkShop 5.0 also improved profile feedback optimization for threaded applications. In SC 4.2, feedback optimization with threaded applications would result in the lack of aggregation of profile data across all the running threads.

The Sun workshop compiler provides a feedback optimization feature that can be used to optimize the performance of the application binaries. By compiling and linking your application with the ‑xprofile=collect switch, you can then execute the application in order to generate profile feedback data. You can then use the feedback profile data to recompile and relink your application using the -xprofile=use switch. This helps improve application performance by optimizing the executable based on the profile feedback data. If your compiler supports feedback optimization, you can use this feature to improve the efficiency of the application executables.

Sun also provides an optimized math library that can be used to improve the performance of your application. The optimized math library (libmopt) is provided with the Sun Workshop and can be linked with your application instead of the standard math library (libm). The libmopt routines support only IEEE style treatment of exceptional cases as opposed to libm which can provide ANSI, POSIX, SVID, X/Open, or IEEE. For SPARC systems, the vector math library (libmvec_mt) provides parallel versions of vector functions that rely on multiple processor parallelization.

4.14 PROGRESS METER

The progress meter is a database feature which allows you to estimate the elapsed time of a long operation, such as a long-running query. The view V$SESSION_LONGOPS maintains information on operations such as the elapsed time in seconds, the amount of work completed at a point in time, and the total amount of work to be completed. The progress meter allows applications to more accurately estimate the elapsed time of a long-running operation. For example, an application installation utility can use the progress meter to report progress of the installation by examining the V$SESSION_LONGOPS view at periodic intervals. The following query reports the status of the long running operations for a particular user.

```
select sid,sofar,totalwork,units,start_time,
       time_remaining, elapsed_seconds,sql_hash_value
from v$session_longops
where username='APPS';
```

SID	SOFAR	TOTALWORK	UNITS	START_TIM	TIME_REMAINING	ELAPSED_SECONDS	SQL_HASH_VALUE
30	197	197	Blocks	09-FEB-2000	0	36	3031356464
30	61	61	Blocks	09-FEB-2000	0	7	1494619776

Applications can also use the DBMS_APPLICATION_INFO.SET_SESSION _LONGOPS API to set the long-running operation information such as the units, amount of work completed at a point in time, and the total amount of work to be completed. The progress meter can be useful for batch operations, installation programs, and reporting programs.

4.15 THE DATA MODEL

The fact that the data modeling section is the last section in this chapter is by no means any indication that its relevance is last. On the contrary, the data model is probably one of the most important aspects of the application. A poor data model will destroy application performance from day one. Tuning init.ora parameters will never be able to address the issue of a nonscalable data model. In general, most OLTP-based databases tend to be highly normalized. The logic is that joins have a small selectivity and usually return a single row or a small number of rows. A normalized database has its advantages and disadvantages. The advantage is that data is not duplicated, which is the main idea behind normalization. However, high degrees of normalization typically require complex SQL statements with numerous joins when producing reports or aggregate information. A disadvantage of denormalizing the database is that it results in longer row lengths, which may slow down DML operations or full-table scans. However, the performance of full-table scans should not be the main design criteria for an OLTP system since these are the types of operations which should be kept to a minimum.

I cannot overemphasize the importance of the data model; it is as crucial to the application as an engine is to the automobile. No matter what type of fuel or tires you use on your automobile, if the engine is poorly designed, the vehicle throughput will be limited. Similarly, if the data model is so complex that developers need to write one-page-long SQL statements with an unreasonable number of table joins, the application performance will be limited. A good example of this is an online application which bases its main query on a view which takes 4 seconds alone just to parse, but only 0.05 seconds to fetch the rows. Such a view is way too complex for an online system. In my application tuning experience, it is often the case that too much time is spent focusing on tuning a particular complex SQL statement or piece of the code, when it would be much easier to revisit the data model so that the code can be simplified. To paraphrase a colleague of mine, the idea behind a data model is to make SQL programming relatively straightforward. If the data model is designed such that developers need three-page SQL statements to produce reports or display data online, then the model needs to be revisited. In short, when designing an application, make sure a considerable amount of time is spent thoroughly reviewing the data model from all aspects, including performance, ease of use, maintainability, and extensibility. The database design is crucial to the system performance, and you should spend a great deal of time researching the design and reviewing it with your company's application staff and database staff. It is also a good idea to review your design with other database specialists and/or consultants. A good design will help foster a high-performance system.

TUNING AN OLTP SYSTEM

This chapter offers recommendations on performance tuning relating to transaction workloads. It assumes that you are familiar with the basic concepts of the Oracle Server and the standard background processes such as SMON, PMON, DBWR, and LGWR. If you are not familiar with the System Global Area (SGA) and the standard processes, refer to the *Oracle8i Concepts Manual.*

The main performance goal of an On-Line Transaction Processing (OLTP) system is the overall transaction processing rate, also referred to as the TPS (transactions per second) rate. The idea is that the individual transactions should be extremely quick and short-lived. Long running transactions are usually submitted in batch. Tuning a system with the primary goal of achieving high TPS rates and high transaction throughput requires that you focus your attention on the relevant areas that can offer the most gain.

The following areas are discussed in this chapter: monitoring database I/O, latches and locks, the database writer, the log writer, SGA caches, shared pool, redo area, rollback segments, OLTP application-related issues, and object management. These are the key areas that can help to maximize the performance of an OLTP system.

5.1 PERFORMANCE MONITORING TOOLS

It is important that you obtain a complete set of database performance monitoring tools for your work environment. I recommend that you use the Oracle Enterprise Manager to monitor your database. The Oracle Enterprise Manager is an excellent tool that provides GUI graphs and charts of the Oracle Server utilization. This tool is available for Windows NT[1], and helps you avoid using manual SQL scripts to monitor performance. As the saying goes, a picture is worth a thousand words. The Enterprise Manager can provide you with utilization and performance statistics for the database server much faster than manual SQL scripts.

The Oracle Enterprise Manager (OEM) can also provide specific performance tuning tips such as recommending the creation of indexes to facilitate more efficient access paths or the creation of materialized views to improve query response times for complex reports. OEM analyzes the database instance in detail and identifies problem areas such as high load SQL statements or latch contention.

5.2   MONITORING EVENT WAITS

The event model in the Oracle server is an extremely useful mechanism for identifying the cause of performance issues. The event model allows you to identify which events are experiencing the most wait time. In Oracle8*i*, there are over 200 events. You can obtain the full list of event names as well as their parameters via the view V$EVENT_NAME. The views V$SESSION_WAIT and V$SYSTEM_EVENT can be used to survey the instance for wait event information. The V$SESSION_WAIT event view reports the event that the session is currently waiting on or the event that the session last waited on. The WAIT_TIME column of the V$SESSION_WAIT view indicates whether the session is currently waiting on an event (WAIT_TIME=0) or the last event that the session waited on (nonzero value for WAIT_TIME). The columns P1, P2, and P3 of the V$SESSION_WAIT view reflect the different parameters for the specific event. For a description of the parameters, you can either query the V$EVENT_NAME view or display the P1TEXT, P2TEXT, and P3TEXT columns of the V$SESSION_WAIT view. For example, the parameters P1, P2, and P3 for the I/O event db file sequential read refer to the file#, block#, and the number of blocks being read, respectively. Wait times are only collected if the init.ora parameter timed_statistics=TRUE is set.

The following query can be used to report the system event information.

```
select event,total_waits, time_waited,average_wait,total_timeouts
from v$system_event
order by time_waited
```

---

1. Because the tool is available for Windows NT, you can monitor all your database servers from a single console using SQL *Net to connect to the different databases.

EVENT	TOTAL_WAITS	TIME_WAITED	AVERAGE_WAIT	TOTAL_TIMEOUTS
direct path write	3926	1	.000254712	0
db file parallel write	13743	7	.00050935	0
file identify	194	9	.046391753	0
log file single write	53	18	.339622642	0
direct path read	133449	66	.000494571	0
db file parallel read	23	94	4.08695652	0
db file single write	1716	315	.183566434	0
SQL*Net message to client	2201422	530	.000240753	0
SQL*Net more data to client	60719	903	.014871786	0
library cache load lock	146	1214	8.31506849	2
LGWR wait for redo copy	172892	2018	.011672026	37
library cache pin	624	3354	5.375	2
SQL*Net more data from client	4685	5853	1.2493063	0
buffer busy waits	12043	6401	.531512082	10
log file sync	44958	12719	.282908492	1
enqueue	231	19974	86.4675325	57
latch free	16536	41388	2.50290276	15228
log file sequential read	75622	44906	.593821904	0
db file scattered read	279159	101686	.364258362	0
log file parallel write	1249034	152801	.122335341	0
SQL*Net break/reset to client	60408	191954	3.17762548	0
db file sequential read	689572	358485	.519865946	0
pipe get	313032	118970943	380.060003	312994
SQL*Net message from client	2193564	1568269800	714.941438	0

The above system event output is sorted by the TIME_WAITED column, which helps quickly identify the events which are causing the longest waits. The event SQL*Net message from client represented the longest wait event in terms of time. However, this particular event does not indicate a problem as the database is simply awaiting a request from the client. In other words, the server process is idle waiting on a client request. The next longest wait time event is the event pipe get, which means that sessions are waiting on a pipe read, and no data exists in the pipe. The next event is the I/O event db file sequential read. The instance waited on this event 689,572 times and consumed a total wait time of 358485 centiseconds, or approximately 1 hour. Averaging the wait of 1 hour across the total number of waits of 689,572 results in an average wait of 5 milliseconds per wait, which is reasonable for I/O. Of course, this is an average, so there may be some I/O requests which waited longer than 5 milliseconds and some I/O requests which waited less than 5 milliseconds. The latch free event represents the number of times a session waited on a latch. The number of latch free waits is not alarming; however, the average time waited is somewhat high. This can be investigated further by examining the V$LATCH view and examining the number of gets, misses, and sleeps for all the latches.

The system event information (V$SYSTEM_EVENT) is useful for analyzing overall instance activity and determining which areas need further attention. The V$SESSION_WAIT view can be used to drill down further on specific sessions which may be experiencing abnormal wait times.

The V$SESSION_WAIT view can be used to identify specific sessions which are waiting on events. The following query reports the sessions currently waiting on events.

```
SQL> select sid,event,p1,p2,p3
     from v$session_wait
     where wait_time=0 and
           event not like '%SQL*Net%' and
           event not like '%pipe get%' and
           event not like 'rdbms ipc message' and
           event not like 'smon timer' and
           event not like 'pmon timer'

     SID  EVENT                        P1        P2       P3
     -------  -----------------------  --------  --------  --------
      81 db file sequential read      105    114819        1
     212 db file sequential read      364     87094        1
     235 db file sequential read      234     80987        1
     144 db file sequential read      126     11913        1
```

The above query lists the sessions which are currently waiting on events. The query filters out idle wait events such as the SQL*Net, pipe get, or smon timer events. In this example, four sessions are waiting on the db file sequential read I/O event. Each session is reading from a different file (P1 parameter is different), and each session is reading one block from the file, which means that the sessions are likely reading a block from an index or data file.

The V$SESSION_WAIT event view is extremely useful in determining areas of contention for specific sessions such as latch contention or I/O contention. You can automate scripts to periodically capture V$SESSION_WAIT information or you can also enable the 10046 event with level 8 for specific sessions.

The view V$SESSION_EVENT reports event wait information for all the events that the session waited on. This view can be useful in terms of listing aggregate information for all the events that a particular session waited on. The following query reports all the events that a specific set of sessions waited on.

```
select sid,event,total_waits,time_waited,average_wait,max_wait
from v$session_event
where sid in (8,17,76,406) and
      event not like '%SQL*Net%' and
      event not like '%pipe get%' and
      event not like 'rdbms ipc message' and
      event not like 'smon timer' and
      event not like 'pmon timer'
order by sid,time_waited
```

SID	EVENT	TOTAL_WAITS	TIME_WAITED	AVERAGE_WAIT	MAX_WAIT
8	file open	14	1	.071428571	1
8	latch free	12	22	1.83333333	2
8	db file sequential read	122	155	1.2704918	27
8	log file sync	703	187	.266002845	23
17	library cache pin	3	10	3.33333333	10
17	log file switch completion	2	17	8.5	11
17	file open	20	85	4.25	37
17	buffer busy waits	1936	368	.190082645	102
17	latch free	580	811	1.39827586	11
17	db file sequential read	135	1121	8.3037037	77
17	wakeup time manager	2527	7725464	3057.16818	3074
76	control file sequential read	3	0	0	0
76	refresh controlfile command	1	0	0	0
76	log file sync	2	0	0	0
76	file open	3	0	0	0
76	db file sequential read	4	5	1.25	2
76	latch free	17	109	6.41176471	32
406	refresh controlfile command	1	0	0	0
406	file open	1	0	0	0
406	control file sequential read	3	1	.333333333	1
406	buffer busy waits	3	2	.666666667	1
406	log file sync	2	5	2.5	3
406	latch free	15	15	1	2
406	library cache pin	2	77	38.5	47

Using the aggregate information provided by the V$SESSION_EVENT view, you can identify which events represented the majority of the total wait time for a particular session. For example, session id 17 spent a considerable amount of time in the wakeup time manager event. The wakeup time manager event is used as part of the Advanced Queues. The event is used by the enqueue process to post the time manager. The session also spent an average of 8.3 centiseconds for each db file sequential read wait event, which is approximately 83 milliseconds. This may be an indication of some I/O contention as an average of 83 milliseconds to read one block is too high.

The wait event views V$SYSTEM_EVENT, V$SESSION_EVENT, and V$SESSION_WAIT are extremely useful and they help alleviate the guesswork involved when trying to diagnose performance issues. You should become familiar with these views and the different events as they will help you further drill down when sessions appear to be waiting more than normal.

5.2.1 BUFFER BUSY WAITS

The buffer busy waits event can be raised due to several reasons, such as a session trying to acquire exclusive access to a buffer in the buffer cache while another session holds an exclusive pin on the buffer. The buffer busy waits event can also be raised when a session is currently reading a buffer into the buffer cache, and another session is waiting for the read to complete. The `V$SESSION_WAIT` view provides the parameter columns `P1`, `P2`, and `P3` for each wait event. These parameters can be used to further diagnose the source of the `buffer busy waits`. For the `buffer busy waits` event, the `P1`, `P2`, and `P3` columns reflect the file#, block#, and id, respectively. The file# corresponds to the data file containing the block in which the session is waiting. The block# refers to the number of the block within the data file. The ID column refers to the reason why the `buffer busy waits` is being raised. Table 5.1 gives example ID values and descriptions.

TABLE 5.1   ID Values and their descriptions

ID VALUE	REASON
0	The block is being read.
1003	The block is being read, possibly with the undo information for the rollback.
1010	Request to acquire the block in share mode, but another session is currently modifying the block.
1012	The buffer is currently in the exclusive current mode, and is being modified.

Using the query below, the file# (`P1`) and block# (`P2`) can be used to determine the name of the segment for the block which is currently being waited on.

```
select segment_name,segment_type
from dba_extents
where file_id = <file#> and
      <block#> between block_id and block_id+blocks - 1
```

In addition to determining the name of the segment that is experiencing `buffer busy waits`, you can also identify the SQL statement that the session is executing.

```
select vs.sid, vsw.p1,vsw.p2,vsw.p3,vsq.sql_text
  from v$sql vsq,
       v$session vs,
       v$session_wait vsw
  where vsw.sid = vs.sid and
        vs.sql_hash_value = vsq.hash_value and
        vsw.event='buffer busy waits' and
        vsw.wait_time = 0
```

`Buffer busy waits` can be caused by several reasons, including too much concurrency for a single block, an insufficient number of free lists or transaction slots, and inefficient SQL statements. You should examine the SQL statement and its execution plan in detail to ensure that the execution plan is optimal. If an SQL statement perfoms a full-table scan on a large-size table and the degree of execution concurrency for the SQL statement is relatively high, sessions may experience `buffer busy waits` due to the hotness of the tail end of the LRU list. The SQL statement may also be performing an index scan using an inefficient or nonselective index, which will adversely effect the performance of the buffer cache. Examining the SQL statements that are causing `buffer busy waits` as well as determining the actual segment which contains the block being waited on will help you pinpoint the root cause of the `buffer busy waits`.

`Buffer busy waits` can also be caused by too many concurrent operations on a single block, such as when applications use indexes on sequence numbers. For example, suppose an application uses a sequence to compute the value of `ORDER_ID`, and an index exists on the `ORDER_ID` column. Since the value of `ORDER_ID` will continue to increase per the sequence definition, new orders which are inserted will result in block contention for the index on `ORDER_ID` since the values of `ORDER_ID` are increasing. Hence, the current index block will be very hot as the majority of the concurrent inserts will likely try to insert into the same block, thus resulting in buffer contention. This is typically referred to as the right-growing index or moving temperature problem, and is typically caused by creating indexes on sequence numbers.

Resolving `buffer busy waits` issues may not always be straightforward since it may require intimate knowledge of the data-access patterns of the application as well as knowledge of the data distribution. In some cases, it may require that you revisit the data model and the data-access patterns of the application.

5.3   LATCHES AND LOCKS

Latches are internal locks used by Oracle to protect structures in the SGA. Locks are user-level dictionary locks that are placed on user objects such as tables, indexes, and other database objects. There are two main types of locks: *DML locks* and *DDL locks*. DML locks are data locks that are used to protect data such as tables and rows. DDL locks are used to protect dictionary objects such as table definitions. Oracle uses the enqueue manager to manage concurrent access to objects. For example, multiple Oracle users can request share-level locks on the same table. An enqueue is managed as a First-In, First-Out (FIFO) queue. A latch, on the other hand, has no order. If a process fails to obtain a latch, the process may spin or sleep for a specified period of time and try to obtain the latch later. While the process is spinning or sleeping, another process could have obtained the latch.

5.3.1   BUFFER CACHE LATCHES

The database buffer cache (`db_block_buffers`) is managed by a Least Recently Used (LRU) algorithm. Entries in the buffer cache are protected by cache latches. The following query shows the relevant buffer cache latches.

```
SQL> select name,
            gets,
            misses,
            sleeps,
            immediate_gets "IMGETS",
            immediate_misses "IMMISSES"
     from v$latch
     where name like 'cache %'
     order by name
```

NAME	GETS	MISSES	SLEEPS	IMGETS	IMMISSES
cache buffer handles	29183890	53376	59	0	0
cache buffers chains	4733033651	11848270	8659	85379432	1113
cache buffers lru chain	3717959	4304	4	136999082	146533
cache protection latch	0	0	0	0	0

The buffer cache latches are used to protect blocks in the buffer cache during simultaneous operation. Oracle 7.3 introduced another tunable init.ora parameter, db_block_lru_latches, that allows you to tune the number of LRU latches. On multiprocessor systems with a large buffer cache and a heavy OLTP user community, contention for the LRU latches can arise.

In the previous example, the misses and sleeps are extremely low in comparison with the number of gets. For example, the cache buffer chains latch was acquired in wait mode 4.7 billion times while 11.8 million misses occurred which represents a miss ratio of less than 1 percent. If you are experiencing buffer cache LRU contention, set db_block_lru_latches=<number of available processors> to reduce the contention for the LRU latches. If buffer cache LRU contention persists, it is a symptom of hot buffers. The application may be consistently accessing the same set of buffers, thereby inducing latch contention. In such a case, you can use the V$SESSION_WAIT to identify those sessions waiting on this latch and coordinate the parameters for this event to the set of buffers for this LRU latch.

5.3.2 REDO LOG BUFFER LATCHES

The redo buffer is the area in the SGA that contains the redo entries. The buffer is a synchronous buffer that is flushed periodically by the LGWR process. The LGWR process writes redo entries out to the redo log disk files. Before a redo entry can be written into the redo buffer, space in the redo buffer must be allocated for the redo entry. Allocating space in the redo buffer is controlled by the allocation latch. The redo entry is then copied into the redo buffer using either the redo copy latch or the redo allocation latch. There is only one redo allocation latch per instance; therefore, in order to avoid a redo bottleneck, the time the redo allocation latch is held should be kept to a minimum.

The `init.ora` parameter `log_small_entry_max_size` specifies in bytes the maximum redo entry size that can be copied to the log buffers using the redo allocation latch without obtaining the redo copy latch. If the redo entry is larger than `log_small_entry_max_size`, the redo copy latch must be used to copy the data into the redo buffer. In this case, the allocation latch is released after space is allocated in the redo buffer and a redo copy latch is obtained. If the redo entry is less than or equal to `log_small_entry_max_size`, the redo entry is copied on the redo allocation latch, and the allocation latch is released following the copy. Therefore, by reducing `log_small_entry_max_size`, more copies will be done through the redo copy latch as opposed to the allocation latch. You can also increase performance by setting the `log_small_entry_max_size=0`, significantly reducing the time that the allocation latch is held.

The `init.ora` parameter `log_simultaneous_copies` regulates the number of redo copy latches available for concurrent writes into the redo buffer. For good performance on a multiprocessor system, you can set `log_simultaneous_copies=<2>` × `<number of CPUs>`. If `log_simultaneous_copies=0`, all writes are considered small and the copies into the redo buffer are made without the copy latch. On a uniprocessor system, redo copy latches are not used since only one process can be actively copying into the redo buffer at a time. By default, `log_simultaneous_copies` = number of processors in the system. It is recommended that `log_simultaneous_copies` be set to anywhere between its default value to a maximum of two times the number of CPUs in the system. The performance gain from tuning these two parameters depends on the amount of redo and transaction activity of the system. Since LGWR needs to get all the redo copy latches when forcing a log, it may not necessarily be a good idea to configure too many redo copy latches since the cost of acquiring all the latches for LGWR will increase. Hence, you need to balance the number of latches with the frequency in which LGWR is obtaining all the redo copy latches.

To determine the hit and miss ratios for the redo log buffer latches such as the redo allocation latch and the redo copy latch, you can query the `v$latch` view by using the following query.

```
select name,
       sum (gets) "Gets",
       sum (misses) "Misses",
       sum (immediate_gets)"IM_Gets",
       sum (immediate_misses) "IM_Misses"
from  v$latch
where name like '%redo%'
group by name;
```

NAME	Gets	Misses	IM_Gets	IM_Misses
redo allocation	35632016	41445	0	0
redo copy	1481	1114	42372547	4001
redo writing	1487858	113	0	0*

(* new in Oracle8)

In this example, the redo latch statistics show some misses for both wait and immediate get requests. The redo writing latch is used to coordinate the writing of the redo log and waiting for redo writes. However, the percentage of misses to gets in the above example is extremely low. Latch misses will normally occur during periods of high-volume concurrent use; however, the percentage of misses to gets should be low. If your statistics show contention (high misses) for the redo latches, you should increase the number of redo copy latches (if running on a multiprocessor system) and set `log_small_entry_` `max_size=0` to reduce the length of time that the redo allocation latch is held. If you are still experiencing contention in Oracle7, try prebuilding redo log entries before the copy latch is requested. The next section describes how to prebuild redo log entries.

The Oracle7 `init.ora` parameter `log_entry_prebuild_threshold` specifies the maximum number of bytes to group together before copying the redo entry to the redo log buffer. A nonzero value of `log_entry_prebuild_threshold` causes user processes to prebuild redo entries before the redo copy latch is requested. For multiprocessor systems, setting this value can help reduce the time that the redo copy latch is held. On a uniprocessor system, set `log_entry_prebuild_threshold=0`. Do not change the default of `log_entry_prebuild_threshold` (which is zero) if your system is experiencing memory shortages or memory contention. To adequately tune this parameter, review the system statistics (`v$sysstat`) to determine the total number of redo entries generated (`redo  entries`) and the total amount of redo generated, expressed in bytes (`redo` `size`). The `redo entries` and `redo size` statistics will give you a good feel for how much redo is being generated, and therefore how much redo should be grouped together.

In Oracle8*i*, the parameters `log_small_entry_max_size` and `log_simul-` `taneous_copies` have been made obsolete. In Oracle8*i*, Oracle uses the redo copy latch on multiprocessor systems, and defaults the number of redo copy latches to 2 × <number of processors>. The number of redo copy latches can be overridden via the `_log_simultaneous_copies` parameter; however, you should generally not need to set this parameter.

5.3.3 VECTOR POSTING

Oracle8 release 8.0.4 provides a performance enhancement to post and wait operations known as vector posting. Vector posting allows a process to post a set (vector) of processes in a single post call. This reduces system call overhead and improves the performance of processes such as LGWR. After writing out redo entries to the redo log files, LGWR may need to post a set of foreground processes. Without the vector post, LGWR would need to separately post each foreground process. By using the vector post feature, LGWR can post the foregrounds in a single post call. For semaphores, enabling vector posting may require you to increase the values of the semaphore kernel parameters such as `SEMOP` (maximum number of operations per `semop()` call). To enable vector posting set the `init.ora` parameter `_use_vector_post=TRUE`. Vector posting has shown a 3–5 percent performance gain for systems with heavy OLTP workloads.

5.3.4 SHARED LATCHES

Oracle8 improves latch utilization by employing shared latches. Shared latches allow multiple processes concurrent read access to a section of memory by using a low-level synchronization mechanism. In Oracle8, the redo copy latches, both parent and children, can be shared. This helps increase redo throughput since multiple processes can simultaneously acquire a redo copy latch in shared mode. Shared latches may not be supported on all platforms, such as platforms that do not support the ability to perform an atomic compare-and-swap. Shared latches are supported on the Sun Ultra systems (sun4u architecture). In future releases, additional latches will use the shared latches model in order to improve concurrency by reducing latch contention.

5.4 MONITORING THE REDO BUFFER

The key to tuning the redo buffer is monitoring the `redo log space wait time` and `redo log space requests` statistics. The `redo log space requests` value reports the number of times a user process had to wait for space in the redo log buffer. This indicates that redo buffers are being filled faster than LGWR can write (free buffers). The `redo log space requests` statistic is incremented when a log switch is forced or a user process had to wait on a log switch. `Redo log space requests` should be zero, meaning sufficient redo buffer space regularly exists for user processes. In addition to the `redo log space requests`, you can monitor the value of `redo log space wait time`, which reports the time spent waiting for log space (in 1/100s of a second). You can monitor `redo log space requests` and `redo log space wait time` by querying the `v$sysstat` table or by using the Oracle Enterprise Manager. The following shows the query against the `v$sysstat` table reporting the number of `redo log space requests`.

```
SQL> select  name,value
     from v$sysstat
     where name = 'redo log space requests';
```

If `redo log space requests` continues to increase, then you should increase the size of the redo buffer by setting the `init.ora` parameter `log_buffer`. The `log_buffer` setting should be a multiple of the database block size (`db_block_size`). Make sure your system has sufficient memory available before you increase the size of `log_buffer`. In general, a reasonable size for the redo log buffer should be 1–2 MB. A larger size redo buffer will not result in noticeable performance benefits. For example, there is no value in configuring a redo log buffer of 100 MB.

5.5　MONITORING DBWR AND LGWR

In order to maximize the performance of the DBWR and LGWR processes, it is important that DBWR and LGWR keep up with the workload. If DBWR or LGWR fall behind, user processes can experience long wait times. Also, it is important that both DBWR and LGWR keep up with the workload in order to avoid situations of recursive waiting. One of the major reasons that cause a slow DBWR or LGWR is due to I/O contention. If data files and redo log files are not distributed properly, DBWR and LGWR can spend a large majority of their time waiting on I/Os to complete. This is turn causes user foreground processes to wait on events such as checkpoints and buffer flushes. You can query the v$system_ event, v$session_event, and v$session_wait views to determine if processes are waiting on I/O. The v$system_event view reports the total number of event waits for all sessions. The v$session_event view reports total number of event waits per session. The v$session_wait view reports the events that sessions have just completed waiting on or are currently waiting on. These views are extremely useful for pinpointing contention. For example, the following query lists the total number of waits and wait times for file I/O events.

```
SQL> select event,
            total_waits,
            time_waited
     from v$system_event
     where event like '%file%'
     order by total_waits desc;
```

EVENT	TOTAL_WAITS	TIME_WAITED
log file parallel write	1345421	170490
db file sequential read	705663	373413
db file scattered read	283361	103910
log file sequential read	88430	53616
log file sync	49327	15485
control file parallel write	27678	4440
db file parallel write	15170	8
file open	10533	996
control file sequential read	2718	589
db file single write	1980	352
refresh controlfile command	229	81
file identify	214	10
log file single write	61	25
log file switch completion	42	601
db file parallel read	23	94
control file single write	8	216
switch logfile command	1	9

The above query shows that the file I/O events log file parallel write, db file sequential read, and db file scattered read, account for a majority of the process event waits. The average wait times are reasonable in terms of typical I/O rates. The db file sequential read event refers to when a foreground process is waiting for a sequential read from the database to complete. The db file scattered read event refers to a full table scan where the database issues a multi-block I/O request. The log file parallel write event refers to when redo entries are written from the redo log buffer to the redo log files. If the init.ora parameter timed_statistics=TRUE, the TIME_WAITED column of the v$system_event view can help determine if I/Os are taking too long. You should check the disk utilization statistics to determine if the disks containing the redo log files are being saturated and if disk contention is occurring. If you determine there is redo log disk contention, you may have to relocate your redo log files onto dedicated disks or reconfigure the redo log files to increase the degree of striping. The log file sync event reports the wait time of LGWR writing redo entries for a given user session. When a user session commits a transaction, the redo information for the session is flushed to the redo log file. The user session posts the LGWR process to write the redo buffer entries to the redo log file, and the LGWR process will then post the user session upon completion. Querying the system event views can help you identify the contention for resources. You can further identify the exact file of the I/O event by querying the v$session_wait view as follows.

```
SQL> select event,
            p1,
            p2,
            p3,
            state
       from v$session_wait;
```

Each event listed in v$system_event or v$session_event can be correlated with the v$session_wait view. The v$session_wait view lists the wait event, session id, and wait event parameters for a given session. Therefore, you can use the v$session_wait view to drill down on the wait event while the session and wait events are in progress. The v$session_wait view provides the event parameter columns p1, p2, and p3 that help you further analyze the reason behind the event wait. For example, for the db file sequential read event, the parameters p1, p2, and p3 refer to the file number of the file being read from, block number, and the number of blocks being read, respectively. You can then correlate the file number with the v$datafile view to determine which Oracle file is being read from.

Using the information provided in the v$system_event, v$session_event, and v$session_wait views can help you determine if DBWR or LGWR are waiting on I/O events. If sessions are spending too much time waiting on file I/O events, this indicates that there is an I/O bottleneck. You will also need to correlate the event wait statistics with the disk utilization statistics (e.g., sar -d) in order to determine if I/O is being distributed across multiple disks and multiple controllers. You should strive to eliminate I/O wait events by ensuring that the Oracle data files and redo log files are configured, sized, and distributed optimally. It is key that you identify and resolve disk I/O contention and bottlenecks in order to ensure that DBWR and LGWR are keeping up with the workload.

The main indication that DBWR is not keeping up with the buffer cache workload is the `free buffer waits` event and the `write complete waits` event. If you observe large number of waits on these events, then it is an indication that DBWR is not keeping up with the workload. It could either be due to I/O contention or insufficient number of database writers. You can determine if the cause is I/O contention by examining the wait times for the I/O events along with the `V$FILESTAT` view and the OS level statistics such as `sar` or `iostat`. If there does not appear to be I/O contention, you may need to configure additional database writers in order to keep up with the workload.

5.6 MONITORING LATCHING

There are two main types of latch requests: `wait` and `nowait`. The view `V$LATCH` provides statistics on the latches such as the number of gets, misses, and sleeps. The `GETS` (`wait`) column reports the number of times a process acquired the latch on its first attempt but had to wait before acquiring the latch. The `MISSES` (`wait`) column reports the number of times a process acquired a latch after failing to acquire the latch on the first attempt. The `SLEEPS` (`wait`) column reports the number of times a process was put to sleep while waiting for a latch. The `GETS` (`no wait`) column reports the number of times a process acquired the latch without waiting. The `MISSES` (`no wait`) column reports the number of times a process failed to acquire a latch and did not wait after failing to acquire the latch.

The *latch free* event in the `v$system_event` view reports the wait time on latches. If no latch contention is occurring, the latch free event will not be reported. If the latch free event occurs, you can review the wait times for the latch free event in the `v$system _event` view to determine the severity of the latch contention. These latch statistics (from the `v$system_event` and `v$latch` views) can help you determine if you are experiencing latch contention. High sleep latch rates indicate latch contention. There are many different latches used within the Oracle kernel, and minimizing latch contention can help foster a high throughput system with minimal wait time. You can use the following query to identify the latches experiencing contention (misses).

```
select l.name,
       round((l.misses/(l.gets+.001))*100,2) "MISS_RATIO",
      round((l.immediate_misses/(l.immediate_gets+.001))*100,2)
                "IMMEDIATE_MISS_RATIO"
 from v$latch l,
      v$latchname ln
 where (l.latch#=ln.latch#) AND
       (((l.misses/(l.gets+.001))*100 > .2) OR
       ((l.immediate_misses/(l.immediate_gets+.001))*100 > .2))
 order by 2
```

NAME	MISS_RATIO	IMMEDIATE_MISS_RATIO
channel handle pool latch	0	31.13
redo copy	0	1.92
channel operations parent latch	.01	92.28
row cache objects	.09	.41
redo allocation	.22	0
redo writing	.43	0
session allocation	1.12	0
user lock	1.18	0
latch wait list	3.11	.81

The following query can be used to list the latch statistics.

```
SQL> select name,
            gets,
            misses,
            sleeps,
            immediate_gets "IM_GETS",
            immediate_misses "IM_MISS"
     from v$latch
     where gets > 0
     order by name;
```

NAME	GETS	MISSES	SLEEPS	IM_GETS	IM_MISS
Active checkpoint queue latch	43465	0	0	0	0
Checkpoint queue latch	2977321	191	0	0	0
Direct I/O Adaptor	2	0	0	0	0
JOX SGA heap latch	15669	0	0	3538	0
NLS data objects	9	0	0	0	0
Token Manager	12802	1	0	14022	0
address list	3	0	0	0	0
archive control	58	0	0	0	0
archive process latch	61	0	0	0	0
begin backup scn array	28	0	0	0	0
cache buffer handles	840346	8	0	0	0
cache buffers chains	858018461	1371526	2022	2867070	1059
cache buffers lru chain	4613812	253	0	1991595	78
channel handle pool latch	41405	0	0	40978	12723
channel operations parent latch	82914	8	1	40978	37720
cost function	1	0	0	0	0
dml lock allocation	5967590	312	0	0	0
dropped object history latch	519	0	0	0	0
enqueue hash chains	10638145	262	1	0	0
enqueues	11789123	2139	5	0	0
event group latch	41385	0	0	0	0
file number translation table	66	0	0	0	0
global transaction	91328	0	0	0	0

global tx free list	28	0	0	0	0
global tx hash mapping	1148	0	0	0	0
job_queue_processes parameter latch	1389	0	0	0	0
ktm global data	303	0	0	0	0
kwqit: protect wakeup time	13378	0	0	0	0
latch wait list	3329	104	4	3240	26
library cache	62063223	55025	3711	617493	411
library cache load lock	213136	8	0	0	0
list of block allocation	3714302	55	0	0	0
loader state object freelist	1350	0	0	0	0
longop free list	623022	0	0	0	0
message pool operations parent latch	3	0	0	0	0
messages	4847631	7847	4	0	0
mostly latch-free SCN	1	0	0	0	0
multiblock read objects	678482	13	0	4	0
ncodef allocation latch	1389	0	0	0	0
process allocation	41385	20	19	41383	2
process group creation	82361	52	12	0	0
redo allocation	12772678	28689	3	0	0
redo copy	2640	0	0	10040397	193083
redo writing	4795087	20859	4	0	0
row cache objects	30356649	26669	3528	14077	58
sequence cache	239836	6	0	0	0
session allocation	17078666	191913	6821	0	0
session idle bit	5097411	16	3	998	0
session switching	2793	0	0	0	0
session timer	43159	0	0	0	0
shared java pool	3995	0	0	0	0
shared pool	13913277	26901	1378	0	0
sort extent pool	1192	0	0	0	0
temporary table state object allocation	25	0	0	0	0
transaction allocation	5112791	151	0	0	0
transaction branch allocation	1425	0	0	0	0
undo global data	6152661	659	0	0	0
user lock	166364	1973	502	0	0
virtual circuit queues	8288	0	0	0	0

5.6.1   IDENTIFYING THE SOURCE OF LATCH CONTENTION

Latch contention is a symptom, rather than a direct problem per se. In other words, there is no magic wand that can be waved to eliminate latch contention, and typically adjusting init.ora parameters will not eliminate latch contention. Latch contention typically surfaces from application performance issues such as the lack of SQL reuse, frequent DDL execution, and inefficient SQL. In order to identify the source of the latch contention, you need to query the V$SESSION_WAIT view (events = 'latch free') and examine the P1, P2, and P3 parameters to determine the latch number which the session is waiting on. For example, if the session is waiting on a library cache latch, you can determine which child latch the library cache refers to by referencing the V$LATCH_CHILDREN view, which maintains latch statistics on the child latches. The V$LATCH_PARENT view provides statistics on the parent latch level.

In some cases, Oracle needs to acquire the parent latch, which is, in effect, all the child latches for a particular latch. For example, during certain library cache events, Oracle needs to acquire all the library cache child latches (i.e., the parent latch) such as during cursor invalidation or object invalidation. For example, suppose a session gathers statistics on a table while other sessions are executing cursors. Once the gathering statistics completes, the data dictionary cache will reflect the new set of statistics, and existing cursors which are dependent on that table will be invalidated so that new cursors can be built which reflect the new set of statistics. Since the intended goal of gathering statistics on a table or index is that the optimizer make use of these new statistics, existing cursors based on the old set of statistics are invalidated, which will result in the session which is invalidating the dependent cursors acquiring the parent latch. During such time, other sessions which may need only a single library cache child latch will not be able to acquire the latch because another session has acquired the parent latch (i.e., all the child latches). The number of library cache child latches is configured automatically upon instance startup. In cases of parent latch contention, such as little application reuse of SQL, a large number of child latches lengthens the time needed to acquire the parent latch. Even though the number of child latches can be overridden, it is recommended that you optimize the application to avoid the symptom of parent latch contention rather than override the internal setting for the number of library cache child latches. Another example of cursor invalidation which would result in the attempt to acquire the parent latch is if the application creates and drops tables dynamically. Since there may be many cursors dependent on the object, the parent latch is needed to purge those cursors which are dependent on an object about to be dropped.

You can diagnose latch contention by identifying the source SQL statement being executed by the session. The following is an example query that lists the session id and the SQL statement being executed for those sessions currently waiting on a latch.

```
select vs.sid, vsw.p1,vsw.p2,vsq.sql_text
from v$sql vsq,
     v$session vs,
     v$session_wait vsw
where vsw.sid = vs.sid and
     vs.sql_hash_value = vsq.hash_value and
     vsw.event = 'latch free' and
     vsw.wait_time = 0
```

The SQL statement will help you further investigate the cause of the latch contention. The SQL statement will identify the SQL statements using literal values in place of bind variables thereby inducing library cache latch contention or SQL statements that perform full-table scans, subsequently inducing buffer cache latch contention.

In summary, latch contention typically stems from application issues such as not sharing cursors and creating and dropping objects. Gathering statistics on database objects also causes cursors to be invalidated; hence you should avoid an over-frequent gathering of statistics.

5.6.2 MINIMIZING THE EFFECT OF LATCH CONTENTION

The `init.ora` parameter `spin_count` controls the amount of CPU ticks (cycles) that a process executes after an initial attempt to acquire a busy resource (latch). After the number of `spin_count` ticks, the process makes a second attempt to acquire the resource. If the resource is still unavailable, the process is put to sleep and is later awakened when the resource becomes available. Oracle uses an exponential back-off mechanism when a process sleeps due to the inability to acquire a latch. Each time the process fails to acquire the latch after awakening from a sleep, Oracle increases the sleep time so as to avoid a frequent wake up-sleep cycle. The `V$LATCH` view provides the columns `SLEEP1–SLEEP11`, which can be used to determine how often processses backed-off for a particular latch. If the values for `SLEEP1`, `SLEEP2`, or `SLEEP3` are high, this indicates that processes are spending a considerable amount of time sleeping due to latch contention.

Putting the process to sleep and later awakening it is an expensive operation. Forcing the process to spin longer before it acquires the resource yields higher performance than putting the process to sleep on a multiprocessor system. The default for `spin_count` on most UNIX platforms is 2,000 (on multiprocessor machines), which is adequate for most applications. Increasing `spin_count` generally results in greater CPU utilization.

If you are seeing a high number of latch sleeps and your system has available processor cycles (i.e., low or medium CPU utilization), increasing `spin_count` may increase your performance over the time spent sleeping. In such as case, you can will need to balance the setting of spin_count with the latch sleep rates and processor utilization rates. When you increase `spin_count`, monitor CPU utilization to ensure that processes are not being starved of CPU time because of the increase in `spin_count`. You may have eliminated latch sleeps, but process elapsed times may have increased due to their inability to obtain CPU time. You can monitor latch statistics by examining the `V$LATCH` view or by using the latch monitor of the Enterprise Manager. The `spin_count` parameter should be set to zero (i.e., no spinning) if running Oracle on a single-processor machine. In Oracle8*i*, the `spin_count init.ora` parameter exists as an underscore parameter (`_spin_count`). Although you can override the default value for `spin_count`, it is still recommended that you pursue application optimization to the utmost maximum in order to eliminate the latch contention rather than try to mask the latch contention.

5.7 TUNING ROLLBACK SEGMENTS

Rollback segments store the pre-image of changed data. The rollback segment contains the data as it existed before the change. It is used to restore the data in the event that the transaction aborts, issues a rollback statement, or terminates abnormally. Rollback segments are also used to create read-consistent views of data for transactions that may have started before the data was modified. Transactions (non read-only transactions) are assigned to rollback segments by Oracle from the pool of rollback segments that are specified in the `init.ora` parameter `rollback_segments`. The two `init.ora` parameters `transactions_per_rollback_segment` and `max_rollback_segments` specify the number of rollback segments brought on-line in the rollback cache in the SGA upon instance startup. The two parameters do not limit the number of rollback segments that can be used by transactions. Oracle always maintains the SYSTEM rollback segment in addition to the user private and public rollback segments. The minimum number of rollback segments that will be brought on-line upon instance startup is defined by the value of

```
CEIL (TRANSACTIONS / TRANSACTIONS_PER_ROLLBACK_SEGMENT)
```

The `CEIL` function rounds up to the next integer. For example, if `TRANSACTIONS=100`, and `TRANSCATIONS_PER_ROLLBACK_SEGMENT=1`, Oracle, upon instance startup, attempts to bring at least 100 rollback segments on-line from the pool of available rollback segments.

The approach to tuning rollback segments is twofold: quantity and sizing. The quantity approach ensures that enough rollback segments exist to service the amount of users and transactions without causing high waits or transaction failures. Sizing refers to the storage parameters of the rollback segments that ensure that rollback segments are not constantly extending, shrinking, and/or wrapping.

5.7.1 NUMBER OF ROLLBACK SEGMENTS

As far as quantity, you should create enough rollback segments to serve the transaction workload. Ideally, each concurrent user (session) should have a separate rollback segment to eliminate rollback segment contention. However, not only will this increase the size of the rollback cache, it may also not even be possible due to space availability. Before you create rollback segments, make sure that the underlying tablespaces housing the rollback segments are striped and spread across multiple disk drives and controllers. Start by creating a default set of rollback segments such as 10 or 20. You can then query the `v$waitstat` and `v$rollstat` views to determine if contention for rollback segments exists. For example, the following query can be used to list the undo wait statistics.

```
SQL>    select class,count,time
        from v$waitstat
        where class in ('free list',
                        'system undo header',
                        'system undo block',
                        'undo header',
                        'undo block')
        order by class;
```

CLASS	COUNT	TIME
free list	0	0
system undo block	0	0
system undo header	0	0
undo block	78	1
undo header	40	0

From this query, you can see that the number of waits for undo blocks and undo headers is relatively small. Rollback segments are also referred to as undo segments because they contain the pre-image of the data that allows the transaction to be undone (rolled back).

The following queries report the total number of requests for data as well as the rollback segment hit ratios.

```
SQL> select sum(value) "Total # Requests of Data"
     from v$sysstat
     where name in ('db block gets','consistent gets');

          Total # Requests of Data
          ------------------------
                   6290459

SQL> select name,waits,gets,
            (100-(waits/gets)) "Hit Ratio"
     from v$rollstat a,v$rollname b
     where (a.usn=b.usn);
```

NAME	WAITS	GETS	Hit Ratio
SYSTEM	0	1004	100.00
RBS_01_SEG1	2	334999	99.99
RBS_01_SEG2	0	346669	100.00
RBS_01_SEG3	0	164525	100.00
RBS_01_SEG4	3	133645	99.99
RBS_01_SEG5	6	230221	99.99
RBS_01_SEG6	1	162901	99.99
RBS_01_SEG7	0	169634	100.00
RBS_01_SEG8	0	208727	100.00
RBS_01_SEG9	3	149909	99.99
RBS_01_SEG10	3	158899	99.99
RBS_01_SEG11	1	344554	99.99
RBS_01_SEG12	2	146403	99.99

If the hit ratios are 95 percent or higher, then the number of existing rollback segments is optimal. If, however, the hit ratios are low and waits are high, you need to add more rollback segments. You can add more rollback segments by issuing the `create rollback segment` statement and adjusting the relevant `init.ora` parameters.

5.7.2 SIZING ROLLBACK SEGMENTS

The sizing of the individual rollback segments is critical to the overall performance. If rollback segments are not sized properly, extends and shrinks can occur frequently, thereby reducing the performance of the transaction. To size a rollback segment appropriately, you will need to estimate the amount of data being modified, inserted, or deleted by each transaction. Remember to consider batch size operations that operate on a number of rows simultaneously as opposed to a single row at a time. For large batch transactions, you may want to consider creating separate rollback segments, as discussed in section 5.7.3. Once you have a good feel for the amount of data being modified, then you should size the initial extents of each rollback segment so that a transaction can always complete by using only the initial extent. This eliminates the need of the transaction to continue extending itself, subsequently resulting in recursive storage management overhead. When a transaction needs another extent, the transaction is extended across another extent within the rollback segment. The number of times a rollback segment extended itself and allocated another extent is reported by the extends column in the v$rollstat view. You can also use the Enterprise Manager to report rollback segment hit and miss ratios. If the number of extends is high, it is an indication that the extent sizes are too small.

The rollback segment storage parameter OPTIMAL specifies the optimal size of the rollback segment when a shrink of the rollback segment occurs. A shrink occurs when multiple rollback segment extents are de-allocated into one large (optimal size) rollback segment extent. The optimal size must be at least larger than (INITIAL + NEXT + ··· up to MINEXTENTS). The OPTIMAL setting can be used to cause rollback segments to shrink down to the optimal size. For long-running transactions, the OPTIMAL parameter should be set large so that the frequency of shrinks is reduced. For short-running transactions, set optimal to the minimum value so that rollback segments will tend to be small, increasing the likelihood they will remain in the cache. You should tune the OPTIMAL setting so that the number of shrinks is extremely low and the average sizes shrunk are high. A high number of shrinks indicates that the OPTIMAL setting is too low.

When you size rollback segments, you should set the INITIAL and NEXT extent values the same. The value for PCTINCREASE for rollback segments is always zero. Setting the INITIAL and NEXT extent to the same value helps prevent fragmentation.

In addition to the rollback statistics columns listed previously, you should also monitor the high-water mark size as well as the number of wraps that occur. The high-water mark reports the maximum space ever used by a rollback segment. The wraps column reports the number of times a transaction continued writing from one extent in a rollback segment to another existing extent. The average active sizes (aveactive) column reports the average number of bytes used by active extents in the rollback segment. These rollback statistics are available through the v$rollstat view. Analyzing the number of wraps, shrinks, extends, and average sizes can help you size your rollback segments more effectively. The goal is to minimize extends and shrinks by maintaining a transaction in a single or few rollback segment extents.

5.7.3 LARGE TRANSACTIONS

If your application consists of long-running transactions that process large amounts of data, you may want to consider creating separate large rollback segments for this purpose. The application can then assign its transaction to the large rollback segment specifically by using the following command.

```
SQL> SET TRANSACTION USE ROLLBACK SEGMENT
     <rollback segment name>;
```

This enables the long transaction to utilize a dedicated rollback segment to ensure that adequate rollback space exists to complete the transaction and to minimize contention with other users issuing small transactions. This technique is also ideal for batch runs that run for an extended period of time (typically overnight).

5.7.4 SNAPSHOT TOO OLD

The classic ORA-1555 snapshot-too-old error typically occurs when writers are interfering with readers. The snapshot-too-old error is raised when a writer wrapped across the rollback segment and overwrote rollback information which was being used to assemble a read-consistent view for readers. There are several ways to handle the snapshot-too-old error. You can either increase the MINEXTENTS on the rollback segments so as to reduce the possibility of a wrap, or you can assign the writer session to a specific rollback segment which can be sized for long running transactions. You can also investigate the application and examine the type of synchronization that is occurring for sessions which are modifying the objects which other sessions are trying to read. You may need to modify the commit cycles and the batch sizes for the writers so as to avoid readers raising the snapshot-too-old error.

5.8   THE SHARED POOL

Oracle7 introduced the concept of the shared pool. The shared pool, as the term suggests, allows multiple users to share SQL and PL/SQL areas. This reduces parsing overhead for multiple repeated SQL. The shared pool consists of three main areas: the library cache, the data dictionary cache, and session information. The size of the shared pool is specified by the init.ora parameter shared_pool_size.

5.8.1 LIBRARY CACHE

The library cache consists of the shared SQL and PL/SQL areas. It helps reduce parsing overhead by maintaining parsed SQL and PL/SQL in the library cache. Therefore, any subsequent execution of the same exact SQL or PL/SQL eliminates the need to reparse the statement. This increases performance, especially for OLTP systems that tend to have a custom application issuing the same generic SQL. Using bind variables in your SQL statements also helps increase the utilization of the library cache.

A library cache miss can occur if a user submits a parse call for a SQL statement that does not exist in the library cache or in the shared SQL area. Oracle will parse the SQL statement and allocate a shared SQL area for the statement. You can reduce the library cache miss ratio by ensuring that users maximize the utilization of the shared SQL area. A library cache miss can also occur if a shared SQL statement was aged-out of the shared pool. This causes the SQL statement, once reexecuted, to be reparsed, and Oracle then has to allocate a shared SQL area for the statement and then execute the statement. Maintaining a high library cache hit ratio can increase performance by reducing parsing and shared SQL area allocation overhead. You can monitor the library cache by querying the v$library-cache view. The following query reports the library cache utilization statistics for the different library cache namespaces.

```
SQL> select NAMESPACE, GETS, GETHITS, trunc(GETHITRATIO,2) GETHITR,
            PINS, PINHITS, trunc(PINHITRATIO,2) PINHITR,
            RELOADS, INVALIDATIONS
      from v$librarycache
```

The output of the query should look as follows.

NAMESPACE	GETS	GETHITR	PINS	PINHITR	RELOADS	INVALIDATIONS
SQL AREA	753572	.93	11866666	.99	42125	39458
TABLE/PROCEDURE	1518658	.99	32641934	.99	326	0
BODY	1535048	.99	1535592	.99	0	0
TRIGGER	75432	.99	75432	.99	1	0
INDEX	212	.49	214	.47	1	0
CLUSTER	2016	.99	2193	.99	0	0
OBJECT	0	1	0	1	0	0
PIPE	1056901	.99	1058782	.99	0	0

The library cache pin hit ratio for the SQL area namespace is 99 percent while the get hit ratio is 93 percent, both of which are good hit ratios. You can maintain a high library cache hit ratio by ensuring that the shared pool is sized appropriately, that SQL statements are sharable, and that cursors are also being reused. You should set the init.ora parameter open_cursors to the maximum number of concurrent cursors that will be opened by a session.

The library cache is dependent on the fact that SQL statements must be exactly the same, character for character. This means that spaces and case sensitivity will affect whether or not a SQL statement is reused. To maximize the use of the library cache, ensure that SQL statements are exact. Also, use bind variables to specify predicate values in the WHERE clause. This will avoid queries in which WHERE clauses are hard-coded with scalar values. Using bind variables allows the SQL statement to be reused because the statement is exactly the same, only the value of the run-time bind variable is changing. Tools such as Oracle Forms help increase the library cache hit ratio since multiple uses of the same application form will likely execute the same SQL.

5.8.2 OPTIMIZING CURSOR EXECUTION

The Oracle server provides a configuration optimization known as cursor space for time. Cursor space for time reduces cursor execution time by using more memory, as the parameter name suggests (cursor_space_for_time). Essentially, when a cursor is parsed and then executed, cursor frames and related buffers need to be allocated for the cursor. For an application which frequently executes the same set of cursors, cursor space for time can help reduce the setup time for cursor execution by maintaining persistence of the cursor frames and buffers used during cursor execution. Cursor space for time also effectively eliminates the expense of a soft parse. In order to enable cursor space for time, you can set the init.ora parameter CURSOR_SPACE_FOR_TIME=TRUE. When set to TRUE, it causes the cursor and related buffers to be pinned at cursor parse time versus cursor execution time. The pin remains in effect until the application issues an explicit close cursor. This can be useful for applications which frequently execute the same set of cursors. This parameter, when set to TRUE, also causes the private SQL area allocated for each cursor to be maintained in the library cache. This improves cursor allocation and initialization time as well as overall SQL execution time. If this parameter is set to FALSE, Oracle needs to scan the library cache to determine if the SQL statement is in the shared SQL area (i.e., soft parse). If set to TRUE, this check is not needed since the shared SQL area cannot be aged-out while at least one active cursor references the SQL statement. Enabling cursor space for time requires a much larger shared pool; therefore you should only set this parameter to TRUE if your shared pool is large enough, and the application can benefit from the cursor space for time optimization.

OBSOLETE IN ORA 7.3 →   Another init.ora parameter SESSION_CACHED_CURSORS can be used to cache multiple reuses of a session cursor. If more than three parse requests are issued on the same SQL statement, the session cursor associated with the statement is moved into the session cursor cache. Subsequent parses on the SQL statement by the same session will be faster because the cursor is in the session cursor cache. An LRU algorithm is used to age-out cursor entries from the session cursor cache.

You can set the SESSION_CACHED_CURSORS through the init.ora file or through the following command.

```
SQL> alter session set session_cached_cursors = <value>;
```

By querying the v$sysstat view, you can obtain statistics on the use of cached session cursors. For example, consider the following output from v$sysstat.

NAME	VALUE
parse count (total)	4277152
session cursor cache hits	3128940
session cursor cache count	14426

Divide the session cursor cache hits by the parse count to determine the percentage of parses that are being serviced from the session cursor cache. In this case, `3128940/4277152` is approximately 73 percent. You should increase the value of `session_cached_cursors` if the percentage is low. You should also monitor the parse count at the session level by querying the `v$sesstat` view. If little gain is observed after increasing the value of `session_cached_cursors`, it is an indication that the application is not reexecuting the same SQL statement within the same session enough times to cause the cursor to be migrated to the cursor cache.

You should also query the `v$db_object_cache` view to list the objects in the library cache. The view maintains statistics such as the number of loads, executions, pins, and locks. The `v$db_object_cache` view allows you to determine the objects loaded in the library cache as well as corresponding object-level statistics. In Oracle8*i*, the execution count (`EXECUTIONS` column) in V$DB_OBJECT_CACHE is zero for PL/SQL units such as packages. Hence, you cannot use this view to determine execution statistics for PL/SQL packages. In releases prior to Oracle8, the execution count is incremented upon the first pin, and not for each execution. For example, if a package P1 calls the package P2 in a loop for 1,000 times, the execution count will not reflect the repeated executions. For this reason, the count was set to zero in Oracle8*i*.

5.8.3 DATA DICTIONARY CACHE

The data dictionary cache is also part of the shared pool. The data dictionary cache is divided into namespaces and is used to cache data dictionary objects such as tables, indexes, internal storage management tables, and other data dictionary objects. You can monitor the cache hit ratio of the data dictionary cache for each namespace by querying the `v$rowcache` view. The following query is an example that reports `v$rowcache` statistics.

```
SQL> select parameter, sum(gets) "DC. Gets",
            sum(getmisses) "DC. Misses",
            round(((1-(sum(getmisses)/
            sum(gets)))*100),2) "DC.Hit Ratio"
       from v$rowcache
       where gets > 0
       group by parameter
```

PARAMETER	DC. Gets	DC. Misses	DC.Hit Ratio
dc_constraints	1277	448	64.92
dc_database_links	43796	20	99.95
dc_free_extents	3918	2067	47.24
dc_global_oids	699	9	98.71
dc_histogram_data	3696	319	91.37
dc_histogram_defs	442136	7183	98.38
dc_object_ids	1531880	11397	99.26

dc_objects	540884	11727	97.83
dc_profiles	20199	1	100.00
dc_rollback_segments	34511	31	99.91
dc_segments	1451976	5042	99.65
dc_sequence_grants	80025	1025	98.72
dc_sequences	40410	2968	92.66
dc_synonyms	175384	1781	98.98
dc_tablespace_quotas	2954	52	98.24
dc_tablespaces	101072	201	99.80
dc_used_extents	27463	1759	93.60
dc_user_grants	570266	119	99.98
dc_usernames	259003	163	99.94
dc_users	911362	209	99.98

In the sample output above, the majority of the cache hit ratios are in the high nineties except for the free extents namespace, which has a hit ratio of 47.24 percent and the constraints namespace which has a hit ratio of 64.92 percent. However, the number of gets for the constraints namespace is significantly less than the other core namespaces, such as the segments or objects namespaces. If you see low cache hit ratios, you need to increase the size of the shared pool. A low data dictionary cache hit ratio can cause a tangible performance degradation because OLTP transactions often result in *recursive* SQL. Recursive SQL refers to a user SQL statement that requires additional backend SQL, such as storage management, object metadata lookups, or statistics lookups, to complete the statement. The CBO makes extensive use of the dictionary cache, especially the objects and histogram namespaces. Insufficient space in the shared pool can cause data dictionary objects to be aged out quickly, thereby decreasing the cache hit ratio and impacting future accesses to the dictionary objects.

5.8.4 MAXIMIZING THE SHARED POOL UTILIZATION

To size the shared pool adequately, you need to monitor four things: the library cache hit ratio, data dictionary cache hit ratio, session cache hit ratio, and memory used. Monitoring the cache hit ratios has been discussed in previous sections. The memory used is also important. You can query the v$sgastat view to determine if the shared pool is too large and is not being utilized. The following query shows the output from the v$sgastat table showing free memory.

```
SQL> select 'shared pool size' NAME,
            trunc(value/1024/1024,2) "Size in MB"
     from v$parameter
     where name='shared_pool_size'
     UNION ALL
     select name, trunc(bytes/1024/1024,2) "Size in MB"
     from v$sgastat
     where name= 'free memory'
```

```
NAME                             Size in MB
-------------------------        ----------
shared pool size                    1049.04
free memory                          119.43
```

In this example, there is 119 MB of free memory in the shared pool, which means that the total size of the shared pool is not being utilized. In this example, the size of the shared pool is approximately 1049 MB (`shared_pool_size=1100000000`). This means that 11 percent of the shared pool is not being used. Large amounts of free memory reported by `v$sgastat` indicate that memory is being wasted and could be better directed to other areas, such as the buffer cache or other user processes.

5.8.5 FRAGMENTATION IN THE SHARED POOL

Fragmentation is also a problem that can cause performance problems with the shared pool. As objects of different sizes are brought in and aged-out of the shared pool, memory can be fragmented. To correct this problem, Oracle provides parameters that help deal with the problem of fragmentation within the shared pool.

The `init.ora` parameters `SHARED_POOL_RESERVED_SIZE` and `SHARED_POOL_RESERVED_MIN_ALLOC` specify the amount of the shared pool memory to be reserved from the total `shared_pool_size` for allocations, and the minimum amount of space to be allocated from the shared pool free list. If a shared pool memory allocation is larger than the value of `SHARED_POOL_RESERVED_MIN_ALLOC`, space can be allocated from the reserved list if the allocation cannot be satisfied from the free list. In Oracle8*i*, the `init.ora` parameter `SHARED_POOL_RESERVED_MIN_ALLOC` is an underscore parameter (`_SHARED_POOL_RESERVED_MIN_ALLOC`).

`SHARED_POOL_RESERVED_SIZE` should be set so that all requests for memory in the shared pool can always be satisfied without having to age objects out of the shared pool. The general rule is to set `SHARED_POOL_RESERVED_SIZE` equal to 10 percent of the total `shared_pool_size`. Be careful when setting `SHARED_POOL_RESERVED_SIZE`, because a high value can cause objects to be aged-out so that sufficient free memory is always reserved. A value of zero for `SHARED_POOL_RESERVED_SIZE` means that no shared pool space is reserved. In Oracle8*i*, set `SHARED_POOL_RESERVED_MIN_ALLOC=4000` so that allocations do not overallocate space and waste memory that other processes could have used. If you enable the shared pool reserve, you should query the `v$shared_pool_reserved` view to obtain statistics on the shared pool reserve area. The `v$shared_pool_reserved` view maintains statistics regarding shared pool reserve usage such as available space, number of requests, misses, request failures, and amount of space used. The statistics from the `v$shared_pool_reserved` view can also aid in sizing the shared pool reserve area.

5.8.6 PINNING OBJECTS IN THE SHARED POOL

When a large object needs to be loaded into the shared pool, Oracle may age out smaller objects to make memory space available for the large object. Memory fragmentation may occur if objects are frequently loaded into the shared pool and then aged out. Oracle8 improved the SGA cache management by using segmented memory structures. This helps reduce the fragmentation that can occur by the loading and unloading of large objects in the shared pool.

The package DBMS_SHARED_POOL can help you improve response time and reduce fragmentation by pinning large objects in the shared pool. The DBMS_SHARED_POOL package provides the procedures DBMS_SHARED_POOL.KEEP and DBMS_SHARED_POOL.SIZES to pin the specified object in the shared pool and display the shared pool objects of a size larger than the size specified by the parameter in the SIZES procedure call. For example, the following SQL can be used to show the objects in the shared pool larger than 5 KB.

```
SQL> SET SERVEROUTPUT ON SIZE 5000
SQL> EXECUTE DBMS_SHARED_POOL.SIZES(5000);
```

The procedures DBMS_SHARED_POOL.KEEP and DBMS_SHARED_POOL.UNKEEP can be used to pin objects in the shared pool, and allow objects to be aged out, respectively The syntax for the procedures is

```
DBMS_SHARED_POOL.KEEP (object, object type);

DBMS_SHARED_POOL.UNKEEP (object, object type);
```

The object parameter is the value that is returned from the DBMS_SHARED_POOL.SIZES procedure call. If you have large objects such as PL/SQL packages, pinning the object in the shared pool can improve overall response time and shared pool utilization. Pinning certain objects can also help reduce shared pool memory fragmentation. The DBMS_SHARED_POOL package is created from the SQL script dbmspool.sql (located in $ORACLE_HOME/rdbms/admin).

5.8.7 LITERAL REPLACEMENT

Oracle8*i* release 8.1.6 provides a feature known as literal replacement, which allows SQL statements that use literal values to be shared. This can improve the performance of applications that do not use bind variables in the SQL statements. The literal replacement feature is aimed at those applications that may currently suffer from latch contention due to the fact that the SQL statements are not sharable. The init.ora parameter cursor_sharing is used to enable literal replacement. If cursor_sharing=FORCE, Oracle replaces literal values in SQL statements with system-generated bind variables, which helps facilitate cursor sharing. For example, consider the following two different SQL statements that use literal values.

```
select ai.invoice_num,ai.invoice_id,ai.amount_paid
from ap_invoices_all ai
where ai.invoice_num = '83092';

select ai.invoice_num,ai.invoice_id,ai.amount_paid
from ap_invoices_all ai
where ai.invoice_num = '569219';
```

Although these two SQL statements are similar, they are actually different because literal values are used for the value of INVOICE_NUM. The result is that these two SQL statements are being individually hard-parsed. If a bind variable was used for the value of the INVOICE_NUM, the SQL statement could be shared across multiple executions. This would normally require application code changes to implement the use of bind variables. The literal replacement feature can be used to improve cursor sharing without necessarily requiring application code changes. By setting the init.ora parameter cursor_sharing=FORCE, Oracle generates a system bind variable which allows the SQL statement to be shared. The V$SQL view (SQL_TEXT column) shows that the SQL statement has been transformed to use bind variables. In addition, the EXECUTIONS column of V$SQL reflects that the SQL statement is being shared across executions as opposed to having a separate copy of the SQL statement for each specified value of INVOICE_NUM. If literal replacement is enabled, the SQL text that appears in V$SQL using the above example, is as follows.

```
select ai.invoice_num,ai.invoice_id,ai.amount_paid
from ap_invoices_all ai
where ai.invoice_num = :SYS_B_0
```

Literal replacement can also effect the execution plan since literal values will no longer be visible by the optimizer. Instead, the optimizer will generate an execution plan for the SQL statement based on the system-generated bind variable, and not the actual literal value. Also, since the cost-based optimizer does not use histogram information to calculate selectivity for predicates using bind variables, the execution plan may differ for those SQL statements that depend on a histogram to attribute data skew. If you plan to utilize the literal replacement feature, you should review the execution plans of the SQL statements with and without literal replacement in order to identify those SQL statements (if any) that result in a suboptimal execution plan when literal replacement is enabled. Literal replacement is an extremely useful feature that can help alleviate the application performance issues caused by a lack of cursor sharing.

5.9   SIZING THE SGA

Oracle creates at least one shared memory segment upon instance startup to hold the SGA. The SGA should be in physical memory. Reads and writes to the SGA are significantly faster than physical reads and writes to the disk. Therefore, it is important that the SGA areas be optimally sized in order to reduce physical I/O and maximize memory utilization. The total amount of shared memory required by the Oracle Server for the System Global Area (SGA) can be calculated by the following formula.

```
total shared memory (size of SGA) = Fixed Size +
                                     Variable Size +
                                     Database Buffers +
                                     Redo Buffers
```

The fixed size is determined by the products that have been installed on the system. The variable size is determined by the majority of the `init.ora` parameters. The database buffer cache size is determined by the value of `<db_block_buffers>` × `<db_block_size>`. The default block size (`db_block_size`) is 2 KB. Therefore, if `db_block_buffers=10000`, the size of the database buffer cache would be 20 MB. The redo buffer size is determined by the `log_buffer` parameter (specified in bytes).

The key to tuning the SGA in terms of obtaining the most optimal values for `db_block_buffers`, `shared_pool_size`, `log_buffer`, and `log_archive_buffers` is to monitor the utilization and respective hit ratios of each. For example, if you have a 97 percent buffer cache hit ratio and 0 `redo log space requests`, start decreasing the size of each buffer by 5 percent to see the effects on the buffer cache hit ratio and `redo log space requests`. If the hit ratio and `redo log space requests` remain the same, then obviously the buffer areas were unnecessarily large. Conversely, if you experience poor hit ratios, continue to increase the size of each area experiencing the poor hit ratio until the hit ratio is optimal. You should target hit ratios of at least 90 percent to allow for future system scalability. Also, be careful when you increase the size of the SGA to make sure paging or swapping does not occur.

5.9.1   SIZING THE BUFFER CACHE

The size of the buffer cache is specified by the `init.ora` parameter `db_block _buffers`. The buffer cache is used to cache database blocks in the SGA in order to reduce the amount of physical I/O. Hence, a larger cache can help increase performance by maintaining changes in the cache as opposed to on the physical disk. If your system is primarily an OLTP system, you should use a smaller database block size, such as 4 KB or 8 KB, allowing more database blocks to be cached in the SGA. To size the buffer cache appropriately, use the following query to query the `v$sysstat` table to report the buffer cache hit ratio.

```
SQL> select round(((1-(sum(decode(name,
              'physical reads',value,0))/
              (sum(decode(name,'db block gets',value,0))+
              (sum(decode(name,'consistent gets',
              value,0))))))
              *100),2) || '%' "Buffer Cache Hit Ratio"
     from v$sysstat;

                  Buffer Cache Hit Ratio
                  _____

                         97.63%
```

Formula:
Hit Ratio = 1 – (physical reads / (db block gets + consistent gets))

In this example, the buffer cache hit ratio is high (97 percent). You should target a buffer cache hit ratio of at least 90 percent to allow for scalability as more users are added to the system. Monitor the cache hit ratio, and continue to increase db_block_buffers until you achieve a high cache hit ratio such as 90 percent or higher. You should also monitor the buffer cache hit ratio at the session level via the v$sesstat view. The v$sesstat view maintains statistics at the session level while the v$sysstat view maintains statistics at the instance level. Monitoring the buffer cache hit ratio at the session level allows you to identify the offending sessions that are causing large displacements in the overall buffer cache hit ratio. In addition, monitoring the buffer cache hit ratio at the session level may also help you identify those sessions that could benefit most from multiple buffer pools. When you increase the size of the buffer cache, be sure that your system has enough memory to accommodate the increase; otherwise paging may increase and swapping may occur. Also, when you tune the buffer cache, make sure you monitor the other areas in the SGA to ensure that increasing the buffer cache did not offset another area.

In Oracle8, you can use the v$recent_bucket view to estimate the gains of increasing the size of the buffer cache. The init.ora parameter db_block_lru_extended_statistics enables the collection of statistics for the v$recent_bucket view. Setting db_block_lru_extended_statistics=500 collects 500 rows of statistics in the v$recent_bucket view. Each row in the v$recent_bucket view corresponds to the addition of a buffer. When db_block_lru_extended_statistics=500, statistics are collected in order to estimate the potential gain of increasing the buffer cache size by an additional 500 buffers. The following query shows the cache hits per interval of 500 additional buffers.

```
SQL> SELECT 500*TRUNC(ROWNUM/500)+1||
              ' to '||500*(TRUNC(ROWNUM/500)+1)
                 "Interval",
           SUM(count) "Buffer Cache Hits"
     FROM V$RECENT_BUCKET
     GROUP BY TRUNC(ROWNUM/500);
```

Interval	Buffer Cache Hits
1 to 500	45320
501 to 1000	17680

The query results show that adding 500 buffers results in 45,320 cache hits. Adding an additional 500 buffers yields 17,680 cache hits in addition to the 45,320 cache hits from the first addition of 500 buffers. This results in a total of 63,000 cache hits when 1,000 buffers are added to the buffer cache. Using the above query can help you optimally size the buffer cache. It will also help you identify the drop-off point of the buffer cache hit ratio whereby adding additional buffers results in minimal (if any) gain.

In Oracle8, you can use the v$current_bucket view to estimate the performance of a reduced size buffer cache. The v$current_bucket view maintains a row for each buffer in the buffer cache and the amount of cache hits thereof. To enable the collection of statistics for the v$current_bucket view, set the init.ora parameter db_block _lru_statistics=TRUE. The v$current_bucket view helps you estimate the number of cache misses that would occur if the buffer cache size were reduced. The following query determines the number of cache hits that occur at each interval set of 1,000 buffers.

```
SQL> SELECT 1000*TRUNC(ROWNUM/1000)+1 ||
            ' to '||1000*(TRUNC(ROWNUM/1000)+1)
             "Interval",
          SUM(count) "Buffer Cache Hits"
      FROM V$CURRENT_BUCKET
      WHERE (ROWNUM > 0)
      GROUP BY TRUNC(ROWNUM/1000);
```

Interval	Buffer Cache Hits
1 to 1000	6370
1001 to 2000	0
2001 to 3000	0
3001 to 4000	0
4001 to 5000	0
5001 to 6000	0
6001 to 7000	0
7001 to 8000	0
8001 to 9000	0
9001 to 10000	0

The above query results show that buffers 9,001–10,000 contribute no cache hits. This query also shows that no cache misses would occur until the buffer cache is reduced to 1,000 or fewer buffers. This indicates that the buffer cache is unnecessarily large and can be reduced significantly in size without incurring cache misses.

Using the buffer cache statistic views v$recent_bucket and v$current_ bucket can help you optimally size your buffer cache. The statistics provided by these views can also help you conserve memory by avoiding configuring large size buffer caches that are not fully utilized. Enabling db_block_lru_statistics and db_block_lru _extended_statistics can impact performance due to the overhead of collecting the statistics. Therefore, you should disable these parameters once you have completed tuning the buffer cache size.

5.9.2 MONITORING THE BUFFER CACHE

In Oracle8*i*, you can use the V$BH view to monitor the buffer cache utilization in order to determine which file or set of files dominate the buffer cache. In Oracle8, the V$BH view does not return any data. However, you can directly access the X$BH table from the SYS user. The following is an example query which references the V$BH view.

```
SQL> select file#, count(block#)     **** Oracle8i
     from v$bh
     group by file#
     order by 2;

SQL> select file#, count(dbablk)     **** Oracle8
     from x$bh
     group by file#
     order by 2;
```

You can also use the V$BH view to determine the number of free buffers, number of buffers being used for consistent read, and the number of buffers being used for exclusive access. The following query illustrates the categorization of the class of buffers.

```
SQL> select status,count(*)
     from v$bh
     group by status;

STATUS    COUNT(*)
-------   ----------
cr          13477
read            2
xcur       111519
```

In the above output from V$BH, 13,477 consistent read buffers exist in the buffer cache while 111,519 exclusive buffers exist in the buffer cache. These statistics can be useful in order to determine if the application is mostly read-intensive or update-intensive. You can also correlate these statistics with the SQL area (v$sql) in order to classify the majority of SQL statements as queries or DML. The equivalent query for Oracle8 is as follows.

```
select decode(state,0,'free',1,'xcur',2,'scur' ,
           3,'cr',4,'read',5,'mrec',6,'irec'), count(*)
from x$bh
group by decode(state,0,'free',1,'xcur',2,'scur' ,
           3,'cr',4,'read',5,'mrec',6,'irec');
```

5.9.3 MULTIPLE BUFFER POOLS

Oracle8 allows you to configure multiple buffer pools in order to improve buffer cache utilization. Object access patterns can vary depending on the application. A very large segment that is frequently accessed can cause the data buffers of other segments to be aged-out of the cache. This reduces the overall benefits of the cache and results in the large segment consuming a large majority of the buffer cache. Multiple buffer pools can improve buffer cache utilization in situations where large segment reads are not occurring frequently enough to synchronize with the flush cycle of the buffer cache. In this case, you can either relocate the large segment to a separate recycle buffer pool, or place the small segments in the keep buffer pool. This helps separate the segments based on the access frequency, thereby maximizing the utilization of the buffer cache. The recycle buffer pool should be smaller than the default cache and is intended for quick reuse of buffers. The keep buffer pool can be used to improve the response time of SQL statements by ensuring that the small segments are not aged out of the buffer cache. This in turn helps reduce cache misses and physical I/O.

A recycle buffer pool is beneficial for very large tables that are experiencing random I/O access. The idea behind the recycle buffer pool is to remove the objects from memory once they are no longer needed. A keep buffer pool is useful for small, frequently accessed tables requiring quick response times. Use the following queries to determine the number of cache buffers used by the particular object or segment and total number of database buffers.

```
SQL> SELECT count(*) "Number of Object Buffers"
     FROM x$bh
     WHERE obj in
             (SELECT data_object_id
              FROM dba_objects
              WHERE (object_name = <object name> ) AND
              (object_type = <object type>));

SQL> SELECT value "Total DB Buffers"
     FROM  v$parameter
     WHERE name = 'db_block_buffers';
```

You can divide the number of object buffers by the total number of database buffers to determine the percentage of cache buffers used by a particular segment.

The `init.ora` parameters `buffer_pool_keep` and `buffer_pool_recycle` specify the number of buffers and latches to be allocated for the keep and recycle buffer pools, respectively. The buffers allocated to the keep and recycle buffer pools are allocated from the total amount of database buffers specified by `db_block_buffers`. The latches for each buffer pool are allocated from the total number of LRU latches specified by `db_block_lru_latches`. Therefore, the aggregate number of buffers and latches for all buffer pools cannot exceed the values of `db_block_buffers` and `db_block_lru_latches`. The following is an example setting of the buffer pool `init.ora` parameters.

```
buffer_pool_keep=(buffers:8500, lru_latches:4)

buffer_pool_recycle=(buffers:1000, lru_latches:2)
```

The storage clause of the `ALTER` or `CREATE` SQL commands allows you to specify the default buffer pool for the object via the `BUFFER_POOL` option. You can also query the object definition views such as `USER_TABLES` and `USER_INDEXES` to determine the buffer pool for an object.

The `V$BUFFER_POOL_STATISTICS` view provides buffer pool statistics that will help you tune and size the individual buffer pools based on the application workload. The logic behind the keep buffer pool is to help reduce physical I/O by maintaining objects in memory. Use the following query to monitor the keep buffer pool cache hit ratio.

```
SQL> SELECT round(1-((physical_reads)/
            (db_block_gets+consistent_gets)),2)
             || '%' "Keep Buffer Hit Ratio"
       FROM v$buffer_pool_statistics
       WHERE name='KEEP';
```

In order to effectively measure the keep buffer pool cache hit ratio, you should compute the hit ratio only after the system has been running for some time, thus allowing time for the buffers to be loaded into the buffer pool. It is important that you size the buffer pools appropriately. An object that continues to grow may no longer fit in the keep buffer pool, subsequently losing its blocks from the buffer cache. It is key that you size the buffer pools optimally according to your workload in order to maximize buffer cache utilization.

In addition to monitoring buffer pool utilization, you should also monitor the LRU latch statistics to determine if there is contention for the LRU latches. The following queries can be used to determine the LRU child latches and associated buffer pool name experiencing LRU latch contention.

```
SQL> SELECT child#,
            misses/gets "LRU Latch Miss Ratio",
            sleeps/gets "LRU Latch Sleep Ratio"
       FROM V$LATCH_CHILDREN
       WHERE (name = 'cache buffers lru chain')
       ORDER by child#;
```

Miss and sleep ratios higher than 1 percent indicate LRU latch contention. Using the following query, you can determine which buffer pool is experiencing LRU latch contention by specifying the `child#` of the LRU latch from the previous query.

```
SQL> SELECT name
      FROM V$BUFFER_POOL
      WHERE (lo_setid <=: child #) AND
            (hi_setid >=: child #);
```

After identifying the child latches and specific pools experiencing the LRU latch contention, you may need to increase the number of LRU latches (`db_block_lru_latches`) or reconfigure the number of latches assigned to each buffer pool.

In Oracle8, if you configure multiple database writers (`db_writer_processes`) with only one buffer pool, the buffer cache is divided up amongst the database writers by LRU latches; whereby each LRU latch manages an LRU list. Each LRU list consists of database block buffers. In such a case, it is important that each DBWR process receive an equivalent distribution of buffers so as to balance the workload among the DBWR processes. This avoids situations where certain DBWR processes receive a large LRU list to process while others receive very small LRU lists. If you configure multiple buffer pools and multiple database writers, the number of LRU latches per pool should be equal to or a multiple of the number of database writers configured. In the case of multiple buffer pools, each buffer pool may have a different block utilization rate. Buffer blocks in the recycle buffer pool are typically frequently modified whereas buffer blocks in the keep pool may be seldom modified. This translates into more writes for the recycle buffer pool than that of the keep buffer pool. Consequently, in order to achieve an optimal load balance, each DBWR process should receive an equal number of LRU lists per pool. When multiple buffer pools are employed, each buffer pool maintains a contiguous range of LRU latches. It is important that you optimally configure the number of LRU latches based on the number of available processors, number of database writers, and buffer pool configuration. This helps ensure an even workload distribution across the database writers thereby maximizing database I/O throughput.

5.9.4 LARGE POOL

Oracle8 provides the ability to configure a separate memory pool to be used for large memory allocations in Multithreaded Server (MTS) environments. Memory allocated for MTS sessions can reduce the amount of shared pool memory available for the shared SQL cache. This may cause additional parses and loads because of SQL statements that may get aged-out of the cache to make space for MTS session memory allocations. Configuring a separate pool for MTS session memory helps reduce contention for shared pool memory. The large pool can also be used for I/O buffers during backups. The `init.ora` parameters `large_pool_size` and `large_pool_min_alloc` specify the size of the large pool and the minimum allocation size when memory is allocated from the large pool, respectively. You can also examine the POOL column of the v$sgastat view to determine in which pool objects reside. The large pool is not managed as a cache, and objects are not aged out of the large memory pool. The large memory pool is a memory allocation heap which can be used for MTS session memory and backup and restore I/O buffers.

In order to size the large pool optimally, you can query the v$sysstat view to determine the amount of session memory allocations.

```
SQL> select name,value
        from v$sysstat
        where (name like '%memory%') AND
              (name like '%session%')
        order by name;
```

NAME	VALUE
session pga memory	44924560
session pga memory max	44924560
session uga memory	365168
session uga memory max	29576300

The session memory allocation statistics provided by the v$sysstat view can be used to size the large pool appropriately. You should also query the v$sesstat view in order to obtain the session memory allocations per session rather than a total at the instance level (v$sysstat). The v$sesstat view allows you to determine the amount of session memory allocated per session. You may find that certain sessions are allocating large amounts of memory while other sessions are using very little session memory.

In Oracle8*i*, the large pool can also be used for parallel execution message buffers. Using the large pool heap helps reduce contention for the shared pool and improves the performance of parallel execution. This also allows database administrators to more effectively size the shared pool for the library and data dictionary caches and separately size the large pool for the parallel execution message buffers.

5.10 TUNING ARCHIVING

If your database is in archive mode, you may want to increase the size of the archive buffers so as to minimize the amount of time LGWR is blocking, awaiting the ARCH (archiver) process to archive a redo log file. If archiving mode is enabled, LGWR cannot switch back to the log file that is currently being archived until the archiver completes the copy of the redo log file.

The init.ora parameter log_archive_buffer_size specifies the size of each archival buffer in redo log blocks size (i.e., 512 bytes). The init.ora parameter log_archive_buffers specifies the number of buffers to allocate for archiving. The default, which is sufficient for most workloads, is 4. Increasing the value of these parameters increases the speed of the archiver process significantly. However, a faster archiver process at the expense of slower background processes decreases overall system performance. Tune these parameters accordingly with the goal of synchronizing the archival rate with the other background processes, such as LGWR and DBWR.

You can also enable archiving I/O slaves if your platform does not support asynchronous I/O or the implementation of asynchronous I/O is not efficient. The `init.ora` parameter `arch_io_slaves` can be used to configure several I/O slaves for the purposes of parallelizing archive I/O requests. You should also monitor the archive destination disks to determine if disk I/O contention is occurring. Disk I/O contention can cause the ARCH process to wait on I/O completion and may also result in LGWR backing up if LGWR needs to switch back to the redo log file that is currently being archived.

Oracle8*i* provides the ability to configure multiple archiver (ARCH) processes to be spawned at instance startup. The `init.ora` parameter `log_archive_max_processes` can be used to specify the number of ARCH processes to be spawned. Configuring multiple archiver processes is useful for situations in which LGWR is writing redo faster than the ARCH process can read redo data from the redo log files and write the redo data to one or more of the archive log destinations. Prior to Oracle8*i*, users had to either use I/O slaves or manual foreground sessions to parallelize the work of the archiver. In addition, Oracle8*i* allows the user to specify multiple archive destinations. The new `init.ora` parameters `log_archive_dest_<n>` and `log_archive_dest_state_<n>` specify the location of the archive destination as well as whether or not the destination is enabled, respectively. The value for `<n>` ranges between 1 and 5.

5.11 THE POST-WAIT DRIVER

The Oracle Server, by default, uses semaphores to coordinate shared resource access. One semaphore is used per Oracle process. A process that needs a lock on an already-locked shared resource will suspend and wait until the resource becomes available. When the resource becomes available, the process's semaphore will be incremented when the process is posted. Semaphores can be an expensive operation for post and wait requests, and have resulted in poor scalability on certain platforms.

In an effort to improve scalability, several platforms provide a post-wait driver as an alternative to expensive semaphore operations for interprocess communication. To enable the post-wait driver in the Oracle Server, set the `init.ora` parameters `use_post _wait_driver=TRUE` and `post_wait_device=<post wait device name>`. Once enabled, Oracle will no longer use semaphores. You can verify this through the `ipcs` command while the Oracle Server is running. The post-wait driver is not available on all platforms. Check with the *Oracle Installation and Configuration Guide* for your specific platform for instructions on enabling the post-wait driver. You can use the post-wait driver to increase performance on certain platforms. If you are running Oracle on a Sequent system, you can choose between the post-wait driver and semaphores. On Sequent, the performance gain offered by the post-wait driver versus semaphores is approximately 5 percent. On Solaris, Oracle uses semaphores because of their demonstrated scalability and high performance.

5.12 TUNING TCP/IP

The default packet size used by SQL*Net V2 and Net8 is 2 KB for the Session Data Unit (SDU). The packet size utilized by the TCP/IP stack and underlying network layer is 1 KB for most platforms. The SDU should be equal to, or a multiple of, the underlying TCP/IP packet size. Extra network overhead may be needed if the packet size is smaller than the SDU size since each SDU packet would be broken down into smaller packet sizes. Some platforms allow to you increase the OS TCP/IP packet size. Increasing the OS packet size to 2 KB allows SQL*Net/Net8 packets and OS TCP/IP packets to be the same size.

5.12.1 SESSION DATA UNIT (SDU)

The Oracle networking layer places data in buffers and then sends the buffers when full or when the data is requested. The Session Data Unit (SDU) is the buffer that is used to send data across the network. By adjusting the SDU unit size from the default of 2 KB, you may be able to increase performance by reducing the number of networking round trips. You should only modify the SDU size if large amounts of data are being transmitted, a Wide Area Network (WAN) is being used where latency is critical, or the packet sizes are consistently the same size. The Transport Data Unit (TDU) is the block used to transmit the data to the underlying protocol adapter. TDU and SDU can be set to different sizes; however, in most cases there is little advantage in doing so.

Before adjusting the sizes of SDU and TDU, you should examine the amount of network traffic by querying the v$sysstat view.

```
SQL> select name,
            value
     from v$sysstat
     where name like '%Net%';
```

```
NAME                                                    VALUE
--------------------------------------------------- ----------
bytes sent via SQL*Net to client                    2089859860
bytes received via SQL*Net from client               310259198
SQL*Net roundtrips to/from client                      4749102
bytes sent via SQL*Net to dblink                         12122
bytes received via SQL*Net from dblink                   78615
SQL*Net roundtrips to/from dblink                           81
```

This query reports the amount of bytes of SQL*Net/Net8 traffic as well as the number of round trips. This information can help you size the SDU and TDU buffers more effectively based on the network traffic. You should also query the v$system_event view to determine if users are waiting on networking events.

```
SQL> select event,
            total_waits,
            time_waited,
            average_wait
     from v$system_event
     where event like '%Net%';
```

EVENT	TOTAL_WAITS	TIME_WAITED	AVERAGE_WAIT
SQL*Net message to client	4776784	1191	.000249331
SQL*Net message to dblink	82	0	0
SQL*Net more data to client	650918	4621	.007099205
SQL*Net message from client	4775666	105374930	22.0649706
SQL*Net more data from client	938	17327	18.4722814
SQL*Net message from dblink	81	184	2.27160494
SQL*Net more data from dblink	30	6	.2
SQL*Net break/reset to client	5794	18150	3.13255091
SQL*Net break/reset to dblink	2	1	.5

After determining the amount of networking traffic and whether users are experiencing waits on networking events, you can adjust the size of SDU and TDU by modifying the tnsnames.ora and listener.ora files on both the client and the server. The main event which indicates whether larger SDU/TDU units would be beneficial is the SQL*Net more data event. The SQL*Net more data event is used when multiple round trips are needed to deliver the data because the data could not fit in the packet size. If the event wait information shows that a considerable amount of time is being spent on the SQL*Net more data event, then increasing the SDU/TDU sizes will likely help improve performance by reducing the number of round trips. In general, performance has increased when setting SDU to a multiple of the database block size. In addition to reviewing the networking statistics and events, you should test your application thoroughly in order to determine the optimal settings for SDU/TDU.

```
TNSNAMES.ORA:

sales= (DESCRIPTION=
       (SDU=8192)   ***** session data unit buffer size
       (TDU=8192)   ***** transport data unit size
       (ADDRESS= (PROTOCOL=tcp)
       (PORT=1521)
       (HOST=myhost))
       (CONNECT_DATA= (SID=prods))
    )
```

```
LISTENER.ORA: The parameters need to appear in the SID_DESC
clause.

SID_LIST_LISTENER =
    (SID_LIST =
        (SID_DESC =
            (SDU = 8192) ***** Connects to this SID
            (TDU = 8192) ***** using an 8k packet size.
            (SID_NAME = prods)
            (ORACLE_HOME = /myhost/unix/oracle)
        )
    )
```

5.12.2 NO DELAY FLAG

TCP often coalesces packets together before transmitting in order to reduce round trips and group small numbers of requests into a single packet. This function of grouping requests may cause delays for a small number of clients requiring immediate responses. If using the TCP/IP protocol adapter with SQL*Net V2 or Net8, you can enable the no delay flag by setting the parameter `tcp.nodelay=yes` in the `protocol.ora` file.

5.13 TUNING THE ORACLE NETWORKING LAYER

Whether you are using SQL*Net V2 or Net8, it is important that you configure the Oracle networking layer optimally in order to improve network utilization and throughput. By utilizing the different options of SQL*Net V2 and Net8, you can maximize the utilization of network resources and improve network transmission efficiency.

5.13.1 OUT-OF-BAND BREAKS

The UNIX TCP/IP stack supports the mechanism utilized by SQL*Net and Net8 TCP/IP for out-of-band breaks. The Net8 and SQL*Net V2 listener process negotiates out-of-band breaks by default. Performance can increase up to 20 percent by using out-of-band breaks over using in-band breaks. For those platforms that do not support out-of-band breaks, the Oracle server process polls periodically to check for client-side interrupts. You can also increase the interval between checks for client-side interrupts by setting the parameter `BREAK_POLL_SKIP` in the `sqlnet.ora` file on the server side. You can set `BREAK_POLL_SKIP` to a very large number to reduce the number of polls that are done (i.e., `BREAK_POLL_SKIP=10000000`). The performance gain offered by tuning `BREAK_POLL_SKIP` is minimal, but it can help reduce system calls and context switches.

5.13.2 DEADMAN ALERT

SQL*Net V2 uses the TNS (Transparent Name Substrate) interface, allowing multiple different stacks to connect to the Oracle Server. SQL*Net V2.1 and above offer an extremely useful feature known as *deadman alert*. Deadman alert probes for dead or invalid connections and terminates the corresponding server processes, thereby freeing up system resources (memory, locks, etc.). Deadman alert is extremely useful for situations where client PCs are often rebooted leaving shadow processes on the server. You can adjust the time that SQL*Net probes for a connection and/or request. If the probe finds a dead connection, the corresponding server process is terminated; this is known as deadman alert. The SQL*Net parameter is `sqlnet.expire` and is set to the number of minutes between SQL*Net probes for dead connections. You can set this parameter in the `sqlnet.ora` file located in the `$ORACLE_HOME/network/admin` directory. The following is an example of the `sqlnet.expire` option.

```
###########################################
# Filename: sqlnet.ora                    #
###########################################
AUTOMATIC_IPC = OFF
SQLNET.EXPIRE_TIME = 30
```

5.13.3 NETWORKING TRACING

Ensure that SQL*Net tracing is disabled both on the client and the server if you are not experiencing any problems and are not trying to debug a SQL*Net issue. Enabling tracing can cause SQL*Net's performance to degrade due to the overhead of the trace calls on the client and server. To determine if tracing is enabled, examine the `sqlnet.ora` and `listener.ora` files in the `$ORACLE_HOME/network/admin` directory.

5.13.4 PRESPAWNING SERVER PROCESSES

The SQL*Net V2 listener listens on a given port (this is specified in the `listener.ora` file in the `$ORACLE_HOME/network/admin` directory). Once a request for a connection comes across the port, the SQL*Net V2 listener (`tnslsnr LISTENER -inherit`) spawns an Oracle process if running in a dedicated server mode, and this new process becomes the dedicated server process for the user (shadow process). The shadow process is also referred to as the dedicated server process. The shadow process communicates with the user (client). The shadow process (acting on behalf of the client) attaches to the SGA and executes the client statements. In a dedicated server mode, each time a user connects to the Oracle Server, a shadow process is created. This can be verified by issuing the `ps -ef | grep LOCAL` command on the server if running SQL*Net V2 or Net8. For example, the following is an example of the `ps` command to list the shadow processes.

```
myhost> ps -ef | grep LOCAL

OWNER      PID    PPID   TIME    COMMAND
─────────────────────────────────────────────────
oracle     25145     1   0:00    oracleSPROD (LOCAL=NO)
```

This example shows a shadow process with `LOCAL=NO`. This means that the connection is a remote connection (from a client or another server).

A new feature of SQL*Net V2.1 (with Oracle 7.1) provides the ability to prespawn connections to the Oracle Server, thereby reducing the user connection time by eliminating the need for the V2 listener to spawn a process for each user connection at connection time. A specified number of prespawned processes can be created, allowing users to attach to these shadow processes immediately.

To configure prespawned processes, set the `PRESPAWN_MAX` parameter in the `listener.ora` file to the maximum number of prespawned servers you want created. You can also set the `POOL_SIZE` parameter in the `listener.ora` file to the number of idle prespawned server processes that the listener should maintain. The `TIMEOUT` parameter specifies the period of time that an idle prespawned server process waits before termination. Without prespawning connection processes, a shadow process is created for each connection, and the shadow process terminates after the user disconnects from the Oracle Server. Setting the `TIMEOUT` parameter can keep a shadow processes active for a specified period of time. If your system has a large number of users constantly connecting and disconnecting (which is very typical in an OLTP application), you may increase performance by prespawning connections, thereby reducing the user connection time.

5.13.5 CONNECTION POOLING

Net8 provides a feature known as connection pooling which maximizes the amount of physical connections to a multithreaded server (MTS) by utilizing idle sessions. Connection pooling allows a dispatcher's set of connections to be shared among client processes. Connection pooling helps maximize the utilization of resources. In order to enable connection pooling, you need to set the `POOL` option of the `init.ora` parameter `mts_dispatchers`. The following example enables connection pooling.

```
mts_dispatchers="(PROTOCOL=TCP)(DISPATCHERS=5)(POOL=ON)"
```

You can also specify whether connection pooling should be enabled for either incoming or outgoing connections or both. You can also specify the timeout (in ticks) for connection pooling for both incoming and outgoing connections. In addition, you can also specify the length of a tick in seconds by using the `TICKS` option of the `init.ora` parameter `mts_dispatchers`. Connections that have been idle for a set period of time can then be reused. Once the idle connection becomes active again, the connection is reestablished with the dispatcher. The following example enables connection pooling for both incoming and outgoing connections and specifies a timeout of 10 for incoming connections, and a timeout of 20 for outgoing connections.

```
mts_dispatchers="(PROTOCOL=TCP)(DISPATCHERS=5)(POOL=ON) \
                 (IN=10)(OUT=20)"
```

Connection pooling is useful for environments with a large number of interactive users whereby users spend more time analyzing the results than submitting requests. Connection pooling effectively increases concurrency and maximizes server utilization. You should also monitor the v$dispatcher and v$queue views to determine if contention for dispatchers or shared server processes is occurring.

5.13.6 CONNECTION MANAGER

Connection Manager is a utility that provides the ability to administer network access, multiplex client sessions, and support multiple protocols. The Oracle Connection Manager replaces the Oracle Multiprotocol Interchange used with SQL*Net V2. You can use the Connection Manager to establish filters and restrictions on access. Connection Manager functions in a manner similar to a router. Connection Manager receives a connection request, negotiates the protocol, and routes the request appropriately. The Connection Manager is invoked and shut down through the Connection Manager Control Utility (cmctl), and is configured via the Connection Manager configuration file (cman.ora). For more information on configuring the Connection Manager, refer to the *Oracle Net8 Administrator's Guide*.

Connection Concentration is a feature of the Oracle Connection Manager that allows multiple client sessions to be multiplexed over a single transport. Connection Concentration reduces the number of server endpoints for incoming connection requests, thus allowing more server sessions. Connection Concentration maximizes network resource utilization by increasing the number of sessions over a fixed number of physical ports. Connection concentration is useful for MTS environments where a large number of users require a constant connection. Using Connection Concentration enables thousands of concurrent user connections. To enable Connection Concentration, set the MULTIPLEX option of the init.ora parameter mts_dispatchers as follows.

```
mts_dispatchers="(PROTOCOL=TCP)(DISPATCHERS=5)(MULTIPLEX=ON)"
```

Connection Manager coupled with Connection Concentration allows you to reduce contention for network resources and maximizes system resources. Connection Manager also provides multiprotocol support as well as mechanisms to control access.

5.13.7 NET8 TNS RAW

Net8 provides an option known as TNS RAW that allows Net8 packets to be transmitted without Net8 headers, if possible. In a networked environment, this can help reduce the amount of data transferred. Net8 has also been optimized to issue low-level API protocol calls.

5.13.8 LISTENER LOAD BALANCING

Net8 provides listener load balancing which helps distribute incoming connection requests over multiple listeners so as to not burden a single listener. Each listener registers itself with a service handler. The service handler maintains load statistics and thus allows the listener to be aware of the load. The listener then redirects the connection to the least busy handler. To enable listener load balancing, configure multiple listeners per database.

5.14   RECURSIVE SQL

You should monitor the number of recursive SQL calls compared to user calls. Recursive calls typically occur due to dynamic storage management or cache misses in the data dictionary or library cache. For example, an INSERT statement may execute recursive SQL in order to allocate additional extents to hold the new rows that are being inserted if sufficient space does not exist. Recursive calls are also generated for the following activities.

❑ data dictionary cache misses.

❑ invocation of database triggers.

❑ Data Definition Language (DDL) statements.

❑ SQL statements executed from within functions, stored procedures, anonymous PL/SQL blocks, and packages.

❑ referential integrity constraints enforcement.

You can use the following query to monitor the rate of recursive SQL.

```
SQL> select name,value
     from v$sysstat
     where name in ('recursive calls','user calls')
     order by name

     NAME                             VALUE
     -------------------- ----------
     recursive calls               75329798
     user calls                    22896655
```

In this example, the ratio of recursive calls to user calls is 75329798 / 22896655 = 3.29:1. This means that each user call on the average required at least 3 recursive calls to complete. Recursive calls can also occur when PL/SQL blocks issue SQL statements that require recursive calls to handle the equivalent of bind and define. To reduce recursive calls, you may have to either redesign the application to group several SQL statements together, or rebuild the objects (tables and indexes) to reduce dynamic storage management. When you rebuild the objects, you can allocate enough space upfront using the storage clause in order to avoid having to extend the object dynamically.

You should also try to minimize the amount of `user calls`. `User calls` are calls made to the Oracle kernel. The `parse count` is the number of times a SQL statement was parsed. You should try to reduce the number of calls made to the Oracle kernel. By using array processing and PL/SQL blocks to group multiple SQL statements into a single statement or single batch, you can reduce the calls made to the kernel. Calculate the ratio of `parse count` to `user calls` by querying the `v$sysstat` view as follows.

```
SQL> select name,value
     from v$sysstat
     where name in ('parse count (total)','user calls',
                    'parse time cpu','parse time elapsed',
                    'parse count (hard)')
     order by name

         NAME                         VALUE
         --------------------    ----------
         parse count (hard)         14108
         parse count (total)       843816
         parse time cpu             52517
         parse time elapsed         64171
         user calls               4872200
```

In this example, the ratio of `user calls` to `parse count` is 4872200/843816 = 5.77:1. This means that on the average a parse occurs for every 5.77 user calls. The parse count (hard) statistic is also useful for determining the number of hard parses in comparison with the total parse count.

5.15 TUNING STORAGE CLAUSES

Setting the storage clauses of database objects can help you reduce dynamic storage extension and thus recursive calls. The high-water mark of a table identifies the portion of the table that has been allocated. You should monitor the table to ensure that the table does not contain a lot of holes—meaning that after a large number of deletions, the high-water mark for the table could be causing the table to waste space. In this event, you can re-create and reload the table to reset the high-water mark to a more optimal position. Oracle 7.3 also provides a new command that you can use to deallocate unused space within a table. The following command can be used to free unused space above the table high-water mark.

```
SQL> alter table <table name> deallocate unused;
```

This will not help you deal with the problem of table holes, but it can free unused space, allowing other objects to make use of the space. To deal with the problem of holes, you can re-create the table using either export/import, create table as select, or SQL*Loader to reload the table. Tuning loads and table creations are discussed in Chapter 6.

The PCTFREE and PCTUSED columns determine the blocking factor of the table. You should always set these parameters explicitly, as the defaults may not be optimal. Using PCTFREE, you can specify the amount of space that will be left free in the object for future inserts. PCTUSED specifies the percentage amount of space used per data block. Sizing PCTUSED and PCTFREE appropriately helps reduce the overhead of dynamic space management. If you expect large amounts of growth, set PCTFREE to a high value to account for future inserts or updates. Do not size PCTUSED and PCTFREE so small that dynamic extension is occurring frequently. If PCTFREE is set too low, sessions may experience buffer busy waits during concurrent updates to the rows. If each block contains a large number of rows, and sessions are concurrently updating different rows in the same block, then sessions may experience contention for the block. This will likely show up as a buffer busy waits event. Buffer busy waits can be caused by several factors; however, it is typically a result of concurrent updates to the same block (i.e., block contention). You can either increase the PCTFREE so that the rows of the table are spread across more blocks, or change the application such that concurrent processing of rows occurs on different blocks.

The PCTINCREASE parameter specifies the growth rate of each subsequent extent following the second extent allocated. The default for PCTINCREASE is 50 percent. In most cases, you should set PCTINCREASE to 0 to prevent fragmentation. Setting it to 0 ensures that each extent is of equal size. You should not rely solely on PCTINCREASE to handle object sizing. You should set the INITIAL and NEXT extent sizes appropriately, as well as PCTUSED and PCTFREE to accommodate future inserts and updates. In Oracle8*i* release 8.1.6, you can alter the INITRANS option of an object, which will take effect for new blocks.

If you are designing a new database, using the Oracle Designer tool can help you with sizing by making use of the volume growth, initial size, and maximum size input data.

5.15.1 THE ONE EXTENT MYTH

Although it is commonly thought that keeping your data in one extent or as few extents as possible increases performance over having many extents, this, however, is not entirely true. The performance problems associated with many extents has to do with the levels of row fragmentation and block packing, not with the number of extents. Furthermore, trying to keep all your table or index data in one extent can be extremely difficult. It is impossible for very large databases on platforms that support only 2 GB data files. For example, with a 10 GB table, it is not possible to load all the data into one extent. Oracle 7.3 removed the limit placed on the maximum number of extents per object. Therefore, with Oracle 7.3, you can have an unlimited number of extents. Using either the Export/Import, create table as select, or SQL*Loader utilities, try re-creating the object to eliminate fragmentation.

A large number of extents for an object will result in more entries in the data dictionary space management tables such as UET$. Hence, it is not advisable to allow an object to grow to the maximum number of extents which is actually 2 GB (unlimited). Locally managed tablespaces should be used in place of dictionary-managed tablespaces. Refer to section 3.18 for more details on locally managed tablespaces.

5.16 THE FREE LIST

Contention for the free list can reduce the performance of an application. The free list contains a list of data blocks allocated for a segment's extents and has free space greater than PCTFREE. When you issue an INSERT, Oracle scans the free list for the first available block and uses it if possible. Deletes and updates that result in the number of used blocks being used by the object being less than PCTUSED cause the blocks to be returned to the free list. You can determine if your system is experiencing high contention for the free list by querying the v$waitstat view.

```
SQL> select class,count
     from v$waitstat
     where class='free list';

     CLASS          COUNT
     ─────────────────────
     free list        33
```

The following query reports the total requests make for data.

```
SQL> select sum(value)
     from v$sysstat
     where name in
     ('db block gets','consistent gets');

          SUM(VALUE)
          ──────────
          5094340
```

In this example, the v$waitstat shows that the number of waits for free blocks is 33. You should compare the number of waits for free blocks with the total requests for data. In the previous example, 5,094,340 requests were made for data. The ratio of waits for free blocks to total requests for data is extremely low. If, however, the ratio was higher than 1 percent, you may want to consider increasing the number of free lists to reduce the contention. You should also monitor the statistic buffer busy waits by querying the v$system_event view. A high number of buffer busy waits may indicate free list contention. Prior to Oracle8*i*, you would need to re-create the table to increase the number of free lists. For example, you can use the following statement (assuming you have sufficient space) to re-create the table.

```
SQL> Create Table neworders
        storage (initial 100M
                next 100M
                pctincrease 0
                freelist groups 10
                freelists 22)
        as select * from orders;

SQL> drop table orders;

SQL> rename neworders to orders;
```

In Oracle8*i* release 8.1.6, you can increase the number of freelists for a table by using the ALTER TABLE command as follows.

```
SQL> alter table ap.ap_invoices_all storage (freelists 32);
```

The ability to alter the number of freelists is extremely useful as it avoids having to recreate the table and reissue the grants. In addition, re-creating the table will invalidate all objects which were based on the table, such as views or PL/SQL units.

5.17 MONITORING LOCKING

Locking can also cause performance problems by causing processes to wait long times before locks on rows or tables can be obtained. You can use the Lock Monitor in the Enterprise Manager to monitor the users holding locks and types of locks being held. In some cases, the DBA might have to kill user sessions explicitly in order to remove locks on objects. PMON is responsible for cleaning up user processes and for freeing any resources held by the process upon termination of a process. You can also query the v$lock and v$session views to show the locks that are being held by users. The following queries can be used to show the DDL and DML locks being held by user processes.

```
SQL> select substr(username,1,12) "User",
            substr(owner,1,8) "Owner",
            substr(name,1,15) "Name",
            substr (a.type,1,20) "Type",
            substr (mode_held,1,11) "Mode held"
        from sys.dba_ddl_locks a,
            v$session b
        where (a.session_id=b.sid);
```

```
SQL> select substr(username,1,12) "User",
            substr(owner,1,8) "Owner",
            substr(name,1,15) "Name",
            substr (mode_held,1,11) "Mode held"
     from sys.dba_dml_locks a,
          v$session b
     where (a.session_id=b.sid);
```

You need to run the `catblock.sql` script located in the `$ORACLE_HOME/rdbms/admin` directory. The `catblock.sql` script will create various different lock views that will enable you to monitor the locks being held by user processes. You can also use the `utllockt.sql` (located in `$ORACLE_HOME/rdbms/admin` directory) to output the current locks being held in tree format.

There is no secret to performance tuning when dealing with locks. The goal of the application is to avoid exclusive locks (unless absolutely needed), and use the finest level of locking possible when acquiring locks. The application should also try to minimize the amount of time that the lock is held. This will allow other processes to obtain the lock without waiting for long periods of time.

You should also monitor the enqueue statistics from the `v$sysstat` view. Oracle uses the enqueue lock manager to manage locks. If `enqueue waits` or `enqueue timeouts` is high, you will need to increase the `init.ora` parameter `enqueue_resources`. The `init.ora` parameter `enqueue_resources` specifies the number of resources that can be locked concurrently. If `enqueue releases` and `enqueue requests` are close in value, this means that sufficient enqueue resources exist. If enqueue requests are much higher than enqueue releases, you need to increase the value of `enqueue_resources`. You may also need to increase the value of the `init.ora` parameter `dml_locks` if the statistics show contention for enqueue locks. The `dml_locks` parameter should be set to the maximum number of users multiplied by the number of tables being modified in a transaction. For example, if four users are modifying three tables, then set `dml_locks=12`.

If you are increasing the number of concurrent locks that can be held, you may also want to consider increasing the `init.ora` parameters `sessions` and `processes`. Recall that if your Oracle Server is configured to use semaphores, one semaphore will be used per process. Therefore, if increasing the `init.ora` parameters `sessions` and `processes`, you may also need to increase the number of available semaphores. You can increase the number of semaphores by increasing the semaphore kernel parameters. See Chapter 2 for a complete list of the semaphore-related kernel parameters.

5.18   REFERENTIAL INTEGRITY

Oracle7 introduced the concept of stored procedures and database triggers. Stored procedures and triggers can be used to perform many database operations including Referential Integrity (RI). When you design an application, avoid placing the equivalent referential integrity logic in the application itself. Use primary keys and foreign keys to enforce referential integrity at the database level. It increases the performance of the application since the RI is done at the Oracle kernel level rather than at the application level. Handling RI at the application level can reduce performance because of the increased number of SQL calls that are needed to verify parent and child relationships. In a networked environment, this increases network traffic as more SQL calls are sent across to the server from the client. This also increases the number of SQL user calls made to the Oracle kernel.

Triggers can also be used to handle distributed transactions that need to insert or update data in other tables (possibly in other servers) following an insert or delete on a certain table. Again, do not handle distributed transactions in the application. Allow the server to perform the distributed transaction through the use of triggers and stored procedures. This can increase the performance of your OLTP system.

5.18.1 DEFERRED CONSTRAINTS

Oracle8 provides the ability to defer constraint checking upon commit rather than upon each statement. For example, you may have several update or insert statements within a single transaction and then issue a commit. If the constraint is marked as immediate, then the constraint is validated at the end of each statement. If you specify the constraint to be deferrable, you can also choose whether you want the constraint initially deferred or initially immediate. Initially deferred starts the transaction in deferred mode, and initially immediate starts the transaction in nondeferred mode. The following example creates a deferred unique column constraint with the constraint marked as initially deferred.

```
CREATE TABLE dealer
      (dealer_no number(8),
       territory_id number(5),
       dealer_desc varchar2(60),
       dealer_streetno number(8),
       dealer_address varchar2(30),
       dealer_city_id number(8),
       constraint udealer_no unique(dealer_no)
            initially deferred deferrable);
```

You can use the NOVALIDATE option of the enable constraint clause which enables the constraint for future inserts, updates, and deletes but does not check the existing rows in the table. This can be useful for large bulk load situations where you want to load the data in parallel and eliminate the constraint checks at load time. Following the load, you can then scan the table in parallel in order to determine if rows exist which violate the constraints. The following example enables a constraint with the NOVALIDATE option.

```
SQL> alter table dealer enable novalidate
            constraint udealer_no;
```

5.19 DISCRETE TRANSACTIONS

Discrete transactions can increase performance over the standard transactions. Discrete transactions do not generate any undo or rollback information because, in a discrete transaction, the block is not modified until the transaction commits. Redo information is generated but is held in a separate location in memory. Once the transaction commits, the database block changes are applied directly to the block, and the redo information is copied to the redo buffer and written out to the redo log file in the normal manner.

Discrete transactions can increase performance depending on the type of OLTP workload. In some cases, using discrete transactions for small, light transactions increased performance 50 percent.

Discrete transactions have some limitations: A database block is never modified more than once in the same transaction, the new modified data does not need to be seen by the process, and tables containing columns of type LONG are not modified. If your transaction meets these requirements, you may be able to use discrete transactions to increase performance.

Because discrete transactions do not actually modify the data block until the transaction commits, you cannot see the changes of your modification as in a normal transaction. To enable discrete transactions, call the procedure DBMS_TRANSACTION.begin_ discrete_transaction from your transaction to indicate that your transaction is a discrete transaction.

Discrete transactions can increase performance by minimizing rollback and redo buffer contention. The discrete transactions feature is ideal for lightweight, short-lived transactions that can live with the restrictions of the discrete transaction.

5.20 HASH CLUSTER

If you have a transaction table that is maintained by a primary or unique key, you can increase the performance of transactions against this table by using a hash cluster key. A hash cluster key uses an internal hash function or the unique key itself as the hash function to locate records. This reduces the number of I/Os needed to locate rows.

In a typical unique index scan, the branch blocks and leaf blocks of the index are searched to find the index data block containing the unique key. Then, the rowid stored in the index data block is used to access the row of the table. For a unique scan, this often translates into two or three physical I/Os to locate the row. For a hash cluster key, the row can often be found with one I/O using the hash function to locate the row. Hash tables cannot be loaded in direct path using SQL*Loader. However, for a transaction-based system, using a hash cluster key on the table for the primary key can increase performance. You should make sure you configure the SIZE parameter and the number of HASHKEYS appropriately; otherwise many more I/Os will be required to locate the row. For more information on creating hash cluster keys, refer to the *Oracle8i SQL Reference Manual*.

5.21 ORACLE PARALLEL SERVER (OPS)

Oracle8 integrated the Distributed Lock Manager (DLM) into the Oracle8 DBMS kernel. This improves administration and performance as well as provides a consistent and portable OPS implementation. In addition to the incorporation of the DLM, Oracle8 OPS also provides the Application Fail-Over mechanism, which maintains a user connection as long as at least one instance in the OPS environment remains available. Oracle8 provides major enhancements to OPS in the areas of administration, performance, and reliability. Oracle is committed to OPS, and future releases of Oracle8 will include significant enhancements to administration, scalability, performance, and reliability.

The performance of OPS is also highly dependent on the configuration of the interconnect between nodes in the OPS cluster. Hardware vendors continue to improve the interconnect technology by providing low-latency, high-bandwidth interconnects. As interconnect technology continues to improve, more nodes can be added to the cluster in order to increase reliability and performance.

Oracle Parallel Server 8i provides a new feature known as Cache Fusion, which replaces the old disk ping model of OPS for foregrounds, which need a consistent copy of a block due to a read-write mix. Cache Fusion, in essence, "ships" the blocks across the interconnect rather than using the disk ping model. In the disk ping model, the foreground process requesting the block posts the DBWR process on the instance holding the block. The database writer process then services the cross-instance call and writes out the dirty block(s). The foreground on the requesting instance then reads the block in order to obtain a consistent version of the block. In the applications space, disk pings can result in a performance degradation due to the nature of the activity as well as the code path associated with pings. Cache Fusion is an attempt to deal with the scalability and performance issues associated with disk pings. Cache Fusion utilizes the high-bandwidth, low-latency interconnect that exists between the nodes in a cluster. There are two phases to Cache Fusion: read-write and write-write. Oracle8i OPS optimizes for the read-write phase, which is known as CR Server (Consistent Read Server). Applications which can be partitioned by module to avoid write-write mixes maximize the scalability of OPS. Applications workloads with a read-write mix can make use of Cache Fusion to improve application scalability in a clustered environment.

5.22 INDEXING ENHANCEMENTS

Oracle 7.3 allows you to rebuild an index by using the following command.

```
SQL> alter index <index name> rebuild;
```

You can also rebuild the index in parallel and choose the unrecoverable or recoverable option in Oracle7 and the nologging or logging option in Oracle8 when rebuilding the index. The index rebuild feature is extremely useful for fragmented indexes and avoids your having to first drop and then re-create the index. In Oracle8*i*, an index can be rebuilt on-line without effecting users by specifying the ONLINE keyword after the REBUILD keyword. On-line index rebuilds allow DML statements to proceed while the index is being rebuilt.

5.22.1 INDEX COMPRESSION

Oracle8*i* allows indexes to be compressed, which improves storage utilization for indexes that have a large number of duplicate keys. If the COMPRESS option is specified as part of the index creation or part of the index rebuild command, duplicate key column values are eliminated. This can have a tremendous amount of benefit in terms of disk storage savings as well as index update performance since there will be less key value pairs. The following example creates a compressed index.

```
SQL> CREATE INDEX AP_INVOICES_C1 ON AP_INVOICE_DISTRIBUTIONS_ALL
         (accrual_posted_flag, invoice_id)
      COMPRESS 1;
```

The integer value following the COMPRESS keyword specifies the number of columns to compress in the index key column pair. The above index will compress the duplicate entries of the ACCRUAL_POSTED_FLAG column values. Since the ACCRUAL_POSTED _FLAG can have either the value 'Y' or 'N', the compression will result in a major disk savings.

5.23 TEMPORARY TABLES

Oracle8*i* allows for the use of temporary tables. Temporary tables are useful for applications that need to hold temporary results for the duration of only a session or transaction. No recovery data is generated for temporary tables. Rollback data is, however, generated for temporary tables. Indexes can also be created on temporary tables and inherit the scope and duration of the underlying table. Temporary tables can be created using the CREATE GLOBAL TEMPORARY TABLE command. In addition, the ON COMMIT DELETE ROWS clause specifies a transaction duration for the table data, while the ON COMMIT PRESERVE ROWS clause specifies a session duration for the table data. The first insert against a temporary table causes the allocation of space. Temporary tables can be useful for those applications that create, drop, or truncate tables dynamically in order to simulate the behavior of temporary tables. If the application commits frequently, you should use the ON COMMIT PRESERVE ROWS attribute for the temporary table so as to minimize the overhead of space management. The following example creates a temporary table with the ON COMMIT PRE-SERVE ROWS attribute.

```
CREATE GLOBAL TEMPORARY TABLE QP_DISCOUNTS_TEMP (
        discount_id number,
        discount_name varchar2(50),
        discount_line_id number,
        discount_percent number)
ON COMMIT PRESERVE ROWS;
```

Oracle8*i* global temporary tables are useful for applications that create and drop tables in the application in order to simulate the behavior of temporary tables. Statistics cannot be gathered on temporary tables, neither through the ANALYZE command nor through the DBMS_STATS package. If you plan to use Oracle8*i* temporary tables, you need to set the statistics using the DBMS_STATS.SET_TABLE_STATS() procedure. For more information on setting statistics via the DBMS_STATS package, refer to the *Oracle8i Supplied PL/SQL Packages Reference Guide.*

Chapter 6

TUNING THE
DATA WAREHOUSE

This chapter offers recommendations on performance tuning for the data warehouse. This chapter assumes that you are familiar with the basic concepts of the Oracle Server as well as the background processes associated with it. Data warehousing has become extremely popular. In the past, companies mastered the art of processing operational data through the use of transaction systems. Now, those same companies are trying to analyze their operational data using complex models to help them predict customer buying power, loyalty, market share, purchase habits, as well as performing other marketing-related studies that help them to better understand their customers and the market. Data warehousing workloads are quite different than OLTP workloads. In an OLTP environment, small and short-lived transactions consist of inserts, updates, and deletes as new data is received and processed. In an OLTP environment, there are typically many concurrent users, each issuing many light transactions. In a data warehousing environment, there are fewer users than in an average OLTP system. The data warehousing users submit much more complex and resource-intensive transactions (queries).

6.1   THE DATA WAREHOUSE

A data warehouse, as defined by the father of data warehousing, Bill Inmon, is a subject-oriented, integrated, time-variant, nonvolatile collection of data used in support of management decisions. Generally, data warehouses are built by extracting and aggregating data from the operational transactional database systems. Figure 6.1 illustrates the concept of a data warehouse.

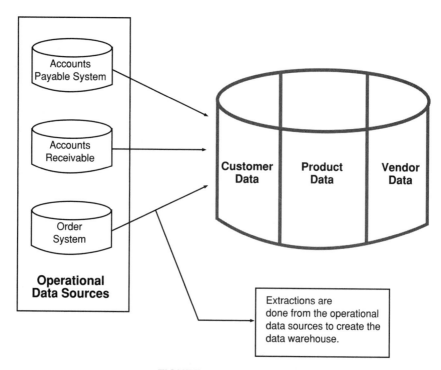

FIGURE 6.1   Data warehousing.

In Figure 6.1, data is extracted from the operational database systems to create the data warehouse. Typically, the data extracted is aggregated by specific metrics such as time or geography. On-Line Analytical Processing (OLAP), as coined by Dr. Codd who developed the relational algebra and the relational calculus, was intended to provide analytical processing and data warehousing technology on-line. The on-line piece of OLAP was meant to indicate that complex analytical processing should occur in almost the same time as OLTP systems can process a transaction. The reality of the situation is that not only is OLAP possible, but also that Oracle and hardware vendors such as Sun, HP, and Sequent have released products that push the limits of parallel processing technology. Oracle7 and Oracle8 provide features that enable customer sites to build large-scale data warehouses, and achieve unparalleled performance. The hardware vendors are also enhancing the hardware systems and operating systems constantly, thus bringing to market larger bus bandwidths, faster processors, enhanced disk I/O subsystems, and larger memory configurations. The disk I/O subsystems have been improved to sustain many more I/Os per second (IOPS). The Sun Ultra Servers such as the Enterprise 10000 and the Sequent NUMA-Q systems are excellent examples of the awesome computing power that is available on the market today. The Oracle DBMS is tailored to take advantage of the specific platforms, providing near linear scalability.

The purpose of this chapter is to offer recommendations based on my personal experiences of building large-scale data warehousing systems. The material presented in the previous chapters as well as in this chapter, will clearly help you to build a high-performance, large-scale data warehouse.

6.2 REQUIREMENTS FOR A DATA WAREHOUSE

A data warehouse is an expansion of a Decision Support System (DSS). Traditionally, DSSs were small-scale, summarized databases of operational data that did not permit many permutations of predicate-based analysis. Because the DSS was presummarized, only certain queries could be executed. A data warehouse enhances the traditional DSS by combining the power of large-scale distributed computing and parallel-aware database management systems. This enables a data warehouse to be a vast collection of data in which the complex analysis is done on-line. The data is provided in its raw form and allows many different types of queries, as opposed to the traditional summarized DSS. In this chapter, I use the terms *data warehousing* and *DSS* synonymously. I use the terms synonymously because although data warehousing and OLAP have revolutionized DSS systems, the concept of a data warehouse and a DSS remains the same: *making better decisions faster.*[1]

Enabling a business analyst to make better decisions faster requires three main components: recent and accurate data, a flexible database design, and a highly parallel hardware and software server environment. Recent and accurate data are needed to make an intelligent decision. Your decision is only as good as the data you use to make the decision. It is also important that the data be recent, so you can make the best decision based on the most recent information. The flexible database design helps you to execute the different types of complex queries in a relatively straightforward manner. The parallel software and hardware help you expedite the processing of your analytical query by breaking down larger tasks into smaller tasks that execute in parallel.

6.3 THE DATA WAREHOUSE DATA MODEL

As mentioned in Chapter 4, database design techniques deserve their own text. There are available many data warehousing database design texts that discuss different design methods such as the star schema design. Designing a database requires detailed knowledge of the business rules as well as a firm understanding of end-user requirements. It is important that the database that is designed meet the requirements of end users by enabling them to satisfy their queries to business questions using the database schema provided. Whether

---

1. Sun Microsystems Computer Corporation. *Data Warehousing White Paper.* February 1995, p.1.

you use a relational database design or star schema approach, the important thing is that the data warehouse should enable the business analyst to get answers to questions quickly. Usually, data warehouse database designs are somewhat de-normalized in order to reduce the amount of joins needed to gather data.

6.4   TUNING I/O

By now, you are probably saying that the subject of tuning I/O has been beaten to death. However, I cannot emphasize enough the importance of tuning I/O. This is extremely critical in a data warehouse environment. If your I/O subsystem is not tuned properly, you will not be able to achieve good performance. Data warehousing environments typically involve large, complex queries that perform full-table scans and sort large amounts of data. If your I/O system is not tuned properly, loads and queries may take a much longer time. Follow the guidelines discussed in Chapter 3 to tune I/O. Use the I/O monitoring utilities to ensure that I/O is being properly balanced. For optimal performance, use a database block size of 16 KB (available in 7.3 and above), and use the guidelines from section 3.4 to optimally select the stripe width. Section 3.15 offers tips on tuning the value of `db_file_multilblock_read_count`. Optimally setting `db_file_multilblock_read_count` improves the efficiency of full-table scans.

6.5   SORTING

The Oracle Server uses the `init.ora` parameter `sort_area_size` to specify the size of in-memory sorts. The `sort_area_size`, specified in bytes, allocates the specified amount of memory to be used for a sort. The `sort_area_size` is part of the PGA (Program Global Area). Once the sort is complete and all that remains is to fetch the rows, the sort memory is released down to the size specified by the `init.ora` parameter `sort_area_retained_size`. The `sort_area_retained_size` specifies the maximum amount of PGA memory (in bytes) to retain following a sort. Once the last row is fetched from the sort space, the memory is freed back to the PGA, not to the Operating System (OS). The `init.ora` parameter `sort_read_fac` specifies the ratio of the amount of time needed to read a single database block to the block transfer rate. The formula for `sort_read_fac` is as follows.

$$sort\_read\_fac = \frac{(avg.seek\ time\ +\ avg.\ latency\ time\ +\ block\ transfer\ time)}{(block\ transfer\ time)}$$

To set `sort_read_fac` properly, obtain the disk seek time, latency time, and block transfer time values for your specific disk I/O subsystem. This helps maximize disk sorting on your platform. When a sort requires more than `sort_area_size`, the sort is done on disk using temporary tablespace extents. There is no multiple allocation of `sort_area _size`. For large sorts, and if memory is plentiful on your system, you may try increasing the value of `sort_area_size`. This helps increase the performance of sorts by performing the sort in memory (assuming the `sort_area_size` is large enough). You can monitor the amount of in-memory sorts versus disk sorts by querying the `v$sysstat` view.

```
SQL> select name,value
       from v$sysstat
       where name like '%sort%'

     NAME                          VALUE
     ───────────────────────────────────
     sorts (memory)                 7003
     sorts (disk)                     54
     sorts (rows)                 163488
```

In this example, the number of sorts done in memory and on disk are reported, as well as the total number of rows sorted. Each sort to disk requires `sort_area_size` memory since the `sort_area_size` is filled first, and anything beyond that is sorted on disk. For optimal performance, set `sort_area_size` so that the ratio of disk sorts to memory sorts is extremely low. Use caution when you increase `sort_area_size` because this can increase paging and possibly cause swapping if it is set too large.

6.5.1 DIRECT SORT WRITES

Oracle 7.2 and Oracle 7.3 provide additional enhancements for large-scale sorts that are primarily performed on disk, such as large data warehousing queries involving order by, or sort-merge joins. The `init.ora` parameter `sort_direct_writes`, originally introduced in Oracle 7.2 and expanded in Oracle 7.3, specifies whether sorts are to be performed directly to disk, thereby reducing the SGA overhead of first writing the temporary sort segment to the cache and then flushing out the sorted block to disk. When set to true, the `sort_direct_writes` parameter allocates additional buffers in memory and writes the buffers directly to disk. When `sort_direct_writes=FALSE`, direct sort writes to disk are disabled, and sort blocks are written to the cache in the usual manner. Oracle 7.3 enables another setting for `sort_direct_writes`. If `sort_direct_writes=AUTO`, Oracle chooses a direct write sort to disk if the `sort_area_size` is at least ten times greater than the direct write buffer size. If `sort_direct_writes=AUTO`, `sort_ write_buffer_size` and `sort_write_buffers` are configured automatically and override any user setting. The `sort_write_buffer_size` parameter is the size of the direct write sort buffer. The default is 32 KB. You can set the value of `sort_write_buffer_size` to the `<stripe interleave size>` ✕ `<number of`

distinct members in the stripe> for optimal performance. For instance, if your
stripe interleave is 64 KB, and your temporary tablespace data files are striped across six
different disks, set sort_write_buffer_size=384 K. This allows sort disk writes to
the temporary tablespace to proceed in parallel since the temporary tablespace is striped.
The sort_write_buffers parameter specifies the number of sort buffers to use when
sort_direct_writes=TRUE. Using direct sorts on queries that require large sorts can
increase performance significantly. Figure 6.2 illustrates the direct write sorts.

Although direct sorts can increase performance for data warehouses, it is important
to note that memory requirements may increase when using direct sorts. When
sort_direct_writes=AUTO, Oracle sets the value of sort_write_buffer_size
and sort_write_buffers automatically. When sort_direct_writes=AUTO, the
memory for the direct write buffers is taken from the sort area. Therefore, when
sort_direct_writes=AUTO, the total amount of memory used for sorting is still
sort_area_size. When sort_direct_writes=TRUE, the memory allocated for
direct write sorts is as follows.

```
(sort_write_buffers *
  sort_write_buffer_size) +
      sort_area_size
```

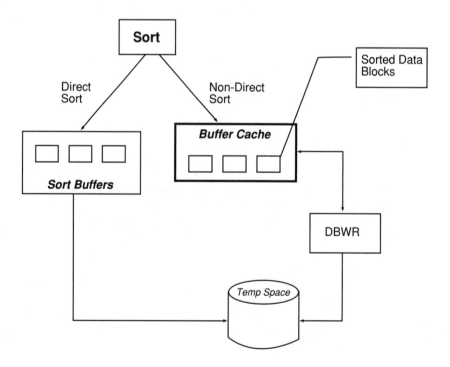

FIGURE 6.2   Direct write sorts.

When `sort_direct_writes=TRUE`, the write buffers are allocated in addition to the `sort_area_size`. Hence, make sure that your system has sufficient memory before you increase the value of `sort_area_size` or you enable direct write sorts. Increasing `sort_area_size` or setting `sort_direct_writes=TRUE` can increase paging and possibly cause swapping if careful effort is not taken to ensure that sufficient memory exists. If your sorts are primarily small, setting `sort_direct_writes=TRUE` will decrease performance. Setting `sort_direct_writes=AUTO` (7.3) allows small sorts to sort in memory and large sorts to use the direct write option. If you are using 7.2, you will need to set `sort_direct_writes` in accordance with your workload. If no sorts are being done (or the sorts are small enough to fit in `sort_area_size`), set `sort_direct_writes=FALSE`. If, however, you are doing a lot of large sorts and sort-merge joins, set `sort_direct_writes=TRUE` in your 7.2 Server.

It is important to note that when you use parallel query to parallelize sorts, each parallel query slave allocates a separate `sort_area_size`. For example, if ten parallel query slaves are parallelizing a sort (meaning the query specified a degree of parallelism of 10), and `sort_area_size=5M`, a total of 50 MB may be allocated for the sort. Thus, you should be careful because memory can be eaten up quickly if a high degree of a parallelism is selected.

6.5.2 IDENTIFYING SORT USERS

Often it becomes necessary to identify the users performing sorts. This helps identify the particular sessions that may be issuing resource-intensive sorts. You can also determine whether an in-memory or disk sort is being performed. The following query lists the users performing sorts as well as the type of sort.

```
SQL> select   vs.username,
              vs.osuser,
              vsn.name,
              vss.value
     from     v$session vs,
              v$sesstat vss,
              v$statname vsn
     where    (vss.statistic#=vsn.statistic#) AND
              (vs.sid = vss.sid) AND
              (vsn.name like '%sort%')
     order by 2,3;
```

In Oracle8, you can use the `v$sort_usage` view to identify the users of temporary sort extents. The `v$sort_usage` view provides sort usage statistics such as the user of the temporary extent, tablespace name, and the number of blocks and extents. The following is an example query which reports sort usage information.

```
SQL>  select user,
             tablespace,
             contents,
             blocks,
             extents
      from v$sort_usage
      order by user;
```

6.5.3 ORACLE8*i* SORT OPTIMIZATIONS

In Oracle8*i*, the sort routines used in the kernel have been rewritten to improve consistency and performance. Prior to Oracle8*i*, a sort that required temporary disk storage in addition to the in-memory sort area would experience a performance degradation when the size of the in-memory sort area size was increased (`sort_area_size`). On the contrary, one would expect that increasing the in-memory sort area size would increase overall sort performance. However, in many cases, the performance would remain the same as with a smaller sort area size. In some cases, the performance of the sort would degrade. The new 8i sorting algorithms improve memory utilization and enable rapid sorts when the in-memory sort area size is increased. This results in proportional performance gains when more memory is available for the sort. In addition, Oracle8*i* always uses direct write sorts for sorts requiring temporary disk storage and automatically adjusts the number and size of the direct write buffers. As a result, the following parameters have been made obsolete: `sort_direct_writes`, `sort_write_buffers`, `sort_write_buffer_size`, and `sort_read_fac`.

6.6 THE TEMPORARY TABLESPACE

Oracle uses temporary tablespaces to perform sorts that cannot entirely be sorted in memory from operations such as queries that contain an order by clause, index create statements, and joins. Data warehousing queries can be very complex, and can require a large temporary tablespace to process sorts and joins. When tuning I/O on a data warehousing system, try to keep temporary tablespace data files separate from data files and redo log files. In a data warehousing environment, consider the temporary tablespace as critical as your data files in an OLTP system. In a data warehousing environment, data modifications are minimal compared to reads. For this reason, you must stripe the temporary tablespace at least as good, if not better, than the Oracle data files in an OLTP system. This improves the performance of queries requiring temporary tablespace extents by minimizing I/O wait time.

Sun offers the Zone Bit Recording (ZBR) technology on its disk drives. ZBR causes the outermost cylinders of the disk to be more efficiently utilized than the inner cylinders on the disk. Therefore, to take advantage of ZBR technology on Sun, configure the temporary tablespace data files by using the `format` utility (or `fmthard` utility) to partition the outer cylinders for the temporary tablespace partitions. Then, if you are using ODS, build a stripe by combining the outer partitions (typically slice 6 or slice 7—s6 or s7) on different disks from different controllers to form the metadevice. Then create the temporary tablespace using the metadevice. This increases the performance of sorts when sort extents are written to disk.

6.7 BITMAP INDEXES

Oracle 7.3 introduced the bitmap index option in addition to the B*-Tree indexes. You can use bitmapped indexes in a data warehouse to increase the performance of queries. Bitmap indexes are ideal for low cardinality columns such as gender, marital status, or account status. Each entry in a bitmap corresponds to a row. Table 6.1 is an example of a bitmap corresponding to the account data.

TABLE 6.1   Example bitmap corresponding to account data

ACCOUNT #	ACCOUNT STATUS	DISTRICT	SERVICE LEVEL
7344	Active	West	Gold
8134	Closed	Central	Silver
8332	Active	East	Gold
8564	Active	East	Bronze
9123	Review	West	Silver

Status='Active'	Status = 'Closed'	Status ='Review'
1	0	0
0	1	0
1	0	0
1	0	0
0	0	1

Suppose that a business analyst wants to know how many active customer accounts in the East or West district maintain a gold service level. The SQL query looks as follows.

```
SQL> SELECT count(*)
     FROM account
     WHERE ((status='Active') and
            (district in ('East','West')) and
            (service = 'Gold'));
```

Using the bitmap index option on these low-cardinality data columns, the optimizer logically combines the bitmaps from the different columns and returns the count. Table 6.2 illustrates the bitmaps used to compute the count.

TABLE 6.2   Boolean operations on bitmap indexes

STATUS='ACTIVE'		DISTRICT='EAST'		DISTRICT='WEST'		SERVICE='GOLD'		
1		0		1		1		1
0	AND	0	OR	0	AND	0	=	0
1		1		0		1		1
1		1		0		0		0
0		0		1		0		0

In Table 6.2, the optimizer combines the bitmaps of the different columns using the logical Boolean operators, and computes the count for the query. Bitmap indexes are substantially faster than having to scan large numbers of rows using the traditional B*-tree index. You can use bitmap indexes to increase performance for data warehouse queries with the following characteristics: The query contains multiple predicates in the WHERE clause of low-cardinality columns, the query selects a large number of rows, and the tables involved in the queries are relatively large. Using bitmap indexes to index low to medium cardinality data can increase performance of complex data warehousing queries significantly.

Traditionally, in order to improve the performance of queries, DBAs created multiple concatenated indexes to handle the different types of queries. However, this not only requires substantial disk space, it also requires the DBA either to index every combination of the concatenated columns or to force queries to use a certain index by always providing certain columns.

For example, suppose an index is created on the above account table with a B*-tree index of Account (Status, District, Service). If a query contains all three columns as predicates, then the index can be used. However, suppose the query only specifies District in the WHERE clause. In this case, the index is not used since the leading column of the index is not specified in the WHERE clause of the query. Multiple single-column bitmap indexes solve this classic dilemma by allowing multiple combinations of the different columns.

A bitmap index on a low-cardinality column typically (this is an estimate of course) consumes one-fourth the disk space of an equivalent B*-tree index. B*-tree indexes are great for high-cardinality data such as unique columns or columns where the selectivity per distinct value is low. Therefore, you should not use bitmap indexes on unique columns, or where a B*-tree index is more suitable. Also, because bitmap indexes are designed for use within data warehousing systems, performance can degrade if you use bitmap indexes within OLTP applications that frequently modify the data. An entry in a B*-tree index contains a single row. The single row is made up of its `rowid`, as well as the column(s) of the index. Hence, when an index entry in a B*-tree is locked, the row is locked. A bitmap index entry can consist of a range of `rowids`. Therefore, when locking a bitmap index entry, the entire range of `rowids` is locked. This can have an adverse affect on concurrency because a larger number of rows are locked, possibly preventing other concurrent users from obtaining locks.

The use of bitmap indexes is not recommended within an OLTP application. However, if you are running a mixed environment (OLTP and Data warehousing on the same database), you may want to consider using bitmap indexes to speed up the data warehousing queries. If your bitmap indexes are updated frequently, make sure you tune the `sort_area_size` appropriately to increase the performance of the updates and inserts on the bitmap index. Follow the recommendations made in Section 6.5 to tune the `sort_area_size` appropriately.

To create a bitmap index, use the `BITMAP` keyword in the `create index` command. For example,

```
SQL> create bitmap index bstatus on Account (status);
```

You can use all the standard index options including the related index storage options for the exception of the `NOSORT` index create option. Bitmap indexes can consist of multiple concatenated columns. To enable bitmap indexes, the `init.ora` parameter `compatible` must be set to 7.3.2 or higher. The standard index object views such as `DBA_INDEXES` or `USER_INDEXES` list bitmap indexes as well as B*-tree indexes. Bitmap indexes have their `UNIQUENESS` column in the `DBA_INDEXES` or `USER_INDEXES` view set to `BITMAP`.

As discussed in Chapter 4, the `INDEX_COMBINE` hint was introduced in version 7.3 to utilize bitmap indexes. You can also use the `INDEX` hint with `BITMAP` indexes. The `INDEX_COMBINE` hint specifies the bitmap indexes that are to be combined when combining Boolean operations on bitmap indexes in a query. The syntax of the `INDEX_COMBINE` hint is `INDEX_COMBINE` (table index1 index2 index3 . . .). If the `INDEX_COMBINE` hint is specified without any arguments, the CBO chooses the Boolean combination of bitmap indexes on the table that is being processed with the best cost.

New `init.ora` parameters—`create_bitmap_area_size`, `bitmap_merge_area_size`, `v733_plans_enabled`—that deal with bitmap indexes were introduced in Oracle 7.3. The `init.ora` parameter `create_bitmap_area_size` specifies the amount of memory that is allocated for creating a bitmap index. The default is 8 MB. However, if your bitmap index has a high cardinality, you can increase `create_bitmap_` `area_size` to speed up the index creation. Conversely, if your bitmap index columns have a very low cardinality, you can reduce the value of `create_bitmap_area_size` since a smaller amount of memory is required. You can alter the value of `create_bitmap_area_size` at the session level as well as at the instance level. The `bitmap_merge_area_size` specifies the amount of memory used to merge bitmaps. Increasing the value of `bitmap_merge_area_size` over the default of 1 MB can increase performance of large sorts because the bitmaps must be sorted before the merge is performed. The Oracle7.3 `init.ora` parameter `v733_plans_enabled=TRUE` causes bitmap indexes to be considered on tables with regular B*-tree indexes and at least one bitmap index. Setting `v733_plans_enabled=FALSE` (the default) disables this option.

Bitmap indexes also appear in an explain plan. The explain plan shows the `BITMAP` keyword followed by the bitmap operation such as `BITMAP CONVERSION`, `BITMAP OR`, `BITMAP MINUS`, `BITMAP INDEX`, or `BITMAP MERGE`. If you use bitmap indexes, you should perform an explain plan on the query to ensure that the bitmap index is being used. If the explain plan does not show that the bitmap index is being used, then rewrite the query using the `INDEX` and/or `INDEX_COMBINE` hint and regenerate the explain plan to confirm that the hint is being accepted.

Oracle8 provides the ability to consider a bitmap index access plan even if the table only has B*-tree indexes. The `init.ora` parameter `b_tree_bitmap_plans=TRUE` enables the optimizer to consider a bitmap access path on a table that only has regular B*-tree indexes. The `rowid` entries for the index are converted to bitmaps and then the various Boolean operations can be applied to the bitmaps. The explain plan shows the `BITMAP CONVERSION FROM ROWIDS` if the optimizer chooses to convert the index `rowid` entries to bitmaps. This feature can increase the performance of queries that combine low-cardinality criteria with highly selective predicates. In Oracle8*i*, the `init.ora` parameter `b_tree_bitmap_plans` has been made an underscore parameter (`_b_tree_bitmap _plans`).

6.8   TUNING QUERIES

In a data warehousing environment, queries are often complex and run for a much longer period of time than a traditional OLTP query. In some cases, data warehousing queries can consume a tremendous amount of CPU, sort space, and disk I/O resources. When you tune a data warehouse query, tune by selectivity. For example, using the `ORDERED` hint, you can specify the join order of the query and force the table that causes the highest selectivity to appear first. By using the `ORDERED` hint, you can use the table that reduces the selectivity the most first in order to cause a reduction in the selectivity before it is joined to the other tables.

6.8.1 THE STAR AND STAR_TRANSFORMATION HINTS

Oracle 7.2 allows the use of the STAR hint. The STAR hint causes a star schema to be used. A star schema consists of a single fact table and multiple dimension tables. For example, the fact table may contain all the customer data (facts about customers). A dimension table could consist of dimensions such as time or geography. The dimension tables are often small tables, and the fact table is usually very large for data warehousing systems. The star hint causes a Cartesian product to be performed on the smaller dimension tables, and the result of the Cartesian product join is then joined to the fact table via a nested loops. This is extremely efficient since the fact table usually contains a concatenated index on the primary key that consists of the foreign key columns used to join to the dimension tables. The logic behind a star query is that the processing of the smaller dimension tables will likely first cause a large reduction in the selectivity of the fact table and thereby reduce the overall elapsed time of the query. To use the star method, you can use the STAR hint explicitly (select /*+ STAR */) or equivalently simulate the star plan by utilizing the ORDERED hint along with the USE_NL hint.

Oracle8 provides an alternate method for executing star queries known as the star transformation method. The traditional method for executing star queries is to perform a Cartesian product on the dimension tables and then join the result via a nested loops index join to the fact table. The Cartesian method is ideal for schemas with a dense fact table and a small number of dimensions. The star transformation approach is more suitable for situations where the fact table is large and there are a large number of dimensions. The star transformation method essentially transforms the star query into subqueries using bitmap index access paths on the individual constraints without the need of performing a Cartesian product and requiring a concatenated index on the fact table. The various bitmap indexes can then be merged together to complete the query. To enable star transformations you can use the STAR_TRANSFORMATION hint or set the init.ora parameter star_transformation_enabled=TRUE.

6.8.2 ANTI-JOIN

Another feature of Oracle 7.3 is the anti-join. The anti-join can be used with the NOT IN subselect query. The anti-join, instead of returning the rows that satisfy the join predicate, returns the rows that do not satisfy the join predicate, as is the case with the NOT IN subselect. The anti-join also enables a hash join or merge-join to be performed, which is much more efficient than the traditional nested loops join. You can use the anti-join feature by using the HASH_AJ or MERGE_AJ hints in the nested subselect portion of the query, or by setting the init.ora parameter always_anti_join=MERGE, or always_anti_join=HASH. The default setting is always_anti_join=NESTED_LOOPS. Using the anti-join feature can increase the performance of NOT IN subselect queries by utilizing a hash or merge join in place of the nested loops join.

6.8.3 SEMI-JOIN

Oracle 8.0.4 provides the ability to perform a semi-join to increase the performance of certain queries. The USE_SEMI, HASH_SJ, and MERGE_SJ hints allow you to specify the use of a semi-join, and whether to use a hash semi-join or merge semi-join, respectively. A semi-join can help improve the performance of certain EXISTS subqueries. A semi-join returns the rows that satisfy an EXISTS subquery and avoids the duplication of rows from the left side of the predicate when the subquery criteria can be satisfied by multiple rows on the right side. You can specify the HASH_SJ or MERGE_SJ hint in your query to use a hash or merge semi-join as opposed to using a nested loops join which is the default for EXISTS subqueries. In order to enable the optimizer to consider semi-join access paths, set the init.ora parameter always_semi_join=HASH or always_semi_join=MERGE.

6.8.4 HISTOGRAMS

Another feature that was added to Oracle 7.3 is the ability to create a histogram. The CBO works well for uniformly distributed data. For nonuniformly distributed data, the execution plan chosen by the CBO may not be optimal. For this reason, Oracle provides for the use of histograms whereby the table column is analyzed and placed into height-balanced buckets. Each height-balanced bucket has the same height. When the data is highly skewed, height-balanced histograms can increase the performance of queries.

The height-balanced histograms enable the CBO to determine the selectivity of the query more effectively by knowing which buckets the predicates of the query affect. Using a histogram on data that is highly skewed can increase the performance of queries. To generate a histogram, you can use the following example.

```
SQL> execute DBMS_STATS.GATHER_TABLE_STATS ('PRODS','ORDERS',
METHOD_OPT => 'FOR COLUMNS SIZE 10 ORDER_STATUS');
```

Make sure you choose the appropriate number of buckets (or bands) so that the effectiveness of the histogram is maximized. A general rule of thumb is to choose the number of buckets greater than the number of distinct values that occur frequently. Keep in mind that histograms are data distribution dependent. If the distribution of the data changes frequently, the histogram may not be useful unless recomputed frequently. You can query the USER_HISTOGRAMS and USER_TAB_COLUMNS views to obtain histogram and column-level statistics.

6.8.5 MERGE-JOINS

In a data warehousing environment, full-table scans are extremely common, and tables are often joined and aggregated. Using the parallel query and the sort-merge join can increase the performance over a nested loops join when a large number of rows are being joined. A merge sort has an order of NlogN, where N is the number of rows being sorted. The Sort-Merge Join (SMJ) can be significantly faster than a nested loops join because two sorted lists can be merged into a sorted list using no more than $(M + N - 1)$ comparisons, where N is the number of elements in table 1 being merged with M number of elements in table 2.[2] The parallel query option can also be used to parallelize the SMJ. Recall that an SMJ uses both interparallelism and intraparallelism. This not only means that the table scan is parallelized, but the join and sort are also parallelized. Use the USE_MERGE hint in conjunction with the PARALLEL hint to parallelize large table joins. Nested loop joins are best used for small tables, or tables that are joined on indexes with good selectivity. Sort-merge joins work well for large joins that scan a large number of rows. An SMJ is only possible on an equi-join. An SMJ cannot be used on an outer join. Therefore, if your query contains outer joins, you may have to rewrite the query in the form of an equi-join to utilize an SMJ.

6.8.6 HASH JOINS

Another feature that was added to Oracle 7.3 is the optimizer's ability to utilize a hash join. Hash joins can be extremely efficient when joining large tables using equi-joins. Oracle processes a hash join by performing a full-table scan on each of the tables. Then, each table is split into as many partitions as possible based on the amount of available memory. The amount of available memory is specified by the init.ora parameter hash_area_size. Partitions that do not fit into the amount of available memory are written to disk. Oracle then builds a hash table from one of the partitions, and uses the partition from the other table to search the hash table. The hash technique allows smaller partitions to build the hash table, and then the larger partitions are used to probe the hash table to determine a match. To enable the hash join option, set the init.ora parameter hash_join_enabled=TRUE. You can also set hash_join_enabled=TRUE by using the alter session command. The init.ora parameter hash_multiblock_io_count specifies the number of blocks read and written simultaneously during a hash join. You can set hash_multiblock_io_count through the init.ora parameter file or by using the alter session command. You can increase the value of hash_multiblock_io _count if your data files are well distributed. This parameter also controls the number of partitions that the data is divided into during the hash join. When tuning hash_multiblock_io_count, ensure that the following formula remains true:

```
R / M <= Po2 (M/C)

      R = size of the left input to the join
      M = hash_area_size * 0.9
Po2 (n) = largest power of 2 smaller than n
      C = (hash_multiblock_io_count * db_block_size)
```

---

2. Rosen, Kenneth H. *Discrete Mathematics and Its Applications*. Random House, 1988, p. 484.

Hash joins can increase performance of data warehouse queries by subdividing the data into smaller partitions and using a hash table to join the pairs. You can also use the USE_HASH hint in your SQL statements to explicitly force the use of a hash join. If using the USE_HASH hint, you should also perform an explain plan on the SQL statement to ensure that a hash join is being performed.

6.8.7 OPTIMIZER ENHANCEMENTS

Oracle8 introduced major enhancements to the Oracle optimizer for complex data warehousing queries. Several new init.ora parameters and hints were added. Oracle 8.0.4 even further enhances the optimizer. A new Oracle 8.0.4 init.ora parameter optimizer_features_enable allows you to control the optimizer behavior by specifying the version number to be considered for optimizer features. For example, setting optimizer_features_enable=8.0.4 enables the new optimizer features such as pushing join predicates, complex view merging, fast full scans, and B*-tree bitmap plans.

Oracle8 provides a method to improve the execution timings of distributed join queries by specifying the driving site for the join. The DRIVING_SITE hint allows you to specify the driving table with the goal of reducing the amount of work needed by selecting the most selective table as the driving table. The DRIVING_SITE hint is useful for tuning distributed join queries that often join local tables with large-size remote database tables. The DRIVING_SITE hint allows you to choose the driving table that makes the most sense, thereby reducing the data transmission and join workload.

The PUSH_PRED and NO_PUSH_PRED hints, added in 8.0.4, allow the optimizer to push the individual join predicates down into the view when the query involves a view with multiple base tables on the right side of an outer join. This enables more efficient execution plans by transforming hash joins into nested loops and full-table scans into index scans. The NO_PUSH_PRED hint prevents the join predicates from being pushed into the view. To enable the optimizer to consider pushing the join predicates, set the init.ora parameter push_join_predicate=TRUE in Oracle8 or _push_join_predicate in Oracle8*i*.

The MERGE and NO_MERGE hints, added in 8.0.4, control whether or not a complex view or subquery within a query is evaluated prior to the surrounding query. The NO_MERGE hint causes the optimizer not to merge the view. The Oracle8 init.ora parameter complex_view_merging=TRUE (or _complex_view_merging=TRUE in Oracle8*i*) enables the optimizer to consider merging the views.

Oracle8 release 8.0.5 provides new init.ora parameters that help influence the behavior of the optimizer when considering index and nested loops join access paths. The init.ora parameter optimizer_index_cost_adj specifies the optimizer cost adjustment factor for an index access path. Values for optimizer_index_cost_adj can range from 1 to 10,000. The value of optimizer_index_cost_adj (other than the default of 100) adjusts the index access path cost at the specified percentage of the regular cost. For example, if optimizer_index_cost_adj=50, the optimizer considers an index access path to be half as expensive as the ordinary cost. The optimizer_index_cost_adj parameter can be used to tune the performance of queries in which the optimizer is either favoring index access paths or not considering index access paths often enough.

The `init.ora` parameter `optimizer_index_caching`, added in Oracle8 release 8.0.5, provides the ability to influence the decision of the optimizer when choosing between nested loops joins and other join methods such as a hash join. The cost of a nested loops join in which an index is used to access the inner table much depends on the caching of that index in the buffer cache. The degree to which the index is cached relies on such factors as user block access patterns as well as the load on the system. These factors are not predictable by the optimizer. The `init.ora` parameter `optimizer_index_caching` can be used to reduce the cost of a nested loops join thereby making the optimizer more likely to choose a nested loops join over a hash join or sort-merge join. You can set `optimizer_index_caching` to a value between 0 and 100. A value of zero for `optimizer_index_caching` results in the traditional behavior of the optimizer. A higher value for `optimizer_index_caching` reduces the cost of a nested loops join by assuming that the percentage of index blocks specified by `optimizer_index_caching` are in the cache.

6.8.8 PARALLELIZING THE DISTINCT

Queries that perform a count of a distinct column can be rewritten to improve parallel processing. For example, consider the following query.

```
select count(distinct acct_id)
from ACCOUNT;
```

This query returns a count of the number of distinct account IDs in the ACCOUNT table. The scan of the ACCOUNT table can be parallelized, however, the distinct portion causes the final sort group by operation (distinct) to be serialized. The query can be rewritten in the form of a subquery which translates into a view operation. This allows both the subquery and the sort operation to be performed in parallel. The following is a rewrite of the above query which improves parallel query execution.

```
select count(*)
from (select acct_id from ACCOUNT group by acct_id);
```

Oracle8*i* allows parallel queries with both an ORDER BY and a GROUP BY to be parallelized using inter-parallelism. Earlier releases executed the GROUP BY and ORDER BY row sources serially. This improves the performance of parallel queries which perform aggregation and sorting on large data sets.

Tuning SQL is often the effort of rewriting the SQL to either do less work or improve the parallelization factor of the query. In any case, it is important that you spend a great deal of time tuning the application SQL statements. Poorly written SQL can cause a great deal of contention resulting in long execution times.

6.8.9 UPDATABLE JOIN VIEWS

Oracle 7.3 introduced the ability to update joined views that are joined on a primary key. This feature can be useful for applications that needed to update joined views but had to manually code the update against the individual tables in releases prior to 7.3. You can use this feature to reduce overall SQL calls by making one update to the view, rather than several updates to the individual tables making up the view.

6.8.10 FAST FULL INDEX SCAN

The fast full scan index feature provides the ability to perform a parallel multiblock index scan. The fast full index scan is available in Oracle7 release 7.3.3, Oracle8, and Oracle8*i*. A fast full scan is useful when the columns of the index contain all the data needed to satisfy the query. In such a case, scanning the table data is not necessary. A fast full scan requires at least one of the columns in the index key to have the NOT NULL constraint. A fast full scan can be parallelized and it uses multiblock reads similar to a full-table scan. A fast full scan can reduce the amount of I/O needed to complete a query. For example, consider an index on a SALES table of 200 GB in size containing two columns, week_no and sale_no. Assume the index is approximately 5 GB in size. A query that needed to count the number of sales for weeks after week 10 could utilize a fast full scan as opposed to scanning the entire table. This results in scanning 5 GB of data versus scanning 200 GB of data. This helps increase the performance of the query by substantially reducing the amount of I/O needed to complete the query. The following is an example of a query and its explain plan showing the use of a fast full index scan.

```
SQL> select /*+ INDEX_FFS (s SALES_WKIDX)
                PARALLEL_INDEX (s,SALES_WKIDX,10) */
     count(*)
     from sales s
     where (s.week_no > 10);
```

ID	EXPLAIN_PLAN	POSITION
0	SELECT STATEMENT	1
1	SORT AGGREGATE	1
2	INDEX FAST FULL SCAN SALES_WKIDX	1
	:Q64000 PARALLEL_TO_SERIAL	

This explain plan shows that a fast full scan is being used and that the fast full scan is being parallelized. To enable the use of the fast full scan feature, set the Oracle8 init.ora parameter fast_full_scan_enabled=TRUE (or _fast_full_scan_ enabled=TRUE in Oracle8*i*). You can also use the INDEX_FFS and the PARALLEL_ INDEX hints to specify the use of a fast full scan and specify the degree of parallelism to be used in the fast full scan. The syntax of the INDEX_FFS and PARALLEL_INDEX hints are INDEX_FFS (table index) and PARALLEL_INDEX (table index tdegree idegree), respectively. The value of tdegree refers to the degree of parallelism to be used on the table, and the value of idegree refers to the degree of cross-instance parallelism. You should also analyze the index to help ensure that the optimizer is able to choose a fast full scan.

6.9   PARTITIONING

Partitioning is the ability to subdivide large tables and indexes into smaller components known as partitions. This allows you to manage the individual partitions rather than the entire table. The Oracle optimizer intelligently employs partition pruning in order to identify the particular partitions needed for a given SQL operation. This avoids having to perform a full-table or full-index scan, thus reducing the amount of work needed to complete the SQL operation.

Oracle 7.3 provides the ability to partition tables by creating a view on the individual tables. The optimizer intelligently decides which tables are needed when processing the predicates of the query on the view. This technique is known as partition views. Partition views was the first phase in providing partitioning capabilities, and Oracle8 expanded the partitioning capabilities by providing the ability to partition a single table based on a partition key. The Oracle8 partitioning feature is a major breakthrough in data warehousing technology and can significantly reduce the amount of I/O needed to process complex queries. The optimizer identifies the partitions of interest based on the partition key range and then scans the relevant partitions. The partitioning capabilities provided in Oracle8 massively improves the performance and manageability of large-scale data warehouses.

6.9.1 PARTITION VIEWS

Partition views are implemented as a view consisting of the UNION ALL set operator. Queries are then executed against the view rather than the underlying tables. Based on the predicates specified in the query against the view, the optimizer determines which tables are needed to satisfy the query. In addition, the subqueries that make up the view can also be parallelized. For example, consider the following query.

```
SELECT account_number
FROM ACCOUNT_95
UNION ALL
SELECT account_number
FROM ACCOUNT_96;
```

The CBO parallelizes the individual subqueries because both translate into full-table scans. When each full-table scan is completed, the rows are returned. The same holds true for the `INTERSECT` operation with the exception that, following the full-table scan, a sort is required to return the rows in common. Because the set operators are parallelized, you can use partition views in Oracle to achieve high performance when you need to query from different tables. For example, suppose you created a view on account tables in which an account table existed for each sales quarter per year. If you wanted to return the accounts that purchased a certain amount in each quarter, the equivalent join query could be rather complex and large. However, you can use a partition view, meaning that the view consists of multiple tables partitioned. This improves the performance of the query because each partition can be parallelized. Also, the CBO will not scan partitions that are not used in the query. For example, consider the view and query in Figure 6.3.

In Figure 6.3, because the query does not require any data from the `ACCOUNT_Q296` and `ACCOUNT_Q496` tables, the CBO does not involve the tables in the query. This reduces processing time significantly and increases the performance of the query. To enable partitioned views, set the `init.ora` parameter `partition_view_enabled=TRUE`. Partitioned views allow you to divide a single large table into smaller tables, thus allowing operations such as loads, index creation, deletes, updates, backups, and restores to be performed at the individual partition level (underlying tables), as opposed to a single, large table.

Partition views represented the first phase in providing partitioning functionality in Oracle. In Oracle8*i*, the partitioning option extends by far the partitioning functionality by providing the ability to partition individual tables and indexes. The performance of partition views seems to drop off as more underlying tables are added to the view. The practical limit highly depends on the sizes of the underlying tables in the view and the degree of parallelism. If you are currently using partition views, I highly recommend that you migrate to Oracle8*i* and utilize the partitioning option. Oracle8*i* partitioning scales extremely well for large size tables and has demonstrated superior performance with large numbers of partitions such as several thousand partitions.

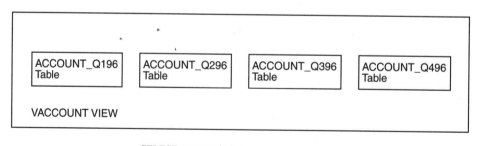

```
SELECT count(*)
from VACCOUNT
WHERE PERIOD IN ('Q196','Q396');
```

FIGURE 6.3 Partition view and query.

6.9.2 PARTITION TABLES

The partitioning option of Oracle8*i* enables you to apportion a very large table into smaller sections known as partitions. Each section represents a range of the partition key. The technique used to partition tables in Oracle 8.0 is via a partition range. Oracle8 table partitioning can be useful for both OLTP and data warehousing systems. In a partitioned table, each partition is independent of each other. This allows you to load and perform DML operations at the individual partition. Partition independence also increases availability since the inability to access a partition due to media failure does not affect the other available partitions. Furthermore, by storing each partition in a separate tablespace, backup and restores can be performed at the partition level. This improves backup administration and helps reduce media recovery time. Figure 6.4 is an example of a sales table partitioned by week range.

The following is the corresponding SQL needed to create the sales table partitioned by the sales week range.

```
CREATE TABLE sales
        (week_no    number(2) not null,
         sale_no    NUMBER(8) not null,
         sale_date  date not null,
         sale_amount number(10,2) not null,
         customer_id number(8) not null)
pctfree 10
pctused 90
initrans 10
storage (initial 1M next 1M pctincrease 0)
parallel (degree 20 instances 1)
PARTITION BY RANGE (week_no)
  (PARTITION sales_w1 VALUES LESS THAN (11)
    TABLESPACE tssw1,
   PARTITION sales_w2 VALUES LESS THAN (21)
    TABLESPACE tssw2,
   PARTITION sales_w3 VALUES LESS THAN (31)
    TABLESPACE tssw3);
```

The above create table statement creates a sales table with three partitions partitioned by week range. Inserting a record with `week_no=10` causes the row to be inserted into the first partition (w1). Inserting a record with `week_no=25` causes the row to be inserted into the last partition (w3) since 25 is larger than 21 but less than 31. If trying to insert a record where `week_no > 31`, the insert will fail because 31 is higher than the partition bound for the highest partition. You can use the `MAXVALUE` keyword in the partition bound value as the last partition (highest partition) to define a partition that holds records with partition key values larger than the bounds defined.

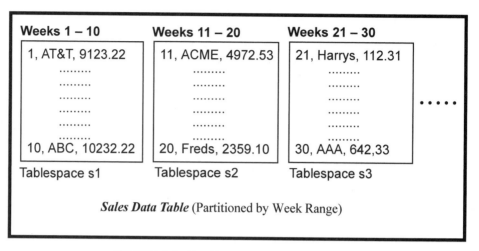

FIGURE 6.4   Partitioned table by week range.

6.9.3   DETERMINING THE PARTITION KEY

In order to maximize the benefits of partitioning, it is crucial that you optimally choose the partition key. The strategy behind selecting the columns that make up the partition key should consider the selectivity of queries and DML statements, partition and tablespace sizing, hot partitions versus seldom accessed partitions, and equi-partitioning versus activity-based partitioning. The partition key is a key factor in the selectivity of queries. If the partition key is too broad or conversely too specific, queries may require more I/O than is necessary by either having to scan a very large partition or scan too many partitions. If certain partitions are accessed much more frequently than others, a uniformly distributed partition key may not be ideal. Date column ranges are also often used in the partition key. Primary keys alone should not be used as partition keys because this translates into having a single row per partition. You may also choose to partition a table based on a date range which may result in certain partitions being more active (recent data) than other partitions (older data).

Two tables or indexes are equi-partitioned when they have identical logical partitioning attributes. Equi-partitioning requires objects to have the same number of partitions as well as the same VALUES LESS THAN boundaries. For example, consider an ACCOUNT table partitioned by ACCOUNT_ID in ranges of 1000 where the first 1000 accounts are stored in the first partition, the second set of 1000 accounts are stored in the second partition, and so on. Then consider an index ACCOUNT_ID_INDEX on the ACCOUNT_ID column of the ACCOUNT table which is also range partitioned on the same boundaries as the ACCOUNT table. This is an example of equi-partitioning. Equi-partitioning tends to improve query performance and optimizer execution plans. It also improves partition administration in the case where partitions need to be split or migrated.

Choosing the partition key that makes the most sense requires that you study in detail the data model, user access frequency, data distribution, data volumes and growth forecasts, performance requirements, tablespace sizing, and database administration requirements. Analyzing these items allows you to have a better understanding of your partitioning needs, subsequently resulting in an optimal choice for a partition key. Whether your focus is performance or administration, you need to spend a fair amount of time in the analysis phase before choosing the partition key.

6.9.4 HASH PARTITIONING

Oracle8*i* expands the partitioning functionality introduced in Oracle8 by allowing additional partitioning methods such as composite and hash partitioning. Oracle8*i* also allows LOBS, Index Organized Tables (IOT), and tables with objects to be partitioned.

Composite and hash partitioning increase performance of data warehousing by further reducing the size of overall partitions, improving intra-partition parallelism and reducing data skew per partition. Hash partitioning improves parallel DML (PDML) performance over range partitioning. In range partitioning, it may not always be possible to ascertain the amount of data that maps into a given range. In addition, the sizes of each partition may differ considerably when using range partitioning due to recent (hot) partitions versus partitions containing historical data. For these reasons, the performance of PDML may not necessarily be optimal. On the other hand, hash partitioning helps reduce data skew per partition, which improves the performance of PDML since the PDML individual slave workload is likely to be more balanced than in the case of range partitioning. Hash partitioning uses a hash function on the partition column(s) to distribute the data into the necessary partitions. The following example shows how a table can be created using the hash partitioning technique.

```
create table product (
    product_id number(8),
    product_category number(3),
    product_desc varchar2(100))
tablespace product_ts
storage (initial 1M)
PARTITION BY HASH (product_category)
PARTITIONS 15;
```

The above example creates a hash partitioned table based on the product category code partitioned into 15 separate hash partitions. You can also specify the names of tablespaces in which to store the hash partitions using either the STORE IN clause or by specifying explicitly the individual partitions and the corresponding tablespaces.

6.9.5 COMPOSITE PARTITIONING

Composite partitioning combines the range partitioning method with the hash partitioning method by employing subpartitions. Composite partitioning increases overall performance through the use of PDML at the subpartition level as well as the ability to support partition-wise joins. Composite partitioning also increases the granularity of partition elimination by being able to prune further down into the subpartitions versus a larger primary range partition. The following creates a composite partitioned table with a range partition as well as a hash subpartition.

```
create table orders (
    order_id number(8),
    order_date date,
    product_id number(8),
    qty         number(4))
PARTITION BY RANGE (order_date)
SUBPARTITION BY HASH (product_id) SUBPARTITIONS 15
STORE IN (ord_ts1,ord_ts2,ord_ts3,ord_ts4)
(PARTITION op1 VALUES LESS THAN (TO_DATE('01-JAN-2000','DD-MON-YYYY')),
 PARTITION op2 VALUES LESS THAN (TO_DATE('01-MAY-2000','DD-MON-YYYY')),
 PARTITION op3 VALUES LESS THAN (TO_DATE('01-SEP-2000','DD-MON-YYYY')),
 PARTITION op4 VALUES LESS THAN (MAXVALUE));
```

The above example creates an order table that is range partitioned on the order date, and subpartitioned via a hash function of the `product_id`. Composite partitioning improves the performance of queries by pruning the subpartitions as opposed to having to scan the entire range partition. For example, if a sales analyst needed to determine the number of products sold for a given product id within a certain sales quarter, the optimizer identifies the partitions needed to satisfy the query and then prunes the subpartitions without the need to scan the entire range partition. Composite partitioning provides the best of both worlds, including the manageability advantages offered by range partitioning as well as the parallelism and data locality advantages offered by hash partitioning. It is also possible to store each hash partition in a separate tablespace by naming the individual subpartitions via the `SUBPARTITION` clause and specifying its respective tablespace name. Local composite indexes can also be created on the composite partitioned tables. DML statements can also explicitly specify the extended composite partition name of the composite partitioned table. For example,

```
UPDATE orders subpartition (SYS_SUBP65) o
set o.qty=1;
```

6.9.6 PARTITION ROW MOVEMENT

Oracle8*i* allows partition keys to be updated by using the new clause ENABLE ROW MOVEMENT of the ALTER TABLE command. If row movement has been enabled, updates to the row partition keys cause the rows to be migrated to the appropriate partition if the update causes the row to no longer belong to its current partition.

6.9.7 PARTITION-WISE JOIN

Oracle8 release 8.0 joins two tables in parallel by splitting each table into separate fragments. Each fragment is then scanned and redistributed on the join key. Oracle8*i* can eliminate the redistribution phase if one or both of the tables are partitioned based on the join key. For example, if the two tables, orders and product, were joined together based on the product id join key, the optimizer would be aware that each partition is hash partitioned on the product id. The result sets of each scan can then be joined without the need of redistributing the data. Eliminating the redistribution phase can significantly reduce memory and temporary storage consumption, thereby increasing overall performance.

The are two types of partition-wise joins: full and partial. In the full partition-wise join, the tables being joined are partitioned on the join key, and the optimizer can determine which partitions should be joined. In the partial partition-wise join, one of the tables is hash partitioned, and the other table is dynamically hash partitioned and then a partial partition wise-join is performed. Figure 6.5 illustrates the partition-wise optimization.

In Figure 6.5, the ORDERS and CUSTOMERS tables are joined on the join key CUSTOMER_ID. Since each table is hash partitioned on the CUSTOMER_ID column, a full partition-wise join can be utilized. The partition-wise join eliminates the need to distribute the rows amongst the slaves and reduces the amount of communication between the query slaves.

FIGURE 6.5 Partition-wise join optimization.

6.9.8 MANIPULATING PARTITIONS

There are many different commands that can be used to manipulate or administer partitions. You can move a partition from one tablespace to another using the MOVE PARTITION option of the ALTER TABLE command. You can also rename a partition using the RENAME PARTITION option of the ALTER TABLE or ALTER INDEX command. The MODIFY PARTITION option of the ALTER TABLE or ALTER INDEX command allows you to modify partition attributes such as nologging or storage parameters. The TRUNCATE PARTITION and DROP PARTITION options of the ALTER TABLE command allow you to truncate the rows from a partition and drop the partition from the partitioned table, respectively. You can also drop a partition from a partitioned index using the ALTER INDEX DROP PARTITION command. The new command ALTER TABLE MERGE PARTITIONS allows adjacent range partitions to be merged into one. The merge partition command can be useful for situations where historical data can be rolled up together into archived partitions.

The SPLIT PARTITION option of the ALTER TABLE or ALTER INDEX command allows you to create two new partitions from an existing partition by specifying the new partition boundaries. The existing partition is then discarded. The SPLIT PARTITION option is useful for situations where a single partition has grown too large or you need to redistribute data on disk to improve I/O performance.

The EXCHANGE PARTITION option of the ALTER TABLE command converts a partition to a nonpartitioned table and a table to a partition of a partitioned table by exchanging their data, and optionally, index segments. The EXCHANGE PARTITION option is useful for situations where an application that was previously using nonpartitioned tables would like to switch to partitioned tables. This can also be useful for migrating from partition views (7.3) to Oracle8*i* table partitions.

The ADD PARTITION option of the ALTER TABLE command is used to add a partition to the high end of the table. The ADD PARTITION option may be useful for scenarios of historical data where new partitions are added at certain periods of time. If you need to add a partition to the middle or beginning of the partitioned table, use the SPLIT PARTITION option.

The REBUILD PARTITION option of the ALTER INDEX command allows you to rebuild a partition of a partitioned index. Rebuilding a section of the index is beneficial as opposed to rebuilding the entire index. For example, you may determine that certain partitions of the partitioned index are very hot as compared to other partitions of the partitioned index. In such a case, the REBUILD PARTITION option can be used to migrate the index partition to another tablespace on another set of disks in order to improve I/O throughput.

Oracle8*i* provides various different options and techniques to administer partitions. This wide variety of partition commands fosters a flexible environment when using partitions. As partitioned objects continue to grow in size and partition access frequency increases, the ability to migrate or split a partition becomes more vital. Partitioned tables and indexes help improve availability, administration, manageability, and performance.

6.9.9   PARTITION INDEXES

There are several types of indexes such as nonpartitioned, global prefixed, local prefixed, and local nonprefixed indexes. Global nonprefixed indexes are not supported by Oracle. The variety of index types allows you to choose the most appropriate index type based on such factors as availability, performance, and manageability. Partitioned indexes are constructed as separate B*-tree structures. A nonpartitioned index is simply a traditional Oracle B*-tree index. A prefixed index has the leftmost columns of the index based on the same columns as the partition key. A unique prefix index requires access to only one index partition in order to retrieve the data when accessing only one row from a DML statement. A nonunique prefixed index where only part of the partition key is provided in the WHERE clause requires that all partitions be scanned. If, however, all the columns that makeup the partition key are specified in the WHERE clause, then only one index partition is accessed. The columns of a nonprefixed index are not based on the same columns as the partition key. A nonprefixed index is range-based partitioned; however, each B*-tree section of each partition is based on the nonprefixed column(s). In order to guarantee uniqueness, the unique nonprefix index must include the partition key as part of the index key. Unique nonprefixed indexes require only one index partition to retrieve the row when accessing only one row via a DML statement. Conversely, a nonunique nonprefixed index must scan all partitions in order to retrieve the row.

The keys in a particular index partition of a global index may refer to rows stored in more than one partition of the underlying table. A global index is created with the GLOBAL attribute of the CREATE INDEX statement and is typically not equi-partitioned with the underlying table. If the global index is equi-partitioned, Oracle does not automatically maintain the equi-partitioning. The optimizer is also not aware of equi-partitioned global indexes and thus cannot eliminate partitions from execution plans. For this reason, equi-partitioned indexes should be created as local indexes. A global index can be unique or nonunique. The highest partition of a global index must be able to hold the maximum value of the indexed columns for the underlying table.

In a local index, all rows in a table partition have a corresponding index entry in the index partition. Hence, a local index is equi-partitioned with the underlying partitioned table. A local index is created by specifying the LOCAL attribute in the CREATE INDEX statement. Local indexes increase availability by ensuring that partition maintenance operations provide partition independence. For example, you could be loading several partitions while concurrent DML statements are occurring on other partitions. Oracle can also generate more efficient plans by taking advantage of the fact that the table and index are equi-partitioned.

6.9.9.1   Local Prefixed Index

A local prefixed index has its partition key based on the leftmost column(s) of the index. For Massively Parallel Processing (MPP) environments, local prefixed indexes provide good data locality. Local prefixed indexes can be unique or nonunique. The following is an example of a local prefixed index that assumes the table is partitioned on the week_no column.

```
SQL> create index sales_lpidx
     on sales (week_no,customer_id)
     local
     (partition w1 tablespace ixw1,
      partition w2 tablespace ixw2,
      partition w3 tablespace ixw3,
      partition w4 tablespace ixw4);
```

Local prefixed indexes tend to offer the best performance, availability, and manageability. The fact that a local prefixed index is equi-partitioned with the underlying table improves the query plan execution by employing partition pruning. For example, a query that specified the values of `week_no` and `customer_id` can take advantage of partition pruning by eliminating the partitions containing weeks other than the ones specified. This improves query performance and reduces the amount of scans needed to execute the query.

6.9.9.2 Local Nonprefixed Index

A local nonprefixed index has its partition key based on something else other than the leftmost column(s) of the index. A local nonprefixed index can be nonunique and can only be unique if the partition key is a subset of the index key. Local nonprefixed indexes are useful in situations where fast access is needed and queries are based on a column which is not part of the partition key of the table. The following is an example of a local nonprefixed index that assumes the table is partitioned on the `week_no` column.

```
SQL> create index sales_lnpidx
     on sales (sale_no)
     local
     (partition w1 tablespace ixw1,
      partition w2 tablespace ixw2,
      partition w3 tablespace ixw3,
      partition w4 tablespace ixw4);
```

It is generally more expensive to scan a nonprefixed index than to scan a prefixed index. Oracle must apply a predicate involving the index columns to all index partitions for a nonprefixed index in order to perform a single key lookup or index range scan. An index range scan also causes Oracle to combine information from other index partitions. Local nonprefixed indexes reduce the degree of partition independence since DML statements using the keys of local nonprefixed indexes results in the probe of all index partitions. However, several index partitions in a local nonprefixed index can be scanned in parallel in cases where queries specify a range on the index key, thus increasing overall performance.

6.9.9.3 Global Prefixed Index

A global prefixed index is partitioned on a left prefix of the columns of the index. Global prefixed indexes are generally not equi-partitioned with the underlying table. In a global prefix index, Oracle maintains only the index structures, and not the partitions themselves. Global indexes increase administration complexity due to the fact that they do not maintain partition independence. As such, operations such as SPLIT, MOVE, DROP, TRUNCATE, or point in time recovery affect all partitions. The following is an example of a global prefixed index:

```
create index sales_gpidx
    on sales (week_no,customer_id)
global
partition by range (week_no)
  (partition w1 values less than (25),
   partition w2 values less than (maxvalue));
```

Global prefixed indexes minimize the number of index probes, thereby increasing performance. Global prefixed indexes are generally more difficult to manage, and the database administrator is responsible for maintaining the partitioning of the global prefixed index. All corresponding entries in a global prefixed index must be restored to the same point in time when recovering the underlying table partition to a point in time. The only way to recover a global prefixed index is to re-create the index since the index entries may be dispersed across all the partitions of the index which may be combined with index entries from other partitions that are not being restored.

6.9.10 PARTITION PRUNING AND THE EXPLAIN PLAN

The Oracle optimizer determines which partitions are needed to satisfy the DML statement based on the predicates specified. Partition pruning can significantly reduce the amount of I/O needed as well as reduce the overall work needed to complete the DML statement. For example, a query might require a hash join and then a sort for a complex join with an order by clause. Without partition pruning, the query might require full-table scans on the tables in the join clause. If the tables listed in the join clause are large in size, the query may take a long time to complete due to the amount of I/O needed as well as the time needed to sort the data. By utilizing partition pruning, the optimizer identifies only those partitions needed to satisfy the query predicates. For example, consider the following query.

```
SELECT *
FROM sales
WHERE sale_date BETWEEN TO_DATE('01-AUG-2000', 'DD-MON-YYYY') AND
                        TO_DATE('15-NOV-2000', 'DD-MON-YYYY') AND
product_id = 55;
```

Figure 6.6 illustrates the concept of partition pruning for the different partitioning schemes: range, hash, and composite.

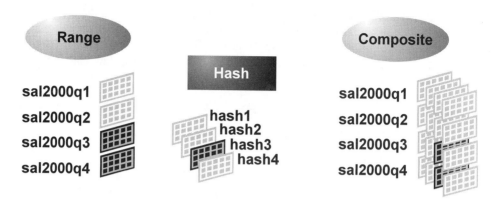

FIGURE 6.6 The concept of partition pruning.

In the range scheme, assuming that the SALES table is range partitioned on the ORDER_DATE in sales quarter ranges, partition pruning would result in the third and the fourth partitions being used because of the query filters on orders (between August 1, 2000 and November 15, 2000). In the hash partition case, if the SALES table was partitioned on the PRODUCT_ID column, then the optimizer would be able to prune to a single partition since the predicate is an equality predicate. In the composite case, if the SALES table was range partitioned by ORDER_DATE in ranges of sales quarters, and subpartitioned by HASH on the PRODUCT_ID column, then the optimizer would prune to the third and fourth partitions; however, it would further prune down to the subpartitions containing orders for PRODUCT_ID=55.

Partition pruning can also be confirmed via the execution plan. For example, consider the following query on a partitioned table.

```
SQL> select count(*)
        from sales
        where (week_no between 1 and 15);
```

The explain plan for the above query looks as follows.

```
ID EXPLAIN_PLAN                                                    POSITION

0  SELECT STATEMENT                                                     1
1    SORT AGGREGATE                                                     1
2      PARTITION CONCATENATED    :Q25000
          PARALLEL_COMBINED_WITH_PARENT   NUMBER(1) NUMBER(2)          1
3        TABLE ACCESS FULL  SALES :Q25000
            PARALLEL_TO_SERIAL   NUMBER(1) NUMBER(2)                   1
```

This explain plan shows that the optimizer is employing partition pruning. The PAR-TITION CONCATENATED operation indicates that more than one partition is involved and that the results from the multiple partition scans will be concatenated. If only one partition were being accessed, there would not be a PARTITION CONCATENDATED operation. Instead, the PARTITION_START and PARTITION_STOP columns would show the same partition being accessed (PARTITION SINGLE). The explain plan table columns PARTITION_START and PARTITION_STOP show the partitions being used. The explain plan above shows the values NUMBER(1) and NUMBER(2) for the columns PARTITION_START and PARTITION_STOP, respectively. This means that partition 1 and partition 2 are needed to satisfy the query. In addition, the explain plan also shows that the query is being parallelized.

The following is another example of an explain plan illustrating partition pruning using an update statement.

```
SQL> update sales_pending
        set sale_amount = sale_amount - (0.10*sale_amount)
     where (week_no between 21 and 30);
```

ID	EXPLAIN_PLAN	POSITION
0	UPDATE STATEMENT	1
1	UPDATE SALES_PENDING	1
2	TABLE ACCESS FULL SALES_PENDING :Q33000	1
	PARALLEL_TO_SERIAL NUMBER(3) NUMBER(3)	

This update statement is used to offer a 10 percent discount on sales still pending for the weeks 21 through 30. The corresponding explain plan shows that partition 3 is being used, and the explain plan also shows that the table access is being parallelized.

Using the explain plan utility, you can determine whether or not a query is employing partition pruning. Furthermore, you can determine which partitions are involved in the SQL operation. You should perform an explain plan on your SQL statements to ensure that partition pruning is being utilized. The explain plan data helps you understand the execution path of your SQL statements. By using the explain plan utility, you can take steps to improve execution times should you determine that the plan being generated is suboptimal. You may have to regenerate table and partition statistics, or rewrite the SQL statement.

6.9.11 PARTITION EXTENDED TABLE NAMES

You can also explicitly specify the name of the partition to be used in a SELECT, INSERT, UPDATE, or DELETE SQL statement. This allows you to view an individual partition as a separate table. If you choose to use partition extended table names, you should use a view in order to insulate the application from the specifics of this SQL extension. In addition, using a view avoids having to hard-code partition names inside the application. The following is an example of explicitly specifying the partition name as part of the SELECT statement.

```
select count(*)
from sales partition (w1)
where (week_no <= 10);
```

The use of views in conjunction with partition extended table names can also help build partition-level security. By building a view against a select statement that uses the partition extended table name feature, you can then grant or revoke privileges to the view to and from other users or roles. This is useful for situations where certain users' access should be restricted to certain partitions within the entire table.

6.9.12 PARTITION TABLESPACE OPTIMIZATION

The beauty of Oracle partitioning is that it allows you to spread your tables and indexes across different tablespaces. This not only allows you to achieve high I/O throughput by distributing your tablespace data files across different disks and controllers, it also allows you to partition by frequency of access. For example, certain partitions of a partitioned table may seldom be accessed because they represent archive or historical data. You may also have certain partitions that are not updated in which case you can employ read-only tablespaces for such partitions. It is important that you lay out your table data and partitions appropriately so as to minimize I/O contention and separate partitions and tablespaces by criteria such as workload, administration requirements, availability, and performance requirements. You may have to stripe certain frequently accessed (very hot) partitions across more disks and controllers more than other infrequently accessed partitions. For example, a frequently accessed partition may be striped across 20 disks with a small stripe interleave while a partition that is seldom accessed may be striped only across 2 disks with a larger stripe interleave. It is vital that you consider the many different factors such as workload, performance, manageability, access frequency, type of access, availability, data distribution, and level of concurrency when planning and sizing table and index partitions. You should also monitor I/O utilization using the Oracle Enterprise Manager as well as the server utilities such as `sar` or `iostat` to determine if I/O contention is occurring. If I/O contention is occurring, you may have to split or move partitions in order to redistribute data.

6.9.13 GATHERING STATISTICS AT THE PARTITION LEVEL

Oracle8 and Oracle8*i* allow you to gather statistics at the partition level for a table and index. This helps you parallelize statistics gathering for very large tables and indexes. By choosing a reasonable sampling size per partition, you can estimate statistics at the partition level if the partitions are too big to perform a compute statistics. For example,

```
SQL> analyze table sales partition (sales_w1)
        estimate statistics sample 5000 rows;
```

Gathering statistics at the partition level improves the performance and manageability of statistics gathering. You should compute or estimate statistics at the partition level so that the optimizer can produce intelligent execution plans. Without statistics, it is difficult for the optimizer to generate efficient execution plans since the default estimates may not be optimal. You can reduce the time it takes to gather statistics by submitting multiple analyze statements in parallel, each against different partitions.

In Oracle8*i*, you can use the DBMS_STATS package to gather statistics on partitioned tables. The GATHER_TABLE_STATS procedure can be used to gather statistics on a single partition using the PARTNAME parameter of the GATHER_TABLE_STATS procedure. If the PARTNAME parameter is null, then statistics are gathered for all partitions. You can also specify whether local partition statistics, global table statistics, or both should be gathered. The GRANULARITY parameter of the DBMS_STATS.GATHER_TABLE_STATS procedure can be used to request the type of partition statistics which to gather. In general, you should gather both local partition statistics and global table statistics in order to allow the optimizer to use the appropriate set of statistics based on the queries.

6.9.14 PARTITION CATALOG TABLES

There are various new Oracle8*i* catalog views that provide information on partitions such as partition ranges, statistics, storage information, and number of partitions. The following are the catalog views pertaining to partitions.

- ❑ ALL_IND_PARTITIONS
- ❑ ALL_IND_SUBPARTITIONS
- ❑ ALL_LOB_PARTITIONS
- ❑ ALL_LOB_SUBPARTITIONS
- ❑ ALL_PARTIAL_DROP_TABS
- ❑ ALL_PART_COL_STATISTICS
- ❑ ALL_PART_HISTOGRAMS
- ❑ ALL_PART_INDEXES
- ❑ ALL_PART_KEY_COLUMNS
- ❑ ALL_PART_LOBS
- ❑ ALL_PART_TABLES
- ❑ ALL_SUBPART_COL_STATISTICS
- ❑ ALL_SUBPART_HISTOGRAMS
- ❑ ALL_SUBPART_KEY_COLUMNS
- ❑ ALL_TAB_PARTITIONS
- ❑ ALL_TAB_SUBPARTITIONS
- ❑ DBA_IND_PARTITIONS
- ❑ DBA_IND_SUBPARTITIONS

- ❑ DBA_LOB_PARTITIONS
- ❑ DBA_LOB_SUBPARTITIONS
- ❑ DBA_PARTIAL_DROP_TABS
- ❑ DBA_PART_COL_STATISTICS
- ❑ DBA_PART_HISTOGRAMS
- ❑ DBA_PART_INDEXES
- ❑ DBA_PART_KEY_COLUMNS
- ❑ DBA_PART_LOBS
- ❑ DBA_PART_TABLES
- ❑ DBA_SUBPART_COL_STATISTICS
- ❑ DBA_SUBPART_HISTOGRAMS
- ❑ DBA_SUBPART_KEY_COLUMNS
- ❑ DBA_TAB_PARTITIONS
- ❑ DBA_TAB_SUBPARTITIONS
- ❑ LOADER_PART_INFO
- ❑ USER_IND_PARTITIONS
- ❑ USER_IND_SUBPARTITIONS
- ❑ USER_LOB_PARTITIONS
- ❑ USER_LOB_SUBPARTITIONS
- ❑ USER_PARTIAL_DROP_TABS
- ❑ USER_PART_COL_STATISTICS
- ❑ USER_PART_HISTOGRAMS
- ❑ USER_PART_INDEXES
- ❑ USER_PART_KEY_COLUMNS
- ❑ USER_PART_LOBS
- ❑ USER_PART_TABLES
- ❑ USER_SUBPART_COL_STATISTICS
- ❑ USER_SUBPART_HISTOGRAMS
- ❑ USER_SUBPART_KEY_COLUMNS
- ❑ USER_TAB_PARTITIONS
- ❑ USER_TAB_SUBPARTITIONS

For more information on the above views and other catalog views, refer to the *Oracle8i Reference Manual*.

6.10 MATERIALIZED VIEWS AND QUERY REWRITE

Oracle8*i* provides a feature known as materialized views, which helps data warehousing applications improve query execution by orders of magnitude. A materialized view, in essence, is an instantiation of an SQL statement that can be used to store summaries of pre-computed results. The result of a materialized view is stored in a table and thus can have different storage attributes than the base tables that make up the materialized view. Indexes can be created on materialized views. Materialized views can also be partitioned. A materialized view can also be refreshed manually or automatically. The refresh method can be specified as part of the materialized view creation command. The refresh methods include a full refresh, fast refresh of DML modifications, fast refresh of direct-load modifications, and a synchronous refresh of DML. A full refresh truncates the existing data and reinserts all the data based on the underlying tables and criteria. Fast refreshes involve applying the changes captured in the log to the materialized view. Fast refreshes can also, if possible, update the materialized view on an incremental basis. For example, suppose a materialized view consists of totals using the SUM() function. In this case, the materialized view can be updated by adding the existing SUM() values to the sum computed from the new rows. The synchronous refresh method refreshes the materialized view upon commit of the changes made to the underlying tables. The DBMS_MVIEW package provides the REFRESH procedure which can be used to refresh materialized views. The DBMS_MVIEW.REFRESH_ALL_MVIEWS procedure can be used to refresh all the materialized views. Refreshes can be queued, in which case they employ job queues to perform the job of the refresh. Hence, it is important that you configure the job queue related init.ora parameters appropriately to ensure enough job queue processes exist (job_queue_processes). In conjunction with materialized views, the Oracle8*i* server utilizes a technique known as query rewrite to improve query performance. Query rewrite enables the optimizer to avoid expensive joins and aggregate operations by utilizing the data available in the materialized view to satisfy the query. Query rewrite is transparent to the application, and is a function of the optimizer similar to that of choosing an index access path for a given query.

Materialized views can be used for replication (i.e., snapshots), the storage of summaries, and the storage of join queries. Materialized views enhance the capabilities of replicating snapshots by being able to perform fast refreshes. This reduces the network traffic between the master and the remote sites by avoiding a full refresh and improves overall refresh performance. Summary materialized views store the results of aggregate queries such as those containing SUM(), AVG(), and GROUP BY operations. Join materialized views store the results of a join between multiple tables. The join materialized view can then be used by the optimizer for queries involving joins of the tables of the join materialized view. Query rewrite and join materialized views can substantially increase query performance by avoiding costly joins as well as eliminating the memory and disk storage needed to perform the joins dynamically.

The following example creates a summary materialized view.

```
CREATE MATERIALIZED VIEW SALES_SUMMARY
   TABLESPACE SALES_TS
   PARALLEL (degree 4)
   BUILD IMMEDIATE
   REFRESH FAST
   ENABLE QUERY REWRITE
   AS
   SELECT s.zip_code,p.product_category,sum(s.amount)
   FROM   SALES S,
          PRODUCT P
   WHERE (s.product_id=p.product_id)
   GROUP BY s.zip_code,p.product_category;
```

The materialized view was created with query rewrite enabled, which enables the optimizer to utilize the summary materialized view for certain queries as opposed to performing the join between the sales and product tables. The following example illustrates the query rewrite feature via the explain plan.

```
select  s.zip_code,p.product_category,sum(s.amount)
from sales s,
     product p
where (s.product_id=p.product_id)
group by s.zip_code, p.product_category;
```

```
Execution Plan
-------------------------------------------------------------------
SELECT STATEMENT Optimizer=CHOOSE (Cost=1 Card=21 Bytes=819)
   TABLE ACCESS* (FULL) OF 'SALES_SUMMARY' (Cost=1 Card=21 Bytes=819)
```

The execution plan shows that the query rewrite feature resulted in the optimizer selecting the materialized view as the access path versus performing the join and aggregating the data. Query rewrite can be used in situations where there is an exact match, aggregate roll-up, aggregate to all, and summary join-back. An exact match refers to when the columns selected and the join conditions of the query match with that of the materialized view. The aggregate roll-up situation occurs when the summary grouping is less than that of the query grouping. For example, if a query was interested in yearly sales statistics, and the summary view contained monthly sales statistics, query rewrite could derive the yearly sales from the monthly sales available in the summary. The aggregate to all situation occurs when there are more dimensions in the summary, such as when the GROUP BY clause of the query contains a subset of the columns specified in the GROUP BY clause of the summary view. Query rewrite can also be enabled in the case of a summary join-back in which a column used in the query is not available in the summary view, but the column can be derived. In such a case, the column can be derived by joining the summary table with the appropriate dimension table in order to obtain the column.

Oracle8*i* allows dimensions and hierarchies to be defined, which is useful for describing business entities and dependencies. Dimensions are also recommended for query rewrites since often constraints are not maintained in a data warehousing environment. Dimensions offer query rewrite additional candidates for execution plans when rewriting queries. The CREATE DIMENSION command can be used to create the dimensions and relationships in one's schema. Dimensions are also useful for OLAP applications that often require the dimensions to be defined. The DBMS_OLAP package can be used to perform dimension-related operations, such as validating a dimension using the DBMS_OLAP.VAL-IDATE_DIMENSION procedure.

Query rewrite is available only with the cost-based optimizer (CBO), and can be enabled by setting the init.ora parameter query_rewrite_enabled=TRUE. The init.ora parameter query_rewrite_integrity allows you to specify the state under which query rewrite should be enabled. QUERY_REWRITE_INTEGRITY=ENFORCE enables query rewrites only if consistency can be guaranteed. QUERY_REWRITE_ INTEGRITY=NOENFORCE enables query rewrites based on declared relationships. However, it is not required that the relationships be enforced. QUERY_REWRITE_INTEGRITY=USE_STALE enables query rewrites for stale materialized views that have not been refreshed since the last DML operation.

Materialized views in conjunction with query rewrite provide a powerful mechanism to considerably improve data warehousing and OLAP performance. Fast refreshes enable a quick and incremental update of the materialized view. Materialized views help reduce the expensive operations such as joins and aggregation. DBAs often create summarized tables in order for applications to avoid long-running SQL statements that consist of complex predicates and large table joins. The DBA would often have to drop the summary table and re-create it in order to refresh the data. Applications would also need to have explicit knowledge of the summary table. Materialized views eliminate the burden of having to frequently drop and re-create summary tables. Furthermore, materialized views provide a transparent view to the application via the automatic query rewrite feature. You should also verify that query rewrite is functioning properly by examining the execution plan of the query (explain plan).

6.11 FUNCTION-BASED INDEXES

Oracle8*i* allows indexes to be created known as function-based indexes that qualify on the value returned by a function or expression. The function or expression value is pre-computed and stored in the index. Function-based indexes can be built based on arithmetic expressions, a PL/SQL function, package function, C callout, SQL function, or an expression involving one or more columns. Function-based indexes can significantly improve query performance in situations where queries often contain predicates consisting of computationally intensive expressions. A common situation where function-based indexes can help improve query performance is the use of the upper() SQL function. For example, consider the following query.

```
select empno,ename,sal
from emp
where upper(ename)='SMITH';
```

In this particular case, the optimizer would not be able to use the employee name index because a function is being performed on the column, thereby changing the value of the data. In this case, a function-based index could be created on the table, thereby allowing the optimizer to utilize the index during SQL execution. The following example creates a function-based index using the `upper()` function.

```
create index ename_idx on emp (upper(ename));
```

Function-based indexes can also be used to perform linguistic sorts based on linguistic sort keys. Function-based indexes can be used to improve query performance by enabling the optimizer to utilize an index access path versus a full-table scan when performing function or expression based column conversions in SQL statements.

6.12 LOADING DATA

Loads are often performed in a data warehousing environment to refresh data. SQL*Loader with the parallel option can reduce the time it takes to load a large table by loading the table in parallel. Do not confuse the parallel query option with the parallel load option. Parallel load does not use query slaves to parallelize the load. Parallel load removes the exclusive lock held on the table, enabling multiple processes to insert into the same table. Each parallel load session loads the data into temporary table extents and then merges the temporary table extents upon completion. You can verify the existence of the temporary table extents by querying the `DBA_EXTENTS` view setting `segment_type='TEMPORARY'` while a parallel load is running.

6.12.1 DIRECT PATH LOADS

As of Oracle7, release 7.1, the SQL*Loader utility provides a parallel load feature. The parallel load feature, along with the direct path option, can load large amounts of data in a relatively small period of time. The direct load option of SQL*Loader bypasses the Oracle SGA by writing directly to disk and updates the high-water mark of the table. You can obtain high I/O throughput during loads by using raw devices, striping, and a volume manager. The parallel load feature enables multiple loads to proceed in parallel on the same table. Without the `parallel=true` SQL*Loader option, an exclusive lock is placed on the table until the SQL*Loader session completes. By parallelizing the load process, you can reduce the amount of time it takes to load a table. You can also use the `FILE` option of SQL*Loader. The `FILE` option enables you to specify which database file Oracle will allocate extents from for the load. Using the `FILE` option, you can achieve high throughput by spreading the data across different files and different disk drives. If you are using SQL*Loader direct path, you may want to decrease the size of the SGA temporarily to enable more memory to be dedicated to the load processes. Because direct load bypasses the SGA, a large SGA is not needed.

6.12.1.1   Direct Path Load API

Oracle8*i* extended the Oracle Call Interface (OCI) to include support for the Direct Path Load services present in the SQL*Loader utility. This allows applications to use the direct load interface without having to directly use SQL*Loader. Applications can use a programmatic interface to read and process data files, and then use the direct load APIs to load the data into the database. The direct load API allows application logic to handle the direct load of the data into the database, and programmatically handle errors. This is superior to using shell scripts which invoke SQL*Loader. The application has much greater control over the direct load and its sequence of steps. The direct load API is available through OCI8*i*. The OCI API *OCIDirPathPrepare()* is used to prepare the direct load interface. For more information on the direct load API, refer to the *Oracle Call Interface Programmer's Guide* for release 8*i*.

6.12.2   CONVENTIONAL PATH LOADS

If you use the conventional load option of SQL*Loader, you can make use of the `bindsize` parameter. SQL*Loader uses the SQL array interface option, and `bindsize` specifies, in bytes, the size of the array for each insert. A larger number of rows can be inserted each time by increasing the `bindsize`. SQL*Loader reads the number of rows that fit into the `bindsize` array and then performs an array insert of the bind array. This reduces the number of SQL calls between the SQL*Loader process and the Oracle Server. It can also pseudo-parallelize the load process by allowing the Oracle Server to insert the bind array while SQL*Loader reads continue to populate the bind array for the next insert. Increasing the bind array maximizes CPU utilization and minimizes I/O wait time. Of course, when you size the bind array, be careful to size it accordingly so that sufficient memory is available for the size of the bind array, and paging and swapping do not occur. If you load through the conventional path, the SGA should be optimally sized so as to accommodate the bind array inserts into the SGA. Please refer to the *Oracle8i Utilities Guide* for more information on the SQL*Loader utility.

6.12.3   PARTITION LOADS

In Oracle8 and Oracle8*i*, you can load data at the partition level. By specifying the name of the partition in the SQL*Loader control file, you can invoke concurrent loads, each loading a separate partition. The following is an example SQL*Loader control file that specifies the name of the partition.

```
— Parallel, direct-path load at the partition level..
— Unrecoverable option used to speed up the load..
—

OPTIONS (DIRECT = TRUE, PARALLEL = TRUE)
UNRECOVERABLE
LOAD DATA
INFILE 'sales.dat'
APPEND
INTO TABLE sales partition (sales_w1)
APPEND
FIELDS TERMINATED BY ',' OPTIONALLY ENCLOSED BY '"'
(
    week_no              integer external,
    sale_no              integer external,
    sale_date            date "MM/DD/YY",
    sale_amount          integer external,
    customer_id          integer external
)
```

This control file example specifies the name of the table partition following the partition clause. The control file also specifies a direct path and parallel load. Loading at the partition level allows you to achieve a high degree of parallelism. By optimally distributing the partition tablespaces, you can reduce the amount of time needed to load the entire table by loading concurrently at the partition level. In order to achieve a high throughput load, it is important that the data files of the underlying table partitions be distributed so as to minimize I/O contention. In an optimal situation with no I/O contention nor resource contention (processor and memory), the time needed to load all the partitions (in parallel) should be roughly near the time it takes to load a single partition. Monitor I/O utilization during the load in order to ensure I/O is being distributed and to determine if I/O contention is occurring.

6.12.4 FIXED FIELD LOADS

Another technique you can use to increase the performance of SQL*Loader loads is through the use of fixed-length fields in the SQL*Loader control file. By using fixed-length columns, as opposed to variable-length fields delimited by a delimiter, you will reduce SQL*Loader parsing. When using variable delimited fields, SQL*Loader spends a considerable amount of time parsing the records by setting the start position and the length of each field for the data records. By using fixed-length record fields in the SQL*Loader control file, parsing time can be reduced significantly and you can increase the performance of the load.

6.12.5 UNRECOVERABLE OPTION

The UNRECOVERABLE option can be used with a direct path load to request that the load data not be logged. Instead, invalidation redo is generated. This helps increase load performance. However, you need to consider media recovery when using the UNRECOVERABLE option since the load data blocks cannot be recovered. You should backup the table following the load to ensure that you will be able to recover the table data should media recovery be necessary.

6.12.6 LOADING THROUGH NFS

When running parallel loads, it is critical that I/O be distributed. Try to place the input files on a striped file system separate from the Oracle data and redo log files. This minimizes I/O contention and thus increases the performance of the load. When loading from a remote file system staging area (not local to the database server), either load from the machine that contains the file system using SQL*Net or Net8, or NFS-mount the file system on the database server and run a local load. As far as Oracle is concerned, it has no idea that the input data is NFS-mounted; this is handled by the OS. NFS tends to have a higher throughput than SQL*Net or Net8 and can therefore reduce the time it takes to load the data. To increase the load performance over an NFS link, you may want to consider setting up a dedicated connection between the database server and file system staging area server using a dedicated Ethernet connection or even a fiber connection. This reduces network contention and may reduce the length that the packet must travel if the dedicated connection is directly connected between one server and another (bypassing routers and other network segments).

By tuning loads appropriately, you can achieve a very fast high-throughput load. In my experience, I have been able to concurrently load 10-GB tables on highly tuned servers in less than 30 minutes by starting multiple loads and distributing I/O as optimally as possible. Load throughput can also be increased by loading at the table partition level. This allows you to sustain more concurrent loads by making sure that each load at the partition level loads a small subset of the data. You should also divide your input data streams (SQL*Loader input data files) into partitions, thus allowing each input data stream to map to an Oracle table partition.

6.13 BUILDING INDEXES

In addition to loading data in parallel, you can also create indexes in parallel and reduce the time it takes to build an index. Oracle 7.1 introduced the parallel index creation option, and Oracle 7.2 introduced the unrecoverable option, further increasing performance. Oracle 7.3 introduced the alter index rebuild option that allows an index to be rebuilt using the existing index. In Oracle8 and Oracle8i, you can rebuild an index at the partition level. To create indexes in parallel, you can use the following example.

```
SQL> Create Index ACCOUNT_INDEX on Account (ACCOUNT_NO)
     unrecoverable         *** Oracle7
     nologging             *** Oracle8
     parallel (degree 4)
     storage (.......);
```

In this example, the ACCOUNT_INDEX is created in parallel using a degree of parallelism of four. The Oracle7 unrecoverable keyword indicates that no redo information will be generated for this index creation. The equivalent to unrecoverable in Oracle8 is nologging. The unrecoverable (Oracle7) or nologging (Oracle8) keyword means that the index cannot be recovered using the redo log files or archived redo log files. However, it can speed up the creation of the index tangibly if redo is a bottleneck on your server. Be careful when choosing the degree of parallelism. Although a degree of parallelism of four is selected, eight slave processes actually will be spawned. Four of the slaves will scan the table gathering the ACCOUNT_NO columns, and four of the slaves will perform the sorting of the ACCOUNT_NO columns. Again, this demonstrates the use of inter-parallelism. Be careful not to choose a high degree of parallelism; otherwise too many processes will be spawned, and the high degree of parallelism may have a negative effect.

6.14 BUILDING TABLES

In a data warehousing environment, tables are often created for the purpose of aggregation or analysis. The tables are often dropped and re-created in order to refresh the data. Building a large table without parallelism can take a long time. Oracle 7.2 provides the parallel table creation option that allows not only the underlying query to be parallelized, but the table creation itself is also parallelized. To create a table in parallel, you can use the following example.

```
SQL> Create Table ORDERS_PER_STATE
     nologging
     parallel (degree 4)
     AS SELECT /*+ ORDERED
                   FULL (A)
                   FULL (O)
                   PARALLEL (A,4)
                   PARALLEL (O,4)
                   USE_HASH (A O) */
        A.STATE_ID,
        count(*) SALES_COUNT
        FROM ACCOUNT A,
             ORDERS O
        WHERE  (A.ACCOUNT_NO=O.ACCOUNT_NO)
        GROUP BY A.STATE_ID;
```

In this example, the ORDERS_PER_STATE table is created in parallel by using a degree of parallelism of four. Both the subselect query and the table creation are parallelized. The nologging keyword (unrecoverable in Oracle7) also can be used with table creations as well as with index creations to eliminate the redo for the table creation. However, keep in mind that using the nologging (or unrecoverable) option prevents you from being able to recover the table through the redo log files or archived redo log files. The performance increase offered by the nologging option can make dealing with the recoverability issue worthwhile. Following the completion of the table create statement, you should make a backup of the table in the event of a media failure. Choosing the appropriate degree of parallelism can help minimize the time needed to create the table.

In a data warehousing environment, it is often necessary to refresh table data. This can be done in many different ways. If there are a small number of rows that need to be refreshed, an update statement can be used to update the table. However, if dealing with a large amount of rows, a Create Table as Select (CTAS) statement is much faster than an update statement. The CTAS operation can be parallelized even on nonpartitioned tables. If you are using update statements to refresh tables in a data warehousing environment, you may want to consider using a CTAS statement in place of the update to re-create the table. When updating a large number of rows, a CTAS statement outperforms an equivalent update statement.

6.15 PARALLEL STORAGE

When you load, index, or create tables in parallel, recall that each slave allocates an initial extent followed by next extents if needed. This means that if you load a table in parallel with INITIAL extent size set to 100 MB, and five parallel loads are running simultaneously on the table, 500 MB (5 × 100 MB) in initial extents are allocated. Therefore, make sure you have enough space for the parallel load, index, or table create.

You should also make sure that your data file extents are distributed and sized properly so as to avoid disk contention and fragmentation. You can use the FILE option of SQL*Loader to specify from which data files Oracle will allocate extents. This allows you to distribute your data across different data files and different disks. When building or loading indexes and tables in parallel, it is essential that you optimally size and distribute the Oracle data files in order to maintain high I/O throughput.

6.16 DEGREE OF PARALLELISM

The degree of parallelism you choose is highly dependent on your system configuration. The number of processors, level of I/O distribution, and the amount of available memory all contribute to the optimal selection of the degree of parallelism. You should balance the degree of parallelism with the number of on-line available processors, and the degree of striping. For example, if your data is spread across only two disk drives and you have ten processors, starting up ten slaves to scan the table (data) will likely saturate the two disks and cause high I/O wait times.

You should balance I/O with available processors when selecting the degree of parallelism. Also, if for example, you are trying to parallelize a query that consists of a large hash join, and the tables' data files are striped across five different disks and controllers, and the temporary tablespace is also striped across five different disks and controllers (different disks and controllers than the tables), and you have ten processors, choosing a degree of parallelism of five is optimal. Recall that a parallel query using a hash join utilizes both inter- and intraparallelism. In this case, a degree of parallelism of five will actually spawn ten query slaves—five of the slaves will attack the table (scanning the table) in parallel, and five slaves will perform the join. For a large hash join, the data blocks may be written out to the temporary tablespace. If so, the five scan slaves and the five join slaves will experience minimal contention since the data files and temporary tablespace files are separated. Use `sar -u` and `sar -d` to monitor processor and disk I/O utilization to help you choose the most effective degree of parallelism.

6.17 PARALLEL QUERY AND THE 9/13 RULE

The Parallel Query Option (PQO) uses a 9/13 rule when it parallelizes queries. First, PQO (when used) converts the base user shadow process into the Query Coordinator (QC). The QC then spawns the number of query slaves needed. If slaves are already available, then the QC uses the available slaves. The QC is responsible for partitioning the work among the parallel query slave processes, managing the workload among the parallel query slaves, and returning the results of the query back to the client. The QC divides the total number of blocks occupied by the table by the number of parallel query slaves assigned to the query, rounding up when necessary. The QC then further subdivides each partition into thirteenths. Each partition is divided into three subpartitions: one 9/13, one 3/13, and the last partition of 1/13.

For example, suppose a query is submitted with a degree of parallelism of four. The QC divides the table being scanned into four equal-size partitions (rounding may be necessary, causing the partitions to be near in size). Figure 6.7 shows the query coordinator and the four query slaves.

Then the QC further subdivides each of the four partitions into three subpartitions of 9/13, 3/13, and 1/13 in size. Then, the QC assigns each slave a 9/13 partition to scan. As each slave finishes its 9/13 partition, the QC then assigns the 3/13 partition on a first-come, first-serve basis. The first slave to finish the 9/13 scan, receives a 3/13 partition to scan until all scans of the 3/13 partitions are completed. Then, the QC distributes the remaining 1/13 partitions to the slaves also on a first-come, first-serve basis. The 9/13 technique minimizes the effects of uneven data distribution. Even if all the data for a table is located in one or a

FIGURE 6.7   The query coordinator and the parallel query slaves.

few areas, the workload of the parallel query slaves will still be distributed. For example, suppose a parallel query with a degree of parallelism of four is executed on a table that has most of the data centered in one area. Some of the slaves likely will finish their 9/13 partition quickly because not much data is located in the partitions. However, one of the slaves will be quite busy scanning the first 9/13 partition because all the data is concentrated in one area. However, because the other slaves returned quickly, they now can start to receive the 3/13 partitions that contain the bulk of the data. This will help keep all the slaves busy until all the partitions are scanned. Therefore, it is apparent that distributing your I/O and data can help maximize the performance of parallel query.

In the 9-3-1 approach, the Query Coordinator (QC) would generate the row id ranges, and then issue each slave a range of row ids to process. The row id ranges could not span partition and extent boundaries. Adjacent extents could be collapsed so that a contiguous set of row id ranges would be issued to the slaves. However, if a table was partitioned and consisted of many small size extents, which is very typical for tables partitioned into a large number of partitions, a 9 size chunk or a 3 size chunk could not be generated. So often, 1 size chunks would be issued to the slaves.

In Oracle8*i*, a new granule algorithm is used to generate row id ranges, and the row id range generator is no longer constrained by extent boundaries. The new algorithm handles data skew (extent and partition) better than the 9-3-1 algorithm.

6.18   MAXIMIZING PARALLEL QUERY PERFORMANCE

The parallel query option provides an extremely fast mechanism to perform large table scans, sorts, joins, and index builds. To maximize the performance of the parallel query option, it is important that your I/O be tuned so that each parallel query slave receives an equal amount of work. This prevents an uneven distribution in which some slaves are scanning large partitions, and other slaves are scanning much smaller partitions. When you build large tables, try to size each table extent near in size. Doing so will ensure that partition sizes are evenly distributed to each parallel query slave. This allows a parallel query slave to complete its work in roughly the same amount of time as the other slaves. However, this is highly dependent on the level of striping and data distribution. You can maximize the performance of the parallel query option by distributing and striping the Oracle data files evenly and by sizing object extents equally to prevent an uneven parallel query workload.

6.18.1 CONFIGURING THE NUMBER OF PARALLEL SLAVES

The `init.ora` parameters `parallel_min_servers`, `parallel_max_servers`, and `parallel_server_idle_time` specify the minimum number of parallel query slaves started upon instance startup, the maximum number of query slaves that can be started, and the period of time that a parallel query slave can be idle (in minutes) before it is shut down, respectively. To reduce startup time overhead, set `parallel_min_servers` to the number of parallel query slaves that will be used in the data warehouse. Ensure that your system has sufficient memory to handle the parallel query slave processes. The `init.ora` parameter `optimizer_percent_parallel` specifies the amount of parallelism to be used in computing CBO cost estimates. A value of 0 means that the objects' degree of parallelism is not considered when computing the cost. A value of 100 means that the objects' degree of parallelism is used when computing the cost of a full-table scan. The `init.ora` parameter `parallel_min_percent` specifies the minimum number of query slaves that must be available to execute a parallel query. For example, if set to 50 (i.e., 50 percent), and a parallel query with a degree of parallelism of ten is specified, at least five slaves must be available. If not, the query terminates, and an error is returned.

6.18.2 CONTENTION FOR THE PARALLEL QUERY SLAVES

To determine if your system is experiencing contention for parallel query slaves, you can query the `v$pq_sysstat` view as follows.

```
SQL> select *
       from v$pq_sysstat
       order by statistic
```

STATISTIC	VALUE
DFO Trees	24
DML Initiated	1
Distr Msgs Recv'd	0
Distr Msgs Sent	0
Local Msgs Recv'd	810
Local Msgs Sent	681

```
Queries Initiated        22
Server Sessions          60
Servers Busy              3
Servers Cleaned Up        0
Servers Highwater        17
Servers Idle              5
Servers Shutdown         58
Servers Started          66
Sessions Active           1
```

These statistics show minimal contention for query slaves since `Servers Busy` is three. If `Servers Busy` were high, you would need to increase the value of `parallel_max_servers`. If increasing `parallel_max_servers`, you may also have to increase the amount of concurrent processes (`MAXUP`) per user, as well as the total number of processes (`NPROC`) in the operating system kernel. Refer to Chapter 2 for specific information on increasing the OS process kernel limits. You should also monitor the views `v$pq_sesstat` and `v$pq_slave`. The `v$pq_sesstat` view provides parallel query statistics at the session level while parallel queries are in progress. The `v$pq_slave` view provides statistics such as processor utilization and messaging statistics at the parallel query slave level. The `v$pq_slave` can help you determine if certain slaves are busier than others.

6.18.3 TUNING THE MESSAGE POOL

When interparallelism is used such as a hash join between two tables whereby one set of slaves is scanning the data while another set of slaves is consuming the data and processing the hash join, messages are sent between the slaves during parallel execution. The Oracle8 `init.ora` parameters `parallel_min_message_pool`, and `parallel_execution _message_size` (added in 8.0.4) specify the size of the minimum amount of memory allocated at startup time from the shared pool to be used for parallel execution messages and the size of each message, respectively. When `parallel_min_servers` is greater than zero, explicitly setting `parallel_min_message_pool` improves performance since memory is allocated in a contiguous section. Before setting `parallel_min_ message_pool`, you should review the statistics from the `v$pq_sysstat` view. The `v$pq_sysstat` view reports the number of messages sent and received both local and distributed messages. This gives you an idea as to the amount of message pool memory that will be required based on your workload. Also, be careful not to set `parallel_ min_message_pool` so high that a memory shortage occurs in the shared pool.

The `parallel_execution_message_size` parameter specifies the size of the message used during parallel execution. The default is 2148 bytes. The default is sufficient for most applications, however, if there is a high amount of messaging occurring, increasing the parameter from its default can improve parallel execution performance. For data warehousing systems that heavily utilize parallel query and parallel execution messaging, setting `parallel_execution_message_size=8192` or `parallel_execution_message_size=16384` results in performance gains of 15–20 percent. A larger message size results in more data being passed in a fewer number of messages. A larger setting for `parallel_execution_message_size` requires more memory for the message pool since the messages are of larger size. Therefore, if increasing the value of the parameter `parallel_execution_message_size`, you may also need to adjust the size of the message pool (`parallel_min_message_pool`) and the size of the shared pool (`shared_pool_size`). Measure the performance gains of your system when adjusting the size of `parallel_execution_message_size` to determine the optimal setting for your environment.

In Oracle8, parallel query allocated parallel execution message buffers from the shared pool. For environments where parallel query and parallel DML (PDML) are frequently used, contention for the shared pool could occur. In Oracle8*i*, parallel execution buffers can be allocated from the large pool heap. Using the large pool heap helps reduce contention for the shared pool. This also allows DBAs to more effectively size the shared pool for the library and data dictionary caches and separately size the large pool for the parallel execution message buffers.

6.18.4 PARALLEL QUERY OPTIMIZATIONS

Oracle8 release 8.0.4 enhances the performance and scalability of parallel query. The performance of parallel query is dependent on many different factors, one of which is the degree of parallelism. Typically, the degree of parallelism is tuned for a single user or a few users. When the number of users increases, contention surfaces and the performance of parallel query degrades. A new `init.ora` parameter `parallel_adaptive_multi_user` provides a mechanism to tune parallel query for multi-user environments. If `parallel_adaptive_multi_user=TRUE`, the degree of parallelism is automatically reduced based on the current number of active parallel query users. This uses an adaptive algorithm to reduce the amount of parallelism based on the degree of parallelism specified by the table or hint divided by the total number of parallel query users. The adaptive algorithm assumes that the degree of parallelism has been tuned for a single-user environment.

Another parallel query enhancement added to Oracle8 improves the performance of hash and merge-joins when a result set of a very large table is being joined with a result set of a very small table. The `init.ora` parameter `parallel_broadcast_enabled`, when set to `TRUE`, causes the optimizer to broadcast via a single table queue the row sources of the small result set to each of the parallel query slaves that are processing the rows of the large set. This improves the performance of the join.

The `init.ora` parameters `parallel_adaptive_multi_user`, `parallel_automatic_tuning`, and `parallel_threads_per_cpu` can be used to tune parallel query. The parameter `parallel_adaptive_multi_user` specifies whether or not the adaptive algorithm for reducing the requested degree of parallelism based on the current number of active PQ users should be enabled. The parameter `parallel_automatic` `_tuning` specifies whether the Oracle server should employ automatic parallel tuning in conjunction with the parameter `parallel_adaptive_multi_user`. The parameter `parallel_threads_per_cpu` specifies the default degree of parallelism. The views `v$px_session` and `v$px_sesstat` provide parallel execution statistics for all active sessions using parallel execution. The `v$pq_sesstat` view also reflects the effect of the multiuser and adaptive algorithms on the slaves allocated to an active session.

6.19 PARALLEL DML

Oracle8 provided the ability to parallelize DML statements such as inserts, updates, and deletes. This helps improve the performance of DML operations in data warehousing environments where data needs to be updated or deleted from large size tables. You can specify the degree of parallelism via a hint or by setting the degree of parallelism at the table level via the `CREATE` or `ALTER TABLE` commands. Parallel DML avoids the traditional technique of parallelizing updates, deletes, and inserts by establishing multiple sessions with each session specifying a range of key values. Parallel DML allows you to submit a single DML statement within a single transaction and have the DML statement automatically parallelized. In an Oracle Parallel Server (OPS) environment, parallel DML affinity is managed by the Oracle server. Oracle employs a partition to device mapping to allocate parallel slave processes to a specific partition, thus allowing OPS to utilize resources across multiple instances. Parallel DML does not require user knowledge of data (partition) affinity distribution.

Parallel insert uses a direct-load insert, meaning that the data is inserted into new blocks and then merged with the table. This is similar to the way SQL*Loader direct path works. The `APPEND` hint is the default behavior for direct-load insert which means that new blocks are appended to the table. The `APPEND` hint causes more space to be used but results in a faster insert operation. You can use the `NOAPPEND` hint to override the default `APPEND` mode. The `NOAPPEND` hint causes the default storage management algorithm to be utilized to hold the new rows to be inserted. The following is an example of a parallel insert direct-load statement.

```
SQL> insert /*+ APPEND PARALLEL (tsales,4) */
            into tsales
        select /*+ FULL (s) PARALLEL (s,4) */
            * from sales s;
```

The following is the explain plan for the above parallel insert statement. The explain plan shows that both the insert and the select operations are being parallelized.

ID	EXPLAIN_PLAN	POSITION
0	INSERT STATEMENT	1
1	PARTITION CONCATENATED :Q53000	1
	PARALLEL_COMBINED_WITH_PARENT NUMBER(1) NUMBER(4)	
2	TABLE ACCESS FULL SALES :Q53000	1
	PARALLEL_TO_SERIAL NUMBER(1) NUMBER(4)	

You can also use parallel DML to parallelize update and delete statements. However, parallelizing update and delete statements requires that the tables be partitioned. The parallelism for delete and update statements is done at the partition level. Therefore, there is no advantage in specifying a degree of parallelism higher than the number of partitions. The following is an example of a parallel update and a parallel delete statement.

```
SQL> update /*+ PARALLEL (sales,4) */
     sales
     set sale_no=sale_no + 1000
     where (week_no <= 21);

SQL> delete /*+ PARALLEL (sales,4) */
     sales
     where (week_no between 1 and 40);
```

To explicitly enable parallel DML at the session level, you must issue the following statement as the first statement in the transaction.

```
SQL> alter session enable parallel dml;
```

You can also explicitly disable parallel DML at the session level by issuing the following command.

```
SQL> alter session disable parallel dml;
```

In Oracle8 release 8.0.3, the use of parallel DML required you to issue either a commit or rollback following the parallel DML statement within your transaction. No other statements could be issued following a parallel DML statement except for either a rollback or commit. As of 8.0.4, you can issue multiple parallel DML, serial DML, or other query operations within a transaction following a parallel DML statement. The only caveat is that you cannot access the same table in the same transaction after modifying it in parallel. In addition, as of 8.0.4 now maintains local and global indexes during parallel insert operations are automatically maintained.

Parallel DML is extremely useful for reducing the time it takes to modify large tables. In addition to distributing file I/O, you should also size and distribute your rollback segments appropriately. Each parallel slave transaction can be assigned to different rollback segments and this is likely given the fact that Oracle will attempt to load balance when assigning transactions to rollback segments. Therefore it is important that you have a sufficient number of rollback segments so as to minimize parallel slave transaction contention for rollback segments. You should also make sure that the rollback segments are sized properly since long-running transactions may require a large amount of rollback segment space. Also, rollback segments should be equal in size when using parallel DML since you cannot be certain which rollback segments get assigned to which parallel slave transactions. If they are not equal in size, certain parallel slave transactions may have enough space in their assigned rollback segment while other rollback segments may not. The statistic `DML Initiated` from the `v$pq_sysstat` view reports the number of DML statements that were initiated. The statistic `DML Parallelized` from the `v$pq_sesstat` view reports the number of DML statements parallelized within the session. You can monitor these statistics to determine the amount of parallel DML activity on your system.

In choosing the degree of parallelism for parallel DML operations, you should consider the degree of data distribution, number of processors, amount of available memory, number of disks and controllers, and amount of concurrency of other users performing parallel query or parallel DML operations. For parallel update or delete operations, you should constrain the degree of parallelism by the total number of partitions. Monitor disk, processor, memory, rollback segment, and parallel slave utilization to determine the optimal degrees of parallelism. Use the guidelines presented in section 6.16 to help determine the optimal degree of parallelism.

6.20   INDEX ONLY TABLES

Oracle8 provided the ability to create index only tables. An index only table has all the table data stored in the index. In data warehousing environments, a DBA often creates many indexes to improve query plan execution so as to avoid full-table scans. However, this can be expensive in terms of the disk storage space required to hold both the table and the additional indexes. The index only table allows you to build a table of the index, meaning that you do not need to store all the table data. This conserves space and improves the performance of DML operations such as inserts, deletes, and updates because only the index needs to be updated. Index only tables store the data as a standard Oracle B*-tree index. Index only tables are useful for data warehousing and OLAP environments, information retrieval applications, and spatial and GIS applications.

To create an index only table, you simply need to add the `ORGANIZATION INDEX` clause to the `CREATE TABLE` statement. For example,

```
SQL>   create table bookindex
         (book_id number(8),
          book_title varchar2(30),
          author_name varchar2(30),
          book_description varchar2(2000),
          constraint bookindex_pk
            primary key (book_id))
         organization index
         tablespace tsbook
         pctthreshold 20
         overflow tablespace tsbook_overflow;
```

In this example, an index only table is created to store information on books. The primary key for the table is the `book_id` column. The PCTTHRESHOLD option allows you to specify an overflow area. In this example, for the rows that are larger than 20 percent of the block size, the nonkey columns of those rows will be stored in the overflow tablespace (`tsbook_overflow`). The overflow area option is useful for situations where large rows are resulting in slow full-index scans. When an overflow area is specified, the index contains only the key value and a pointer to the columns in the overflow area. The IOT_TYPE column of the USER_TABLES view has a value of IOT for index only tables and is set to NULL for all other tables. You can use standard DML operations, direct path insert, SQL*Loader, Export, and Import on index only tables.

The INCLUDING clause of the IOT creation should be used to specify which columns should be included in the primary key segment along with the primary key columns. If the row lengths are fairly small, and the IOT is not often updated, then you should include all the columns making up the IOT. However, if the row lengths are fairly long or you have some columns such as VARCHAR2(2000) or VARCHAR2(4000), which are mostly populated, then you should include those columns which are searched on or specified as filters in the query.

In Oracle8*i*, index only tables were extended to allow support for range partitioning and secondary indexes. In Oracle8*i*, the universal `rowid` was added in order to facilitate secondary index creation on index only tables. Hence, you can create indexes similar to a regular table index on columns of the IOT. Also, in Oracle8*i*, you can range partition an index only table.

6.21 REVERSE KEY INDEXES

Oracle8 provided the ability to create reverse key indexes. Reverse key indexes reverse the bytes of each indexed column for the exception of `rowid` and still maintain the column order. Reverse key indexes are useful for when specific index blocks are extremely hot due to the organization of the keys and in Oracle Parallel Server (OPS) environments. In certain cases, concurrent updates to a table may result in contention for index blocks due to the organization of the index key. Sessions may wait on the event `buffer busy waits` because the index key is such that concurrent updates to different rows are resulting in a lot of sessions touching the same set of index blocks. In such a case, a reverse key index can be used to redistribute the rows in the index such that data is more evenly distributed across the index blocks, and buffer busy waits are reduced.

In an OPS environment, modifications to indexes are focused on a small set of leaf blocks. Reversing the keys of the index allows insertions to be distributed across all the leaf keys in the index. Reverse key indexes prevent queries from performing an index range scan since lexically adjacent keys are not stored next to each other. Reverse key indexes can also be used in situations where users insert ascending values and delete lower values from the table, thus helping to prevent skewed indexes. To create a reverse key index, simply add the keyword `REVERSE` to the `CREATE INDEX` statement. For example,

```
SQL>     create index tsales_index
         on tsales (week_no,sale_no)
         reverse;
```

6.22 INTER-NODE PARALLEL QUERY

Oracle Parallel Server 7.3 introduced the Internode Parallel Query (IPQ) feature. IPQ enables multiple nodes in the parallel server cluster to each execute a query in parallel. This means not only that a query can be executed in parallel on a single node, but also that the query can be executed in parallel across several nodes. This helps make use of all the nodes' processors and disks by distributing the workload across the nodes. To enable IPQ, set the Oracle7 `init.ora` parameter `use_internode_pqo=TRUE`. For example, if each node in the cluster has six processors and the table is very large, you can distribute the query by allowing six slaves to be created on each node. This is much faster than having only six slaves execute on only one machine. Oracle Parallel Server (OPS) handles the creation of the IPQ slaves as well as the communication among the IPQ slaves.

In Oracle8 and Oracle8*i*, the `init.ora` parameter `use_internode_pqo` has been made obsolete. However, you can achieve the same result by setting the value of `INSTANCES` in the parallel settings for the table or index. You can also specify the value of `INSTANCES` via the `PARALLEL` hint. The syntax for the `PARALLEL` hint is `PARALLEL` (table *tdegree idegree*). The *tdegree* is the degree of parallelism used for the table, and the *idegree* is the degree of parallelism used across the instances. The following is an example of setting the value of `INSTANCES`.

```
SQL> alter table customer parallel (degree 10 instances 4);
```

In this example, a degree of parallelism for the table is set to ten, and the degree of parallelism across the instances is set to four. You can also set the value of the `init.ora` parameter `parallel_default_max_instances` which specifies the default degree of parallelism to be used for cross-instance parallelism. The setting for `parallel_default_max_instances` is used if the value of `INSTANCES` in the parallel settings for the table or index is set to the keyword `DEFAULT`.

6.23   ORACLE8*i* ANALYTICAL FUNCTIONS

Oracle8*i* provides a new set of analytical SQL functions to perform such functions as `ROLLUP`, `NTILE`, and `RANK`. In addition, Oracle8*i* provides windowing, reporting, and statistical functions which can be used to perform OLAP functions. The Oracle8*i* analytical functions are built into the server; hence, the performance of these functions is far superior to third-party products, which typically use a middle-tier product and application code to provide similar analytical functionality.

The new Oracle8*i* analytical functions can be used to simplify complex code by referencing the analytical functions directly in the SQL statement. Using the native analytical functions avoids multiple passes of the data, which would typically be needed in order to implement the same functionality in the application. In addition, the analytical functions avoid having to code procedure logic, such as PL/SQL, to prepare OLAP-like reports.

The `CASE` operator is one example of the new Oracle8*i* SQL extensions. The `CASE` operator can be used to pivot within a dataset and aggregate values based on certain conditions. For example, consider the following query which pivots on the `ORDER_DATE`.

```
select inventory_item_id AS ITEM,organization_id
      AS ORG,order_type,
      count(case when to_char(order_date,'MON-YYYY')='JAN-2000'
      then 1 else null end) as JAN2000_CNT,
      count(case when to_char(order_date,'MON-YYYY')='FEB-2000'
      then 1 else null end) as FEB2000_CNT,
      count(case when to_char(order_date,'MON-YYYY')='MAR-2000'
      then 1 else null end) as MAR2000_CNT
FROM MSC_DEMANDS
group by inventory_item_id,organization_id,order_type

SAMPLE OUTPUT:
```

ITEM	ORG	ORDER	JAN2000_CNT	FEB2000_CNT	MAR2000_CNT
101	1	INT	10	8	6
102	2	EXT	10	8	6

For more information on the Analytical functions, refer to the *Oracle8i Data Warehousing Guide*.

MEDIA RECOVERY

As databases continue to grow in size, the task of backing up the database can become tedious and time consuming. There are many customer sites running hundreds of gigabyte- and terabyte-size databases in production. Backing up a very large database of several hundred gigabytes or even a terabyte is an enormous task that requires careful thought and precision planning. The slightest mistake can invalidate an entire backup. Not only are the logistics of backing up a very large database an issue, attaining a reasonable level of performance is also an issue that warrants legitimate concern. In some cases, backups that run slowly may still fit within the backup service time window. However, if you have to backup a 300 GB database and the system can only be down for a few hours, performance of the backup is critical. In many production sites, the database server must be available seven days a week, 24 hours a day with no down time. In this chapter, I offer recommendations based on my personal experience backing up and restoring large databases.

7.1 THE SYSTEM IS DOWN

If your system becomes unavailable due to some sort of hardware or software failure, it is important that you execute your recovery efforts carefully and thoroughly. First and foremost, do not panic. This will only make matters worse by possibly disrupting the proper sequence of events needed to recover the system. It is important that you study the situation in complete detail to determine the cause of the failure, the effects of the failure, and the set of possible solutions to the problem of recovering the system in the most efficient manner. Do not start by executing media recovery commands and scripts before you understand completely what happened, and which sections were affected.

When you deal with a down system, it is important that you work in a coordinated environment. You need to coordinate your efforts with the system administrator, database administrator, and network administrator. The system administrator is responsible for administrating the hardware and the operating system (OS). The system administrator is able to brief others on the cause of the failure, and the subsequent effects. The database administrator, after being briefed by the system administrator, knows which sections of the database are affected from the system failure. Finally, the network administrator helps coordinate network backups and restores to ensure that the network is not taken off-line for administration purposes.

Even if your restores are performed locally (on the system itself), you may still need to coordinate your efforts with the network administrator in the event that your commands are being submitted remotely (across the network) from a workstation or another console. If the network is taken off-line for some reason, all your recovery work may be lost. In addition, the system may be left in a state of inconsistency if the restore terminated before successful completion.

It is also important that when backing up a system, you maintain a detailed catalog of the backup, including a list of the files backed up, date and time stamps, size of the files backed up, and type of backup (complete, incremental, etc.). Make sure that backup tapes are kept in a safe and secure area. Also, ensure that each tape is properly labeled. Most mission-critical sites have a tape vault (or a secure area for tapes) as well as a tape management system to catalog tapes.

Restoration of a down system requires precise and attentive steps to bring the system back on-line. Therefore, it is important that at a minimum you follow the recommendations made previously to help ensure a smooth backup and restore. Despite the famous system administration claim *the best backup is the one that never needs to be used,* your system may fail and proper steps need to be taken to ensure that the system and data are restored in the shortest time possible.

7.2   SYSTEM ARCHITECTURE

It is vital that you design a complete system architecture to handle the tasks of backing up and restoring your systems. The architecture needs to consider such things as

- ❏ Amount of data to be backed up per system
- ❏ Service time window for each backup
- ❏ Can the system be taken off-line?
- ❏ Media device data transfer speeds
- ❏ Network data transfer speeds

❑ Performance requirements

❑ Multiplatform issues

❑ Version control system

❑ Tape management system

❑ Permissions required for the backup and/or restore

❑ Off-line and on-line backups

❑ Complete, incremental, and cumulative backup

❑ Multiple task (scripts) dependencies

The architecture must address issues such as the service time window in which the backup needs to complete, multiplatform issues if a heterogeneous environment of different hardware and software platforms is to be backed up, and the tape management system. Architectural design must be a coordinated effort between database, system, and network administrators, as well as with end users. Working closely with the end users helps administrators to better understand the end users' backup and restore requirements. It also provides end users with a complete understanding of the tasks and subtasks involved when systems are backed up or restored. This informs the end user of the time that is required to perform each task as well as the dependencies between tasks. Often, when a system becomes unavailable, end users contact the system or database administrator constantly during the restoration process and ask, "What is taking so long? Why is the system still down?" Explaining the backup and restore process to the end user completely can help to reduce end users' level of frustration as well as misunderstanding.

You should use a version control system to manage backup and restore scripts as part of the backup and restore architecture. This helps to maintain a repository of the backup and restore scripts as well as any changes that are made to the scripts. Using the version control system helps coordinate system administration efforts, especially in a situation in which multiple system administrators manage the same environment.

In addition to the version control system, you should thoroughly comment all of your backup and restore scripts (line by line). Your scripts may be run by someone other than you, and the comments you make in the scripts can help the person who runs the script to better understand each step. The comments also help you to remember the purpose and the logic underlying the script in the event that future changes are necessary.

7.3 HARDWARE REQUIREMENTS

The design of a complete backup and restore architecture is highly dependent on the hardware configuration of your environment. To backup a very large database, you must have a multiprocessor system with an appropriate number of high-speed backup devices (tape drives). To obtain optimal backup and restore performance, you must configure an appropriate number of backup devices so that backups and restores can proceed in parallel. If your environment consists of very large databases, you must choose the right number of backup devices as well as the right type of backup device, such as an autoloader or jukebox. For large system configurations, you need to implement a backup and recovery system that is fully automated, fast, and reliable. An automated system reduces the tedious manual effort required to load tapes and start backups and/or restores. A fast system enables you to backup and restore large quantities of data in a small period of time. The new backup and recovery systems often multiplex the workload and thereby substantially reduce the time needed to complete the backup and/or restore.

7.4 SELECTING THE BACKUP AND RECOVER TOOLS

Implementing a complete backup and recovery system requires that you select both the appropriate type of backup system as well as the number of backup devices. For example, trying to backup a 500 GB database on a Sun Enterprise 6000 using a single, or even a few, 8-mm 5 GB external tape drives is impractical and will take an enormous amount of time. It is critical that you choose the correct number of backup devices in addition to the type of backup system.

Before you select the number of backup devices, you need to obtain a complete set of backup and restore tools for your environment. If you run a heterogeneous environment, you will need a tool that supports multiple platforms. You may also need the capability to perform network-based backups. There are many backup and restore tools available. When you select a tool, try to select it based on the following criteria.

- ❏ Complete backup and restore catalog system
- ❏ Database support (preferably native)
- ❏ Automated (scheduled) backups and restores
- ❏ Ability to schedule events
- ❏ Distributed capabilities
- ❏ Backups and restores are parallelized
- ❏ Supports file systems and raw devices
- ❏ Supports complete, incremental, and cumulative backups
- ❏ Supports on-line and off-line backups
- ❏ Multiplatform support
- ❏ Supports a wide variety of tape media devices
- ❏ Tool maintains a high level of performance
- ❏ Easy to use and easy to configure
- ❏ GUI functionality (browser interface)

Selecting a backup and restore tool based on the above criteria enables you to manage your environment smoothly and flexibly.

The tool should enable you to perform network-based and distributed backups, possibly from one server to another. The tool should parallelize backups and restores. This can make a magnitude of a difference for large databases and large system backups. The tool can significantly reduce the amount of time needed to perform a backup and/or restore by utilizing multiple processors and multiple tape drives. It is also important that the tool you choose supports both file systems and raw devices. Raw devices are commonly used with large databases to achieve a high level of performance. Therefore, the tool must be able to backup and restore both file system-based files as well as raw devices.

The tool should also support the different levels of backup, such as complete, incremental, and cumulative. If you manage a heterogeneous environment, it is also imperative that the tool support multiple platforms. This avoids you having to use many different tools to manage your environment. In fact, choosing a tool that enables you to manage your entire environment from a single console is the ideal choice for a heterogeneous environment. Try to choose a tool that is easy to use and configure. Some tools are extremely complicated and require too much technical knowledge to be implemented. Keep in mind that the backup and restore tool may have to be used by persons other than yourself who may not have as much detailed knowledge of your systems. You should also choose a tool that uses a catalog and thereby enables you to search the catalog quickly without having to scan the entire tape for the existence of a file.

There are several backup and restore tools that you can use to manage your environment. Sun provides the Solstice Backup tool. The Sun Solstice Backup tool is basically a rebundle of the Legato Networker backup product. Legato's Networker product provides a tremendous amount of functionality. In addition, Legato provides an Oracle database module that performs Oracle database backups and restores. EMC provides the Epoch Enterprise Backup tool that also allows you to backup your Oracle databases.

7.5   CONFIGURING AND SIZING THE MEDIA DEVICES

Selection of the backup device type depends on the amount of data you need to backup. For example, purchasing an expensive autoloader or jukebox when you only need to backup less than 1 GB is overkill. By the same token, using a few tape drives to backup a several hundred gigabyte database is less than adequate. The most popular backup media device seems to be the DLT drives. The DLT 4700 is an autoloader tape backup device that allows up to seven DLT cartridges with each cartridge having a maximum capacity of 20 GB (40 GB compressed). This allows a single DLT 4700 autoloader to backup 140 GB (280 GB compressed) of data. The Quantum DLT 8000 uses a past-wide SCSI-2 connection that can yield a data transfer rate of 6 MB per second. There are other tape backup device vendors that also provide autoloaders and tape libraries. When you select the type of backup device, make sure that tape loads are automatic so that your backup and restore can be automated, thereby eliminating the need for someone to manually load tapes.

It is important that you try to obtain a tape media device with the highest data transfer rate. This increases the performance of your backups and restores. Also, try at least to match the data transfer rate of the tape media system with your disk I/O subsystem. For example, if your disk I/O subsystem has a 20 MB per second (fast-wide differential SCSI) maximum data transfer rate, selecting a tape media device of 5 MB per second will not enable you to maximize the performance of your I/O subsystem. In this case, you will need to synchronize the disk I/O subsystem transfer rate with the tape media system in order to avoid saturation of the tape media device. Disk I/O subsystems are constantly improving, and as more of the disk I/O subsystem vendors move toward a fiber optic-oriented design, data transfer rates are likely to increase to 100 MB per second. Therefore, it is important that the tape media device be synchronized with the disk I/O subsystem so that the utilization of the system is maximized.

In order to choose the optimal number of backup media devices, you need to consider your backup window as well as the data transfer rates of the media devices. For example, suppose the average data transfer rate for a given media device is 10 GB per hour. If you need to backup your 400 GB database in at most two hours, you will need a minimum of 20 of these media devices, each offering you 10 GB per hour. Of course, this assumes that the system can handle this many media devices running concurrently while the 10 GB per hour average throughput is maintained. The reality of the situation is that having this many devices on a single system that perform backups simultaneously will more than likely saturate the SCSI bus and the central bus. For this reason, you may need to distribute your backup devices such that the 20 backup devices are distributed evenly across two or three systems rather than a single system. The optimal number of tape media devices that should be attached to a single system depends on the number of available processors on the system. For example, if your system has ten processors, try not to configure or attach more than ten or fifteen tape drives or tape media systems to the system. Backups and restores can be CPU-intensive operations when compression is used. Therefore, to maximize performance and processor utilization, try to balance the number of tape drives with the number of available processors. This helps to avoid CPU saturation and helps prevent backup and restore processes from waiting for long periods of time for an available processor. This also improves the utilization of the tape drive because each processor can service a separate tape drive.

7.6   EXPORT AND THE BUFFER OPTION

You can use the Oracle Export (EXP) utility to export data from an Oracle database, or to perform a backup of the database. You can reduce the amount of time it takes to export the data from the database by using the BUFFER option of the EXP utility. The BUFFER option defines the size (in bytes) of the data array. The array is used to perform an array fetch from the database and allows a larger number of rows to be returned at each fetch. Using the array fetch feature by increasing the value of the BUFFER parameter can reduce the SQL parse and call overhead of the EXP process. It can also increase CPU utilization and I/O throughput. The following is an example of how to use the Export BUFFER option.

```
#####################################
#Name: exparray.par
#Sample Export Parameter File
#Using the Array/Buffer Option
#
#####################################
USERID=test/test
FULL=N
BUFFER=10485760      # Set Buffer Size to 10MB
FILE=exparray.DMP
TABLES=(ACCOUNT,ORDERS,PARTS)
COMPRESS=N
GRANTS=Y
INDEXES=Y
ROWS=Y
CONSTRAINTS=Y
LOG=exparray.log
```

This Export parameter option file shows the use of the BUFFER option. To use the parameter file, invoke the Export utility and specify the name of the parameter file as follows.

```
myhost> exp parfile=exparray.par
```

If your system has plenty of memory, you can use the BUFFER option to substantially accelerate exports. On the other hand, if your system does not have sufficient memory, or your system experiences memory shortages, setting BUFFER to too high a value can increase paging and possibly cause swapping. On a system that has sufficient free memory, values of 5 MB or 10 MB are reasonable for the export BUFFER parameter and offer optimal performance for large exports. If you are performing a large export, it is better to execute multiple smaller exports rather than one large export. This helps parallelize the exports and reduces the overall time that is needed to export the database objects. You should monitor the SGA and system memory utilization while running exports to determine if the value you selected for BUFFER is optimal.

7.7 THE DIRECT EXPORT OPTION

Oracle 7.3 introduced a new direct export option that enables exports to read the data directly from the database and avoid the evaluation buffer. The direct export option also helps reduce the number of data copies. Figure 7.1 illustrates the difference between the direct export path and the conventional export path.

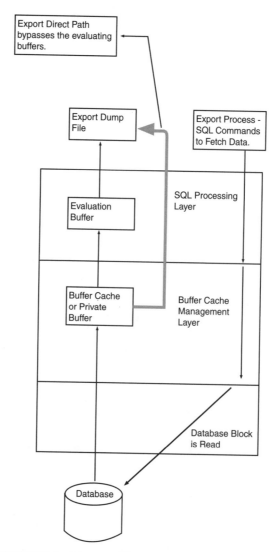

FIGURE 7.1   Direct and conventional export paths.

Figure 7.1 shows the traditional export path as well as the direct path that avoids the evaluation buffer. Avoiding the buffer evaluation enables the export to read from the database directly. This reduces the overhead of the SGA and SQL call interface. To use the direct export option, you must ensure that the catexp.sql script has been run on your database. The catexp.sql script is located in the $ORACLE_HOME/rdbms/admin directory. You can use the direct export option by specifying the DIRECT=Y option when you invoke the export utility. The following is an example export parameter file that uses the direct export option.

```
#####################################
#Name: expdirect.par
#Sample Export Parameter File
#Using the Direct Option
#
#####################################
USERID=test/test
FULL=N
DIRECT=Y
FILE=exparray.DMP
TABLES=(ACCOUNT,ORDERS,PARTS)
COMPRESS=N
GRANTS=Y
INDEXES=Y
ROWS=Y
CONSTRAINTS=Y
LOG=exparray.log
```

This example export parameter file shows the direct option being used (DIRECT=Y). Also, because the direct path option avoids the buffer evaluation, the BUFFER parameter has no affect. The BUFFER parameter is used with the conventional path to specify the array fetch size. Exporting large databases with the direct option can increase the performance of the export up to 100 percent.

7.8 IMPORT AND THE BUFFER OPTION

The Oracle Import (IMP) utility is used to import data from an Oracle Export file (using the Oracle Export utility) into the Oracle database. Importing large objects or large files can often take a long period of time. For this reason, you can utilize the BUFFER option to specify the size of the import insert array. You can reduce the amount of time it takes to import the data into the database by using the BUFFER and COMMIT option of the IMP utility. The BUFFER option defines the size (in bytes) of the data array. The array is populated by reading the size of BUFFER bytes from the export file into the array. The import then performs an array insert into the database. You should also use the COMMIT=Y option to ensure that commits are performed at each array insert. Otherwise, your rollback space requirements will increase as the load continues. This allows a larger number of rows to be inserted at each insert call. To specify the size of the import buffer, you can use the import command to specify the name of an import parameter file. The following is an example of the import BUFFER option using an import parameter file to specify the size of the buffer.

```
####################################
#Name: imparray.par
#Sample Import Parameter File
#Using the Array/Buffer Option
#
####################################
USERID=test/test
FULL=N
BUFFER=10485760        #Set buffer to 10MB
FILE=export.DMP
SHOW=N
TABLES=(ACCOUNT,ORDERS)
IGNORE=Y
GRANTS=Y
INDEXES=Y
COMMIT=Y
ROWS=Y
LOG=imparray.log

myhost> imp parfile=imparray.par
```

Using the array insert feature by increasing the value of the BUFFER parameter can reduce the SQL parse and call overhead of the IMP process. It can also increase CPU utilization and I/O throughput. Importing large export files into the database using a large BUFFER and the COMMIT=Y option have resulted in performance gains of 50–100 percent. To reduce the amount of time needed to import objects, use the BUFFER option and invoke multiple imports to help parallelize the imports. If you have a multiprocessor system with a large amount of memory, starting multiple imports with each import using the BUFFER option can decrease the total import time by parallelizing the imports and using the array insert option.

7.9   EXPORTING AND IMPORTING BY PARTITION

Oracle8 and Oracle8i allow you to export and import tables at the partition level. This can be used to parallelize exports and imports by invoking multiple sessions of exports or imports with each processing different partitions. This also helps reduce disk contention assuming each partition is separated from the other in terms of disk data distribution. Exporting at the partition level can also help you deal with the export file size limit. Instead of exporting the entire table, you can export the individual partitions. The following is an example of an export by partition using an export parameter file.

```
####################################
#Name: exppart.par
#Sample Export Parameter File
#Exporting by Partition
#The syntax for exporting by table partition
#is TABLE:PARTITION
####################################
USERID=prod/prod
FULL=N
DIRECT=Y
FILE=exppart.DMP
TABLES=(SALES:SALES_W2)
COMPRESS=N
GRANTS=Y
INDEXES=Y
ROWS=Y
CONSTRAINTS=Y
LOG=exppart.log
```

You can also import by partition by specifying the name of the partition in the TABLES clause. The following is an example of an import by partition.

```
####################################
#Name: imppart.par
#Sample Import Parameter File
#Importing by Partition
#The syntax for importing by partition
#is TABLE:PARTITION
####################################
USERID=prod/prod
FULL=N
FILE=exppart.DMP
TABLES=(SALES:SALES_W2)
IGNORE=Y
GRANTS=Y
INDEXES=Y
ROWS=Y
LOG=imppart.log
```

Importing by partition also allows you to parallelize the import of a large table by invoking multiple sessions of import, each processing a distinct and disjoint partition. The import by partition option is extremely useful for large size tables when used in conjunction with the export by partition option.

7.10   EXPORT/IMPORT AND THE 2 GB FILE LIMIT

If you are exporting to a file system-based file, a single file cannot exceed 2 GB on most UNIX platforms. Oracle8 and Oracle 8*i* for HP-UX support large files for the Export and Import utilities. The 64-bit releases of Oracle8 and Oracle 8*i* also support large files. If your platform does not support large files and you need to export an object larger than 2 GB, you can export the object to tape. Therefore when you build export scripts, remember to divide the objects across multiple exports so that no single export dump file exceeds 2 GB. Also, if you have a single object that is larger than 2 GB, you should use some other technique to backup the object. You should use a backup and restore tool to backup large database objects. You can use the dd utility if your Oracle data files are on raw devices, or use a file system utility to backup the Oracle data files. When you use the dd or file system utility, the database must be shut down if it is running in noarchivelog mode. Backing up large databases using Export and Import is not often possible due to the limitations. For this reason, some sites have elected to use the Oracle7 Enterprise Backup Utility (EBU) or the Oracle8 Recovery Manager (RMAN).

7.11   EXPORTING DATA USING THE QUERY OPTION

Oracle8*i* provides the ability to export a subset of a table using the QUERY option, which is added as part of the export criteria for a table. This can be extremely useful for exporting a very large table because the table can be exported in ranges of its primary key using the QUERY clause of the Export command. The following is an example of using the QUERY clause of the Export utility to export a section of a table.

```
myhost> exp userid=ap/ap tables=ap_invoices_all \
          query=\"where invoice_id between 10000 and 20000\"
```

The above example exports the data from the AP_INVOICES_ALL table where the invoice_id is between 10,000 and 20,000. The QUERY clause can be used to export a large table into smaller chunks by executing parallel export streams each operating on a different range of rows.

7.12   ORACLE7 ENTERPRISE BACKUP UTILITY (EBU)

The Oracle7 Enterprise Backup Utility (EBU) offers users the ability to backup large databases in parallel. EBU works in conjunction with the tape media management software, such as Legato or Epoch, to parallelize the backup and/or restore. EBU cannot be used to backup an Oracle8 or Oracle 8*i* database, and EBU supports only Oracle7 databases. EBU provides the ability to perform hot and cold backups. EBU release 2.2 provides a GUI interface via the Oracle Enterprise Manager (OEM).

EBU uses tape management media software such as the Legato Oracle Database Module to perform the backups and restores of the Oracle database. The Legato Oracle Database Module provides a shared library (`libobk.so`) that EBU uses to perform the database backups and restores. EBU uses a separate database (other than the database that is being backed up) to store the backup catalog.

EBU enables the database administrator to parallelize backups and restores. If your system has multiple processors and multiple tape drives, you can increase significantly the performance of your backup and restore. EBU can spawn multiple processes to help parallelize the work of the restore or backup. EBU offers two different I/O models, the asynchronous I/O model and the shared memory model. For those model platforms that support both, the user can select either the asynchronous I/O model or the shared memory model by using the EBU parameter `use_io_model`. You can set `use_io_model=AIO` to direct EBU to use the asynchronous I/O model, or you can set `use_io_model=SHM` to employ the EBU shared memory model. Figure 7.2 illustrates the shared memory model architecture of EBU using a degree of parallelism of three.

In Figure 7.2, multiple processes are spawned to parallelize the backup or restore. The `ebu` is the main control process and spawns the instance manager process (`brd`). The `brio` processes handle the reads and writes of the disk and tape files. Multiple `brio` processes are spawned for each parallel I/O stream.

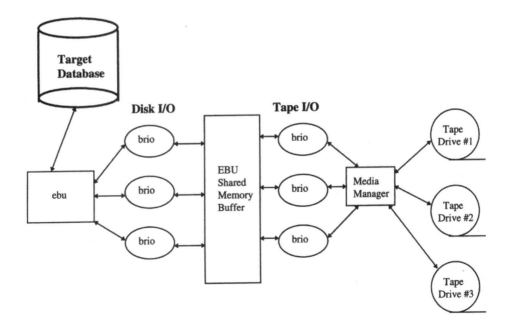

FIGURE 7.2   EBU shared memory model architecture.

EBU uses a shared memory buffer to improve the performance of backups and restores. Each disk `brio` process reads the database disk files and writes into the shared memory buffer. The tape `brio` processes then write the contents of the shared memory buffer out to the tape device via the media manager software. You can achieve high throughput backups and restores by tuning the degree of parallelism as well as the size of the shared buffer. EBU provides many parameters that you can set via the EBU parameter file. Table 7.1 shows the main EBU parameters affecting performance.

Each `brio` process allocates the size specified by `BUFFER_SIZE` for the shared memory buffer. Therefore, the total amount of shared memory allocated can be calculated as follows.

```
Total Shared Memory = (BUFFER_SIZE × db_block_size × NBRIO)
```

`NBRIO` refers to the number of `brio` processes. To increase the performance of EBU, set `parallel=<number of tape drives>`. This will maximize the performance of the backup and restore by parallelizing the backup and/or restore across all available tape drives. If you have more tape drives than you have processors available, try to set the parallel parameter so that you balance the number of available tape drives with the number of processors.

TABLE 7.1   EBU parameters

PARAMETER	DEFAULT	DESCRIPTION
PARALLEL	1	Degree of parallelism.
DISK_IO_SIZE	16	The number of database blocks read or written per disk I/O.
TAPE_IO_SIZE	32	The number of database blocks read or written per tape I/O.
BUFFER_SIZE	128	Size of the EBU shared memory buffer (specified in database blocks).

The following is an example EBU parameter file.

```
##EBU Sample Parameter File:
backup on-line
db_name="SALES"
oracle_sid="SALES"
tablespace = "ORDERS_TS"
parallel=5
log="/oracle7/obackup/log/obkSALES.log"
buffer_size=16384
tape_io_size=32
disk_io_size=16

## End of EBU Parameter file
```

In this example, a degree of parallelism of five is selected, and the database is backed up on-line (hot backup). The `ORDER_TS` tablespace is backed up. The output from obackup will be sent to the log file specified in the parameter file (`log="/oracle7/obackup/log/obkSALES.log"`).

7.12.1 EBU AND COLD BACKUPS

If you are performing a cold backup, meaning the database is shut down prior to starting the backup, you can create a large shared memory buffer. Because the database is shut down, the memory for the SGA and the Oracle database processes can instead be used by EBU. In this case, set `BUFFER_SIZE=<db_block_buffers> / (NBRIO)`. For example, if your `db_block_buffers=65536`, set `BUFFER_SIZE = ((65536) / (NBRIO))`. This optimally sizes the total EBU shared memory buffer in accordance with the degree of parallelism. Declaring a large shared memory buffer can increase the performance of EBU. The large shared memory buffer also minimizes wait time between the tape processes and disk processes. A large buffer allows enough space in which tape processes can be writing out buffers to the tape drives, while the disk reader processes can be writing data into the shared memory buffer. The `BUFFER_SIZE` parameter must be a power of two, and at least equal to the greater of the `DISK_IO_SIZE` and `TAPE_IO_SIZE` values.

7.12.2 EBU AND HOT BACKUPS

Performing a hot backup requires that the database be available and in archive log mode. Because the instance is running, the SGA may consume a large portion of the system's physical memory. In addition, database and user processes also may be using additional memory. Therefore, you will need to set `BUFFER_SIZE` to a much smaller value than the size recommended for a cold backup. If you are performing a hot backup, try to estimate the amount of free memory that is available on the system. This estimate should take into consideration future user connections and processes. Then set `BUFFER_SIZE` using the following recommendation.

$$BUFFER\_SIZE \ = \ \frac{(amount \ of \ free \ memory \ - \ free \ pool)}{(NBRIO) \times (db\_block\_size)}$$

The free pool is the amount of memory that should be left free for future processes and/or database connections. Recall that the `BUFFER_SIZE` parameter must be a power of two. For example, if your system has 2 GB of memory, and the existing SGA is 1 GB in size, you may consider setting the total EBU shared memory to 128 MB or 256 MB in order to allow sufficient memory for other user processes. The optimal setting for `BUFFER_SIZE` is highly dependent on your system configuration and system workload. You should start with the default setting and then continue to tune `BUFFER_SIZE` until EBU performance is maximized. It is important that you not degrade the performance of the SGA and the user processes when tuning EBU parameters for a hot backup.

7.12.3 DISK AND TAPE I/O SIZES

The defaults for DISK_IO_SIZE and TAPE_IO_SIZE are usually optimal; however, if your disk data files are striped, you can increase the value of DISK_IO_SIZE to allow more database blocks to be processed to disk per I/O. Similarly, if your tape drive system supports high-speed data transfer rates, you can increase the value of TAPE_IO_SIZE to allow more database blocks to be written to tape per I/O. If your database files are striped, you can set DISK_IO_SIZE = (stripe size) + (number of members in the stripe) in order to maximize EBU performance. This allows a single read to utilize all the physical disks in the stripe. For example, if your database block size is 8 KB and you have a striped volume that consists of six disks with a stripe size of 64 KB, set DISK_IO_SIZE=48 (384 KB). The optimal value of TAPE_IO_SIZE depends on the media manager software and tape management system being used. Each media manager software may have its own optimal I/O size for tape I/O operations. In general, you should set TAPE_IO_SIZE=DISK_IO_SIZE and tune DISK_IO_SIZE such that a single I/O utilizes all the disks in the stripe.

You can also increase backup performance by multiplexing different database files into a single Backup File Set (BPS). Multiplexing effectively integrates the database blocks from multiple database files into a single logical stream. Using the multiplexing feature can help increase disk throughput if each of the multiple database files are striped across different disks. To enable the multiplexing feature, use the EBU parameter mux to specify the database files to be multiplexed.

Compression may also reduce the stream throughput by not keeping the tape drives busy. Certain data may be more compressible than other data. In this case, there may be a throughput imbalance between certain tape drives processing files with high-compression ratios versus other tape drives processing files with low-compression ratios. Therefore, try to balance the mix of files in terms of compression ratios so that the overall compression ratio results in a medium-compression ratio.

If your platform supports both the shared memory model and asynchronous I/O model, you can set the parameter use_io_model=AIO to direct EBU to use the asynchronous I/O model (AIO). In the asynchronous I/O model, EBU uses the capabilities of the operating system to issue asynchronous I/O to disk. However, some operating systems may not support asynchronous I/O on database files residing on file systems. Irrespective of the I/O model used, the goal is to maximize the disk transfer rates and overall I/O throughput. By tuning the I/O size parameters and the number of I/O processes, you can maximize the performance of EBU as well as the disk and tape I/O throughput.

7.12.4 TUNING EBU PARAMETERS

The performance of EBU depends on the configuration of your database and system. You can achieve a high backup and restore throughput by tuning the database system and EBU appropriately. You should benchmark EBU extensively and continue to tune the parameters until you achieve the best performance. EBU is an excellent utility that can help achieve phenomenal backup and restore rates. On a Sun Ultra Enterprise 6000 server, I have been able to achieve an 85 GB per hour backup and restore rate. Some sites have achieved even higher rates by using more backup tape drives, thereby increasing the degree of parallelism. For more information on the Enterprise Backup Utility, refer to the *Oracle7 Enterprise Backup Utility Administrator's Guide.*

7.13 RECOVERY MANAGER

Oracle8 introduced a new utility known as the Recovery Manager (RMAN) to manage database backups. For Oracle8 and Oracle 8*i* databases, RMAN replaces the Oracle7 EBU utility. RMAN is a more comprehensive utility and integrates the backup and restore functionality inside the Oracle kernel. This not only simplifies the architecture of RMAN, it also allows you to utilize the Oracle Enterprise Manager (OEM) to schedule, perform, and administer database backups. You can think of RMAN as another database service rather than an external component like EBU. RMAN uses a recovery catalog to maintain the repository of information used for managing backup and restore operations. RMAN also supports tertiary storage subsystems such as Epoch, Legato, StorageTek, and HP. RMAN can backup individual tablespaces or data files as well as only changed blocks. RMAN can automate media recovery operations and can generate a log of all backup and restore activities. RMAN can also parallelize backups and restores as well as automatically compress unused blocks. RMAN can be used via the command-line interpreter in interactive mode or via the OEM GUI tool. Figure 7.3 illustrates the architecture of RMAN.

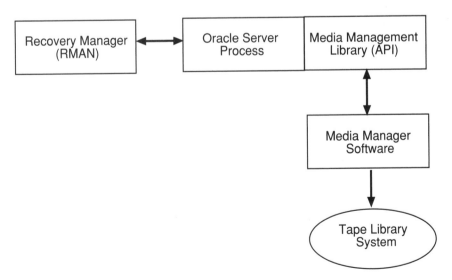

FIGURE 7.3   RMAN architecture.

In the RMAN architecture diagram in Figure 7.3, the Media Management Library (MML) is a vendor-supplied API that is used to interface to Oracle. The Oracle server process invokes the MML routines to backup and restore the Oracle database files to media devices managed via the media manager software.

The RMAN recovery catalog should be maintained in a separate database. The `catrman.sql` script located in `$ORACLE_HOME/rdbms/admin` is used to create the RMAN catalog tables and views. The recovery catalog contains information about the data files and archive log backup sets, data file copies, archive redo log files, physical structure of the target database, and named sequences of commands call stored scripts.

Oracle8*i* made several enhancements to RMAN including the ability to monitor the progress of RMAN jobs via the views `V$BACKUP_SYNC_IO` and `V$BACKUP_ASYNC_IO`. These views can be used to determine the progress of RMAN jobs such as a backup or restore. The view columns `ELAPSED_TIME`, `TOTAL_BYTES`, and `EFFECTIVE_BYTES _PER_SECOND` can be used to determine the progress of the RMAN job. Oracle8*i* also improved the RMAN integration with OPS by automatically discovering the appropriate node in the OPS cluster from which to restore the backups. Oracle8*i* also includes a new release of the media management API (release 2.0) while maintaining backward compatibility with the release 1.1 media management API.

7.13.1 PARALLELIZING BACKUPS AND RESTORES

RMAN uses two main command options to parallelize backups and restores: channels and files per set. The `channel` control commands specify the degree of parallelism to be used for backup operations and also specify the size of the backup pieces. The `channel` command can be used to specify limits on I/O bandwidth. Each channel establishes a connection to a target database instance and each connection operates on one backup set at a time. If multiple connections are established, than each connection operates on a separate file copy or backup set. Using the `allocate channel` command, you can parallelize your backup operation by configuring multiple channels. The `release channel` command releases the channel and terminates the connection, thus allowing the channel to be reused. The `setlimit channel` command can be used to set the maximum number of kilobytes that the backup command will attempt to write to a backup piece. The `setlimit channel` command allows you to specify the readrate which specifies the number of blocks read per second by a backup or copy command. The `filesperset` option of the backup command specifies the maximum number of files that will be placed in a single backup set. If the number of files to be backed up is greater than `filesperset`, then the backup sets will result in the creation of multiple backup sets. By allocating a channel per device (disk or tape), you can achieve a high-throughput backup. This allows you to parallelize the backup across the different devices. You should also balance the number of active concurrent channels with the number of tape media devices. Too many concurrent channels may cause contention for the tape media devices. The `filesperset` option can also be used to control the degree of multiplexing. Data files within the same backup set are multiplexed and sent as a stream to the tape media device.

You can also utilize I/O slaves to parellelize RMAN reads and writes. The Oracle8 `init.ora` parameters `backup_tape_io_slaves` and `backup_disk_io_slaves` specify whether or not I/O slaves should be used for backups. To enable I/O slaves, set `backup_tape_io_slaves=TRUE` and `backup_disk_io_slaves=<N>` where `N` refers to the number of slaves per channel. Monitor I/O utilization to determine the optimal number of backup I/O slaves. I/O slaves can be especially useful for situations where asynchronous I/O is either inefficient or not available.

By tuning the number of channels, files per set, and I/O slaves, you can increase the performance of your backup and restore. You should monitor tape drive, disk, and processor utilization in order to choose optimal settings for the number of channels, files per set, and I/O slaves. RMAN provides a tremendous amount of functionality and number of performance features that allow you to effectively manage your database backups while achieving high-backup and restore throughput. Incorporating the recovery management functionality in the Oracle DBMS allows you to utilize the OEM tool to manage your backups. For more information on RMAN, refer to the *Oracle8i Recovery Manager User's Guide and Reference*.

7.14 PARALLEL RECOVERY

As of release 7.1, the Oracle Server provides the capability to accelerate database recovery time by employing multiple slave processes to parallelize the recovery work. This can reduce significantly the elapsed recovery time by an almost linear factor. In order to take full advantage of the parallel recovery option, the system should have multiple processors and should be configured with well-balanced I/O striped devices (using the volume manager). The degree of parallelism for recovery can be controlled through the `init.ora` parameter `recovery_parallelism`. To minimize the recovery time, set `recovery_parallelism=<number of available processors in the system>`. For example, setting `recovery_parallelism=4` will spawn four processes during the instance or media recovery phase, and each process (slave) will read a different section of the redo files and apply the changes in parallel. The effectiveness of parallel recovery is inherently dependent on the system's I/O distribution. If the redo log files are poorly distributed or are located on one disk or a few disks, spawning many processes to read the same disk will not produce any gains. This simply results in an I/O bottleneck where the traditional synchronous recovery process of one single process performing the recovery probably would be faster. If your system has multiple processors and your redo log files are striped, set `recovery_parallelism` to the number of available processors limited by the degree of the I/O distribution of the redo log files. This helps expedite instance or media recovery.

Oracle8i provides the ability to parallelize the recovery of parallel transactions. In Oracle8, parallel transactions that failed are rolled back serially by the background process. This increases transaction recovery time and impacts the availability of the database. Parallel transaction recovery is enabled when the SMON process determines that the amount of recovery work is above a certain threshold. The threshold is defined by the amount of work at which the time it takes to complete recovery in parallel becomes less than the time it takes to recover in serial. The `init.ora` parameter `fast_start_parallel_rollback` controls the number of parallel transaction recovery server processes. If `fast_start_parallel_rollback=FALSE`, parallel transaction recovery is disabled. If `fast_start_parallel_rollback=low`, 2 × CPUs recovery server processes are started. If `fast_start_parallel_rollback=high`, 4 × CPUs recovery server processes are started. The views `v$recovery_servers` and `v$recovery_transactions` provide statistics for the recovery transactions and servers.

Another recovery improvement of Oracle8*i* is the ability to perform on-demand block level transaction recovery. On-demand block level transaction recovery recovers dead transactions one block at a time, but only on demand. This improves database availability by reducing the time that data is locked by large dead transactions. Previously, users would be blocked until the dead transaction is recovered in its entirety. This new feature recovers only the blocks under consideration, thus allowing the user to proceed. The remaining blocks of the dead transaction are recovered in the background via the SMON process. SMON may also choose to recover the blocks in parallel using the parallel transaction recovery servers (if enabled). The on-demand block level transaction recovery improves database availability and provides an asynchronous method of recovery, allowing users to proceed with other operations.

7.15 STANDBY DATABASE

Oracle 7.3 introduced the standby database feature which allows another system to act as a backup system in the event of a failure on the primary system. A standby database is a copy of the primary database on a separate system that is in a constant state of media recovery. If the primary system fails, the standby database can be brought on-line relatively quickly by applying the archive redo logs from the primary database to make the standby database consistent with the primary database prior to the system failure. This allows the standby database to continue serving the user community so as to minimize downtime while the primary database can be recovered. The users can continue using the standby database until the primary system becomes available. Using a standby database can help reduce the amount of down time.

In Oracle8*i*, a standby database can be opened in read-only mode. This is useful for two reasons: it allows you to test that the archive logs are being applied correctly, and that the database could be opened successfully if the primary system were to fail. In addition, by allowing the standby database to be opened in read-only mode, some of the read-only load from the primary system, such as queries and reports, can be directed to the standby database.

7.16 TABLESPACE POINT-IN-TIME RECOVERY

Oracle8 introduced a new feature known as Tablespace Point-in-Time Recovery (TSPITR) which allows a tablespace to be recovered to a point-in-time different from that of the rest of the database. TSPITR is most useful for scenarios such as recovering from a `drop` or `truncate table` statement, recovering a table that has become corrupted, or recovering from an invalid batch job. TSPITR builds on top of the Oracle7 export and import functionality for recovering a subset of the database. TSPITR allows the user to make a copy of the relevant data files of the recovered database referred to as the clone database. The data file copies along with the corresponding data dictionary information are transferred over to the production database. Both the Export and Import utilities support tablespace point-in-time recovery. TSPITR is a complex process, and you should fully understand all the steps required to configure TSPITR. You should also thoroughly test TSPITR to ensure that it is working and the correct steps have been taken to configure and use TSPITR. For more information on TSPITR, refer to the *Oracle8i Backup and Recovery Guide*.

7.17 TRANSPORTABLE TABLESPACES

Oracle8*i* provides the ability to transport tablespaces from one database to another through a new feature known as transportable tablespaces. Transportable tablespaces are platform-dependent, meaning that you can transport tablespaces within the same operating system environment. For example, you can transport tablespaces from one Solaris SPARC system to another Solaris SPARC system. Transportable tablespaces are very useful for shipping a portion of a database to another system so that the tablespaces can be plugged into the destination database. For example, you may want to use transportable tablespaces to transport a certain set of tablespaces from the main OLTP system to the data warehousing system. Transportable tablespaces can also be used to publish data to customers. The customer can import the tablespace as opposed to having to manually import the schema objects and related data.

The `TRANSPORT_TABLESPACE` option of the Export/Import utilities is used to initiate an export of the transportable tablespace. The Import utility is then used on the receiving side to import the transportable tablespace. For more information on the use of transportable tablespaces, refer to the *Oracle8i Administrator's Guide*.

Chapter 8

INTERNET COMPUTING
MODEL AND OBJECTS

Oracle8*i* is the database management software for the Internet. Oracle8*i* and Oracle tools are focused on providing Internet computing solutions. The goal of Internet computing is to reduce computing complexity and cost, and to improve manageability. The Internet computing model is also centered around open systems and distributed computing. Oracle8*i* is an object-relational database management system combining the functionality of relational databases with the ability to create and manage complex objects. Oracle8 represented the first phase of database object functionality, and Oracle8*i* further expanded object functionality as well as provided such features as the ability to code stored procedures in Java.

8.1 THE INTERNET COMPUTING MODEL

Oracle's Internet computing model is a paradigm shift in computing that emphasizes the easy access, power, and stability of distributed computing. For large-scale systems, the traditional two-tier client-server model is insufficient. Large-scale systems that require a high level of performance, interoperability and security require a multi-tier approach that distributes the computing workload across application and database servers. There are several tiers of the Internet computing model consisting of thin clients on the client side, such as network computers, an application server in the middle tier to manage business objects and logic, and a data server to manage the objects and their data. Oracle products such as Developer and JServer are examples of Internet-enabling products that allow you to build high-performance distributed systems. Figure 8.1 illustrates the Internet computing model. One of the core components of the Internet computing model is the concept of cartridges. In essence, cartridges combine business objects and rules into software components. They consist of applications or application components written in many different languages, such as JAVA, PL/SQL, Perl, or C. The beauty of cartridges is that they enable the dynamic expansion and addition of functionality at any of the tiers of the Internet computing model. It is important that you begin to adopt and utilize the Internet computing model when designing new applications. The Internet computing model is centered around the concepts of easy access, open systems, and distributed computing. The cartridges further demonstrate the openness and deployment ease of Internet-based applications.

The Internet computing model centers around the ability to easily add cartridges to either the database server, application server, or client. The time series, spatial, and image cartridges are examples of database server cartridges in Oracle8. The intercartridge exchange provides a common protocol for information exchange between cartridges. The cartridge model allows you to easily deploy new cartridges that provide new application functionality.

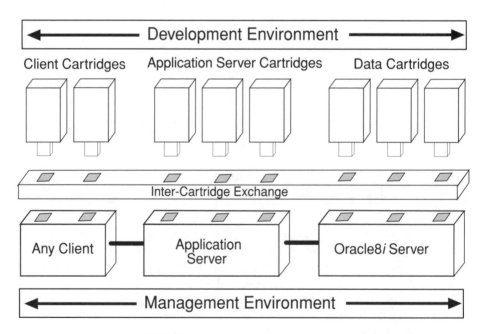

FIGURE 8.1   Internet computing model.

8.2   ORACLE OBJECTS

Oracle8 introduced the ability to create object types with member functions. You can then create a table based on the object type. Using object types allows you to encapsulate the supported operations within the object type. This allows application languages such as C++ to encapsulate the data with its methods. SQL, PL/SQL, and the precompilers have been extended to support operations on object types. Although object types can simplify data models and provide an elegant interface to the application developer, it is important that you consider performance when designing and creating object types.

8.2.1   MAP VERSUS THE ORDER METHOD

When creating object types in Oracle, you can choose to use the MAP or ORDER comparison methods. A MAP method returns the relative position of a record within the order of records within the object. The ORDER method must be called for every two objects being compared. The MAP method is called only once per object. When sorting a set of objects, an ORDER method is called more than the number of times that a MAP method would be called. Scalar value comparisons are very efficiently complemented by the fact that invoking a user-defined function is slower than calling a kernel implemented function; sorting objects using the ORDER method is relatively slow as compared to sorting the mapped scalar values that are returned by the MAP function.

8.2.2   BLOB VERSUS THE BFILE

The BLOB datatype can be used to store unstructured binary data inside the database. The BFILE datatype can be used to store unstructured binary data outside the database, via operating system files. As opposed to BFILE data, the data for a BLOB/CLOB is stored inside the database. BFILE data is stored in an operating system file and is therefore stored external to the database. A user can read and write data to a BLOB or CLOB. However, database access to a BFILE is read-only since the main purpose of a BFILE is to support access to data on read-only devices. A BLOB or CLOB participates in database transactions and is also recoverable. BLOBs and CLOBs maintain all ACID properties. BFILEs maintain integrity by the operating system and through the application. BLOB and CLOB data is backed up along with other database data whereas BFILE data is not backed up. BFILE data is not replicated whereas BLOB and CLOB data is replicated. Future releases of Oracle in which partitioning is supported for LOBs, allows the BLOB and CLOB data to be partitioned. With LOB partitioning capabilities, only the BFILE locator will be partitioned, and not the actual BFILE data. Although BLOBs and BFILEs have relatively similar read performance, it is important that you consider all the different constraints when choosing between a BLOB or a BFILE.

8.2.3 VARRAYS VERSUS NESTED TABLES

Nested tables can be fully manipulated via SQL and PL/SQL whereas manipulating VARRAYs can be done only through PL/SQL or OCI. You cannot access an individual element of a VARRAY within SQL. Nested tables are stored in a storage table with every element mapping to a row in the storage table. VARRAYs, on the other hand, are stored as opaque objects (raw or blob). VARRAYs are a good choice if your application primarily retrieves an entire collection as a value. If the collection is very large and the application needs only a small subset of the collection, then nested tables are more appropriate. Nested tables also allow you to pin the object using REFs in the object cache, thus increasing performance if the application continues to access the object. Inserts on nested tables can consume more time since the insert operation needs to follow the nested operations.

8.2.4 ORACLE REFS

An Oracle REF can be thought of as a database pointer to an instance of an object in an object table. Collections can contain elements that are REFs to objects that exist in object tables or objects that exist only within the collection. Objects that have significance outside of the object in which they are contained should generally be made referenceable. For example, employees have significance outside of any specific department to which they may be assigned; therefore they should be referenceable. Also, each department may consist of a large number of employees. Therefore, selective queries on personnel within a department are often typical, thus making a nested table with REFs to employees an optimal solution. VARRAYs and a VARRAY of REFs can be fetched in a single-server round trip. Nested tables can vary in size. Although a nested table can be fetched in a single-server round trip, the amount of data needed to be transferred can result in a large amount. VARRAYs typically generate less network traffic than a nested table.

8.2.5 ORACLE8*i* LOB ENHANCEMENTS

Tables containing object types, collection types, REF columns, and LOBs may also be partitioned in Oracle8*i*. LOB types such as BLOB, CLOB, NCLOB, as well as the LOB data, can be partitioned. LOB data may be stored in different data segments from the actual table data. This is typically referred to as out-of-line storage. LOB data may be stored external to the table segments if the LOB exceeds 4,000 bytes, even if out-of-line storage is not explicitly requested. The ability to partition object type tables and LOBs improves administration, availability, scalability, and performance. The following is an example of how to partition a table containing LOB data types.

```
CREATE TABLE lob_tab (cid number,
                      c_blob BLOB,
                      c_clob CLOB,
                      c_nclob NCLOB)
  LOB (c_blob,c_nclob) STORE AS (STORAGE (NEXT 15K))
```

```
LOB (c_clob) STORE AS (TABLESPACE TS_CLOB)
PARTITION BY RANGE (cid)
 (PARTITION lobp1 VALUES LESS THAN (MAXVALUE)  TABLESPACE TS_LOBP
     LOB (c_blob) STORE AS (TABLESPACE TS_BLOB),
     LOB (c_clob) STORE AS (PCTVERSION 20),
     LOB (c_nclob) STORE AS (STORAGE (NEXT 10K)))
TABLESPACE TS_LOBP;
```

Oracle8*i* also provides the ability to create a temporary LOB. Temporary LOBs are transient objects and exist for a maximum period of the creating session. Temporary LOBs can also be managed using the DBMS_LOB and OCI interfaces. Temporary LOBs do not generate rollback data. Oracle8*i* improves LOB performance by reducing the number of reads and writes performed during LOB manipulation. Oracle8 used system generated object and nested table ids. If an object or nested table is not being used in a distributed environment, the space used to store the system-generated id is wasted. Oracle8*i* allows the primary key of the table to serve as the object id, avoiding the need to create system-generated ids.

8.3 JDBC PERFORMANCE

Oracle provides two types of JDBC drivers: the thick JDBC driver and the the thin JDBC driver. The thin JDBC driver is a type IV driver that is Java-based. The thin JDBC driver does not require an Oracle client environment. The thick JDBC driver is a type II driver based on the native OCI driver. There are several tuning tips that can be used to improve the performance of the JDBC-based applications such as the use of batch operations or the prefetch feature.

8.3.1 BATCH OPERATIONS

The JDBC drivers allow applications to perform operations such as inserts and updates in batch as opposed to per row. Batch operations improve performance by reducing the number of database server round trips. The concept of batch operations is similar to that of the bulk operations in PL/SQL 8i or array processing in PRO*C/OCI. The size of the batch can be controlled via the method setExecuteBatch (<batch size>). If the value of the batch size is greater than 1, then JDBC accumulates insert and update statements and sends the statements to the database server once the batch size has been reached. Batch operations increase the efficiency of the application and reduce the number of round trips to the database server.

8.3.2 PREFETCH

JDBC-based applications can also use the prefetch feature to improve query performance. The prefetch feature fetches the specified number of rows into the client JDBC cache, which helps reduce the number of database server round trips. The method `setDefault-RowPrefetch (<prefetch size>)` can be used to specify the number of rows to prefetch. For example, `setDefaultRowPrefetch (15)` specifies that 15 rows should be fetched at each database fetch call. Hence, as the application uses the `next()` method to navigate through the result set, an actual database fetch would not be issued until after 25 rows have been read by the client via the `next()` method.

8.3.3 USING THE DEFINE TYPE METHODS

The JDBC driver provides the `defineColumnType` method, which can be used to specify the data type of an out-bind variable. There are two versions of the `defineColumnType` method.

```
defineColumnType (<column position>,<type>)
```

or

```
defineColumnType (<column position>,type,<length>)
```

You should use the three-argument version of the `defineColumnType` method so that the maximum length of the out-bind variables can be specified. For VARCHAR columns, if the maximum length of the out-bind variable is not specified, then JDBC allocates 4 KB of memory for the bind buffer for each VARCHAR column. This can significantly increase the memory footprint of the application for those queries which select many columns of type VARCHAR. In addition, using the `defineColumnType` method avoids the extra server round trip that would be needed by JDBC in order to determine the data type.

8.4 ORACLE8*i* CACHE

Internet applications typically use a multitier model which consists of Web servers and applications servers. In cases where the application is based entirely on a single database server and the application uses a great deal of server-side PL/SQL units or Java stored procedures, the scalability of the application may be limited by the resources of the database server. The Oracle product, Oracle8*i* Cache, helps alleviate such a situation by utilizing a middle-tier cache to disseminate the application workload across an available pool of Oracle8*i* Cache servers. Oracle8*i* Cache effectively transforms a database server into a middle-tier cache by allowing queries and PL/SQL units to be executed on the middle-tier Oracle8*i* Cache sytem as opposed to the origin database server. Oracle8*i* Cache transparently routes queries to the Oracle8*i* Cache tier via the Oracle Call Interface (OCI) layer. Applications that are based on OCI can utilize Oracle8*i* Cache to improve application scalability by distributing query workload across the pool of Oracle8*i* Cache middle-tiers. Java applications which use the thick JDBC driver can also utilize Oracle8*i* Cache. You can choose which tables to cache in the Oracle8*i* Cache middle-tier by using the Oracle Enterprise Manager. Oracle8*i* Cache version 1 (V1) is designed to improve application scalability for those Internet-based applications that perform mostly read-only queries (i.e., lookups). Oracle8*i* Cache version 2 (V2) will expand the capabilities of Oracle8*i* Cache V1 by allowing PL/SQL units and SQL statements such as inserts, updates, or deletes to be executed in the Oracle8*i* Cache middle-tier.

Oracle8*i* Cache is an extremely useful product that allows Internet-based applications to distribute the database workload across a pool of middle-tier caches. Oracle8*i* Cache V1 is primarily intended to cache read-only table or tables that may not change frequently. This helps improve the scalability of Internet-based application in which the proportion of reads is much higher than writes. For example, an Internet-based online bookstore application will likely have a higher proportion of reads as compared to writes since users are more likely to browse the catalog several times before ordering a book. In addition, many users may simply browse the online bookstore without actually purchasing a book. In this case, Oracle8*i* Cache can be used to distribute the query workload across multiple middle-tiers as opposed to directing all the queries to a single database server. Oracle8*i* Cache V2 allows an Oracle8*i* Cache middle-tier to service additional client requests, including the execution of PL/SQL units and DML-based SQL statements such as deletes, inserts, and updates. This helps further improve application scalability by distributing the application workload across the available pool of Oracle8*i* Cache middle-tiers.

INSTALLING AND CONFIGURING UNIX FOR OPTIMAL PERFORMANCE

This appendix summarizes installation and configuration tips for the UNIX operating system. It is organized into the following sections.

- ❏ A Corporate Architecture
- ❏ Determining the Type of System
- ❏ Sizing the File Systems
- ❏ Mirroring the Operating System
- ❏ Installing the UNIX Operating System
- ❏ Naming Service
- ❏ Post-Installation Procedures

A.1 A CORPORATE ARCHITECTURE

If you are managing many different UNIX systems, it can be extremely helpful to define a complete UNIX systems architecture such as host name standards, networking standards, security standards, and configuration standards. The architecture will help you to more effectively manage your environment by implementing a consistent set of standards across all the UNIX systems. Defining the UNIX systems architecture must be a coordinated effort among the system, database, and network administrators, as well as the application staff who use these systems to develop applications.

A.2 DETERMINING THE TYPE OF SYSTEM

Before you install the UNIX operating system on your system, you must determine the main purpose of the system. Will the system be a server, a client workstation, an NFS server, and so on? The type of system is important because the system may require extra packages and/or patches. Determining the main purpose of the system will also help during the post-configuration phase.

A.3 SIZING THE FILE SYSTEM

It is extremely important that you size the file systems appropriately before you install the operating system. If the file systems are not sized properly, you may not have enough space to install certain operating system packages. The root (/) file system is the most critical file system. My recommendation is that you always leave at least 100 MB of free space in the root file system to account for kernel rebuilds and kernel patches. Also, use separate file systems for the / (root), /usr, /var, and /opt directories. This helps keep separate the operating system binaries from user software packages and system administration files. The /usr file system typically contains operating system utilities as well as operating system-related applications. The /var file system typically contains patches, e-mail, and system administration log files. The /opt directory typically contains operating system packages. Therefore, separating these directories into separate file systems can help reduce the chances of the / (root) file system from filling up.

A.4 MIRRORING THE OPERATING SYSTEM

Most software and hardware volume managers provide you with the ability to mirror your operating system file systems, such as the / (root), and /usr file systems. Doing so helps reduce system down time should a media failure occur on the / (root), or other operating system file systems. Refer to the volume manager documentation for your platform for specific details on how to set up operating system mirroring. Enabling mirroring helps reduce system downtime and increases the reliability of the system. As always when mirroring, distribute the submirrors across multiple disk drives and controllers so that the members of the mirror are not on the same disk and controller.

A.5 INSTALLING THE UNIX OPERATING SYSTEM

When you install the operating system, try to install it in its entirety upon your system, depending on space. This enables you to utilize any of the system packages easily without having to add the software package later. Installing the entire OS upfront may also help reserve disk space for the operating system which may not be available in the future.

During the installation, make sure that you configure a sufficient amount of swap space. You can also configure and add the swap space following the OS installation by using the swap command. Chapter 3 discusses how to list the current swap devices as well as how to add swap devices.

Following the installation, it is critical that you determine the patches that are needed for your system. Obtain the relevant patches from the appropriate vendor and install the patches. If you are installing a new operating system release, make sure you obtain the recommended patch list from the OS vendor to determine if your system needs the patches.

A.6 NAMING SERVICE

If you plan to manage a medium-to-large-size UNIX environment, you should configure a naming service such as NIS (YP) or NIS+. This improves the ease of administration by allowing a root master server to push the namespace maps such as the password, hosts, and services tables. This avoids having to edit these files manually on all the different systems. If your environment consists primarily of Sun Solaris Servers, you should use the NIS+ naming service. HP-UX 11.0 also provides support for NIS+. For more information on configuring YP or NIS+, refer to your platform's system administration documentation.

If you plan to configure a naming service such as YP or NIS+, make sure you configure at least one replica server in the event that the root master server fails. Creation of multiple replica servers on different subnets can increase performance by minimizing the network traffic and distributing the NIS calls to the root master and the replicas.

A.7 POST-INSTALLATION PROCEDURES

After the operating system has been installed and configured successfully, you must make sure that any operating system or kernel patches were also installed successfully. If you are configuring a database or application server, you may need to increase the amount of semaphores in the system. You may also need to increase the maximum amount of shared memory if, for example, you will be configuring a large SGA. You may also need to set kernel process, file size, and memory size limits. After you set the kernel parameters, you must rebuild the kernel and reboot the system for the changes to take effect.

In addition to the kernel parameters, you may also need to alter the security configuration of the system, such as disabling certain `inetd` services. Most system administrators tend to disable finger, remote shell, and other `inetd` services in order to increase the security of the system. You may want to configure a set of post-install scripts. This will enable you to automate the post-install process.

INSTALLING ORACLE FOR OPTIMAL PERFORMANCE

This appendix summarizes installation and configuration tips for the Oracle software. It is organized into the following sections.

- ❏ A Corporate Architecture
- ❏ Determining the Type of System
- ❏ Sizing the File Systems
- ❏ Directories and File Locations
- ❏ Installing the Oracle DBMS
- ❏ Configuring SQL*Net/Net8
- ❏ Post-Installation Procedures

B.1   A CORPORATE ARCHITECTURE

If you plan to manage many different Oracle systems, it can be extremely helpful to define a complete Oracle architecture such as database standards, application standards, security standards, and configuration standards. The architecture will help you manage your environment more effectively by implementing a consistent set of standards across all the Oracle database systems. Defining the Oracle database systems architecture must be a coordinated effort between the operations and application staff.

B.2   DETERMINING THE TYPE OF SYSTEM

Before you install the Oracle software, it is important that you determine the main purpose of the system. Will the server be an application server, or will the server be a DSS or OLTP database server? The type of system is important because not only may the system require different packages and/or patches, the system may also require a different release of Oracle. For example, certain versions of Oracle tools or Oracle Applications may also require a specific release of the Oracle Server. Determining the main purpose of the system also will help during the post-configuration phase.

B.3   SIZING THE FILE SYSTEMS

It is vital that you size the file systems appropriately before you install the Oracle software. If the file systems are not sized properly, you may not have enough space to install the Oracle software packages. I recommend that you create a separate file system dedicated to Oracle software. Separate the disks used for the Oracle software file system from other operating system disks to help distribute I/O.

B.4   DIRECTORIES AND FILE LOCATIONS

I recommend that you keep a consistent set of directory names across all the database servers. This will help you to locate trace files and database startup scripts more easily. Create a dbs directory (separate from the $ORACLE_HOME/dbs), and use the following directory structure.

```
../../../dbs/$ORACLE_SID/    — main directory

                adump       - audit dump destination
                bdump       - background dump destination
                cdump       - core dump destination
                create      - database creation scripts
                export      - export scripts/files
                import      - import scripts/files
                pfiles      - parameter files (init.ora)
                udump       - user dump destination
```

Use this structure to help you organize files in a consistent manner. This structure also helps organize files for single servers that run multiple databases. Because the directory structure is organized by $ORACLE_SID, each database will have its own directory and set of related subdirectories.

Remember to create at least three control files and place them on separate disks and controllers to minimize the probability of losing a control file. You can generate a control file creation script by issuing the command:

```
SQL> alter database backup controlfile to trace;
```

The trace file then can be edited and used to re-create the database control file if needed.

B.5 INSTALLING THE ORACLE DBMS

When you install the Oracle DBMS, install those options that you have licensed from Oracle. It is a good idea to select the relink option in the installer. This causes products being installed to be relinked on your specific platform. You should also make sure that the Oracle software file system has sufficient space for future upgrades and patches.

Oracle8*i* provides the new Oracle Universal Installer. This installer provides a GUI interface that makes the task of installing a great deal easier. I recommend that you use the GUI installer to install the Oracle products.

Following the installation, you may need to run the root.sh script generated by Oracle that performs post-installation actions as the root user. The root.sh file needs to be run as the root superuser account. After the installation completes, review the contents of the root.sh file to determine if you need to execute the root.sh script.

B.6 CONFIGURING THE SQL *NET/NET8

SQL*Net V2 and Net8 provide a tremendous amount of new functionality. SQL*Net V2 and Net8 allow multiple protocol adapters to be used. SQL*Net V2 and Net8 enable you to prespawn connection processes so that user connection time is minimized. Chapter 5 discusses how to tune SQL*Net V2 and Net8.

SQL*Net V2 and Net8 also enable you to configure a name server so that managing SQL*Net V2 and Net8 configuration files can be done from a central server. SQL*Net V2 and Net8 also provide a NIS agent to enable SQL*Net V2or Net8 to work in conjunction with NIS servers.

You will need to configure the listener.ora, sqlnet.ora, and/or tnsnames.ora files after installing SQL*Net V2 or Net8. You can use the Oracle Network Manager tool to administer the SQL*Net V2 configuration files and Net8 Assistant to manage the Net8 configuration files. Using a central name server can help you reduce the manual effort of maintaining the SQL*Net V2 and Net8 configuration files on all the different database servers and clients.

B.7 PASSWORD MANAGEMENT

Oracle8 introduced password management services such as account locking, password aging and expire, password history, and password complexity verification. The script utlpwdmg.sql located in $ORACLE_HOME/rdbms/admin needs to be run in order to enable password management. Using the CREATE USER and ALTER USER commands, database administrators can lock, unlock, and expire database accounts. Password limits are set up in the user profiles and are always enforced. By using the CREATE PROFILE command, the database administrator can establish rules for password aging and password history. Additionally, the DBA can also code his or her own complex PL/SQL function for password verification and then specify the use of the function within the CREATE PRO-FILE or ALTER PROFILE statement. Password management is a useful feature and should be used by the DBA to increase the security of the Oracle database.

B.8 POST-INSTALLATION PROCEDURES

After you install the Oracle software, you may need to run the root.sh post-configuration script. You may also need to set some new environment variables that are specific to the new version of the Oracle products. You should add the environment variables to the appropriate user startup scripts to ensure that the environment variables are set automatically upon a user login. You should also check with Oracle to determine if you need to install patches for the products you are installing. Oracle generally provides README files and installation and configuration documentation that report any required patches. The CD often contains a patches directory with README files describing the purpose of each patch.

You may also need to alter the ksms.s file (SGA mapping file) and relink the Oracle Server executable if you are configuring a large SGA. If you are configuring a large SGA, you may also need to alter the relevant UNIX kernel parameters. If you install new versions of the Oracle Server and PRO*C, I recommend that you recompile a few of your PRO*C programs to ensure that your applications are working properly. You should also perform a complete set of regression tests on the new software versions in order to ensure that your existing applications are completely functional. The regression tests may also help you resolve problems (if any) with the new versions of the software packages.

REFERENCES

1. Cockcroft, Adrian and Richard Pettit. *Sun Performance and Tuning*, 2nd ed. Englewood Cliffs, NJ: Prentice Hall, 1998.

2. Cockcroft, Adrian. *Sun Performance and Tuning*. Englewood Cliffs, NJ: Prentice Hall, 1995.

3. Date, Chris J. *An Introduction to Database Systems*, 5th ed. Addison-Wesley, 1990.

4. Deitel, Harvey M. *Operating Systems*, 2nd ed. Addison-Wesley, 1990.

5. Kulihin, Julia, Mary L. Fox, and Joan Nester. *System Administration for Intel Processors UNIX SVR4.2MP*, Vol. 2, UNIX Press. Englewood Cliffs, NJ: Prentice Hall, 1993.

6. Rosen, Kenneth H. *Discrete Mathematics and Its Applications*. Random House, 1988.

7. *Oracle7 for Sun Performance Tuning Tips*. Oracle Corporation, 1995.

8. *Oracle7 for UNIX Performance Tuning Tips*. Oracle Corporation, 1995.

9. *Oracle8i Reference Release 8.1.6 Manual*. Oracle Corporation, 1999.

10. *Oracle8i Backup and Recovery Guide Release 8.1.6*. Oracle Corporation, 1999.

11. *Oracle8i Administrator's Guide Release 8.1.6*. Oracle Corporation, 1999.

12. *Oracle8i Concepts Manual*. Oracle Corporation, 1999.

13. *Oracle8i Data Warehousing Guide Release 8.1.6*. Oracle Corporation, 1999.

14. *Oracle8i SQL Reference Manual*. Oracle Corporation, 1999.

15. *Oracle8i Designing and Tuning for Performance Release 8.1.6.* Oracle Corporation. 1999.

16. *Oracle8i Utilities Manual.* Oracle Corporation. 1999.

17. *Oracle Net8 Administrator's Guide Release 8.1.6.* Oracle Corporation, 1999.

18. *Oracle8i PL/SQL User's Guide and Reference Release 8.1.6.* Oracle Corporation, 1999.

19. *Oracle8i Application Developer's Guide Release 8.1.6.* Oracle Corporation. 1997.

20. *Oracle Enterprise Manager Administrator's Guide Release 2.1.* Oracle Corporation, 1999.

21. *Performance Tuning an Application.* SPARCWorks SunPro, Part Number 800-6018-11, Revision A, October 1992.

22. *Programmer's Guide to the Oracle PRO*C/C++ Precompiler.* Oracle Corporation, 1994, 1996.

23. *Pro*C/C++ Precompiler Programmer's Guide Release 8.0.* Oracle Corporation, 1997.

24. *SQL*Plus User's Guide and Reference Release 8.1.6.* Oracle Corporation, 1999.

25. *Symmetry Multiprocessor Architecture Overview.* Sequent Computer Systems, Inc. Part Number 1003-50113-03, 1994.

26. *Solstice DiskSuite Tool 4.0 User's Guide.* SunSoft, Sun Microsystems Computer Corporation. Part Number 802-1724-10, Revision A, March 1995.

27. *Solstice DiskSuite 4.0 Administration Guide.* SunSoft, Sun Microsystems Computer Corpororation. Part Number 802-2422-10, Revision A, March 1995.

28. *Configuration and Capacity Planning for Sun Servers*, 3rd ed. Sun Microsystems Computer Corporation, Technical Product Marketing. Part Number 801-6876-01, Revision A, January 1994.

29. *Data Warehousing White Paper.* Sun Microsystems Computer Corporation, February 1995.

30. *Multithreaded Applications Programming.* SunService Division, Sun Microsystems, Inc. Technical Education Services. Part Number SI-260-02, Revision SunSoft 2.1.

31. *Sun OS 5.X Internals.* SunService Division, Sun Microsystems, Inc. Technical Education Services. Part Number SP-365, Revision B.1, September 1993.

32. *SVM Configuration and Administration Guide.* Sequent Computer Systems, Inc., 1994.

INDEX

Oracle Desk Reference

Guy Harrison 2000, 400 pp., Paper, 0-13-013294-2, $34.99

Finally, there's a quick and handy printed reference to all the Oracle information you need most! Don't waste time searching Oracle's slow, unwieldy help system when you can find it faster right here, in the *Oracle Desk Reference*! This one-stop source delivers the information you need every day — organized for super-fast access. Here's just some of what you'll find in *Oracle Desk Reference*: Coverage of all SQL commands, functions, operators, and datatypes; PL/SQL and Oracle PL/SQL packages; the Data Definition Language (DDL), SQL*Plus, even Oracle Java and JDBC. There's more: detailed information on database configuration parameters and files, a handy Oracle glossary, even an Internet resource list. If you want to maximize your productivity with Oracle, you can't make a better investment!

Oracle SQL High Performance Tuning , Second Edition

Guy Harrison 2001, 500 pp., Paper, 0-13-012381-1, $49.99

This second Edition of *Oracle SQL High Performance Tuning* zeroes in on SQL, showing how to achieve performance gains of 100% in many applications. Expert Oracle developer, Guy Harrison, gives Oracle developers and DBAs a single source for guidance on every aspect of Oracle 8i SQL and PL/SQL tuning. This book starts with a detailed overview of SQL processing in Oracle, and then introduces SQL tuning guidelines that improve virtually any application. Learn how to trace SQL statement execution, create more effective indexes, identify and resolve Oracle Server bottlenecks, and fix poorly performing SQL code. The book outlines up-front design techniques for enhancing application efficiency; includes detailed real-world tuning guidelines for both SQL and PL/SQL; and presents opportunities to improve performance by substituting PL/SQL or Java for SQL.

Oracle 8I and UNIX® Performance Tuning

Ahmed Alomari 2001, 450 pp., Paper, 0-13-018706-2, $49.99

Now, the #1 guide to Oracle tuning on UNIX platforms has been thoroughly updated for Oracle 8i! Oracle Senior Performance Engineer, Ahmed Alomari, covers every relevant optimization technique for every leading application and approach, including Web-centered development, OLTP, OLAP/DSS, and object-relational database systems. This book covers the entire system lifecycle, showing how to achieve breakthrough performance by tuning both Oracle 8i and your underlying UNIX platform. Coverage includes: choosing Oracle 8/8i and UNIX installation options that maximize performance, optimizing the UNIX kernel, Oracle 8/8i optimizer and PRO*C enhancements, expert techniques for eliminating SQL bottlenecks, state-of-the-art database performance benchmarking and specific solutions for Solaris, HP-UX, and Sequent. No matter how long you've been running Oracle and UNIX, you'll run them faster—and smarter—with *Oracle8i and UNIX Performance Tuning*.

Oracle 8I and Java: From Client/Server to E-Commerce

Elio Bonazzi and Glenn Stokol 2001, 750 pp., Paper, 0-13-017613-3, $49.99

All things Oracle must be Internet or E-Business oriented, and that also means JAVA. Java programmers who want to create e-business solutions, must learn Oracle since 90% of all e-business solutions include Oracle. Oracle has proclaimed that the internet changes everything, and so it changes Oracle. Use the tips and techniques offered in this new book to help eliminate SQL code bottlenecks and learn new techniques for optimizing object-rational databases.

Prentice Hall PTR

Oracle Forms Developer's Handbook

Albert Lulushi 2001, 1000 pp., Paper w/CD-ROM, 0-13-030754-8, $54.99

In *Oracle Forms Developer's Handbook,* one of the world's leading Oracle developers presents powerful techniques for leveraging Oracle Forms in both web-centered and client/server environments. This is the first Oracle Forms book to reflect the brand-new Version 6i. *Oracle Forms Developer's Handbook* presents the reader with step-by-step instructions for using every tool in the Forms environment, including the Forms Designer, Object Navigator, and the Layout Editor. Next, learn how to use PL/SQL in Forms applications; master all of the methods and objects available to Forms programmers; and learn how to apply object-oriented programming practices to Forms development, including inheritance, reusability, encapsulation, and polymorphism. Oracle Forms is the single most important tool used to create sophisticated applications for Oracle databases. The latest versions of Oracle Forms have reflected Oracle's Internet-centered strategy, adding powerful capabilities for building Web-centered applications to the product's traditional client/server focus.

Oracle Interactive Workbooks

These integrated book-and-Web learning workbooks teach all of the Oracle skills you need, through hands-on, real-world labs, exercises, projects, and our great Web-based training site. Your free Web-based training module includes a Virtual Study Lounge where you can interact with the author, interactive Q&As, new projects, book updates, and more! Every Prentice Hall Interactive Workbook is fully integrated with its own exclusive Web site, giving you all this and more:

- "Test Your Thinking" project solutions and detailed explanations
- Author's Corner: Your personal connection to this book's expert author
- Additional self-review exercises with instant feedback and explanations
- An exclusive Virtual Study Lounge where you can interact with other learners!

You'll learn hands-on, through practical exercises, self-review questions and real-world answers. Exclusive "Test Your Thinking" projects guarantee you'll go beyond rote knowledge to really master the subject! It's an integrated learning system that's proven to work!

Oracle Forms Interactive Workbook

Baman Motivala 2000, 488 pp., Paper, 0-13-015808-9, $39.99

Oracle DBA Interactive Workbook

Douglas Scherer and Melanie Caffrey 2001, 400 pp., Paper, 0-13-015742-2, $39.99

Oracle PL/SQL Interactive Workbook

Benjamin Rosenweig and Elena Silvestrova 2000, 472 pp., Paper, 0-13-015743-0, $39.99

Oracle SQL Interactive Workbook

Alex Morrison and Alice Rischert 2000, 544 pp., Paper, 0-13-015745-7, $39.99